Drupal 8 Module Development

Build and customize Drupal 8 modules and extensions efficiently

Daniel Sipos

BIRMINGHAM - MUMBAI

Drupal 8 Module Development

First published: October 2017

Production reference: 1251017

Published by Packt Publishing Ltd.
Livery Place
35 Livery Street
Birmingham
B3 2PB, UK.

ISBN 978-1-78216-877-5

www.packtpub.com

Credits

Author
Daniel Sipos

Reviewers
Todd Zebert
Tracy Charles Smith

Commissioning Editor
Amarabha Banerjee

Acquisition Editor
Nigel Fernandes

Content Development Editor
Aditi Gour

Technical Editor
Diksha Wakode

Copy Editor
Dhanya Baburaj

Project Coordinator
Ritika Manoj

Proofreader
Safis Editing

Indexer
Rekha Nair

Graphics
Jason Monteiro

Production Coordinator
Shantanu Zagade

About the Author

Daniel Sipos is a senior web developer specializing in Drupal. He has been working with Drupal sites since version 6 and started, like many others, as a site builder. He's a self-taught programmer with many years of experience in working professionally on complex Drupal 7 and 8 projects. In his spare time, he runs `webomelette.com`, a Drupal website where he writes technical articles, tips, and techniques related to Drupal development.

About the Reviewers

Todd Zebert has been involved with Drupal since shortly after the launch of version 6. He is a full stack web developer, is proficient in a variety of technologies, and is currently a lead web developer for Miles. He has also been a technical reviewer for the Packt books *Developing with Drush* and *Drupal 8 Development Cookbook*, and the related video series *Drupal 8 Development Solutions*.

He's a frequent presenter at conferences on Drupal, JavaScript, and frontend technologies. He has a technology blog at Medium.

Todd has a diverse background in technology, including infrastructure, network engineering, project management, and IT leadership. His experience with web development started shortly after the release of the original Mosaic graphical web browser, with SHTML/CGI and Perl.

Todd is an entrepreneur and is involved with the Los Angeles start-up community. He's a believer in volunteering, open sourcing, the Maker movement, and contributing back. He's also an advocate for STEAM (Science, Technology, Engineering, Art, and Math) education.

I'd like to thank the Drupal community, especially the Los Angeles Drupal group.

Finally, I'd like to thank my teen son with whom I get to share my interest in technology and science , often while doing Maker-ish things together, with microcontrollers and other electronics.

Tracy Charles Smith began working with computers at the age of 10 years. His background includes network support, web development, customer service, project management, and financial management.

His entrepreneurial spirit is a key component to his success in interacting with clients and team members on business and user-experience related technology solutions. In fact, he used that passion to found his own technology-consulting firm called Alpha Geek Tech, LLC. He also served as the technology director for Quiddities Dev. Inc., in Santa Cruz, CA, before moving back to the DC area to join Phase2 in 2010 as a senior developer. Tracy now works as a senior project manager at Phase2, supporting growth and support clients in government and private enterprise. His diverse development background complements his project management skills.

Tracy was also the lead programmer and architect for 12seconds.tv in 2007 (a video messaging platform), which leveraged Drupal. He also authored Drupal Intranets with Open Atrium.

He earned a BS in computer information systems and business administration from Wingate University.

www.PacktPub.com

For support files and downloads related to your book, please visit www.PacktPub.com. Did you know that Packt offers eBook versions of every book published, with PDF and ePub files available? You can upgrade to the eBook version at www.PacktPub.com and as a print book customer, you are entitled to a discount on the eBook copy. Get in touch with us at service@packtpub.com for more details.

At www.PacktPub.com, you can also read a collection of free technical articles, sign up for a range of free newsletters and receive exclusive discounts and offers on Packt books and eBooks.

https://www.packtpub.com/mapt

Get the most in-demand software skills with Mapt. Mapt gives you full access to all Packt books and video courses, as well as industry-leading tools to help you plan your personal development and advance your career.

Why subscribe?

- Fully searchable across every book published by Packt
- Copy and paste, print, and bookmark content
- On demand and accessible via a web browser

Customer Feedback

Thanks for purchasing this Packt book. At Packt, quality is at the heart of our editorial process. To help us improve, please leave us an honest review on this book's Amazon page at `www.amazon.in/dp/178216877X`.

If you'd like to join our team of regular reviewers, you can email us at `customerreviews@packtpub.com`. We award our regular reviewers with free eBooks and videos in exchange for their valuable feedback. Help us be relentless in improving our products!

Table of Contents

Preface

Drupal 8 is a powerful web-based content management system (CMS) that can be used to build anything from simple websites to powerful applications. While it is useful out of the box, it is designed with developers in mind.

The purpose of this book is to talk about the most common ways a Drupal 8 website can be extended to provide new functionality. In doing so, the book will cover a number of extension points, but also illustrate many subsystems and APIs that can help you model, structure, and wire your business requirements.

Alongside the obligatory theoretical explanations, it will use a practical, example-based approach in order to break down complex topics and make them easier to understand. So, join me on this journey to discover exactly how powerful Drupal 8 actually is.

What this book covers

Chapter 1, *Developing for Drupal 8,* provides an introduction to module development in Drupal 8. In doing so, it introduces the reader to the various subsystems and outlines the requirements for running a Drupal 8 application.

Chapter 2, *Creating Your First Module,* gets the ball rolling by creating the first Drupal 8 module of the book. Its main focus is to explore the most common things module developers need to know from the get-go.

Chapter 3, *Logging and Mailing,* is about the tools available for doing something every web-based application does and/or should be doing, that is, sending emails and logging events.

Chapter 4, *Theming,* presents the theme system from a module developer's perspective in Drupal 8.

Chapter 5, *Menus and Menu Links,* explores the world of menus in Drupal 8 and shows how to programmatically create and work with menu links.

Chapter 6, *Data Modeling and Storage,* looks at the various types of storage available in Drupal 8, from the state system to configuration and entities.

Chapter 7, *Your Own Custom Entity and Plugin Types*, takes a hands-on approach creating a custom configuration and content entity type, as well as custom plugin type to wire up a practical functional example.

Chapter 8, *The Database API*, presents the database abstraction layer and how we can work directly with data stored in custom tables.

Chapter 9, *Custom Fields*, exemplifies the creation of the three plugins necessary for creating a custom field that can be used on a Drupal 8 content entity type.

Chapter 10, *Access Control*, explores the world of access restrictions in Drupal 8, from roles and permissions to route and entity access checks.

Chapter 11, *Caching*, looks at the various cache mechanisms available for module developers to improve the performance of their functionality.

Chapter 12, *JavaScript and the AJAX API*, introduces module developers to the specificities of writing JavaScript in Drupal 8, as well as the powerful AJAX system, which can be used to build advanced interactions.

Chapter 13, *Internationalization and Languages*, deals with the practices Drupal 8 module developers need to observe in order to ensure that the application can be properly translated.

Chapter 14, *Batches, Queues, and Cron*, explores the various ways module developers can structure their data processing tasks in a reliable way.

Chapter 15, *Views*, looks at the various ways module developers can programmatically interact with Views and even expose their own data to them.

Chapter 16, *Working with Files and Images*, explores the various file and image APIs that allow module developers to store, track, and manage files in Drupal 8.

Chapter 17, *Automated Testing*, explores the various types of automated test module developers can write for their Drupal 8 applications to ensure stable and resilient code.

What you need for this book

Readers don't need much to follow along with this book. A local environment setup capable of installing and running Drupal 8 (preferably with Composer) should suffice.

Who this book is for

The primary target of this book is Drupal 7 developers who want to learn how to write modules and do development in Drupal 8. It is also intended for Drupal site builders who have basic object-oriented programming skills, as well as PHP programmers without that much Drupal experience.

A little bit of Symfony experience is helpful but not mandatory.

Conventions

In this book, you will find a number of text styles that distinguish between different kinds of information. Here are some examples of these styles and an explanation of their meaning.

Code words in text, database table names, folder names, filenames, file extensions, path names, dummy URLs, user input, and Twitter handles are shown as follows: "Just assign the names of the layers you want to activate to the `admin/reports/dblog` environment variable."

A block of code is set as follows:

```
hello_world.logger.channel.hello_world:
    parent: logger.channel_base
    arguments: ['hello_world']
```

New terms and **important words** are shown in bold. Words that you see on the screen, for example, in menus or dialog boxes, appear in the text like this: "Users can now reach this page from the module administration page by clicking on the **Help** link for each individual module that has this hook implemented."

Warnings or important notes appear in a box like this.

Tips and tricks appear like this.

Reader feedback

Feedback from our readers is always welcome. Let us know what you think about this book-what you liked or disliked. Reader feedback is important for us as it helps us develop titles that you will really get the most out of.

To send us general feedback, simply e-mail feedback@packtpub.com, and mention the book's title in the subject of your message.

If there is a topic that you have expertise in and you are interested in either writing or contributing to a book, see our author guide at www.packtpub.com/authors.

Customer support

Now that you are the proud owner of a Packt book, we have a number of things to help you to get the most from your purchase.

Downloading the example code

You can download the example code files for this book from your account at http://www.packtpub.com. If you purchased this book elsewhere, you can visit http://www.packtpub.com/support and register to have the files e-mailed directly to you.

You can download the code files by following these steps:

1. Log in or register to our website using your e-mail address and password.
2. Hover the mouse pointer on the **SUPPORT** tab at the top.
3. Click on **Code Downloads & Errata**.
4. Enter the name of the book in the **Search** box.
5. Select the book for which you're looking to download the code files.
6. Choose from the drop-down menu where you purchased this book from.
7. Click on **Code Download**.

You can also download the code files by clicking on the **Code Files** button on the book's webpage at the Packt Publishing website. This page can be accessed by entering the book's name in the **Search** box. Please note that you need to be logged in to your Packt account.

Once the file is downloaded, please make sure that you unzip or extract the folder using the latest version of:

- WinRAR / 7-Zip for Windows
- Zipeg / iZip / UnRarX for Mac
- 7-Zip / PeaZip for Linux

The code bundle for the book is also hosted on GitHub at `https://github.com/PacktPublishing/Drupal-8-Module-Development`. We also have other code bundles from our rich catalog of books and videos available at `https://github.com/PacktPublishing/`. Check them out!

Downloading the color images of this book

We also provide you with a PDF file that has color images of the screenshots/diagrams used in this book. The color images will help you better understand the changes in the output. You can download this file from `https://www.packtpub.com/sites/default/files/downloads/Drupal8ModuleDevelopment_ColorImages.pdf`.

Errata

Although we have taken every care to ensure the accuracy of our content, mistakes do happen. If you find a mistake in one of our books-maybe a mistake in the text or the code-we would be grateful if you could report this to us. By doing so, you can save other readers from frustration and help us improve subsequent versions of this book. If you find any errata, please report them by visiting `http://www.packtpub.com/submit-errata`, selecting your book, clicking on the **Errata Submission Form** link, and entering the details of your errata. Once your errata are verified, your submission will be accepted and the errata will be uploaded to our website or added to any list of existing errata under the Errata section of that title.

To view the previously submitted errata, go to `https://www.packtpub.com/books/content/support` and enter the name of the book in the search field. The required information will appear under the **Errata** section.

Piracy

Piracy of copyrighted material on the Internet is an ongoing problem across all media. At Packt, we take the protection of our copyright and licenses very seriously. If you come across any illegal copies of our works in any form on the Internet, please provide us with the location address or website name immediately so that we can pursue a remedy.

Please contact us at copyright@packtpub.com with a link to the suspected pirated material.

We appreciate your help in protecting our authors and our ability to bring you valuable content.

Questions

If you have a problem with any aspect of this book, you can contact us at questions@packtpub.com, and we will do our best to address the problem.

1
Developing for Drupal 8

Drupal is a web-based **Content Management System (CMS)**. While it is useful out of the box, it is designed with developers in mind. The purpose of this book is to explain how Drupal can be extended in many ways and for many purposes. To this end, the version we will use will be the latest one at the time of writing this book--Drupal 8.2. In this book, we will cover a wide range of development topics. We'll discuss how to create a Drupal 8 module, and as we go through the chapters, many concepts and tips that will help you build what you need will be introduced. The goal is not only to explain how things work but also to go through some examples to demonstrate them. Since no book can contain everything, I hope that after reading this book, you'll be able to expand on this knowledge on your own using the resources I reference and by looking into the Drupal code yourself. As helpful as such a book can be for learning any kind of software development, if you really want to progress, you will need to apply the knowledge you learned and explore the source code yourself. Only by doing this you will be able to understand complex systems with many dependencies and layers.

This chapter introduces the terminology, tools, and processes for developing Drupal 8. While subsequent chapters focus on code, this chapter focuses on concepts. We'll talk about the architecture of Drupal and how you can hook into Drupal at strategic places to extend it for accomplishing new tasks.

The following are the major topics we will be covering in this chapter:

- An introduction to Drupal development
- Drupal 8 architecture
- The major subsystems
- Tools for developing in Drupal

By the end of this chapter, you will understand the architectural aspects of Drupal and be ready to start writing code.

Introducing Drupal (for developers)

Out of the box, Drupal performs all of the standard functions of a web-based content management system:

- Visitors can view published information on the site; navigate through menus, view listings, and individual pages; and so on
- Users can create accounts and leave comments
- Administrators can manage the site configuration and control the permissions levels of users
- Editors can create, preview, and then publish content when it is ready
- Content can be syndicated to RSS, where feed readers can pick up new articles as they are published
- With several built-in themes, even the look and feel of the site can be changed easily

With Drupal 8, the scope of what a site builder can do has greatly increased. Core multilingual capabilities make it much easier to configure the site to use multiple languages, creating content listings a few clicks away out of the box, and content management, in general, has greatly improved.

Developing for Drupal 8

As fantastic as these features are, they will certainly not satisfy the needs of all users. To that end, Drupal's capabilities can be easily extended with modules, themes, and installation profiles. Take a look at Drupal's main website, (`http://drupal.org`), and you will find thousands of modules that provide new features and thousands of themes that transform the look and feel of the site.

The fact that almost all aspects of Drupal's behavior can be intercepted and transformed through the module and theme mechanisms has led many to claim that Drupal isn't just a CMS, but a **Content Management Framework** (**CMF**) capable of being re-tooled to specific needs and functional requirements. This is particularly the case with Drupal 8--the latest version of Drupal and the focus of this book--as great progress has been made on the extensibility front too.

Establishing whether Drupal is rightly called a CMS or CMF is beyond our purpose here, but it is certain that Drupal's most tremendous asset is its extensibility. Want to use a directory server for authentication? There's a Drupal module for that. Want to export data to **Comma-Separated Version** (**CSV**) files? There are several modules for that (depending on what data you want to export). Interested in Facebook support, integration with Twitter, or adding a Share This button? Yup, there are modules for all of these too--all of which are available at Drupal.org and provided by developers like you.

Want to integrate Drupal with that custom tool you wrote to solve your special business needs? There may not be a module for that, but with a little bit of code, you can write your own. In fact, that is the subject of this book--providing you with the knowledge and tools to achieve your own goals.

In summary, the purpose of this book is to get you ramped up (as quickly as possible) for Drupal 8 module development. As we move chapter by chapter, we will cover the APIs and tools that you will use to build custom Drupal sites, and we won't stick to theory. Most chapters provide working, practically oriented example code designed to show you how to implement the concepts we talk about. We will follow Drupal coding conventions and utilize Drupal design patterns in an effort to illustrate the correct way to write code within the Drupal development context.

While I certainly can't write the exact code to meet your needs, my hope is that the code mentioned in these chapters can serve as a foundation for your bigger and better applications.

So let's get started with a few preliminary matters.

Technologies that drive Drupal

Installing Drupal 8 in the traditional way is documented both on Drupal.org and in the `INSTALL.txt` file found inside the `/core` folder of the installation, so I won't go into it here. I will, however, mention that a better way of installing Drupal 8, especially for developers, is using the accepted Composer template for Drupal 8 projects found on GitHub (`https://github.com/drupal-composer/drupal-project`). However, the instructions for setting up your site are well covered there as well.

Instead, let's talk a bit about the technologies that power (or are needed by) Drupal 8.

PHP

Drupal is written in the PHP programming language. PHP is a widely supported, multiplatform, and web-centric scripting language. Since Drupal is written in PHP, this book will largely feature code written in PHP, albeit with Drupal standard practices being kept in mind.

It is very important to note that the minimum version of PHP required for Drupal 8 to run (and install via Composer) is 5.5.9. Moreover, since the current version of PHP (at the time of writing this book) is PHP 7, I personally recommend that you run Drupal 8. It's best to start off right.

Regarding the style of PHP, a very important change compared to Drupal 7 is the heavy use of object-oriented code and design patterns. Granted, many procedural style approaches remain throughout the Drupal 8 code base, but the use of a good number of popular external libraries (such as Symfony components) has pushed the overall Drupal code to be more modern. For this reason, it is also quite important that you have at least some basic understanding of **object-oriented programming** (**OOP**), especially PHP related, if you want to do Drupal 8 development.

Databases and MySQL

In the past, Drupal has supported two databases--MySQL and PostgreSQL. Drupal 7 and 8 have moved beyond this. Drupal now uses the powerful **PHP Data Objects** (**PDO**) library that is standard in PHP 5/7. This library is an abstraction layer that allows developers to support numerous databases, including MySQL, PostgreSQL, SQLite, and MariaDB.

The minimum database versions for Drupal 8 are as follows:

- MySQL 5.5.3/MariaDB 5.5.20/Percona Server 5.5.8 or higher with PDO and an InnoDB-compatible primary storage engine
- PostgreSQL 9.1.2 or higher with PDO
- SQLite 3.7.11 or higher

Additionally, Drupal provides a powerful database API along with some SQL coding conventions that make it easy to interact with your database--both combined allow you to write safe and portable SQL. However, more and more abstractions have been made at different levels, removing the need for SQL writing almost completely. However, we will still see some examples just so your toolbox does not miss anything, as well as cover all the tools at your disposal for querying your database.

The web server

Apache has long been the predominant web server, but it is by no means the only server. While Drupal was originally written with Apache in mind, many other web servers (including IIS, Lighttpd, and NGINX) can run Drupal.

We do not explicitly cover the web server layer anywhere in this book, primarily because development rarely requires working at that low level. However, Drupal expects a fair amount of processing from the web server layer, including handling of URL rewriting. For more information on what you can expect, you can consult the relevant documentation page on `https://www.drupal.org/docs/8/system-requirements/web-server`.

HTML, CSS, and JavaScript

The de facto web data format is **HTML (Hypertext Markup Language)** styled with **CSS (Cascading Style Sheets)**. Client-side interactive components are scripted with JavaScript. As Drupal developers, we will encounter all three of these technologies in this book. Although you don't need to be a JavaScript ninja to understand the code here, you will get the most from this book if you are comfortable with these three technologies.

Drupal architecture

In the preceding section, we introduced the technologies that drive Drupal. However, how do they all fit together? How is Drupal code organized? In this section, we provide an overview of Drupal's architecture, with a focus on Drupal 8.

Drupal core, modules, and themes

From an architectural standpoint, we can break up Drupal into three pieces--its core, modules, and themes.

When we discuss Drupal 8 core, we can interpret it in two ways. A more restrictive interpretation sees it as a functionality covered in all the code it ships with, without modules and themes. The more widespread interpretation sees it as the total code base it ships with (*out of the box*).

Although the most widespread interpretation is the latter (not least because it differentiates all the functionalities its standard installation contains versus all others provided by contributed modules and themes), it is interesting to consider the first one as well, even if just for a minute. In this way, we can distinguish, architecturally, the base code from the modules and themes that provide various functionalities and layouts (both from the core installation and from external modules and themes). Along these lines will be also the hooks and events that glue everything together, allowing us to intercept and inject ties to our own functionality.

The core libraries are made up of code belonging to the Drupal project and those from the wider PHP community, which Drupal borrows under open source licensing. This latter approach is new in Drupal 8 and has been regarded by many as a positive shift toward getting off the Drupal island and embracing outside libraries, frameworks, and communities.

Essentially, the core libraries provide the functions and services used throughout Drupal. Facilities for interacting with the database, translating between languages, sanitizing user data, building forms, encoding data, and many such utilities are found in Drupal's core libraries.

The modules (both core and contributed) are where most of the actual functionality and business logic is. If enabled, they can provide functionality or extend the existing functionality. Most of the core modules are needed and cannot be disabled due to their importance in the standard Drupal installation. However, contributed ones can be installed and uninstalled as needed.

The themes (both core and contributed) are an important part of the theme system and are used in the presentation logic. They provide HTML templates within which content and data can be rendered to the user, as well as CSS styling and even client-side scripting for some nice visual interactions. Themes can extend other themes and can also contain some PHP logic to process the data before being rendered.

Hooks, plugins, and events

Now that we have seen what the core libraries, modules, and themes do, let's talk briefly about hooks and events to understand how they are all connected.

Hooks are a very typical Drupal procedural concept that allows Drupal core and modules to basically ask for data from other modules and themes (or expose it). By doing this, the latter can provide a new functionality or alter the existing ones. It is the responsibility of the code that calls the hook to make use of whatever the hook implementations return. The *format* and *interface* for what the latter need to return is usually documented in the hook documentation.

Concretely, hooks work by scanning installed modules and themes and looking for a function that follows a specific naming pattern (in other words, a *hook implementation*). This is, in most cases, in the following format--module_name_hook_name. Additionally, there are also alter hooks, which have the word alter tacked on the end of the function name and are used to change data passed as a reference to the hook implementation. We will see examples of hooks later in the book.

 Developers with a background in OOP or with a strong knowledge of design patterns might recognize this as being similar to the event handling paradigm captured in the Passive Observer pattern. When some particular event occurs, Drupal allows modules the opportunity to respond to that event.

In previous versions of Drupal, hooks were KING. Yes, I wrote this with capital letters, my *Caps Lock* did not get stuck. This is because they were the way to add or extend a functionality in modules. As such, they were the single most important aspect of Drupal programming. In Drupal 8, however, although still important, they took a backseat to new concepts, such as plugins and events.

In Drupal 8, I dare to say that plugins are king. Much of the functionalities that used to be tied to Drupal via hooks is now added in through another Drupal typical concept--**plugins** (not to be confused with WordPress plugins). Drupal 8 plugins are discoverable bits of the functionality centralized by a manager and that are used for certain tasks and features. We will see more about plugins and provide many examples later in the book.

A third extension point introduced in Drupal 8 is the event system. Unlike the first two, however, this is not specific to Drupal, but is, in fact, the actual Symfony EventDispatcher component (http://symfony.com/doc/current/components/event_dispatcher.html). Events are primarily used in Drupal to intercept certain actions or flows in order to either stop or modify them. Many *request to response* tasks that were handled via hooks in the past are now being handled by dispatching events to check whether any modules are interested in, for example, delivering the response to the user.

Services and the dependency injection container

Another architecturally important element of Drupal 8 is the Symfony dependency injection component (`http://symfony.com/doc/current/components/dependency_injection.html`), concretely represented by the service container.

This component is a staple of modern OOP PHP programming and as such has become foundational to Drupal 8. It allows us to create *services* that can be injected in various places (and receive themselves services as dependencies). They are then used for the heavy business logic of our functionality. Additionally, they are at times also used as an extension point because the service container is able to collect certain services that are marked as serving a specific purpose and use them automatically. In other words, simply by defining a simple service, we can provide our own functionality or even change the existing logic.

We will encounter many services, and we will see how we can declare our own later in this book.

From request to response

Now that we have listed the most important architectural pieces of Drupal, let's briefly see how these are used in delivering responses to the requests a user makes on a Drupal 8 website. To this end, we will analyze a very simplified example of a typical request as it is handled on a Drupal 8 website:

- A user enters the `http://example.com/node/123` URL in a web browser and presses *Enter*.
- The browser contacts the web server at `example.com` and requests the resource at `/node/123`.
- The web server recognizes that the request must be handled by PHP and starts up (or contacts) a PHP environment to handle the request.
- PHP executes Drupal's front controller file (`index.php`), which then creates a new `Request` object from the resource that was requested.
- Symfony's HTTPKernel handles this request object by dispatching a number of events, such as `kernel.request`, `kernel.controller`, `kernel.response`, and `kernel.view`.
- The route that maps to that request is identified through the `kernel.request` event.

- The route controller is identified, and the `kernel.controller` event is used to perform any alterations on the used controller and to resolve the arguments that need to be passed to it. In our case, this route is registered by the Node module through the main Entity system, which identifies the entity ID, loads it, and builds the markup to be returned as part of `Response`.
- If the respective controller (or handler) returns something other than a `Response` object, the `kernel.view` event is dispatched to check whether there is any code that can transform that into a `Response` object. In most cases, in Drupal 8, we typically return *render arrays*, which are transformed into `Response` objects.
- Once a `Response` is created, the front controller returns it to the browser and terminates the request.

In this context, as Drupal 8 module developers, we spend most of our times inside controllers and services, trying to figure out what we need to return to the page. We then rely on Drupal to transform our render array into a proper response to the user, but we can also return one ourselves directly. Moreover, the theme system comes into play here, as well as the block system, because our content gets to be wrapped into a block that is placed in a region surrounded by other regions that contain blocks. However, if it sounds complicated now, don't worry, we will cover in detail all these aspects with examples, and it will become clear in no time.

However, as a quick conclusion, we can see that events are mostly used (but not only) at the highest levels of a request, whereas plugins and hooks are mostly used at lower levels, within the process of calculating, building a page, or handling a specific business logic.

Drupal's major subsystems

In the preceding section, we took a bird's-eye view of Drupal's architecture. Now, we will refine our perspective a bit. We will walk through the major subsystems that Drupal 8 has to offer.

Routing

It all starts with a route, doesn't it? Any interaction with a Drupal 8 website has its beginning in a user (or system) accessing a certain path (or resource). This translates into a route, which maps that resource to a flow that (hopefully) returns a successful response back or at least a graceful failure.

The Drupal 8 routing system is a major shift away from how it was in its previous versions. In Drupal 7 and earlier versions, the routing system was a very Drupal-specific thing (a *drupalism*, if you will). Many of us remember `hook_menu` as a staple hook each Drupal developer had to know very well. All of that has been abandoned in Drupal 8 in favor of the Symfony Routing component (`http://symfony.com/doc/current/components/routing.html`). Also, since I mentioned `hook_menu`, I will also mention that its other main functions have also been taken over in Drupal 8 by other subsystems, such as plugins.

In this book, we will see how we can define our own route and map it to a controller that will render our page. We will cover a few of the more important route options and take a look at how we can control access to these routes.

Entities

Progressively, entities have become a very powerful way of modeling data and content in Drupal. The most famous type of entity has always been the Node, and it has been historically the cornerstone of content storage and display. In Drupal 8, the entire entity system has been revamped to make other entity types potentially just as important. They have been brought to the forefront and have been properly connected with other systems.

All entity types can have multiple `bundles`, which are different *variations* of the same entity type and can have different fields on them (while sharing some fields).

Drupal core still ships with the Node entity type, with a few bundles such as Basic Page and Article. In addition, it comes with a few other entity types, such as `User`, `Comment`, and `File`. However, creating your own entity type in Drupal 8 has become much more standardized compared to Drupal 7 where contributed modules had to be brought into play.

These are not the only types of entities we have in Drupal 8. The examples mentioned previously are all content entity types. Drupal 8 introduced a new type, configuration entity types. The former are oriented toward content, but in reality, they are for anything that holds data that can be input into the database and is specific to that environment. They are not used for storing configuration, though. Users and content are great examples, as they do not need to be (usually) deployable from one environment to other. The latter, on the other hand, are exportable items of the configuration of which there can be more than one. For example, a content entity *bundle* is a great example because there can be more than one bundle for a certain entity type; they have some metadata and information stored that can differ from bundle to bundle, and they need to be deployed on all environments. That is, they are fundamental to the correct functioning of the site.

Understanding the entity system is indispensable for doing development in Drupal 8 because it provides a powerful way of modeling custom data and content that goes past the traditional nodes that previously were used and is, in my opinion, too much way past their purpose.

Fields

Now that we have an idea of what entities are, let's take a look at how data is actually stored on these entities.

I have alluded in the preceding section to how certain entity bundles can have various fields. This means that each entity type bundle can have any number of fields that are responsible for holding data. Additionally, each entity type itself can have fields for storing data. Okay, but what? Let's break this down.

There are two types of Fields in Drupal 8--base fields and configurable fields. The former are fields that are defined in the code for each entity type you define (or alter), whereas the latter are usually created and configured in the UI and attached to a bundle of that entity type and exported via configuration. So, essentially, both types can end up in the code to be deployed.

Fields can also be of multiples types, depending on the data they store. For example, you can have string (or text) fields, numeric fields, date fields, email fields, and so on. As developers, we can create our own field types if the existing ones are not good enough for our data.

In this book, we will take a look at how we can define base fields on a certain entity type and create our own field type with its own data input widget and output formatter. Site builders can then use this field type on any entity type.

Menus

Any site needs some sort of navigation, right? Drupal not only maintains content, but also provides details about how the site itself is organized, that is, it structures how content is related.

The principle way that it does this is through the menu subsystem. The latter provides APIs to generate, retrieve, and modify elements that describe the site structure. Put in common parlance, it handles the system's navigational menus.

Menus are hierarchical, that is, they have a tree-like structure. A menu item can have multiple children, each of which may have their own children, and so on. In this way, we can use the menu system to structure our site into sections and subsections.

In this book, we will see how we can work programmatically with menus and menu links.

Views

Listing of content and data is always an important capability content management systems covet; this is what Views provides in Drupal 8, and it does so well.

If you've been building (not even necessarily developing) sites in previous versions of Drupal, you'll understand everything with this simple phrase--Views is now in Drupal core. If you haven't, Views has always been a staple Drupal contributed module used on probably all Drupal installations to a certain extent and is an indispensable tool for site builders and even developers.

The purpose of the Views module is to expose data and content in a way that allows the creation of configurable listings. It includes things such as filters, sorts, display options, and many other features. As developers, we often find a need to write our own field or filter plugin to work with Views or expose data from our custom entities or external data sources.

Views is a core Drupal 8 module tied to the general architecture and used for most list pages (especially, admin pages) provided by Drupal core. Although it's a very site building-oriented tool, in this book, we will take a look at how we can create plugins that extend its capabilities to offer site builders even more.

Forms

Unless your site has three pages and five paragraphs of text, the likelihood that you will need to capture user input via some type of form is very high. Also, if you've been coding PHP applications, you know how forms have always been a pain from the point of view of securely and efficiently rendering and processing the submitted data. As soon as you use a PHP framework such as Symfony, you will note that an API is in place to take much of that load off your shoulders.

The same goes with Drupal 8 and its powerful Form API. Historically, it has been a great abstraction over having to output your own form elements and deal with posted values. It allows you to define your own form definition in OOP and handle validation and submission in a logical way. Its render and processing is taken care of by Drupal securely, so you don't have to worry about any of that. In Drupal 8, theming form elements have become much easier than in previous versions.

In this book, we will encounter some forms and see how they actually work in practice.

Configuration

One of the major pet-peeves of Drupal developers (and developers of other popular CMSes for that matter) has always been the way configuration is handled and deployed from one environment to the next. Drupal 7 stored most of its configuration in the database, so various solutions had to be concocted by developers to get that moved up the latter as development progressed.

In Drupal 8, great advancements have been made in this respect with the introduction of a centralized configuration system that although stores all configuration in the database, allows it all to be exported into YML files (and then reimported). So, from a development point of view, we have it much easier now if certain features depend on configuration (for example, a new Field).

Configuration is also of two kinds--simple and complex (configuration entities we noted in the *Entities* section). The difference between the two is that the former is always singular in that it stores just a value (or multiple values together), once--the site name and email address, for example. You only have one site name. The latter, on the other hand, represents multiple instances of the same configuration type, for example, multiple View definitions or multiple entity bundles. In this book, we will see a bit of both.

Plugins

Plugins are new to Drupal in its latest version and are an elegant solution to an important problem--the encapsulating and reusing functionalities. Right off the bat, you should not confuse them with things such as the WordPress plugins, which are more akin to Drupal modules. Instead, you should think of plugins as components of reusable code that can be used and managed by a central system. They are typically used to allow others to contribute their own distinct functionality within your own system. Looking at it from the other direction, Drupal core, for example, handles many things in a certain way, but allows you to provide your own plugins to handle those things in a different way.

An interesting way of looking at plugins is also as being opposite to entities, not for data storage, but for functionality. Instead of creating a type of data that gets stored, you create a type of functionality that is used. The two usually work hand in hand, especially when it comes to manipulating the data in different ways.

Plugins are a great new extension point for developers to add their own functionality and are a critical subsystem for Drupal 8 developers to know. An important aspect of how they work is their discoverability. Most plugin types (but definitely not all) are discovered via something called *Annotations*. Annotations are a form of DocBlock comments, borrowed from the Doctrine library (`http://docs.doctrine-project.org/projects/doctrine-common/en/latest/reference/annotations.html`), by which we can describe classes, methods, and even properties with certain metadata. This metadata is then read to determine what that item is without the need for instantiating the class. In Drupal 8, we use annotations only at a class level to denote that it is a plugin implementation with certain characteristics. That is how most plugins are discovered in Drupal 8.

The second most common discoverability method for plugins is via a YAML file, and a popular example of these are menu links (as we will see later in the book). However, for now, you should know that plugins are very widely used, and we will create quite a few plugins in this book.

The theme system

The responsibility of theming a given piece of data is spread out over the Drupal core, modules, and the themes themselves. So, as a module developer, it is important to know that both modules and themes can theme data or content.

In this book, we will focus on the aspects that happen at the module level. We will not concern ourselves with styling or layouts, but work primarily with theming definitions and templates that are needed within the module. Typically, it is the best practice to ensure that modules are able to theme their data. If done right, themes can then come into play and override that theming to change the presentation.

A major shift in Drupal 8 compared to older versions is the move to the open source Twig templating system (`https://twig.sensiolabs.org/`). This makes the separation of logic from a presentation that much clearer and makes fronted developers' job much easier, not to mention more secure.

Caching

The last major subsystem that I will include here is the caching layer. Drupal 8 has gone to great lengths to improve the performance of building pages and rendering data. To this end, the caching system has become an important part to consider whenever we either do complex or heavy calculations or render content.

From a module developer's perspective, there are two main pillars of the caching system. The first one provides developers a cache backend to store the result of complex data calculations. This data can be read in the next requests to avoid the need for redoing those calculations. This goes hand in hand with cache invalidation when something in the system changes that would require the calculations to be redone. The second pillar is the render cache, which allows developers to wrap their data output with metadata that describe in what context and when that data output needs to be invalidated or changed. The entire markup of that bit gets cached and invalidated based on the rules of the metadata.

We will see these in action in a later chapter dedicated to caching.

Other subsystems

There are other subsystems in Drupal 8 of varying importance. I chose to include the preceding ones because I deemed them to be the most important to be introduced up front and especially from the point of view of a module developer. However, as we progress through the book, we will definitely encounter others.

Tools for developing in Drupal

Drupal is a sophisticated platform, and from the glimpse provided in this chapter, we can already see that there are numerous systems and structures to keep track of. In this section, I will provide tools that simplify or streamline the development process.

Going forward, I assume that you have your own web server stack and your own PHP development tools. However, if you are just getting started, you may want to look at Acquia Dev Desktop from Acquia (http://acquia.com). It offers entire application stacks to get you started on Windows, Linux, or macOS X. Alternatively, if you are even just a bit more advanced, you can consider the Drupal VM (https://www.drupalvm.com/), a Vagrant and Ansible-based local development environment ready for Drupal.

As for a code editor, I personally use PhpStorm (as many others do), but you are free to use whatever IDE you want because Drupal itself doesn't require anything special. Also, while running a PHP debugger is certainly not necessary, you may find running Xdebug or the Zend Debugger to be useful. I personally recommend a PHP debugger wholeheartedly, not only for debugging itself, but also for understanding the processes that happens under the hood.

Version control

Any software development needs to happen through a version controlled environment. By now, Drupal is universally using Git. So, you should make sure that you have Git installed locally, even if just to be able to check out the code examples we write in this book, which will be hosted on GitHub.

Composer

As I alluded to earlier, installing Drupal 8 is best done via a Composer template project. However, you may also install it straight from Git by checking out the latest tag or commit in the Drupal.org Git repository (`https://www.drupal.org/project/drupal/git-instructions`). If you do this, you will need to install its dependencies via Composer, and Drupal has many.

To this end, you will need to have Composer available on your development environment and have a basic understanding of how to use it.

The API site and coding standards

A lot of background knowledge is required for writing good Drupal code. Of course, the aim of a book such as this is to try to provide as much of that background knowledge as possible. However, self-documentation and research still remain key, and there are a number of resources that a Drupal developer should have on-hand.

The first is the official online API documentation. Just about every function in Drupal is documented using in-line code documentation. The Doxygen program is then used to extract that documentation and format it. You can access the full API documentation online at `http://api.drupal.org`.

Along with using the Drupal APIs, we strive to comply with Drupal's coding conventions. Best practices in software development include keeping code clean, consistent, and readable. One aspect of this is removing nuances in code formatting by following a fixed standard.

This is particularly important on a platform such as Drupal, where thousands of developers all contribute to the code. Without coding standards, the code would become a cluttered mishmash of styles, and valuable development time will be spent merely deciphering code instead of working on it.

The Drupal site has a manual on coding standards that each Drupal developer needs to become familiar with (`https://www.drupal.org/docs/develop/standards/coding-standards`). It won't happen overnight; you will get better with experience, but you can also configure your IDE to, for instance, flag any issues with your code formatting.

A third resource for developers new to Drupal 8 but who have experience with Drupal 7 is the change records database (`https://www.drupal.org/list-changes/drupal`). On this page, you'll find an inventory of the most important API and usage changes with some handy explanations that will be extremely helpful for Drupal 7 developers looking up how certain functions have been changed.

The developer (Devel) module

On your development environment, you can install a handy module called Devel (`http://drupal.org/project/devel`), which provides several sophisticated tools designed to help developers create and debug Drupal code.

The following are a few of the features of this module:

- Functions used for dumping objects and arrays into formatted Drupal output
- Tools for analyzing database usage and performance
- A content generator for quickly populating your site with testing content

Drush (the Drupal shell)

Sometimes, it is much easier to run some tasks with a single command in a console. Drush (`http://drupal.org/project/drush`) provides a command-line Drupal interface. It can be used to execute tasks with a few keystrokes at the console.

When developing, we often have to clear caches, run specific tasks, or deploy data to a remote server. Drush can help accomplish tasks like this. Additionally, we can write our own Drush commands that perform various custom tasks, for example, to be used in cron jobs. So having Drush installed is a must for any serious Drupal developer.

Drupal Console

If Drush is a tool that has been around for many years, the Drupal Console (`https://drupalconsole.com/`) project is new to Drupal 8. Its purpose is similar to that of Drush, and in this way, it complements it, if at times even overlaps with it. However, one thing is clear--its scope is much broader, especially in its handy commands that generate boilerplate code, which can get quite lengthy.

Although in this book we won't be using this tool, it's recommended that you install it as you progress with learning Drupal 8 module development and start generating certain code structures faster. That being said, I advise caution in using it at the expense of actually understanding what the code it generates actually does. Always strive to understand what you are doing, and never give in to blindly copying and pasting code from Stack Overflow or any other resource without grasping fully what it does.

Developer settings

While doing local development, it's beneficial to (sometimes) disable things such as caching in order to be quicker. Drupal 8 takes caching to a whole new level, so many hook implementations, for example, get cached. To circumvent this, we can use some local settings that disable caching, prevent CSS and JavaScript file aggregation, and do similar things.

These settings are found inside the `example.settings.local.php` file in the `/sites` folder of the installation. To benefit from these, you will need to make sure that they are included in your main `settings.php` file (either by copying them inside or including a file such as this).

A word of caution--do keep in mind that by developing with caching disabled at all times, you run the risk of overlooking certain aspects that won't work properly with caching enabled (such as invalidations). So, do try to toggle on/off these settings to ensure a production-like environment will work just as well as under your development conditions.

Summary

This chapter has been an overview of Drupal 8 for developers. We saw what technologies Drupal uses. We took a look at Drupal's architecture. We took a cursory glance at several prominent subsystems of Drupal. We also got a feel of which developer-oriented tools are to be used while working with Drupal.

Starting with the next chapter, we will be working with code. In fact, each of the subsequent chapters will focus on practical aspects of working with Drupal.

In the next chapter, we will create our first Drupal 8 module with the obligatory Hello World example.

2
Creating Your First Module

Now that we have covered some of the introductory aspects of Drupal 8 module development, it's time to dive right into the meat of what we are doing here--module creation.

Here are some of the important topics that we will cover in this chapter:

- Creating a new Drupal 8 module--the files that are necessary to get started
- Creating a route and controller
- Creating and using a service
- Creating a form
- Creating a custom block
- Working with links
- Using the Event Dispatcher

Concretely, in this chapter, we will create a new custom module called *Hello World*. In this module, we will define a route that maps to a Controller and that outputs the age-old programming message. So, this will be our first win.

Next, we will define a service that our Controller will use to pimp up our message. After all, we don't want the same message presented to the user all day long. This simple example, however, will illustrate what services are and how to interact with the Service Container in order to make use of them.

Then, we will create a form where an administrator will be able to override the message shown on our page. It will be stored in a configuration, and we will alter our service to make use of that configuration. The key takeaway here will be the use of the Form API. However, we will also discuss how to store some basic configuration values and add dependencies to our existing services.

Finally, we want to become a bit more flexible. Why should users only be greeted on a specific page? We will create a custom block that can be placed anywhere on the site and will display the same message. Here, we will see how block plugins are defined and how they can expose their own configuration forms to be more flexible.

Although not strictly related to our Hello World example, we will also look at how to work with links programmatically in Drupal 8. It's a very common task any Drupal 8 developer needs to do very often. So, we will cover the basics, and some pointers as to where to look for more info will be given. Moreover, we will also look at using the Event Dispatcher component, and more importantly, subscribing to events. We'll illustrate this with a fairly common example of why you'd need to do this--performing redirects from incoming requests.

By the end of this chapter, you should have the foundational knowledge necessary to build your own module from scratch. Moreover, you should be able to understand and implement some of the most commonly used techniques in Drupal 8 module development.

Creating a module

Creating a simple Drupal 8 module is not difficult. You only need one file to get it recognized by the core installation and to be able to enable it. In this state, it won't do much, but it will be installable. Let's first take a look at how to do this, and then we will progressively add meat to it in order to achieve the goals set out at the beginning of the chapter.

Custom Drupal 8 modules typically belong inside the `/custom` directory of the `/modules` folder found inside the root Drupal installation. You would put contributed modules inside a `/contrib` directory instead, in order to have a clear distinction. This is a standard practice, so that is where we will place our custom module, called *Hello World*.

We will start by creating a folder called `hello_world`. This will also be the module's machine name used in many other places. Inside, we will need to create an info file that describes our module. This file is named `hello_world.info.yml`. This naming structure is important--first, the module name, then `info` and followed by the `.yml` extension. You will hear about this file being often referred to as the module's `info` file (due to it having had the `.info` extension in the past before Drupal 8 used YAML).

Inside this file, we will need to add some minimal info that describes our module. We will go with something like this:

```
name: Hello World
description: Hello World module
type: module
core: 8.x
package: Custom
```

Some of this is self-explanatory, but let's see what these lines mean. The first two represent the human-readable name and description of the module. The `type` key means that this is a module info file rather than a theme. In Drupal 8, this has become mandatory. The `core` key specifies that this module works with the version 8 of Drupal, and it won't be installable on previous or future versions. Finally, we will place this in a generic `Custom` package so that it gets categorized in this group on the modules administration screen.

That is pretty much it. The module can now be enabled either through the UI at `/admin/modules` or via Drush using the `drush en hello_world` command.

Before we move on, let's see what other options you can add (and probably will need to add at some point or another) into the info file:

Module dependencies: If your module depends on one or more other modules, you can specify this in its info file like so:

```
dependencies:
  - drupal:views
  - ctools:ctools
```

The dependencies should be named in the `project:module` format, where `project` is the project name as it appears in the URL of the project on Drupal.org and `module` is the machine name of the module. You can even include version restrictions, for example, `ctools:ctools (>=8.x-3.x)`.

Configuration: If your module has a general configuration form that centralizes the configuration options of the module, you can specify the route of that form in the info file. Doing so will add a link to that form on the `admin/modules` UI page where modules are being installed.

Your first hook implementation

The module as it stands doesn't do much. In fact, it does nothing. However, do pat yourself on the back, as you have created your first Drupal 8 module. Before we move on to the interesting stuff we planned out, let's implement our first hook responsible for providing some helpful info about our module.

As we hinted at in the first chapter, when Drupal encounters an event for which there is a hook (and there are hundreds of such events), it will look through all of the modules for matching hook implementations. Now, how does it find the matching implementations? It looks for the functions that are named in the `module_name_hook_name` format, where `hook_name` is replaced by the name of the hook being implemented. The name of a hook is whatever comes after `hook_`. We will see an example below when we implement `hook_help()`. However, once it finds the implementations, it will then execute each of them, one after another. Once all hook implementations have been executed, Drupal will continue its processing.

Depending on the module size, it's recommended that you place all your hook implementations inside a `.module` file. There will be cases, however, when you'll organize them in other files, either by including those files inside the `.module` file yourself or using specific file naming conventions that gets them included by Drupal. However, for now, we stick with the default.

So, let's create a `.module` file in our module folder called `hello_world.module` and place an opening PHP tag at the top. In previous versions of Drupal, a `.module` PHP file was also required to get started with, but in Drupal 8, it is no longer necessary. That being said, we will create one now. Then, we can have the following `hook_help()` implementation inside (and typically all other hook implementations):

```php
use Drupal\Core\Routing\RouteMatchInterface;

/**
 * Implements hook_help().
 */
function hello_world_help($route_name, RouteMatchInterface $route_match) {
  switch ($route_name) {
    case 'help.page.hello_world':
      $output = '';
      $output .= '<h3>' . t('About') . '</h3>';
      $output .= '<p>' . t('This is an example module.') . '</p>';
      return $output;

    default:
  }
```

```
}
```

As you can see, the name of the function respects the above-mentioned format--`module_name_hook_name`--because we are implementing `hook_help`. So, we replaced `hook` with the module name and `hook_name` with `help`. Moreover, this particular hook takes two parameters that we can use inside it; though, in our case, we only use one, that is, the route name.

The purpose of this hook is to provide Drupal some help text about what this module does. You won't always implement this hook, but it's good to be aware of it. The way it works is that each new module receives its own route inside the main p module, where users can browse this info--ours is `help.page.hello_world`. So, in this implementation, we will tell Drupal (and more, specifically, the core `Help` module) the following--if a user is looking at our module's help route (page), show the info contained in the `$output` variable. And that's pretty much it.

According to the Drupal coding standards, the DocBlock message above the hook implementation needs to stay short and concise, as in the preceding example. We do not generally document anything further for Drupal core hooks or popular `contrib` module hooks because they should be documented elsewhere. If, however, you are implementing a custom hook defined in one of your modules, it's okay to add a second paragraph describing what it does.

Users can now reach this page from the module administration page by clicking on the **Help** link for each individual module that has this hook implemented. Easy, right?

Even though we are not really providing any useful info through this hook, implementing it made helped us understand how a hook is implemented and what the naming convention is for doing so. Additionally, we saw an example of a traditional (procedural) Drupal extension point that module developers can use. In doing so, we literally extended the capability of the **Help** module by allowing it to give more info to users.

Now, let's move on to creating something of ours own.

Route and controller

The first real piece of functionality we set out to create was a simple Drupal 8 page that outputs the age-old *Hello World* string. For doing this, we will need two things--a route and a controller. So, let's start with the first one.

The route

Inside our module, we will need to create our routing file that will hold all our statically defined routes. The name of this file will be `hello_world.routing.yml`. By now, I assume that you understand what the deal is with the file naming conventions in a Drupal 8 module. However, in any case, this is another YAML file in which we will need to put the YAML formatted data:

```
hello_world.hello:
  path: '/hello'
  defaults:
    _controller:
'\Drupal\hello_world\Controller\HelloWorldController::helloWorld'
    _title: 'Our first route'
  requirements:
    _permission: 'access content'
```

This is our first route definition. It starts with the route name (`hello_world.hello`) followed by all the necessary info about it, below, in a YAML formatted multidimensional array. The standard practice is to have the route name start with the module name it is in, followed by route qualifiers as needed.

So, what does the route definition contain? There can be many options here, but, for now, we will stick with the simple ones that serve our purpose. For more info about all that you can configure, visit the relevant documentation page on `https://www.drupal.org/docs/8/api/routing-system/structure-of-routes`. It is a good resource to keep on hand.

First, we have a path key, which indicates the path we want this route to work on. Then, we have a `defaults` section, which usually contains info relevant to the handlers responsible for delivering something when this route is accessed. In our case, we set the controller and method responsible for delivering the page and the title of the page. Finally, we have a `requirements` section, which usually has to do with conditions that need to be met for this route to be accessible (or be hit)--things such as permissions and format. In our case, we will require users to have the `access content` permission, which most visitors will have. Don't worry, we will cover more about access in a later chapter.

That is all we need for our first route definition. Also, note that the Drupal 8 routing system is essentially identical to that of Symfony, albeit with some modifications here and there, and although our route definition is done, we will now need to create the Controller that maps to it and can deliver something to the user.

Before we do that, let's look at an example of a very common routing requirement you will most likely have to use really soon. We don't need this for the functionality we're building in this chapter, so I won't include it in the final code. However, it's important that you know how this works.

Route variables

A very common requirement is to have a variable route parameter (or more) that gets used by the code that maps to the route, for example, the ID or path alias of the page you want to show. These parameters can be added by wrapping a certain path element into curly braces, like so:

```
path: '/hello/{param}'
```

Here, `{param}` will map to a `$param` variable that gets passed as an argument to the controller or handler responsible for this route. So, if the user goes to the `hello/jack` path, the `$param` variable will have the `jack` value and the controller can use that.

Additionally, Drupal 8 comes with parameter converters that transform the parameter into something more meaningful. For example, an entity can be autoloaded and passed to the Controller directly instead of an ID. Also, if no entity is found, the route acts as a 404, saving us a few good lines of code. To achieve this, we will also need to describe the parameter so that Drupal knows how to autoload it. We can do so by adding a route option for that parameter:

```
options:
  parameters:
    param:
      type: entity:node
```

So, we have now mapped the {param} parameter to the node entity type. Hence, if the user goes to hello/1, the Node with the ID of 1 will be loaded (if it exists).

We can do one better. If, instead of {param},we name the parameter {node} (the machine name of the entity type), we can avoid having to write the parameters option in the route completely. Drupal will figure out that it is an entity and will try to load that node by itself. Neat, no?

So keep these things in mind the next time you need to write dynamic routes.

Namespaces

Before moving on with the Controller we set out to write, let's break down the namespace situation in Drupal 8 and how the folder structure is inside a module.

Drupal 8 uses the PSR-4 namespace autoloading standard. In effect, this means that the namespace of all Drupal core and module classes starts with \Drupal. For modules, the base namespace is \Drupal\module_name, where module_name is the machine name of the module. This then maps to the /src folder found inside the module directory (for main integration files). For PHPUnit tests, we have a different namespace, as we will see later in the book.

So essentially, we will need a /src folder inside our module to place all of our classes that need to be autoloaded. So, we can go ahead and create it.

The Controller

Now that we have found out more or less where we have to place our Controller, let's begin by creating a `Controller` folder inside our module's `/src` folder. Although not mandatory, this is a standard practice for Controller placement. Inside this folder, we can have our first Controller class file, that is, `HelloWorldController.php`.

Inside the file, we again have something simple (after the opening PHP tags):

```
namespace Drupal\hello_world\Controller;

use Drupal\Core\Controller\ControllerBase;

/**
 * Controller for the salutation message.
 */
class HelloWorldController extends ControllerBase {

  /**
   * Hello World.
   *
   * @return string
   */
  public function helloWorld() {
    return [
      '#markup' => $this->t('Hello World')
    ];
  }

}
```

As expected, we start with the namespace declaration. If you read the preceding section, the namespace choice will make sense. Then, we have our Controller class that extends the Drupal 8 `ControllerBase`, which happens to provide some helper tools (such as the `StringTranslationTrait`, which I will explain later in the book). If you remember our route definition, we have a `helloWorld` method that returns an array.

If you've worked with previous versions of Drupal, this array (called a *render array*) will be familiar. Otherwise, what you need to know right now is that we are returning simple markup with the `Hello World` text wrapped in the translation service I hinted at in the previous paragraph. After the Controller returns this array, there will be an `EventSubscriber` that takes this array, runs it through the Drupal theme layer, and returns the HTML page as a response. The actual content returned in the Controller will be wrapped in the `Main page content` block that is usually placed in the main content region.

Now, our simple Controller is done. If we now clear the cache, we can go to /hello where we should encounter a new page that outputs the **Our first route** title and the **Hello World** content. Success!:

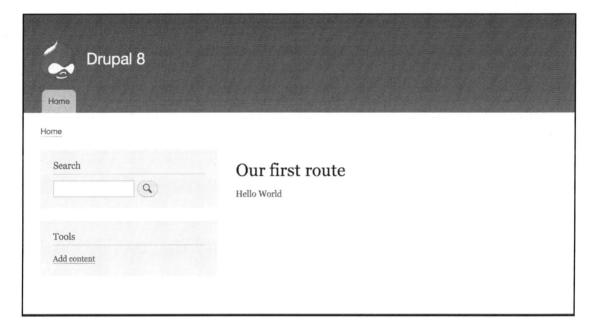

Services

I don't like the Controller making the decision on how to greet my users, first of all, because Controllers need to stay lean. I want my users to be greeted a bit more dynamically, depending on the time of day, and that will increase the complexity. Second of all, maybe I will want this greeting to be done elsewhere also (as, it turns out, I will do), and there is no way I am copying and pasting this logic somewhere else, nor am I going to misuse the Controller just to be able to call that method. The solution? We delegate the logic of constructing the greeting to a service and use that service in our Controller to simply output the greeting.

What is a service?

A service is an object that gets instantiated by a Service Container and is used to handle operations in a reusable way, for example, performing calculations and interacting with the database, an external API, or any number of things. Moreover, it can take dependencies (other services) and use them to help out. Services are a core part of the **dependency injection (DI)** principle that is commonly used in modern PHP applications and in Drupal 8.

If you don't have any experience with these concepts, an important thing to note is also that they are globally registered with the service and instantiated only once per request. This means that altering them after you requested them from the container means that they stay altered even if you request them again. In essence, they are singletons. So, you should write your services in such a way that they stay immutable, and most of the data they need to process is either from a dependency or passed in from the client that uses it (and does not affect it).

Many Drupal 8 core service definitions can be found inside the `core.services.yml` file located in the root `/core` folder. So, if you are ever looking for service names to use, your best bet is to look there. Additionally, core modules also have service definitions inside their respective `*.services.yml` files. So, make sure that you also check there.

The HelloWorldSalutation service

Now that we have a general idea as to what a service is, let's create one to see all this in practice.

As I mentioned earlier, I want my greetings to be more dynamic, that is, I want the salutation to depend on the time of day. So, we will create a (`HelloWorldSalutation`) class that is responsible for doing that and place it in the `/src` folder (or module's namespace root):

```php
namespace Drupal\hello_world;

use Drupal\Core\StringTranslation\StringTranslationTrait;

/**
 * Prepares the salutation to the world.
 */
class HelloWorldSalutation {

  use StringTranslationTrait;
```

```
/**
 * Returns the salutation
 */
public function getSalutation() {
  $time = new \DateTime();
  if ((int) $time->format('G') >= 06 && (int) $time->format('G') < 12) {
    return $this->t('Good morning world');
  }

  if ((int) $time->format('G') >= 12 && (int) $time->format('G') < 18) {
    return $this->t('Good afternoon world');
  }

  if ((int) $time->format('G') >= 18) {
    return $this->t('Good evening world');
  }
}
}
```

By now, I assume that the namespace business is clear, so I won't explain it again. Let's see what else we did here. First, we used the `StringTranslationTrait` in order to expose the translation function (I will explain this later on). Second, we created a rudimentary method that returns a different greeting depending on the time of day. This could probably have been done better, but for the purposes of this example, it works just fine.

 If there is any reason to believe that you will have more than one salutation services, you should create an interface this class can implement. This way, you'll be able to always type hint that interface instead of the class and make the implementations swappable.

Now that we have our class, it's time to define it as a service. We don't want to be going all `new HelloWorldSalutation()` all over our code base, but instead, register it with the Service Container and use it from there as a dependency. How do we do that?

First, we will need, yet again, a YAML file in our `hello_world.services.yml` module. This file starts with the `services` key, under which will be all the service definitions of our module. So, our file will look like this (for now):

```
services:
  hello_world.salutation:
    class: Drupal\hello_world\HelloWorldSalutation
```

This is the simplest possible service definition you can have. You give it a name (`hello_world.salutation`) and map it to a class to be instantiated. It is a standard practice to have the service name start with your module name.

Once we clear the cache, the service will get registered with the Service Container and will be available to use.

Tagged services

Service definitions can also be tagged in order to inform the container as to a specific purpose that they serve. Typically, these are picked up by a collector service that uses them for a given subsystem. As an example, if we wanted to tag the `hello_world.salutation` service, it would look something this:

```
hello_world.salutation:
  class: Drupal\hello_world\HelloWorldSalutation
  tags:
    - {name: tag_name}
```

Tags can also get a priority, as we will see in some examples later in this book.

Using services in Drupal 8

Before we go and use our service in the Controller we created, let's take a breather and run through the ways you can make use of services once they are registered.

There are essentially two ways--statically and injected. The first is done by a static call to the Service Container, whereas the second uses dependency injection to pass the object through the constructor (or in some rare cases, a setter method). However, let's check out how, why, and what is the real difference.

Statically, you would use the global `Drupal` class to instantiate a service:

```
$service = \Drupal::service('hello_world.salutation');
```

This is how we use services in the `.module` files and classes, which are not exposed to the Service Container and into which we cannot inject--although the latter instances are rare. A few popular services also have shorthand methods on the `\Drupal` class, accessing them faster (and easier for IDE autocompletion), for example, `\Drupal::entityTypeManager()`. I recommend that you inspect the `\Drupal` class and take a look at the ones with shorthand methods available.

It is not the best practice, and for me, it is personally unacceptable to use the static method of service instantiation inside a Controller, service, plugin or any other class where an injection is an option. The reason is that it defeats much of the purpose of using a service, as it couples the two, and it becomes a nightmare to test. Inside hook implementations and other Drupal-specific procedural code, on the other hand, we have no choice, and it is normal to do so.

 Just because a code is inside a `.module` file, it doesn't mean that it should be there. In general, these modules should only contain things such as hook implementations or any other implementations that require a certain naming convention to be respected. They should also be lean and have their work delegated to services.

The proper way to use services is to inject them where needed. Admittedly, this approach is a bit more time-consuming, but, as you progress, it will become second nature. Also, since there are a few different ways to inject dependencies (based on the receiver), we will not cover them here. Instead, we will see how they work throughout this book, at the right time. We will take a look at a very important example right now in the next section.

Injecting the service into our Controller

We have now closed the parenthesis on how services can be used. Let's take a look at how to inject our newly created service into our Controller.

We will need to add some code to our Controller (typically at the beginning of the class so that we can immediately identify the presence of this code when looking at it):

```
/**
 * @var \Drupal\hello_world\HelloWorldSalutation
 */
protected $salutation;

/**
 * HelloWorldController constructor.
 *
 * @param \Drupal\hello_world\HelloWorldSalutation $salutation
 */
public function __construct(HelloWorldSalutation $salutation) {
  $this->salutation = $salutation;
}

/**
 * {@inheritdoc}
 */
```

```
public static function create(ContainerInterface $container) {
  return new static(
    $container->get('hello_world.salutation')
  );
}
```

In addition to this, ensure that you include the relevant use statements at the top of the file:

```
use Drupal\hello_world\HelloWorldSalutation;
use Symfony\Component\DependencyInjection\ContainerInterface;
```

So, what is going on here? First, we give the Controller a constructor method, which takes our service as an argument and stores it as a property. For me, this is usually the very first method in the class, but how does this constructor get its argument? It gets it via the create() method, which receives the Service Container as a parameter and is free to choose the service(s) needed by the Controller constructor. This is usually my second method in a class. I prefer this order because it's very easy to check whether they are present. Also, their presence is important, especially when inheriting and observing what the parent is injecting, but how does this injection business work in reality?

In a nutshell, after the route is found and the responsible Controller is resolved, a check is made to see whether the latter implements ContainerInjectionInterface. Our Controller does so via its parent ControllerBase. If it does, the Controller gets instantiated via the create() method and the container is passed to it. From there, it is responsible for creating a new static version of itself with the required services from the container--not that complicated, really!

The create() method is a staple practice in the Drupal 8 dependency injection pattern, so you will see it quite a lot. However, one thing to keep in mind is that you should never pass the entire container to the class you instantiate with it because you are no longer doing dependency injection then.

A note about ControllerBase, which we are extending--it is a standard practice to extend it. It provides some nice traits, implements interfaces that are required and shows what the class purpose is immediately. However, from the point of view of dependency injection, I advise against using the helper methods that return services (for example, entityManager()). They, unfortunately, load services statically, which is not the best practice in this case. You should instead inject them yourself as we did earlier in this chapter.

Okay, now to turn back to our example. Now that we have the service injected, we can use it to render the dynamic salutation:

```
return [
  '#markup' => $this->salutation->getSalutation(),
];
```

There we have it. Now, our greeting is dependent on the time of day and our Controller is dependent on our salutation service.

One thing I would like to specify about our example is that I disregarded caching for the sake of simplicity. With the cache turned on, the page would be cached and served with potentially the wrong salutation. However, we'll have an entire chapter dedicated to caching, where we will cover all these intricacies, so there is no point in complicating our example.

The form

So, now, our page displays a greeting dynamically depending on the time of day. However, we now want an administrator to specify what the greeting should actually be, in other words, to override the default behavior of our salutation if they so choose.

The ingredients for achieving this will be as follows:

- A route (a new page) that displays a form that the administrator can add the greeting with
- A configuration object that will store the greeting

In building this functionality, we will also take a look at how to add a dependency to our existing service. So, let's get started with our new route that naturally goes inside the `hello_world.routing.yml` file:

```
hello_world.greeting_form:
  path: '/admin/config/salutation-configuration'
  defaults:
    _form: '\Drupal\hello_world\Form\SalutationConfigurationForm'
    _title: 'Salutation configuration'
  requirements:
    _permission: 'administer site configuration'
```

Most of this route definition is the same as we saw earlier. There is one change, though, that it maps to a form instead of a Controller. This means that the entire page is a form page. Also, since the path is within the administration space, it will use the administration theme of the site. What is left to do now is to create our form class inside the /Form folder of our namespace (a standard practice directory for storing forms, but not mandatory).

Due to the power of inheritance, our form is actually very simple. However, I will explain what goes on in the background and guide you on your path to building more complex forms. So, here we have our form:

```
namespace Drupal\hello_world\Form;

use Drupal\Core\Form\ConfigFormBase;
use Drupal\Core\Form\FormStateInterface;

/**
 * Configuration form definition for the salutation message.
 */
class SalutationConfigurationForm extends ConfigFormBase {

  /**
   * {@inheritdoc}
   */
  protected function getEditableConfigNames() {
    return ['hello_world.custom_salutation'];
  }

  /**
   * {@inheritdoc}
   */
  public function getFormId() {
    return 'salutation_configuration_form';
  }

  /**
   * {@inheritdoc}
   */
  public function buildForm(array $form, FormStateInterface $form_state) {
    $config = $this->config('hello_world.custom_salutation');

    $form['salutation'] = array(
      '#type' => 'textfield',
      '#title' => $this->t('Salutation'),
      '#description' => $this->t('Please provide the salutation you want to
use.'),
      '#default_value' => $config->get('salutation'),
    );
```

```
        return parent::buildForm($form, $form_state);
    }

    /**
     * {@inheritdoc}
     */
    public function submitForm(array &$form, FormStateInterface $form_state)
{
        $this->config('hello_world.custom_salutation')
          ->set('salutation', $form_state->getValue('salutation'))
          ->save();

        parent::submitForm($form, $form_state);
    }
}
```

Before going into the explanation, I should say that this is it. Clearing the cache and navigating to admin/config/salutation-configuration will present you with your simple **configuration** form via which you can save a custom salutation message:

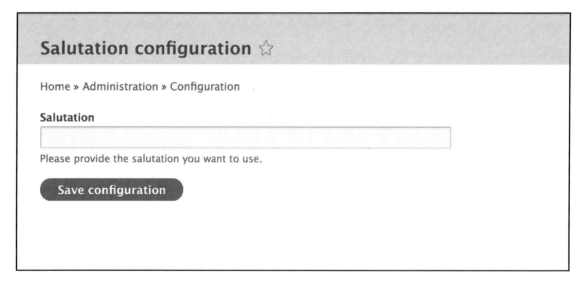

Later on, we will make use of that value. However, first, let's talk a bit about forms in general, and then this form in particular.

A form in Drupal 8 is represented by a class that implements `FormInterface`. Typically, we either extend from `FormBase` or from `ConfigFormBase`, depending on what its purpose is. In this case we created a configuration form so we extended from the latter class.

There are four main methods that come into play in this interface:

- `getFormId()`: Returns a unique, machine-readable name for the form.

- `buildForm()`: Returns the form definition (an array of form element definitions and some extra metadata, as needed).

- `validateForm()`: The handler that gets called to validate the form submission. It receives the form definition and a `$form_state` object that contains, among others, the submitted values. You can flag invalid values on their respective form elements, which means that the form is not submitted but refreshed (with the offending elements highlighted).

- `submitForm()`: The handler that gets called when the form is submitted (if validation has passed without errors). It receives the same arguments as `validateForm()`. You can perform operations, such as saving the submitted values, or trigger some other kind of flow.

Defining a form, in a nutshell, means creating an array of form element definitions. The resulting form is very similar to the render array we mentioned earlier and which we will describe in more depth in the `Chapter 5`, *Creating Your First Module*. When creating your forms, you have a large number of form element types to use. A complete reference of what they are and what their options are (their definition specificities) can be found on the Drupal Form API reference page (`https://api.drupal.org/api/drupal/elements/8.2.x`). Keep this page close to you throughout your Drupal 8 development.

From a dependency injection point of view, forms can receive arguments from the Service Container in the same way we injected the salutation service into our Controller. As a matter of fact, `ConfigFormBase`,which we are extending in our preceding form above, injects the `config.factory` service because it needs to use it for reading and storing configuration values. This is primarily why we extend from that form--so that we don't have to write this code ourselves. Drupal is full of these helpful classes we can extend and provides a bunch of useful boilerplate techniques that are very commonly used across the Drupal ecosystem.

If the form you are building is not storing or working with your configuration, you will typically extend from `FormBase`, which provides some static methods and traits and also implements some interfaces. The same word of caution goes for its helper service methods as for the `ControllerBase`.

Let's turn to our preceding form class and dissect it a bit now that we know a thing or two about forms.

Check the `getFormId()` method that we have now. We also have a `buildForm()` and `submitForm()`, but not `validateForm()`. The latter is not mandatory, and we don't actually need it for our example, but if we did, we could have something like this:

```
/**
 * {@inheritdoc}
 */
public function validateForm(array &$form, FormStateInterface
$form_state) {
   $salutation = $form_state->getValue('salutation');
   if (strlen($salutation) > 20) {
     $form_state->setErrorByName('salutation', $this->t('This salutation
is too long'));
   }
}
```

In this validation handler, we basically check whether the submitted value for the `salutation` element is longer than 20 characters. If so, we set an error on that element (to turn it red usually) and specify an error message on the form state specific to this error. The form will then be refreshed and the error will be presented, and the submit handler, in this case, will not be called.

For the purposes of our example, this is, however, not necessary, so I will not include it in the final code.

If we return to our form class, we will also see a strange `getEditableConfigNames()` method. This is required by the `ConfigFormBaseTrait`, which is used in the `ConfigFormBase` class that we are extending, and it needs to return an array of configuration object names that this form needs and which this form intends to edit. This is because there are two ways of loading configuration objects: editable and immutable. With this method, we inform it that we want to edit that configuration item.

As we see on the first line of `buildForm()`, we are using the `config()` method of the above-mentioned trait to load up our editable configuration object from the Drupal 8 configuration factory. This is to check the value that is currently stored in it. Then, we define our form elements (one, in our case, a simple text field). As `#default_value` (the value present in the element when the user goes to the form) on that form element, we will put whatever is in the configuration object. The rest of the element options are self-explanatory and pretty standard across all element types. Consult the Form API reference to see what other options are available and for which element types. Finally, at the end of the method, we also called the parent method because that provides the form's submit button, which for our purposes is enough.

The last method we wrote is the submit handler, which basically loads up the editable configuration object, puts the submitted value in it, and saves it. Finally, it also calls the parent method, which then simply sets a success message to the user on the screen using `drupal_set_message()`--a standard way of showing the user success or error messages from a code context.

That is pretty much it; this will work just fine.

From the point of view of configuration, we used `ConfigFormBase` to make our lives easier and combine the form aspect with that of the configuration storage. In a later chapter, we will talk a bit more about the different types of storage and also cover how to work with the configuration objects in more detail, as well as what these entail.

Altering forms

Before going ahead with our proposed functionality, I would like to open a parenthesis and discuss forms in detail. One of the principal things that you will do as a module developer in Drupal is alter forms defined by other modules or Drupal core. So, it behooves us to talk about it early on and what better moment than now when defining the form itself is still fresh in our minds.

Obviously, the form we just created belongs to us and we can change it however we want. However, many forms out there have been defined by others, and there will be just as many times that you will want to make changes to them. Drupal provides us with a very flexible, albeit still procedural way, of doing so--a suite of *alter* hooks, but what are alter hooks?

The first thing we did in this chapter was implement `hook_help()`. That is an example of an invoked hook by which a caller (Drupal core or any module) asks all other modules to provide input. This input is then aggregated in some way and made use of. The other type of hooks we have in Drupal are the *alter* hooks, which are used to allow other modules to make changes to an array or an object before that array or object is used for whatever it is used for. So, in the case of forms, there are some alter hooks that allow modules to make changes to the form before it's processed for rendering.

You may be wondering why am I saying that for making changes to a form we have more than one alter hook. Let me explain by giving an example of how other modules could alter the form we just defined:

```
/**
 * Implements hook_form_alter().
 */
function my_module_form_alter(&$form, \Drupal\Core\Form\FormStateInterface
$form_state, $form_id) {
  if ($form_id == 'salutation_configuration_form') {
    // Perform alterations.
  }
}
```

In the preceding code, we implemented the generic `hook_form_alter()`, which gets fired for all forms when being built. The first two arguments are the form and form state (the same as we saw in the form definition), the former being passed by reference. This is the typical *alter* concept--we make changes to an existing variable and don't return anything. The third parameter is the form ID, the one we defined in the `getFormId()` method of our form class. We check to ensure that the form is correct and then we can make alterations to the form.

This is, however, almost always the wrong approach because the hook is fired for all forms indiscriminately. Even if we don't actually do anything for most of them, it's still a useless function call, not to mention that if we want to alter 10 forms in our module, there will be a lot of `if` conditionals in there--the price we pay for procedural functions. Instead, though, we can do this:

```
/**
 * Implements hook_form_FORM_ID_alter().
 */
function my_module_form_salutation_configuration_form_alter(&$form,
\Drupal\Core\Form\FormStateInterface $form_state, $form_id) {
  // Perform alterations.
}
```

Here, we are implementing `hook_form_FORM_ID_alter()`, which is a dynamic alter hook in that its name contains the actual ID of the form we want to alter. So, with this approach, we ensure that this function is called only when it's time to alter our form, and the other benefit is that if we need to alter another one, we can implement the same for that and have our logic neatly separated.

Custom submit handlers

So, up to now, we have seen how other modules can make changes to our form. That means adding new form elements, changing existing ones, and things like that, but what about our validation and submit handlers (those methods that get called when the form is submitted). How can those be altered?

Typically, for the forms defined as we did, it's pretty simple. Once we alter the form and inspect the `$form` array, we can find a `#submit` key, which is an array that has one item--`::submitForm`. This is simply the `submitForm()` method on the form class. So, what we can do is either remove this item and add our own function or simply add another item to that array:

```
/**
 * Implements hook_form_FORM_ID_alter().
 */
function my_module_form_salutation_configuration_form_alter(&$form,
\Drupal\Core\Form\FormStateInterface $form_state, $form_id) {
  // Perform alterations.
  $form['#submit'][] = 'hello_world_salutation_configuration_form_submit';
}
```

And the callback we added to the `#submit` array above can look like this:

```
/**
 * Custom submit handler for the form_salutation_configuration form.
 *
 * @param $form
 * @param \Drupal\Core\Form\FormStateInterface $form_state
 */
function my_module_salutation_configuration_form_submit(&$form,
\Drupal\Core\Form\FormStateInterface $form_state) {
  // Do something when the form is submitted.
}
```

So, the cool thing is that you can choose to tack on your own callback or replace the existing one. Keep in mind that the order they are in that array is the order they get executed. So, you can also change the order.

There is another case though. If the submit button on the form has a `#submit` property specifying its own handler, the default form `#submit` handlers we saw just now won't fire anymore. This was not the case with our form. So, in that situation, you will need to add your own handler to that array. Hence, the only difference is the place you tack on the submit handler. A prominent example of such a form is the Node add/edit form.

Finally, when it comes to the validation handler, it works exactly the same as with the submit, but it all happens under the `#validate` array key.

Feel free to experiment with altering existing forms and inspect the variables they receive as arguments. I strongly encourage you to become familiar with the common form data and keep the documentation on form elements close by (`https://api.drupal.org/api/drupal/elements/8.2.x`).

Rendering forms

Staying on forms for just a bit longer, let's quickly learn how to render forms programmatically. Also, we have already seen how to map a form to a route definition so that the page being built contains the form when accessing the route path. However, there are times where we need to render a form programmatically, either inside a Controller or a block or wherever you want. We can do this using the `FormBuilder` service.

The form builder can be injected using the `form_builder` service key or used statically via the shorthand:

```
$builder = \Drupal::formBuilder();
```

Once we have it, we can build a form, like so:

```
$form =
$builder->getForm('Drupal\hello_world\Form\SalutationConfigurationForm');
```

In the preceding code, `$form` will be a render array of the form that we can return, for example, inside a Controller. We'll talk more about render arrays a bit later on, and you'll understand how they get turned into actual form markup. However, for now, this is all you need to know about rendering forms programmatically--you get the form builder and request from it the form using the fully qualified name of the form class.

With this, we can close the parenthesis on forms.

Service dependencies

In the preceding section, we created a form that allows administrators to set a custom salutation message to be shown on the page. This message was stored in a configuration object that we can now load in our `HelloWorldSalutation` service. So, let's do just that in a two-step process.

First, we will need to alter our service definition to give our service an argument--the Drupal 8 configuration factory (the service responsible for loading config objects). This is how our service definition should look:

```
hello_world.salutation:
    class: Drupal\hello_world\HelloWorldSalutation
    arguments: ['@config.factory']
```

The addition is the argument's key, which is an array of service names proceeded by `@`. In this case, `config.factory` is the responsible service name, which if we check in the `core.services.yml` file, we will note that it maps to the `Drupal\Core\Config\ConfigFactory` class.

So, with this change, the `HelloWorldSalutation` class will be passed an instance of `ConfigFactory`. All we need to do now is to adjust our class to actually receive it:

```
/**
 * @var \Drupal\Core\Config\ConfigFactoryInterface
 */
protected $configFactory;

/**
 * HelloWorldSalutation constructor.
 *
 * @param \Drupal\Core\Config\ConfigFactoryInterface $config_factory
 */
public function __construct(ConfigFactoryInterface $config_factory) {
  $this->configFactory = $config_factory;
}
```

There's nothing too complicated going on here. We added a constructor and set `config` `factory` in a property. We can now use this config factory to load our configuration object that we saved in the form. However, before we do that, we should also *use* the `ConfigFactoryInterface` class at the top of the file:

```
use Drupal\Core\Config\ConfigFactoryInterface;
```

Now, at the top of the `getSalutation()` method, we can add the following bit:

```
$config = $this->configFactory->get('hello_world.custom_salutation');
$salutation = $config->get('salutation');
if ($salutation != "") {
  return $salutation;
}
```

With the preceding code, we can load the configuration object we saved in the form, and from it, we request the `salutation` key, where if you remember, we stored our message. If there is a value in there, we will return it. Otherwise, the code will continue and our previous logic of time-based greeting apply.

So, now if we reload our initial page, the message we saved through the form should show up. If we then return to the form and remove the message, this page should default back to the original dynamic greeting. Neat, right?

Let's now take a look at how we can create a custom block that we can place anywhere we like and which will output the same thing as our page.

Blocks

Custom blocks in Drupal 8 are plugins. Finally, we encounter our first plugin type. For the sake of full disclosure, the *content* blocks that you create through the UI to place in a region and the custom blocks that are placed in a region are content entities. So, the block system is a good example of how entities and plugins work hand in hand in Drupal 8, and not to make matters too complex for you, configuration entities (about which we will learn in a later chapter) also play a big role here.

The block system in Drupal 8 is a great shift from its predecessor. Before, you had to implement two obligatory hooks plus two optional hooks if you wanted the block to have a configuration, and the latter was always saved somewhere that had nothing to do with the block itself. In Drupal 8, we work with a simple plugin class that can be made container-aware (that is, we can inject dependencies into it) and we can store configuration in a logical fashion.

So, how do we create a custom block plugin easily? All we need is one class, placed in the right namespace--Drupal\module_name\Plugin\Block. In this case (with plugins), the folder naming is important. The plugin discoverability is dependent on the plugin type itself, and this one has the Plugin\Block namespace bit in it. Enough talk, let's create a simple block that just renders the same as our Controller did previously, and I will explain things along the way.

Our first block plugin

So, this is our plugin class--HelloWorldSalutationBlock--that does just that:

```
namespace Drupal\hello_world\Plugin\Block;

use Drupal\Core\Block\BlockBase;
use Drupal\Core\Plugin\ContainerFactoryPluginInterface;
use Symfony\Component\DependencyInjection\ContainerInterface;
use Drupal\hello_world\HelloWorldSalutation as HelloWorldSalutationService;

/**
 * Hello World Salutation block.
 *
 * @Block(
 *   id = "hello_world_salutation_block",
 *   admin_label = @Translation("Hello world salutation"),
 * )
 */
class HelloWorldSalutationBlock extends BlockBase implements
ContainerFactoryPluginInterface {

  /**
   * Drupal\hello_world\HelloWorldSalutation definition.
   *
   * @var \Drupal\hello_world\HelloWorldSalutation
   */
  protected $salutation;

  /**
   * Construct.
   *
   * @param array $configuration
   *   A configuration array containing information about the plugin
instance.
   * @param string $plugin_id
   *   The plugin_id for the plugin instance.
   * @param string $plugin_definition
```

```
 *    The plugin implementation definition.
 * @param \Drupal\hello_world\HelloWorldSalutation $salutation
 */
public function __construct(array $configuration, $plugin_id,
$plugin_definition, HelloWorldSalutationService $salutation) {
    parent::__construct($configuration, $plugin_id, $plugin_definition);
    $this->salutation = $salutation;
}

/**
 * {@inheritdoc}
 */
public static function create(ContainerInterface $container, array
$configuration, $plugin_id, $plugin_definition) {
    return new static(
        $configuration,
        $plugin_id,
        $plugin_definition,
        $container->get('hello_world.salutation')
    );
}

/**
 * {@inheritdoc}
 */
public function build() {
    return [
        '#markup' => $this->salutation->getSalutation(),
    ];
}
}
```

Before even going through the explanation, you should know that clearing the cache and placing this block through the UI block management will do what we wanted. However, let's understand what is going on here first.

Perhaps the strangest thing you'll note is the DocBlock comment at the top of the class, which denotes that this is a `Block` plugin--the annotation. As I mentioned in the first chapter, annotations are the most common discovery mechanisms for plugins in Drupal core. In this case, the plugin definition we need is made up of an ID and administration label.

Properly defined plugin types have an `AnnotationInterface` implementation, which describes the properties that one can or should use in the annotation. So, if you are unsure what needs to be used, ensure that you look for this class for that specific plugin type.

Then, we see that our class extends `BlockBase` and also implements the `ContainerFactoryPluginInterface`. The former, similar to the Controller and Form we saw earlier, provides a number of helpful things a block plugin needs. However, we cannot really get around to extending this class because block plugins are quite complex, working with things such as context and configuration. So, ensure that you always extend this class. The latter is, however, optional. That interface makes this block plugin Container-aware, that is, at the moment of instantiation, it uses the `create()` method to build itself using the container for dependencies, and, sure enough, we have our `create()` method below.

Before moving on to the actual block building, we will need to talk a bit about the dependency injection in plugins. As you see, the signature of this `create()` method is different to the one we saw in the Controller. This is also why we are using a different container-aware interface. The reason is that plugins are constructed with a few extra parameters: `$configuration`, `$plugin_id`, and `$plugin_definition`. The first contains any configuration values that were stored with the plugin (or passed when building), the second is the ID set in the plugin annotation (or other discovery mechanism), and the third is an array that contains the metadata on this plugin (including all the info found in the annotation). However, apart from this, it's business as usual when it comes to dependency injection. If a plugin type base class doesn't implement this interface, you can do so yourself directly in your plugin. You can do this with most plugins (there are a few exceptions, which cannot be made container-aware unfortunately, but very rare).

Finally, we have a `build()` method, which is responsible for building the block content. It needs to return a render array (just like our Controller did), and as you can see, we are using our injected service and it returns the same greeting. That is pretty much what we need to do to achieve our goal. There are other important aspects to block plugins we will cover later, such as caching and access, but we have specific chapters for those topics.

Block configuration

Before we close the book on our custom block plugin, though, let's take a look at how we can add a configuration form to it. This way, we can practice using some more Form API elements and see how we can store and use block configuration.

Even though our functionality is complete (for the moment), let's imagine that we need a Boolean-like control on our block configuration so that when an admin places the block, they can toggle something and that value can be used in the `build()` method. We can achieve this with three to four methods on our plugin class.

First, we will need to implement the `defaultConfiguration()` method, in which we can describe the items of configuration that we are storing for this block and the default values of these items. So, we can have something like this:

```
/**
 * {@inheritdoc}
 */
public function defaultConfiguration() {
  return [
    'enabled' => 1,
  ];
}
```

We return an array of keys and values that will be in the configuration. Also, since we said we are going with a Boolean field, we'll use the number 1 as the value to a fictitious key, `enabled`.

Next, we will need to implement the `blockForm()` method, which provides our form definition for this configuration item:

```
/**
 * {@inheritdoc}
 */
public function blockForm($form, FormStateInterface $form_state) {
  $config = $this->getConfiguration();

  $form['enabled'] = array(
    '#type' => 'checkbox',
    '#title' => t('Enabled'),
    '#description' => t('Check this box if you want to enable this
feature.'),
    '#default_value' => $config['enabled'],
  );

  return $form;
}
```

Let's not forget the *use* statement at the top of the file:

```
use Drupal\Core\Form\FormStateInterface;
```

As you can see, this is a typical Form API definition for one form element of the type `checkbox`. Additionally, we are using the `getConfiguration()` handy method of the parent class to load up the configuration values that get saved with this block. If none have been saved, you'll note that the `enabled` key will be present in it with the default value we set above (1).

Lastly, we will need the submit handler that will do the necessaries to store the configuration. I used inverted commas because we don't actually have to do anything related to storage, but just map the value submitted in the form to the relevant key in the configuration. The block system does it for us. Also, no extra processing is needed, in our case, either:

```
/**
 * {@inheritdoc}
 */
public function blockSubmit($form, FormStateInterface $form_state) {
   $this->configuration['enabled'] = $form_state->getValue('enabled');
}
```

It couldn't be simpler than this. Now when we place our custom block somewhere, the form we are presented with will incorporate our form elements that allow us to toggle the `enabled` key. What remains to be done is to make use of this value inside the `build()` method. We can do that similarly to how we loaded the configuration values inside the `buildForm()` method:

```
$config = $this->getConfiguration();
```

Alas, we don't really need this configuration in our example block, so we won't be adding it to our code. However, it is important for you to know how to do it, so we covered it here. Moreover, before moving on, I also want to specify that you can use an optional method to handle validation on the configuration form, that is, `blockValidate()`, which will take the same parameters as `blockSubmit()` and will work the same way as the validation handler we saw when we built our standalone form. So, I won't repeat that here.

Working with links

One of the principle characteristics of a web application is the myriad of links between its resources. They are in fact the glue that brings it together. So, in this section, I want to show you a few common techniques used while working with links programmatically in Drupal 8.

There are two main aspects when talking about link building in Drupal--the URL and the actual link tag itself. So, creating a link involves a two-step process that deals with these two, but can also be shortened into a single call via some helper methods.

The URL

URLs in Drupal 8 are represented with the `Drupal\Core\Url` class, which has a number of static methods that allow you to create an instance. The most important of these is `::fromRoute()`, which takes a route name, route parameters (if any are needed for that route), and an array of options to create a new instance of `Url`. There are other such methods available that turn all sorts of other things into a `Url`, most notably, the `::fromUri()` method that takes in an internal or external URL. Sometimes, these methods are very helpful, especially when dealing with dynamically obtained data (such as a URL). However, when hardcoding, it's always best to work with route names because that allows you to later change the actual path behind that route without affecting your code.

There are many options that can be passed to the `Url` when creating it, inside the `$options` array. You can pass an array of query parameters, a fragment, and others. These will then help construct a URL as complex as you need without having to deal with strings yourself. I suggest that you check out the documentation above the `::fromUri()` method because it describes them all. Also, keep in mind that the options are pretty much the same, regardless of the method that you use to create the `Url` object.

The link

Now that we have a `Url` object, we can use it to generate a link. We can do this in two ways:

- Use the `LinkGenerator` service (named `link_generator`) and call its `generate()` method passing the link text and the `Url` object we have obtained. This will return a `GeneratedLink` object, which contains the actual string representation of the link, that is, the markup.

- Use the `Link` class, which wraps a render element (we will talk more about render elements in the `Theming` chapter) to represent the link.

Let's take a look at an example of both, from start to finish.

Consider this example of generating a link using the service:

```
$url = Url::fromRoute('my_route', ['param_name' => $param_value]);
$link = \Drupal::service('link_generator')->generate('My link', $url);
```

We can then directly print `$link` because it implements the `__toString()` method.

Now, consider this example of generating a link using the `Link` class:

```
$url = Url::fromRoute('my_other_route');
$link = Link::fromTextAndUrl('My link', $url);
```

We now have `$link` as a `Link` object whose `toRenderable()` returns a render array of the `#type => 'link'`. Behind the scenes, at render time, it will also use the link generator to transform that into a link string.

If we have a `Link` object, we can also use the link generator ourselves to generate a link based on it:

```
$link = \Drupal::service('link_generator')->generateFromLink($linkObject);
```

Which way to link?

As we saw, we have a number of ways to create links and URL representations, but when it comes to creating a link, which method should we use? There are advantages and disadvantages for each one.

When it comes to URL, as mentioned, it's a good idea to stick to hardcoding routes rather than URIs. However, if you are working with dynamic data, such as user input or stored strings, the other methods are perfectly valid. I recommend that you look at the `Url` class in detail because you will be using it quite a bit as you develop Drupal 8 modules.

Regarding the actual links, using the service to generate a link means that you are creating a string at your point in the code. This means that it cannot be altered later in the process. On the other hand, using the `Link` class falls nicely in line with the entire render array rationale of delaying the actual generation to the last possible moment. We will talk more about render arrays later on. So, the choice you make depends on the link you need to generate and your answer to the following question: is the link something that might have to be alterable by other modules/themes? If so, proceed with the render array. Otherwise, you might consider generating if you can inject the service properly.

Event Dispatcher and redirects

A common thing you'll have to do as a module developer is to intercept a given request and redirect it to another page, and more often than not, this will have to be dynamic, depending on the current user or other contextual info. Drupal 7 developers know very well that this has always been an easy task. Simply implement `hook_init()`, which gets called on each request and then use the famous `drupal_goto()` function. This, however, is no longer the case in Drupal 8. What we have to do now is subscribe to the `kernel.request` event (remember this from the preceding chapter?) and then change the response directly. However, before seeing an example of this, let's take a look at how we can perform a simpler redirect from within a Controller.

Redirecting from a Controller

In this chapter, we wrote a Controller that returns a render array. We know from the preceding chapter that this is picked up by the theme system and turned into a response. In `Chapter 4`, *Theming*, we will go into a bit more detail and see how this process is done. However, this render pipeline can also be bypassed if the Controller returns a response directly. Let's consider the following example:

```
return new Response('my text');
```

This will bypass much of Drupal, in fact, and return a blank white page with only the "my text" string on it. The `Response` class we're using is from the Symfony HTTP Foundation component.

However, we also have a handy `RedirectResponse` class that we can use, and it will redirect the browser to another page:

```
return new RedirectResponse('node/1');
```

The first parameter is the URL where we want to redirect. Typically, this should be an absolute URL; however, browsers nowadays are smart enough to handle a relative path also, as in the preceding example. So, in this case, the Controller will redirect us to that path.

Redirecting from a subscriber

Many times, our business logic says that we need to perform a redirect from a certain page to another if various conditions match. For these, we can subscribe to the request event and simply change the response--essentially bypassing the normal process, which would have gone through all the layers of Drupal. However, before we see an example, let's talk about the Event Dispatcher for just a bit.

The central player in this system is the `event_dispatcher` service, which is an instance of the `ContainerAwareEventDispatcher` class. This service allows the dispatching of named events that take a payload in the form of an `Event` object, which wraps the data that needs to be passed around. Typically, the code responsible for dispatching an event will create an `Event` subclass with some handy methods for accessing the data that needs to be passed around. Finally, instances of `EventSubscriberInterface` listen to events that have certain names and can alter the `Event` object that has been passed. Essentially, then, this system allows subscribers to change data before the business logic uses it for something. In this respect, it is a prime example of an extension point in Drupal 8. Finally, registering event subscribers is a matter of creating a service tagged with `event_subscriber` and that implements the interface.

Let's now take a look at an example event subscriber that listens to the `kernel.request` event and redirects it to the home page if a user with a certain role tries to access our Hello World page. This will demonstrate both how to subscribe to events and how to perform a redirect. It will also show us how to use the current route match service to inspect the current route.

Let's create this subscriber by first writing the service definition for it:

```
hello_world.redirect_subscriber:
  class: \Drupal\hello_world\EventSubscriber\HelloWorldRedirectSubscriber
  arguments: ['@current_user']
  tags:
    - {name: event_subscriber}
```

As you see, we have the regular service definition with one argument and with the `event_subscriber` tag. The dependency is actually the service that points to the current user (either logged in or anonymous) in the form of an `AccountProxyInterface`. This is a wrapper to the `AccountInterface`, which represents the actual current user. Also, when I say user, I mean an object that has certain data about the user and not the actual entity object with all the field data. Certain things about the user are, however, accessible from the `AccountInterface`, such as the ID, the name, roles, and email. I recommend that you check out the interface for more info. However, for our example, we will use it to check whether the user has the `non_grata` role, which will trigger the redirect I mentioned.

Next, let's look at the event subscriber class itself:

```
namespace Drupal\hello_world\EventSubscriber;

use Drupal\Core\Session\AccountProxyInterface;
use Symfony\Component\EventDispatcher\EventSubscriberInterface;
use Symfony\Component\HttpFoundation\RedirectResponse;
use Symfony\Component\HttpFoundation\Request;
use Symfony\Component\HttpKernel\Event\GetResponseEvent;
use Symfony\Component\HttpKernel\KernelEvents;

/**
 * Subscribes to the Kernel Request event and redirects to the homepage
 * when the user has the "non_grata" role.
 */
class HelloWorldRedirectSubscriber implements EventSubscriberInterface {

  /**
   * @var \Drupal\Core\Session\AccountProxyInterface
   */
  protected $currentUser;

  /**
   * HelloWorldRedirectSubscriber constructor.
   *
   * @param \Drupal\Core\Session\AccountProxyInterface $currentUser
   */
  public function __construct(AccountProxyInterface $currentUser) {
    $this->currentUser = $currentUser;
  }

  /**
   * {@inheritdoc}
   */
  public static function getSubscribedEvents() {
    $events['kernel.request'][] = ['onRequest', 0];
```

```
      return $events;
  }

  /**
   * Handler for the kernel request event.
   *
   * @param \Symfony\Component\HttpKernel\Event\GetResponseEvent $event
   */
  public function onRequest(GetResponseEvent $event) {
    /** @var Request $request */
    $request = $event->getRequest();
    $path = $request->getPathInfo();
    if ($path !== '/hello') {
      return;
    }

    $roles = $this->currentUser->getRoles();
    if (in_array('non_grata', $roles)) {
      $event->setResponse(new RedirectResponse('/'));
    }
  }
}
```

As expected, we store the current user as a class property so that we can use it later on. Then, we implement the `EventSubscriberInterface::getSubscribedEvents()` method. This method needs to return a multidimensional array, which is basically a mapping between event names and the class methods to be called if that event is dispatched. And this is how we actually register methods to listen to one event or another, and we can listen to multiple events in the same subscriber class. It's typically a good idea to separate these, however, into different, more topical, classes. The callback method name is inside an array whose second value represents the priority of this callback compared to others you or other modules may define. The higher the number, the higher the priority, the earlier in the process it will run.

In our example, we listen to the `kernel.request` event I mentioned in the previous chapter. This event is dispatched by Symfony's `HttpKernel`, passing an instance of `GetResponseEvent` which basically wraps the `Request` object. The name of the `Event` class usually well describes the purpose of the event. In this case it is looking for a `Response` object to deliver to the browser. If we inspect the class, we can note that it has a `setResponse()` method on it, which we can use to set the response. If a subscriber provides one, it stops the event propagation (none of the other listeners with a lower priority are given a chance) and the response is returned.

So, in our `onRequest ()` callback method, we check the current path being requested, and if it is ours and the current user has the `non_grata` role, we set the `RedirectResponse` onto the event to redirect it to the home page. This will do the job we set out to do. If you go to the `/hello` page as a user with that role, you should be redirected to the home page. That being said, I don't like many aspects about this implementation. So, let's fix them.

First, we will hardcode the `kernel.request` event name (I did, can't blame you for that). Any decent code that dispatches events will use a class constant to define the event name. The subscribers should also reference that constant, and Symfony has the `KernelEvents` class just for that. Check it out and see what other events are dispatched by the HttpKernel, as they are all referenced there.

So, instead of hardcoding the string, we can have this:

```
$events[KernelEvents::REQUEST][] = ['onRequest', 0];
```

Second, the way we do the path handling in the `onRequest ()` method is all sorts of wrong. We are hardcoding the `/hello` path in this condition. What if we change the route path because our boss wants the path to be `/greeting`? I also don't like the way we passed the path to the `RedirectResponse`. The same thing applies (although in the case of the home page, not so much): what if the path we want to redirect to changes? Let's fix these problems using routes instead of paths. The are system specific and are unlikely to change because of business requirements.

We are now unable to understand which route is being accessed from the `Request` object. Instead, we can use the `current_route_match` service--a very popular one you'll use often--which gives us loads of info about the current route. So, let's inject that into our event subscriber. By now, you should know how to do this on your own (check the final code if you still have trouble). Once that is done, we can do this instead:

```
public function onRequest (GetResponseEvent $event) {
  $route_name = $this->currentRouteMatch->getRouteName ();

  if ($route_name !== 'hello_world.hello') {
    return;
  }

  $roles = $this->currentUser->getRoles ();
  if (in_array ('non_grata', $roles)) {
    $url = Url::fromUri ('internal:/');
    $event->setResponse (new RedirectResponse ($url->toString ()));
  }
}
```

From the `CurrentRouteMatch` service, we can figure out the name of the current route, the entire route object, parameters from the URL, and other useful things. Do check out the class for more info on what you can do, as I guarantee that they will come in handy.

Instead of checking against the pathname, we now check against the route name. So, if we change the path in the route definition, our code will still work. Then, instead of just adding the path to the `RedirectResponse`, we can build it first using the `Url` class used in the preceding section. Granted, in our example, it is probably overkill, but had we redirected it to a known route, we could have built it based on that, and our code would have been more robust. Additionally, using the `Url` class, we can also check other things such as access, and its `toString()` method simply turns it into a string that can be used for the `RedirectResponse`.

With this, we will get the same redirect, but in a much cleaner and more robust way.

Dispatching events

Since we have discussed how to subscribe to events in Drupal 8, it would only be fair to quickly take a look at how we can dispatch our own events. After all, the Symfony Event Dispatcher component is one of the principle vectors of extensibility in Drupal 8.

To demonstrate this, we will create an event to be dispatched whenever our `HelloWorldSalutation::getSalutation()` method is called. The purpose is to inform other modules that this happened and potentially allow them to alter the message that comes out of the configuration object-not really a solid use case, but good enough to demonstrate how we can dispatch events.

The first thing that we will need to do is to create an event class that will be dispatched. It can go into the root of our module's namespace:

```
namespace Drupal\hello_world;

use Symfony\Component\EventDispatcher\Event;

/**
 * Event class to be dispatched from the HelloWorldSalutation service.
 */
class SalutationEvent extends Event {

  const EVENT = 'hello_world.salutation_event';

  /**
   * The salutation message.
```

```
   *
   * @var string
   */
  protected $message;

  /**
   * @return mixed
   */
  public function getValue() {
    return $this->message;
  }

  /**
   * @param mixed $message
   */
  public function setValue($message) {
    $this->message = $message;
  }
}
```

The main purpose of this event class is that an instance of it will be used to transport the value of our salutation message. This is why we created the $message property on the class and added the getter and setter methods. Moreover, we use it to define a constant for the actual name of the event that will be dispatched. Finally, the class extends from the base Event class that comes with the Event Dispatcher component as a standard practice. We could also use that class directly, but we would not have our data stored in it as we do now.

Next, its time to inject the Event Dispatcher service into our HelloWorldSalutation service. We have already been injecting config.factory, so we just need to add a new argument to the service definition:

```
  arguments: ['@config.factory', '@event_dispatcher']
```

Of course, we will also receive it in the constructor and store it as a class property:

```
  /**
   * @var \Symfony\Component\EventDispatcher\EventDispatcherInterface
   */
  protected $eventDispatcher;

  /**
   * HelloWorldSalutation constructor.
   *
   * @param \Drupal\Core\Config\ConfigFactoryInterface $config_factory
   * @param \Symfony\Component\EventDispatcher\EventDispatcherInterface
$eventDispatcher
   */
```

```
public function __construct(ConfigFactoryInterface $config_factory,
EventDispatcherInterface $eventDispatcher) {
  $this->configFactory = $config_factory;
  $this->eventDispatcher = $eventDispatcher;
}
```

We will also have the obligatory *use* statement for the EventDispatcherInterface at the top of the file:

```
use Symfony\Component\EventDispatcher\EventDispatcherInterface;
```

Now, we can make use of the dispatcher, and it's actually pretty simple. Instead of using the following code:

```
if ($salutation != "") {
  return $salutation;
}
```

We can have the following code:

```
if ($salutation != "") {
  $event = new SalutationEvent();
  $event->setValue($salutation);
  $event = $this->eventDispatcher->dispatch(SalutationEvent::EVENT,
$event);
  return $event->getValue();
}
```

We decided that if we are to return a salutation message from the configuration object, we want to inform other modules and allow them to change it. So, we first create an instance of our Event class and feed it the relevant data (the message). Then, we dispatch the named event and pass the event object along with it. The Event Dispatcher returns the event that has been dispatched with any changes that might have been applied to it. So, we get the data from that instance and return it.

Pretty simple, isn't it? What can subscribers do? It's very similar to what we saw regarding the example on redirects in the preceding paragraph. All a subscriber needs to do is listen for the SalutationEvent::EVENT event and do something based on that. One thing that it can do is use the setValue() method on the received event object to change the salutation message. It can also use the stopPropagation() method from the base Event class to inform the Event Dispatcher to no longer trigger other listeners that have subscribed to this event.

Summary

In this chapter, we covered a great deal of info about the things you need to know when developing Drupal 8 modules. The first thing we did was create our very own module skeleton that can be installed on a Drupal 8 site. Then, we saw how to create a new page at a specific path (route) and show some basic data on that page. Nothing too complex, but enough to illustrate one of the most common tasks you will do as a module developer. We then took that to new level and abstracted the logic for that data calculation into a service. Not only that, but we also saw how we can use that service, and, more importantly, how we should use it. Next, we saw how we can work with the Form API in Drupal 8 to allow administrators to add some configuration to the site. A very important takeaway here was also that the Form API page in Drupal 8 will prove invaluable going forward because you have many different types of form elements at your disposal. So, keep that close by. Also, since we talked about forms, we also saw how we can alter the existing forms defined by other modules--an invaluable technique for any module developer.

Next, we created our first custom block in Drupal 8, which allowed us to reuse our service and be more flexible with where we show our data.

Then, we looked at how to create URLs and links programmatically in Drupal 8. In the functionality we built in this module, we don't need any links, yet. However, it is a common practice to work with them, so we had to learn early how to generate links and work with URLs properly in Drupal 8.

In our last section, we explored the Symfony *Event Dispatcher* component, a bit that allows us to dispatch and subscribe to events. We saw some examples of how we can subscribe to one of the main Kernel events in order to redirect the page, but we also saw how to dispatch our own event. The latter was meant to allow subscribers to make changes to our data, but we also saw how we can invoke our own alter hooks for the same purpose.

Most of the topics we covered in this chapter were meant to give you an initial boost and the tools to start developing modules in Drupal 8. They represent the absolute most common things--I believe--any new Drupal developer encounters and has to do. You will probably find that many of the things you will learn in the rest of this book will serve you only after some of the things we covered in this chapter are done in your module.

In the next chapter, we will look at two important aspects most applications will need to use. One is logging--the better your site logs its errors and important actions, the easier it will be to debug and trace back issues. Another is mailing--websites usually need to send out emails to users in one way or another, so it's important that we see how that works in Drupal 8.

3
Logging and Mailing

In the preceding chapter, we learned how to do some of the more common things most Drupal 8 module developers will have to know how to do, starting with the basics, that is, creating a Drupal module.

In this chapter, we will take things further and cover some other important tasks that a developer will have to perform.

- We will take a look at how logging works in Drupal 8. In doing so, we will cover some examples by expanding on our *Hello World* module.
- We will look at the Mail API in Drupal 8, namely, how we can send emails with the default setup (PHP mail). However, more than that, I will show you how to create your own email system to integrate with your (perhaps external) mail service; remember plugins? This will be yet another good example of using a plugin to extend existing capabilities.
- At the end of the chapter, we will also look at the Drupal 8 token system. We'll do so in the context of us being able to replace certain *tokens* with contextual data so that the emails we send out are a bit more dynamic.

By the end of this chapter, you should be able to add logging to your Drupal 8 module and feel comfortable sending emails programmatically. Additionally, you'll understand how tokens work, and as a bonus, see how you can define your own tokens.

Logging

The main logging mechanism in Drupal is a database log by which client code can use an API to save messages into `watchdog` table. The messages in there are cleared after they reach a certain number, but meanwhile they can be viewed in the browser via a handy interface (at `admin/reports/dblog`):

Alternatively, a core module that is disabled by default, Syslog, can be used to complement/replace this logging mechanism with the Syslog of the server the site is running on. For the purpose of this book, we will focus on how logging works with any mechanism, but we will also take a look at how we can implement our own logging system in Drupal 8.

Drupal 7 developers are very familiar with the `watchdog()` function they use for logging their messages. This is a procedural API for logging that exposes a simple function that takes some parameters, which make the logging flexible--`$type` (the category of the message), `$message`, `$variables` (an array of values to replace placeholders found in the message), `$severity` (a constant), and `$link` (a link to where the message should link to from the UI). It's pretty obvious that this solution is a very Drupal-specific one and not really common to the wider PHP community.

In Drupal 8, this has changed. The Database Logging module remains, the table for storing the messages is still called `watchdog`, but this logging destination is just one possible implementation that can be done. This is because the logging framework in Drupal 8 has been refactored to be object-oriented and PSR-3 compatible, and Database Logging is just the default implementation.

The Drupal 8 logging theory

Before going ahead with our example, let's cover some theoretical notions regarding the logging framework in Drupal 8. In doing so, we will try to understand the key *players* we will need to interact with.

First, we have `LoggerChannel`, which represents a category of logged messages. They resemble the former `$type` argument to the Drupal 7 `watchdog()` function. A key difference, however, is that they are objects through which we do the actual logging via the logger plugins themselves. In this respect, they are used by our second main *player*, `LoggerChannelFactory`, a service that is normally our main *contact* with the logging framework as a client code.

To understand these things better, let's consider the following example of a simple usage:

```
\Drupal::logger('hello_world')->error('This is my error message');
```

That's it. We just used the available registered loggers to log an error message through the `hello_world` channel. This is our own custom channel that we just came up with and that simply categorizes this message as belonging to the `hello_world` category (the module we started in the preceding chapter). Moreover, you'll see that I used the static call. Under the hood, the logger factory service is loaded, a channel is requested from it, and the `error()` method is called on it:

```
\Drupal::service('logger.factory')->get('hello_world')->error('This is my
error message');
```

When you request a channel from `LoggerChannelFactory`, you give it a name, and based on that name, it creates a new instance of `LoggerChannel`, which is the default channel. It will then pass to that channel all the available loggers so that when we call any of the `RfcLoggerTrait` logging methods on it, it will delegate to those.

We also have the option of creating our own channel. An advantage of doing this is that we can inject it directly into our classes instead of the entire factory from where we can request the channel. Also, we can do it in a way in which we don't even require the creation of a new class, but will inherit from the default one. We'll see how to do that in the next section.

The third main player is `LoggerInterface` implementation, which follows the PSR-3 standard. If we look at the `DbLog` class, which is the database logging implementation we mentioned earlier, we will note that it also uses `RfcLoggerTrait` that takes care of all the necessary methods so that the actual `LoggerInterface` implementation only has to handle the main `log()` method. This class is then registered as a service with `logger` tag, which in turn registers it with `LoggerChannelFactory` (that also acts as a service collector).

As we saw in `Chapter 2`, *Creating Your First Module*, tags can be used to categorize service definitions and we can have them collected by another service for a specific purpose. In this case, all services tagged with `logger` have a purpose, and they can be gathered and used by `LoggerChannelFactory`.

I know that I have thrown quite a few theories at you, but these are some concepts important to understand. However, don't worry; as usual, we will go through some examples.

Our own logger channel

I mentioned earlier how we can define our own logger channel so that we don't have to always inject the entire factory. So, let's take a look at how to create one for the *Hello World* module we're now writing.

Most of the time, all we have to do is add the following definition to our `hello_world.services.yml` file:

```
hello_world.logger.channel.hello_world:
    parent: logger.channel_base
    arguments: ['hello_world']
```

Before talking about the actual logger channel, let's see what this weird service definition actually means because this is not something we've seen before--I mean, where's the class?

The `parent` key means that our service will inherit the definition from another service. In our case, the parent key is `logger.channel_base`, and this means that the class used will be `Drupal\Core\Logger\LoggerChannel` (the default). If we look closely at the `logger.channel_base` service definition in `core.services.yml`, we'll also see a `factory` key, which means that this service class is not being instantiated by the service container but by another service, namely `logger.factory` service's `get()` method.

The `arguments` key is also slightly different. First of all, we don't have the @ sign. That is because this sign is used to denote a service name, whereas our argument is a simple string. As a bonus tidbit, if the string is preceded and followed by a %, it denotes a parameter that can be defined in any `*.services.yml` file.

Getting back to our example then, if you remember the logger theory, this service definition will mean that requesting this service will perform, under the hood, the following task:

```
\Drupal::service('logger.factory')->get('hello_world');
```

It uses the logger factory to load a channel with a certain argument. So, now we can inject our `hello_world.logger.channel.hello_world` service and call any of the `LoggerInterface` methods on it directly in our client code.

Our own logger

Now that we have a channel for our module, let's assume that we want to also log messages elsewhere. They are fine to be stored in the database, but let's also send an email whenever we encounter an error log. In this section, we will only cover the logging architecture needed for this and defer the actual mailing implementation to the second part of this chapter when we discuss mailing.

The first thing that we will need to create is `LoggerInterface` implementation, which typically goes in the `Logger` folder of our namespace. So, let's call ours `MailLogger`; the following is the code for it:

```
namespace Drupal\hello_world\Logger;

use Drupal\Core\Logger\RfcLoggerTrait;
use Psr\Log\LoggerInterface;

/**
 * A logger that sends an email when the log type is error.
 */
class MailLogger implements LoggerInterface {
```

```
use RfcLoggerTrait;

/**
 * {@inheritdoc}
 */
public function log($level, $message, array $context = array()) {
  // Log our message to our logging system.
}
}
```

The first thing to note is that we are implementing the PSR-3 `LoggerInterface`. This will require a bunch of methods, but we will take care of most of them via `RfcLoggerTrait`. The only one left to implement is the `log()` method, which will be responsible for doing the actual logging. For now, we will keep it empty.

By itself, having this class does nothing. We will need to register it as a tagged service so that `LoggingChannelFactory` picks it up and passes it to the logging channel when something needs to be logged. Let's take a look at what that definition looks like:

```
hello_world.logger.hello_world:
  class: Drupal\hello_world\Logger\MailLogger
  tags:
    - { name: logger }
```

As it stands, our logger doesn't need any dependencies. However, you will note a new property called `tags` via which we literally tag this service with `logger` tag. This will register it as a specific service that another service (called a collector) looks for. In this case, the latter is`LoggingChannelFactory`, if you remember.

Clearing the cache now should enable our logger. This means that when a message is being logged, via any channel, our logger is also used, together with any other enabled loggers (by default, the database one). The preceding service definition that we wrote is used to toggle that. So, if we want our logger to be the only one, we will need to disable the DB Log module from Drupal core.

We will continue working on this class later in this chapter when we will cover sending out emails programmatically.

Logging for Hello World

Now that we have all the tools at our disposable, and, more importantly, understand how logging works in Drupal 8, let's add some logging to our module.

There is one place where we can log an action that may prove helpful. Let's log an info message when an administrator changes the greeting message via the form we wrote. This should naturally happen in the submit handler of SalutationConfigurationForm.

If you remember my rant in the preceding chapter, there is no way we should use a service statically if we can instead inject it, and we can easily inject services into our form. So, let's do this now.

First of all, FormBase already implements ContainerInjectionInterface, so we don't need to implement it in our class, as we are extending from it somewhere down the line. Second of all, ConfigFormBase class we are directly extending already has config.factory injected, so this complicates things for us a bit--well, not really. All we need to do is copy over the constructor and create() method, add our own service, store it in a property, and pass the services it needs to the parent constructor call. It will look like this:

```
/**
 * @var \Drupal\Core\Logger\LoggerChannelInterface
 */
protected $logger;

/**
 * SalutationConfigurationForm constructor.
 *
 * @param \Drupal\Core\Config\ConfigFactoryInterface $config_factory
 *   The factory for configuration objects.
 */
public function __construct(ConfigFactoryInterface $config_factory,
LoggerChannelInterface $logger) {
  parent::__construct($config_factory);
  $this->logger = $logger;
}

/**
 * {@inheritdoc}
 */
public static function create(ContainerInterface $container) {
  return new static(
    $container->get('config.factory'),
    $container->get('hello_world.logger.channel.hello_world')
  );
}
```

And the relevant *use* statements at the top:

```
use Drupal\Core\Config\ConfigFactoryInterface;
use Drupal\Core\Logger\LoggerChannelInterface;
use Symfony\Component\DependencyInjection\ContainerInterface;
```

As you can see, we get all the services any of the parents need and the one we need (our logger channel) via the `create()` method. Also, in our constructor, we store the channel as a property and then pass the parent arguments to the parent constructor. Now, we have our `hello_world` logger channel available in our configuration form class. So, let's use it.

At the end of the `submitForm()` method, let's add the following line:

```
$this->logger->info('The Hello World salutation has been changed to
@message', ['@message' => $form_state->getValue('salutation')]);
```

We are logging a regular information message. However, since we also want to log the message that has been set, we use the second argument, which represents an array of context values. Under the hood, the database logger will extract the context variables that start with @, !, or % with the values from the entire context array. This is done using the `LogMessageParser` service (standard syntax in Drupal), and we'll see more of this in a later chapter when we will discuss internationalization. If you implement your own logger plugin, you will have to handle this yourself as well--but we'll see that in action soon.

Now, we are done with logging a message when the salutation configuration form is saved.

Logging summary

In this first section, we saw how logging works in Drupal 8. Specifically, we covered few theories so that you understand a bit how things play together and you don't just mindlessly use the logger factory without actually having a clue what goes on under the hood.

As examples, we created our own logging channel, which allows us to inject it wherever we need without having to always go through the factory. We will use this channel going forward for the *Hello World* module. Additionally, we created our own logger implementation. It won't do much at the moment, except getting registered, but we will use it in the next section to send emails when errors get logged to the site.

Finally, we used the logging framework (and our channel) in our salutation configuration form to log a message whenever the form is submitted. In doing so, we also passed the message that was saved so that it also gets included in the log. This should already work with the database log so go ahead and save the configuration form and then check the logging UI for that information message.

Mail API

Now that we know how to log things in our application, let's turn our attention to the Drupal 8 Mail API. Our goal for this section is to see how we can send emails programmatically in Drupal 8. In achieving this goal, we will explore the default mail system that comes with the core installation (which uses PHP mail), and also create our own system that can theoretically use an external API to send mails. We won't go all the way with the latter because it's beyond the scope of this book. We will stop after covering what needs to be done from a Drupal point of view.

In the next and final section, we will look at tokens so that we can make our mailings a bit more dynamic. However, before we do that, let's get into the Mail API in Drupal 8.

The theory of the Mail API

Like before, let's first cover this API from a theoretical point of view. It's important to understand the architecture before diving into examples.

Sending emails programmatically in Drupal is a two-part job. The first thing we will need to do is define something of a *template* for the email in our module. This is not a template in the traditional sense, but rather a procedural data wrapper to the email you want to send. It's referred to in our code as the *key* or *message ID*, but I believe that *template* is a better word to describe it, and it works by--you guessed it--implementing a hook.

The second thing that we will need to do is use the Drupal mail manager to send an email using one of the defined *templates* and specifying the module that defines it. If this sounds confusing, don't worry, it will become clear with the example that follows its explanation later on.

The *template* is created by implementing `hook_mail()`. This hook is a special one, as it does not work like most others. It gets called by the mail manager when a client (some code) is trying to send an email for the module that implements it and with a certain *template* ID it defines.

The `MailManager` is actually a plugin manager that is also responsible for sending the emails using a mail system (plugin). The default mail system is `PhpMail`, which uses PHP's native `mail()` function to send out email. If we create our own mail system, that will mean creating a new plugin. Also, the plugin itself is the one delivering the mails as the manager defers to it. As you can see, we can't go even a chapter ahead without creating plugins.

Each mail plugin needs to implement `MailInterface`, which exposes two methods-- `format()` and `mail()`. The first one does the initial preparation of the mail content (message concatenation, and so on), whereas the latter finalizes and does the sending.

However, how does the mail manager know which plugin to use? It checks a configuration object called `system.mail`, which stores the default plugin (`PhpMail`) and can also store overrides for each individual module and any module and *template* ID combination. So, we can have multiple mail plugins each used for different things. A quirky thing about this configuration object is that there is no admin form where you can specify which plugin does what. You have to adjust this configuration object programmatically as needed. One way you can manipulate this is via `hook_install()` and `hook_uninstall()` hooks. These hooks are used to perform some tasks whenever a module is installed/uninstalled. So, this is where we will change the configuration object to add our own mail plugin a bit later.

However, now that we have looked at few theories, let's take a look at how we can use the default mail system to send out an email programmatically. You remember our unfinished logger from the preceding section? That is where we will send our email whenever the logged message gets an error.

Implementing hook_mail()

As I mentioned earlier, the first step for sending mails in Drupal 8 is implementing `hook_mail()`. In our case, it can look something like this:

```
/**
 * Implements hook_mail().
 */
function hello_world_mail($key, &$message, $params) {
  switch ($key) {
    case 'hello_world_log':
      $message['from'] = \Drupal::config('system.site')->get('mail');
      $message['subject'] = t('There is an error on your website');
      $message['body'][] = $params['message'];

      break;
  }
}
```

This hook receives three parameters--the message key (*template*) that is used to send the mail, the message of the email that needs to be filled in, and an array of parameters passed from the client code. As you can see, we are defining a key (or *template*) named `hello_world_log`, which has a simple static subject, and as a body, it will have whatever comes from the `$parameters` array in its message key. Since the email *From* is always the same, we will use the site-wide email address that can be found in the `system.site` configuration object. You'll note that we are not in a context where we can inject the configuration factory as we did when we built the form. Instead, we can use the static helper to load it.

Additionally, you'll note that the body is itself an array. This is because we can build (if we want) multiple items in that array that can be later imploded as paragraphs in the mail plugin's `format()` method. This is in any case what the default mail plugin does, so here we need to build an array.

Another useful key in the `$message` array is the `header` key, which you can use to add some custom headers to the mail. In this case, we don't need to because the default `PhpMail` plugin adds all the necessary headers. Also, if we write our own mail plugin, we can then add our headers in there as well--and all other keys of the `$message` array, for that matter. This is because the latter is passed around as a reference, so it keeps getting built up in the process from the client call to the `hook_mail()` implementation to the plugin.

That is about all we need to do with `hook_mail()`. Let's now see how to use this in order to send out an email.

Sending emails

We wanted to use our `MailLogger` to send out an email whenever we are logging an error. So let's go back to our class and add this logic.

This is what our `log()` method can look like:

```
/**
 * {@inheritdoc}
 */
public function log($level, $message, array $context = array()) {
  if ($level !== RfcLogLevel::ERROR) {
    return;
  }

  $to = $this->configFactory->get('system.site')->get('mail');
  $langode = $this->configFactory->get('system.site')->get('langcode');
  $variables = $this->parser->parseMessagePlaceholders($message,
```

```
$context);
    $markup = new FormattableMarkup($message, $variables);
    \Drupal::service('plugin.manager.mail')->mail('hello_world',
'hello_world_log', $to, $langode, ['message' => $markup]);
}
```

First of all, we stated that we only want to send mails for errors, so in the first lines, we check whether the attempted log is of that level and return otherwise. In other words, we don't do anything if we're not dealing with an error and rely on other registered loggers for those.

Next, we determine who we want the email to be sent to and the langcode to send it in (both are mandatory arguments to the mail manager's mail() method). We opt to use the site-wide email address (just as we did for the *From* value). We also use the same configuration object as we used earlier in the hook_mail() implementation. In the next code snippet, we will take care of injecting the config factory into the class.

When we talk about langcode, we refer to the machine name of a language object. In this case, that is what is being stored for the site-wide default language. Also, we'll default to that for our emails. In a later chapter, we will cover more aspects regarding internationalization and multilingual in Drupal 8.

Then, we prepare the message that is being sent out. For this, we use the FormattableMarkup class to which we pass the message string and an array of variable values that can be used to replace the placeholders in our message. We can retrieve these values using the LogMessageParser service the same way as the DbLog logger does. With this, we are basically extracting the placeholder variables from the entire context array of the logged message.

Lastly, we will use the mail manager plugin to send the email. The first parameter to its mail() method is the module we want to use for the mailing. The second is the key (or *template*) we want to use for it (which we defined in hook_mail()). The third and fourth are self-explanatory, whereas the fifth is the $params array we encountered in hook_mail(). If you look back on that, you'll note that we used the message key as the body. Here, we populate that key with our markup object, which has a _toString() method that renders it with all the placeholders replaced.

You may wonder why I did not inject the Drupal mail manager as I did in the rest of the dependencies. Unfortunately, the core mail manager uses the logger channel factory itself, which in turn depends on our `MailLogger` service. So if we make the mail manager a dependency of the latter, we find ourselves in a circular loop. So when the container gets rebuilt, a big fat error is thrown. It might still work, but it's not alright. So, I opted to use it statically, because, in any case, this method is very small and would be difficult to test due to its expected result being difficult to assert (it sends an email). Sometimes, you have to make these choices, as the alternative would have been to inject the entire service container just to trick it. However, that is a code smell and would not have helped anyway had I wanted to write a test for this class.

Even if I did not inject the mail manager, I did inject the rest. So, let's take a look at what we have now at the top:

```
/**
 * @var \Drupal\Core\Logger\LogMessageParserInterface
 */
protected $parser;

/**
 * @var \Drupal\Core\Config\ConfigFactoryInterface
 */
protected $configFactory;

/**
 * MailLogger constructor.
 *
 * @param \Drupal\Core\Logger\LogMessageParserInterface $parser
 * @param \Drupal\Core\Config\ConfigFactoryInterface $config_factory
 */
public function __construct(LogMessageParserInterface $parser,
ConfigFactoryInterface $config_factory) {
    $this->parser = $parser;
    $this->configFactory = $config_factory;
}
```

Let's check out the relevant *use* statements:

```
use Drupal\Core\Logger\LogMessageParserInterface;
use Drupal\Core\Config\ConfigFactoryInterface;
```

There seems nothing out of the ordinary. We just take in the services I mentioned above. Also, let's quickly see the service definition of our mail logger as it looks now:

```
hello_world.logger.hello_world:
    class: Drupal\hello_world\Logger\MailLogger
    arguments: ['@logger.log_message_parser', '@config.factory']
    tags:
      - { name: logger }
```

We simply have two new arguments--nothing new to you by now.

Clearing the caches and logging an error should send the logged message (with the placeholders replaced) to the site email address (and from the same address) using the PHP native `mail()` function. Congratulations! You just sent out your first email programmatically in Drupal 8.

Altering someone else's emails

Drupal is powerful not only because it allows us to add our own functionality but also because it allows us to alter the existing functionality. An important vector for doing this are the *alter* hooks. Remember these from Chapter 2, *Creating Your Own Module*? These are hooks that are used to change the value of an array or object before it is used for whatever purpose it was going to be used for. When it comes to sending mails, we have an alter hook that allows us to change things on the mail definition before it goes out-- `hook_mail_alter()`. For our module, we don't need to implement this hook. However, for the sake of making it complete, let's take a look at how we could use this hook to, for example, change the header of an existing outgoing email:

```
/**
 * Implements hook_mail_alter().
 */
function hello_world_mail_alter(&$message) {
  switch ($message['key']) {
    case 'hello_world_log':
      $message['headers']['Content-Type'] = 'text/html; charset=UTF-8;
format=flowed; delsp=yes';
      break;
  }
}
```

So, what is going on here? First of all, this hook implementation gets called in each module it is implemented in. It's not like `hook_mail()` in this respect, as it allows us to alter mails defined in our module and sent from other modules as well. However, in our example, we will just alter the mail we defined earlier.

The only parameter (passed by reference as it is usual with alter hooks) is the `$message` array, which contains all the things we built in `hook_mail()`, as well as the key (*template*) and other things added by the mail manager itself, such as the headers. So, in our example, we are setting an HTML header so that whatever is getting sent out *could be* rendered as an HTML. After this hook is invoked, the mail system formatter is also called, which, in the case of the `PhpMail` plugin, transforms all HTML tags into plain text, essentially canceling out our header. However, if we implement our own plugin, we can prevent that and successfully send out HTML emails with proper tags and everything.

So, that is basically all there is to altering existing outgoing mails. Next, we will take a look at how we can create our own mail plugin that uses a custom external mail system. We won't go into details here, but we will prepare the architecture that will allow us to bring in the API we need and use it easily.

Custom mail plugins

In the preceding section, we saw how we can use the Drupal 8 mail API to send emails programmatically in Drupal 8. In doing so, we used the default PHP mailer, which although is good enough for our example, might not be so for our application. For example, we might want to use an external service via an API.

In this section, we will teach you how to do this. To this end, we will need to write our own mail plugin that does just that, and then simply tell Drupal to use that system instead of the default one. Yet another plugin-based, noninvasive, extension point.

Before we start, I would like to mention that we won't go into any kind of detail related to the potential external API. Instead, we will stop at the Drupal 8-specific parts, so the code you will find in the repository won't do much--it will be used as an example only. It's up to you to use this technique if you need to.

The mail plugin

So let's start by creating our Mail plugin class, and if you remember, plugins go inside the Plugin folder of our module namespace. Mail plugins belong inside a Mail folder. So this is what a simple skeleton mail plugin class can look like:

```
namespace Drupal\hello_world\Plugin\Mail;

use Drupal\Core\Mail\MailFormatHelper;
use Drupal\Core\Mail\MailInterface;
use Drupal\Core\Plugin\ContainerFactoryPluginInterface;
use Symfony\Component\DependencyInjection\ContainerInterface;

/**
 * Defines the Hello World mail backend.
 *
 * @Mail(
 *   id = "hello_world_mail",
 *   label = @Translation("Hello World mailer"),
 *   description = @Translation("Sends an email using an external API
specific to our Hello World module.")
 * )
 */
class HelloWorldMail implements MailInterface,
ContainerFactoryPluginInterface {

  /**
   * {@inheritdoc}
   */
  public static function create(ContainerInterface $container, array
$configuration, $plugin_id, $plugin_definition) {
    return new static();
  }

  /**
   * {@inheritdoc}
   */
  public function format(array $message) {
    // Join the body array into one string.
    $message['body'] = implode("\n\n", $message['body']);

    // Convert any HTML to plain-text.
    $message['body'] = MailFormatHelper::htmlToText($message['body']);
    // Wrap the mail body for sending.
    $message['body'] = MailFormatHelper::wrapMail($message['body']);

    return $message;
  }
```

```
/**
 * {@inheritdoc}
 */
public function mail(array $message) {
    // Use the external API to send the email based on the $message array
    // constructed via the `hook_mail()` implementation.
}
}
```

As you can see, we have a relatively easy plugin annotation, no unusual arguments there. Then, you will note that we implemented the mandatory `MailInterface`, which comes with the two methods implemented in the following paragraph.

I mentioned the `format()` method earlier and stated that it is responsible for doing certain processing before the message is ready to be sent. The preceding implementation is a copy from the `PhpMail` plugin to exemplify just what kind of task would go there. However, you can do whatever you want in here, including allowing HTML tags. Imploding the body is something you will probably want to do anyway, as it is kind of expected that the mail body is constructed as an array by `hook_mail()`.

The `mail()` method, on the other hand, is left empty. This is because it's up to you to use the external API to send the email. For this, you can use the `$message` array we encountered in the `hook_mail()` implementation.

Lastly, note that `ContainerFactoryPluginInterface` is another interface that our class implements. If you remember, that is what plugins need to implement in order for them to become container aware (for the dependencies to be injectable). Since this was only example code, it doesn't have any dependencies, so I did not include a constructor and left the `create()` method empty. Most likely, you will have to inject something, such as a PHP client library, that works with your external API. So, it doesn't hurt to see this again.

That is pretty much it for our plugin class. Now, let's take a look at how we can use it because for the moment, our `hello_world_log` emails are still being sent with the default PHP mailer.

Using mail plugins

As I mentioned earlier, there is no UI in Drupal to select which plugin the mail manager should use for sending emails programmatically. It figures it out in the getInstance() method by checking the system.mail configuration object, and more specifically, the interface key inside that (which is an array).

By default, this array contains only one record, that is, 'default' => 'php_mail'. That means that, by default, all emails sent use the plugin with the php_mail ID. In order to get our plugin in the game, we have a few options:

- We can replace this value with our plugin ID, which means that all emails will be sent with our plugin
- We can add a new record with the key in the module_name_key_name format, which means that all emails sent for a module with a specific key (or *template*) will use that plugin
- We can add a new record with the key in the module_name format, which means that all emails sent for a module will use that plugin (regardless of their key)

For our example, we will set all emails sent from the hello_world module to use our new plugin. We can do this using the hook_install() implementation that runs whenever the module is installed:

```
/**
 * Implements hook_install().
 */
function hello_world_install() {
  $config = \Drupal::configFactory()->getEditable('system.mail');
  $mail_plugins = $config->get('interface');
  if (in_array('hello_world', array_keys($mail_plugins))) {
    return;
  }

  $mail_plugins['hello_world'] = 'hello_world_mail';
  $config->set('interface', $mail_plugins)->save();
}
```

As you can see, in this function, we load the configuration object as editable (so we can change it), and if we don't yet have a record with hello_world in the array of mail plugins we set it and map our plugin ID to it. Lastly, we save the object.

Install (and uninstall) hooks need to go inside a .install PHP file in the root of our module. So this function goes inside a new hello_world.install file. Also, if our module has been already enabled, we will need to first uninstall it and then install it again to get this function to fire.

The opposite of this function is hook_uninstall(), which goes in the same file and--expectedly--gets fired whenever the module is uninstalled. Since we don't want to change a site-wide configuration object and tie it to our module's plugin, we should implement this hook as well. Otherwise, if our module gets uninstalled, the mail system will fail because it will try to use a nonexistent plugin. So, let's tie up our loose ends:

```
/**
 * Implements hook_uninstall().
 */
function hello_world_uninstall() {
  $config = \Drupal::configFactory()->getEditable('system.mail');
  $mail_plugins = $config->get('interface');
  if (!in_array('hello_world', array_keys($mail_plugins))) {
    return;
  }

  unset($mail_plugins['hello_world']);
  $config->set('interface', $mail_plugins)->save();
}
```

As you can see, what we did here is basically the opposite. If the record we set previously exists, we unset it and save the configuration object, and that's it.

So, now, any mails sent programmatically for the hello_world module will use this plugin. Easy, right? However, since the plugin we wrote is not ready, the code you find in the repository will have the relevant line from the hook_install() implementation commented out so that we don't actually use it.

Tokens

The last thing we will cover in this chapter is the Token API in Drupal 8. We will cover a few theories and, as usual, demonstrate them via examples on our existing "Hello World" module code. We will do this in the context of the mails we are sending out for error logs.

It would be nice if we could include some personalized information in the mail text without having to hardcode it in the module code or configuration. For example, in our case, we might want to include in the email the username of the current user that is triggering the error log that is being emailed.

Let's first understand how the Token API works, before going into our "Hello World" module.

The Token API

Tokens in Drupal are a standard formatted placeholder, which can be found inside a string and replaced by a real value extracted from a related object. The format tokens use is `type:token`, where `type` is the machine-readable name of a token type (a group of related tokens), and `token` is the machine-readable name of a token within this group.

The power of the Token API in Drupal is not only given by its flexibility but also by the fact that it is already a popular API. It is flexible because you can define groups, which contain related tokens, linked by the data object that contains their value (for example, a Node object or User object). It is popular because in previous versions of Drupal, it was the contributed module many others were dependent on to define their own tokens, and it is now available in Drupal 8 core with many tokens already defined out of the box. So, you'll find many existing tokens that you can use in your code, and if not, you can define your own.

There are three main components of this API--at least from the point of view of a Drupal 8 module developer. These components are two hooks--`hook_token_info()` and `hook_tokens()`--and the `Token` service, which is used to perform the replacement.

The first hook is used to define one or more token types and tokens. It essentially registers them with the system. The second is fired at the moment a token is found inside a string (a replacement is attempted by the service) and is used to do the replacement of the tokens based on the data that is passed to it from the service. For example, the User module defines two token types and a number of tokens inside `hook_token_info()`. Inside `hook_tokens()`, it checks whether the token is one of its own and tries to replace it with the contextual data (either a User object or the currently logged-in User object). To read the documentation related to each of these in detail and to see an extended example, you can find them either on the Drupal.org API page or inside the `token.api.php` file. There, you will also find *alter* hooks that correspond to these two and can be used to alter either the defined token information or logic to replace these tokens written by other modules or Drupal core.

The Token service is what you can use as module developers if you have to replace tokens found inside a string. We will see how this is used in the next section.

Using tokens

If you remember, the custom `MailLogger` we wrote had a `$context` array as an argument to its `log()` method. This contains some relevant information to the *thing* being logged-- `channel`, `uri`, `timestamp`, `user`, and others. We could use this data in conjunction with the token API to include information about the user who was signed in at the moment the error happened and was logged-in in the email. This can be useful information.

We will need to do two simple things to achieve this. First, we will need to alter our `MailLogger::log()` method to get the user account that was signed in and pass it to the mailer in the `$param` array:

```
/**
 * {@inheritdoc}
 */
public function log($level, $message, array $context = array()) {
  if ($level !== RfcLogLevel::ERROR) {
    return;
  }

  /** @var AccountProxyInterface $account */
  $account = $context['user'];
  $to = $this->configFactory->get('system.site')->get('mail');
  $langode = $this->configFactory->get('system.site')->get('langcode');
  $variables = $this->parser->parseMessagePlaceholders($message,
$context);
  $markup = new FormattableMarkup($message, $variables);
  \Drupal::service('plugin.manager.mail')->mail('hello_world',
'hello_world_log', $to, $langode, ['message' => $markup, 'user' =>
$account]);
  }
```

An important thing to note here is that we are talking about the currently logged-in user, which means that it is not a fully loaded user, but a simple `AccountProxyInterface`, which is a more shallow object rather than the full entity--the user session basically. If you are ever dealing with this object and need the entire User entity, you'll need to load it by its ID. However, in our case, the user module's `hook_tokens()` implementation does that for us, as we will see in a moment.

Finally, we will need to alter our `hook_mail()` implementation to handle this user and add another string to our mail body and, of course, replace a token:

```
/**
 * Implements hook_mail().
 */
function hello_world_mail($key, &$message, $params) {
  switch ($key) {
    case 'hello_world_log':
      $message['from'] = \Drupal::config('system.site')->get('mail');
      $message['subject'] = t('There is an error on your website');
      $message['body'][] = $params['message'];
      if (isset($params['user'])) {
        $user_message = 'The user that was logged in: [current-user:name]';
        $message['body'][] = \Drupal::token()->replace($user_message,
['current-user' => $params['user']]);
      }

      break;
  }
}
```

As you can see, if we receive the `user` parameter, we will add a new paragraph to our email. This is a simple string that informs us about the user who was logged in. However, in doing so, we use the `token` service (statically) to replace that string with the token value. The `replace()` method of the service takes a string and optionally an array of data objects keyed by the type (group) of the tokens they should be used for.

The choice of a token and type in this case is important. The User module defines the `user` and `current-user` types. The difference between the two types, if you check inside `user_tokens()`, is that the latter simply delegates to the former after it loads a full user entity. We could, alternatively, have done that ourselves and then passed the `user` type, but why should we? If somebody has done that for us already, we should not have to do it again.

So, that's it. Now, the email message will get an extra line that contains the dynamically generated username of the currently logged-in user at the time the error happened. Under the hood, the token service scans the string, extracts the token, and calls all `hook_tokens()` implementations. The User module is the one that can return the replacement for this token based on the User object it receives.

Defining new tokens

We just saw how we can programmatically use existing tokens inside our strings and get them replaced with minimal effort. All we need is the token service and the data object that can be used to replace the token. Keep in mind that there are tokens which don't even require any data objects due to their global nature. The hook_tokens() implementation will take care of that--let's see how.

In the preceding chapter, we created functionalities for a dynamic "Hello World" message, which are either calculated or loaded from a configuration object. How about we expose the message to a token? This would make its usage more flexible because our string becomes exposed to the entire token system.

As mentioned, we will start with the hook_token_info() implementation:

```
/**
 * Implements hook_token_info().
 */
function hello_world_token_info() {
  $type = [
    'name' => t('Hello World'),
    'description' => t('Tokens related to the Hello World module.'),
  ];

  $tokens['salutation'] = [
    'name' => t('Salutation'),
    'description' => t('The Hello World salutation value.'),
  ];

  return [
    'types' => ['hello_world' => $type],
    'tokens' => ['hello_world' => $tokens],
  ];
}
```

In here, we will need to define two things--the types and the tokens. In our case, we are defining one of each. The type is hello_world and comes with a human-readable name and description in case it needs to be rendered somewhere in the UI. The token is salutation and belongs to the hello_world type. It also gets a name and description. At the end, we return an array that contains both.

What follows is the `hook_tokens()` implementation in which we handle the replacement of our token:

```
/**
 * Implements hook_tokens().
 */
function hello_world_tokens($type, $tokens, array $data, array $options,
\Drupal\Core\Render\BubbleableMetadata $bubbleable_metadata) {
  $replacements = [];
  if ($type == 'hello_world') {
    foreach ($tokens as $name => $original) {
      switch ($name) {
        case 'salutation':
          $replacements[$original] =
\Drupal::service('hello_world.salutation')->getSalutation();
          $config = \Drupal::config('hello_world.custom_salutation');
          $bubbleable_metadata->addCacheableDependency($config);
          break;

      }
    }
  }

  return $replacements;
}
```

There is a bit more going on here, but I'll explain everything. This hook gets fired for each type located inside a string (after all have been scanned and grouped accordingly), and the `$type` is the first parameter. Inside `$tokens`, we get an array of tokens located in that string, which belong to the `$type`. The `$data` array contains the objects needed to replace the tokens, keyed by the type. This array can be empty (as it will be in our case).

Inside the function, we loop through each token of this group and try to replace it. We only know of one, and we use our `HelloWorldSalutation` service to determine the replacement string.

Finally, the function needs to return an array of all replacements found (which can be multiple if multiple tokens of the same type are found inside a string).

The `bubbleable_metadata` parameter is a special cache metadata object that describes this token in the cache system. It is needed because tokens get cached, so if any dependent object changes, the cache needs to be invalidated for this token as well. By default, all objects inside the `$data` array are read and included in this object. However, in our case, it is empty, yet we still depend on a configuration object that can change--the one that stores the overridden salutation message. So, we will need to add a dependency on that configuration object even if the actual value for the salutation we compute uses the same `HelloWorldSalutation` service we used before. So, we have a simple example here, but with a complex twist.

That's all there is to defining our token. It can now also be used inside strings and replaced using the `Token` service. Something like this:

```
$final_string = \Drupal::token()->replace('The salutation text is:
[hello_world:salutation]');
```

As you can see, we pass no other parameters. If our token were dependent on an entity object, for example, we would have passed it in the second parameter array and would have made use of it inside `hook_tokens()` to compute the replacement.

Token summary

The token system is an important part of Drupal because it allows us to easily transform raw data into useful values using placeholder strings. It is a widely used and flexible system that many contributed modules build (and will build) upon. The great thing about tokens is the UI component. There are modules that will allow users to define strings in the UI but make it possible to fill it up with various tokens that it will replace. Also, this is something you can do as a module developer.

Summary

In this chapter, we discussed many things. We saw how logging works in Drupal 8, how the mail API can be used programmatically (and extended), and how the token system can be employed to make our text more dynamic.

While going through this chapter, we also enriched our *Hello World* module. So, apart from understanding the theory about logging, we created our own logging channel service and logger plugin. For the latter, we decided to send out emails when log messages were of the type *error*. In doing this, we took a look at the mail API and how we can use it programmatically. We saw that, by default, PHP's native `mail()` function is used to send out emails, but we can create our own plugin very easily to use whatever external service we want--yet another great example of extensibility via plugins.

Lastly, we looked at tokens in Drupal 8. We saw what components make up the API, how we can programmatically use existing tokens (replace them with the help of contextual data), and how we can define our own tokens for others to use. These are the main tenets of extensibility (and sharing)--using something someone else has exposed to you, and exposing something for someone else to use.

In the next chapter, we will look at another great topic--theming. Even though you may think that this falls within the purview of a frontend developer, module developers play an important role. Yes, much of the styling, client-side scripting, and visual architecture can be, and is, done by what we call *themers*. However, module developers need to understand and use theming tools to ensure that their data is rendered in the proper way. So, in the next chapter, we will focus on that.

4
Theming

The most obvious part of Drupal's theming system is the **Appearance** admin page found at `admin/appearance`, which lists all the themes installed on your website. The page is shown in the following screenshot:

When you choose a theme from the **Appearance** page, you are applying a specific graphic design to your website's data and functionality. However, the applied theme is in reality only a small part of the entire theming layer.

This book mostly focuses on building modules that encapsulate chunks of a functionality. However, since we're ultimately building a web application, everything outputted by our functionality will need to be marked up with HTML. In Drupal, this process of wrapping data in HTML and CSS is called theming.

In this chapter, we will discuss how our module should integrate with the theme layer. We will talk about the architecture of the system, theme templates, hooks, render arrays, and others. Then, we will provide some practical examples.

Business logic versus presentation logic

We will start this chapter by discussing an important architectural choice modern applications make--how to turn data into a presentation.

So, what would be the best way to get our data and functionality marked up? Do we simply wrap each piece of data in HTML and return the whole as a giant string, as shown in the following example?

```
return '<div class="wrapper">' . $data . '</div>';
```

No, we don't. Like all other well-designed applications, Drupal separates its business logic from its presentation logic. It's true, previous versions of Drupal did have this kind of approach, especially when it came to theme functions, but even so, they were easily overridable. So, constructs like these were not found smack in the middle of business logic but were encapsulated in a special theming function that was called by the client code. So, the separation of business logic from presentation logic was clearly there, if at times, not so much one between PHP and HTML code.

Traditionally, the primary motivations for this separation of concerns were as follows:

- To make the code easier to maintain
- To make it possible to easily swap out one layer's implementation without having to rewrite the other layers

As we will see, Drupal takes the "swapability" aspect quite far. You might think that the theme you select on the **Appearance** page is responsible for applying the HTML and CSS for the website. This is true, but only to some extent. There are thousands of contributed modules on Drupal.org. Also, you can write a bunch of your own. Should the theme be responsible for marking up all of those modules' data? Obviously not.

Since a module is most intimately familiar with its own data and functionality, it is its own responsibility to provide the default theme implementation (a *theme hook*)--that initial look and feel that is independent of design but that should be displayed correctly, regardless of the theme. However, as long as the module uses the theme system properly, a theme will be able to override any HTML and/or CSS by swapping the module's implementation with its own.

In other words, after data is retrieved and manipulated inside the module (the business logic), it will need to provide the default theme implementation to wrap it inside its markup. Sometimes a particular theme will need to override this implementation in order for it to achieve a specific design goal. If the theme provides its own implementation, Drupal will use the theme implementation instead of the module's default implementation. This is usually called *overriding*. Otherwise, the default fallback will still be there. The theme also provides the option of applying styling via CSS only and leaving the markup provided by the module intact.

Twig

Theme engines are responsible for doing the actual output via template files. Although previous versions of Drupal were capable of using different theme engines, one stood out and was used 99.9 percent of the time (statistic made up by me on the spot)--PHPTemplate. This theme engine used PHP files with `.tpl.php` extension and contained both markup and PHP. Seasoned Drupal developers grew accustomed to this practice, but it was always more difficult for frontend developers to use and theme against.

In Drupal 8, it was abandoned in favor of the Twig templating engine created by SensioLabs (the people responsible for the Symfony project). As mentioned, theme functions were also deprecated in favor of outputting everything through a `Twig` file. This brought about many improvements to the theme system and quite some joy to the frontend community. For example, it improved security and readability and made it much less important to be actually versed in PHP to be able to take part in the theming of a Drupal site.

All Twig template files in Drupal 8 have `.html.twig` extension.

Theme hooks

Since we have covered some of the principles behind the Drupal theme system--most notably, the separation of concerns--let's go a bit deeper and take a look at how they are actually put into practice. This all starts with the theme hooks. Yes, Drupal always loves to call things *hooks*.

Theme hooks define how a specific piece of data should be rendered. They are registered with the theme system by modules (and themes) using `hook_theme()`. In doing so, they get a name, a list of variables they output (the data that needs to be wrapped with markup), and other options.

The modules and themes that register theme hooks also need to provide an implementation (one that will be used by default). In Drupal 7, this was done in the following two ways-- either via a PHP function that returned a string (markup) or a `PHPTemplate` template file. Both were equally important, but the latter was always more "correct" in my (and many people's) opinion. This is also supported by the fact that the functions in Drupal 8 have been completely ditched in favor of `Twig` templates. Also, together with a complete overhaul of the theme system, almost everything is now outputted via a Twig template file, which is great.

As an example, let's take a look at two common ways of registering a theme hook we'll often find. For this, we will use Drupal core examples:

```
function hook_theme($existing, $type, $theme, $path) {
  return [
    'item_list' => array(
      'variables' => array('items' => array(), 'title' => '', 'list_type'
=> 'ul', 'wrapper_attributes' => array(), 'attributes' => array(), 'empty'
=> NULL, 'context' => array()),
    ),
    'select' => array(
      'render element' => 'element',
    ),
  ];
}
```

In the preceding `hook_theme()` example, I included two theme hooks from Drupal core. One is based on variables, whereas the other is based on a render element. There are, of course, many more options that can be defined here, and I strongly encourage that you read the Drupal.org API documentation page for this hook.

However, right off the bat, you can see how easy it is to register a theme hook. In the first case, we have `item_list`, which, by default (if not otherwise specified), will map to the `item-list.html.twig` file for outputting the variables. In its definition, we can encounter the variables it uses, with some handy defaults in case they are not passed in from the client. The second theme hook is `select`, which doesn't use variables but a render element (that we will discuss soon). Also, its template file is easy to determine--`select.html.twig`. I encourage you to check out both these template files in the core code (provided by the System module).

In addition to the actual implementation, the modules and themes that register a theme hook can also provide a default template preprocessor. In the Drupal world, this concept is very familiar, but in a nutshell, its responsibility is to "preprocess" (that is, prepare) data before being sent to the template. For example, if a theme hook receives an entity (a complex data object) as its only variable, a preprocessor can be used to break that entity into tiny pieces that are needed to be output in the template (such as title and description).

Template preprocessors are simply procedural functions that follow a naming pattern and are called by the theme system before the template is rendered. As I mentioned earlier, the modules and themes that register a theme hook can also provide a default preprocessor. So, for a theme hook named `component_box`, the default preprocessor function would look like this:

```
function template_preprocess_component_box(&$variables) {
  // Prepare variables.
}
```

The function name starts with the word `template` to denote that it is the original preprocessor for this theme hook, then follows the conventional `preprocess` word, and the name ends with the name of the theme hook. The argument is always an array passed as a reference and contains some info regarding that theme hook, and more importantly, the data variables that were defined with the theme hook and passed to it from the calling code. That is what we are usually working with in this function. Also, since it's passed by a reference, we don't return anything in this function, but we always manipulate the values in the `$variables` array. In the end, the template file is available to print out variables named after the keys of this array. The values will be, of course, the values that map to those keys.

Another module (or theme) can override this preprocessor function by implementing its own. However, in its naming, it needs to replace the word `template` with the module name (to avoid collisions). If one such override exists, both preprocessors will be called in a specific order. The first is always the default one, followed by the ones defined by modules and then the ones defined by themes. This is another great extension point of Drupal because altering data or options found inside the preprocessor in many cases can go a long way in customizing the existing functionality to your liking.

Alternatively, to follow the preceding naming convention, you also have the option to register the preprocessor function names in the `hook_theme()` definition when you register the theme hook. However, I recommend that you stick to the default naming convention because it's much easier to spot what the purpose of the function is. As you become more advanced, you'll, in turn, appreciate being able to quickly understand these *convention* functions at a quick glance.

I mentioned a bit earlier that modules and themes can also override theme hooks defined by other modules and themes. There are two ways to do this. The most common one is for a theme to override the theme hook. This is because of the rationale I was talking about earlier--a module defines a default implementation for its data, but a theme can then take over its presentation with ease. Also, the way themes override a theme hook is by simply creating a new Twig file with the same name as the original and placing it somewhere in its `templates` folder. If that theme is enabled, it will be used instead. A less common but definitely valid use case is for a module to override a theme hook defined by another module. For example, this might be because you need to change how data is rendered by a popular contributed module. To achieve this, you will need to implement `hook_theme_registry_alter()` and change the template file used by the existing theme hook. It's also worth adding that you can change the entire theme hook definition using this hook if you want, not just the template. Also, since we mentioned this hook, note that theme hooks, upon definition, are stored and cached in a theme *registry* for optimized performance, and that registry is what we are altering with this hook. This also means that we regularly need to clear the cache when we make changes to the theme registry.

All this is good and fine, but the business logic still has to interact with the theme system to tell it which particular theme hook to use. In Drupal 7, we had the `theme()` function, which took the hook name as an argument and was responsible for everything--determining which template file (or function) was to be used, calling the preprocessors, processors, and so on. In Drupal 8, the `theme()` function no longer exists and has been replaced with a more robust system based on render arrays, which contain the theme hook information, the variables, and any other metadata on how that component needs to be rendered. We will also talk about render arrays in this chapter.

Theme hook suggestions

A great thing about theme hooks is their reusability. However, one problem you'll encounter is that theme hook templates lose context when a theme hook is reused. For example, the `item_list` theme hook whose definition we saw in the previous section has no idea what list it is theming. And this makes it difficult to style differently depending on what that content is. Fortunately, we can provide context to the theme system using a theme hook pattern instead of the original theme hook name, and this pattern looks something like this:

```
base_theme_hook__some_context
```

The parts of the pattern are separated with a double underscore, since some theme hooks could be confusing if we were to use a single underscore to delineate the parts of the pattern, and together they are called a *theme hook suggestion*. However, how does this work?

Client code (the render arrays as we will see soon), when using a theme hook to render a piece of data, can append the context to the theme hook. The theme system will then check for the following:

- If there is a template file that matches that suggestion (inside a theme), it uses it instead of the original theme hook template
- Alternatively, if there is a theme hook registered which has that actual name it uses that instead
- Alternatively, it checks for the base theme hook and uses that instead (the fallback)

In this case, the caller (the render array) is responsible for "proposing" a suggestion. For example, consider the following render array:

```
return [
  '#theme' => 'item_list__my_list',
  '#items' => $items
];
```

The base theme hook is `item_list`, which is rendered using the `item-list.html.twig` template file provided by Drupal core. If there is no `item-list--my-list.html.twig` template file in the theme, and there is no `item_list__my_list` theme hook registered, the default `item_list` theme hook will be used. Otherwise, we will follow the order that I mentioned before. A module can register that suggestion as a hook, which will be used instead. However, a theme can override that further by just creating the template file with that name.

And all this is done so that when rendering something with a reusable theme hook, we give the possibility to themers and manipulators to determine what exactly is being themed. However, the example we saw just now is static in the sense that we hardcoded `my_list` as the theme hook suggestion. We can do better than that.

A module that registers a theme hook can also provide a list of suggestions that should go with that theme hook automatically. It does so by implementing `hook_theme_suggestions_HOOK()`, where `HOOK` is the theme hook name. This hook is fired at runtime by the theme system, trying to determine how a certain render array needs to be rendered. It receives the same `$variables` array as an argument as we do when implementing a template preprocessor. This means that we can make use of those variables and dynamically provide theme hook suggestions. We will see an example of this later in the chapter.

Moreover, as module developers, we can also provide a list of theme hook suggestions to theme hooks registered by other modules or Drupal core. We can do so by implementing `hook_theme_suggestions_HOOK_alter()`, where we receive available suggestions for that theme hook in addition to the variables.

In summary, theme hook suggestions are a powerful way of adding some context to the generic theme hooks that are responsible for rendering multiple things.

Render arrays

Render arrays also existed in the previous versions of Drupal and they were important to the theme system. In Drupal 8, however, they have become the thing--a core part of the Render API that is responsible for transforming markup *representations* into actual markup.

Acknowledging my limits as a writer, I will defer to the definition found in the Drupal.org documentation that best describes what render arrays are:

> *... a hierarchical associative array containing data to be rendered and properties describing how the data should be rendered.*

Simple, but powerful.

One of the principle reasons behind having render arrays is that they allow Drupal to delay the actual rendering of something into markup to the very last moment. In Drupal 7, often-times as module developers, we would call the actual rendering service on an array in order to turn it into markup,for example, in preprocessor functions so that the resulting strings can be printed in the template. However, this made it impossible to change that data later in the pipeline,for example, in another preprocessor that comes after the one which did the rendering.

For this reason, in Drupal 8, we no longer have to/should render anything manually (except in very specific circumstances). We work with render arrays at all times, including the time up to them being printed in the template. Drupal will know how to turn them into markup. This way, modules and themes can intercept render arrays at various levels in the process and make alterations.

We will now talk about render arrays and the different aspects of working with them.

The structure of a render array

Render arrays are rendered by the `renderer` service (`RendererInterface`), which traverses the array and recursively renders each level. Each level of the array can have one or more elements, which can be two types--properties and children. The properties are the one whose keys are preceded by a # sign, whereas children are the ones which are not. The children can be themselves an array with properties and children. However, each level needs to have at least one property in order to be considered a level because it is responsible for telling the render system how that level needs to be rendered. As such, property names are specific to the Render API and to the actual thing they need to render while the names of children can be flexible. In addition to these two types (yes, I lied, there can be more than two), we can also have the variables defined by a theme hook, which are also preceded by the # sign. They are not properties per se, but are known by the theme system because they have been registered.

There are many properties the Render API uses to process a render array. Some of them are quite important, such as `#cache` and `#attached`. However, there are a few that are mandatory in order for a render array to make sense, in that they define their core responsibility. The following are the properties from among which each render array needs to have at least one.

#type

The `#type` property specifies that the array contains data that needs to be rendered using a particular *render element*. Render elements are plugins (yes, plugins) that encapsulate a defined piece of a renderable component. They essentially wrap another render array, which can use a theme hook or a more complex render array to process the data they are responsible for rendering. You can think of them as essentially standardized render arrays.

There are two types of render elements--generic and form input elements. Both have their respective plugin types, annotations and interfaces. They are similar in that they both render a standardized piece of HTML; however, the form input elements have the complexity of having to deal with form processing, validation, data mapping, and so on. Remember, when we defined our form in `Chapter 2`, *Creating Your First Module*, we encountered arrays with # signs. These were (form) render elements with different options (properties).

To find examples of these two types of render elements, look for plugins that implement the `ElementInterface` and `FormElementInterface` interfaces.

#theme

The `#theme` property ties in strongly with what we've been talking earlier in this chapter-- theme hooks. It specifies that the render array needs to render some kind of data using one of the theme hooks defined. Together with this property, you will usually encounter other properties that map to the name of the variables the theme hook has registered in `hook_theme()`. These are the variables the theme system uses to render the template.

This is the property you will use in your business logic to convey that your data needs to be rendered using a specific theme hook. If you thought that you can only use theme hooks you registered, you'd be incorrect. There are many theme hooks that have been already registered by Drupal core and also contributed modules that make the life of a Drupal developer much easier. Just look inside `drupal_common_theme()` for a bunch of common theme hooks that you can perhaps use.

#markup

Sometimes, registering a theme hook and a template for outputting some data can be overkill. Imagine that all you have is a string you need to wrap in a `<span>` tag or something. In this case, you can use the `#markup` property, which specifies that the array provides directly the HTML string that needs to be output. Note, however, that the provided HTML string is run through `\Drupal\Component\Utility\Xss::filterAdmin` for sanitization (mostly, XSS protection). This is perfectly fine because if the HTML you are trying to include here is stripped out, it's a good indication that you are overusing the `#markup` property and should instead be registering a theme hook.

Going a bit further than just simple markup is the `#plain_text` property via which you can specify that the text provided by this render array needs to be escaped completely. So, basically if you need to output some simple text, you have the choice between these two for very fast output.

Now, if you remember, in Chapter 2, *Creating Your First Module*, our controller at some point returned this array:

```
return [
  '#markup' => $this->t('Hello World')
];
```

This is the simplest render array you'll ever see. It has only one element, a tiny string output using the `#markup` property. Later in this chapter, we will adjust this and use a render array provided by our `HelloWorldSalutation` service in order to make things a bit more themable. That will be the section where we put into practice many of the things we learn here.

However, as small as you see this array here, it is only a part of a larger hierarchical render array that builds up the entire Drupal page and that contains all sorts of blocks and other components. Also, responsible for building this entire big thing is the Drupal render pipeline.

The render pipeline

In Chapter 1, *Developing for Drupal 8*, when we outlined a high level example of how Drupal 8 handles a user request in order to turn it into a Response, we touched on the render pipeline. So, let's see what this is about, as there are essentially two render pipelines to speak of--the Symfony render pipeline and the Drupal one.

As you know, Drupal 8 uses many Symfony components, one of which being the HTTPKernel component (http://symfony.com/doc/current/components/http_kernel.html). Its main role is to turn a user request (built from PHP super globals into a `Request` object) into a standardized response object that gets *sent* back to the user. These objects are defined in the Symfony HTTP Foundation component (http://symfony.com/components/HttpFoundation). To assist in this process, it uses the Event Dispatcher component to dispatch events meant to handle the workload on multiple layers. As we saw, this is what happens in Drupal 8, as well.

Controllers in Drupal 8 can return one of two things--either a Response object directly or a render array. If they return the first, the job is almost done, as the Symfony render pipeline knows exactly what to do with that (assuming the response is correct). However, if they return a render array, the Drupal render pipeline kicks in at a lower level to try to turn that into a Response. We always need a Response.

The `kernel.view` event is triggered in order to determine who can take care of this render array. Luckily, Drupal 8 comes with the `MainContentViewSubscriber` that listens to this event and checks the request format and whether the controller has returned a render array. Based on the request format, it instantiates a `MainContentRendererInterface` object (which by default--and most of the time--will be the HTML-based `HtmlRenderer`) and asks it to turn the render array into a Response. Then, it sets the Response onto the event so that the Symfony render pipeline can continue on its merry way.

In addition to the HTML renderer, Drupal 8 comes with a few others that need to handle different types of requests:

- The `AjaxRenderer` handles Ajax requests and integrates with the Ajax framework. We'll see examples of an Ajax-powered functionality later in the book.
- The `DialogRenderer` handles requests meant to open up a dialog on the screen.
- The `ModalRenderer` handles requests meant to open up a modal on the screen.

Returning to the HTML renderer, let's see what *it* does to turn our render arrays into actual relevant HTML on a Response object. Without going into too much detail, here is the high-level of what it does:

- Its first goal is to build a render array which has the `#type => 'page'` as a property because this is the render element responsible for the entire page. So, if the controller has it, it's done in this respect. However, usually, it won't have it so it dispatches an event to determine who can build this render array.
- By default, the `SimplePageVariant` plugin is used for building up the page array, but with the Block module enabled, the `BlockPageVariant` plugin is used, taking things even further down some levels in the render pipeline. The main content area gets wrapped with blocks in the sidebar, header, footer, and so on.
- Once it has the page render array, it wraps it into yet another render element which is the `#type => 'html'` (responsible for things such as the <head> elements).

- Once it has the main render array of the entire page, it uses the `Renderer` service to traverse it and do the actual rendering at each level (and there can be many). It does so by translating render elements (`#type`), theme hooks (`#theme`), simply markedup text (`#markup`), or plain text (`#plain_text`) into their respective HTML representations.

So, as you see, the render pipeline starts at the Symfony level, goes down into Drupal territory when it encounters render arrays, but continues going down to build each component found on a page around the main content returned by the Controller. Then, it comes back up those levels all the way until a great render array is created and can be turned into HTML. Also, as it goes back up, various metadata can bubble up to the main render array.

I purposefully left out caching from this equation, which, although very important, we will cover in a later chapter. However, suffice it to say, cache metadata is one such example that bubbles up from the lower levels all the way to the top and is gathered to determine page level caching, but more on that later on.

Assets and libraries

Now that we know more about the render arrays, how they are structured and the pipeline they go through, we can talk a bit about asset management from a module development perspective, as although it is usually a theme responsibility, module developers also often have to add and use CSS and JS files to their modules, and it all happens in the render arrays.

Working with CSS and JS files has become standardized in Drupal 8 compared to its preceding version, where you had more than one way to do things. It is doing so via the concept of Libraries, which are now in Drupal 8 core and also work differently than their D7 contrib module counterpart (*Libraries API*). So, let's see what we have by going through some examples of making use of some CSS of JS files.

There are three steps to this process:

1. Creating your CSS/JS file.
2. Creating a library that includes them.
3. Attaching that library to a render array.

Libraries

Assuming that you already have the CSS/JS files, libraries are defined inside a `module_name.libraries.yml` file in the module root folder. A simple example of a library definition inside this file would look like this:

```
my-library:
  version: 1.x
  css:
    theme:
      css/my_library.css: {}
  js:
    js/my_library.js: {}
```

At the top in the preceding example, we have the library machine name, whereas we have its definition at the bottom. We can specify a version number for our library and then add as many CSS and JS file references. The file paths are relative to the module folder this library definition is in and we can add some options between the curly braces (more advanced, but we will see an example in a moment).

Additionally, you'll note that the CSS file has an extra level key called `theme`. This is to indicate the type of CSS to be included and can be one of the following (based on SMACSS(https://smacss.com/) standards):

- `base`: Usually contains CSS reset/normalizers and HTML element styling
- `layout`: High-level page styling, such as grid systems
- `component`: UI elements and reusable components
- `state`: Styles used in client-side changes to components
- `theme`: Visual styling of components

The choice here is also reflected in the weighting of the CSS file inclusion, the latter being the "heaviest", meaning that it will be included last.

Another important aspect of using libraries in any application is the ability to include externally hosted files (usually from a CDN) for better performance. Let's take a look at an example library definition that uses externally hosted files:

```
angular.angularjs:
  remote: https://github.com/angular/angular.js
  version: 1.4.4
  license:
    name: MIT
    url: https://github.com/angular/angular.js/blob/master/LICENSE
    gpl-compatible: true
```

```
js:
    https://ajax.googleapis.com/ajax/libs/angularjs/1.4.4/angular.min.js: {
type: external, minified: true }
```

This example is taken from the Drupal.org (`https://www.drupal.org/docs/8/creating-custom-modules/adding-stylesheets-css-and-javascript-js-to-a-drupal-8-module`) on defining libraries in Drupal 8. However, as you can see, the structure is the same as our previous example, except that it has some more meta information regarding the external library. And instead of a local path reference, we have a remote URL to the actual resource. Moreover, we also see some options within the curly braces by which we can specify that the file is actually externally located and it is minified.

An important change when it comes to JS in Drupal 8 is that Drupal no longer always includes all libraries such as jQuery. It does so only where and when it's needed. This has, therefore, brought the concept of library dependencies to the forefront, as certain scripts require other libraries to be loaded for them to work.

Let's assume that `my-library` depends on jQuery and specify it as a dependency. All we need to add to our library definition is the following; keep in mind that the `dependencies` key is at the same YML level as `css` and `js`:

```
dependencies:
    - core/jquery
```

With this, we declare the Drupal core jQuery library to be required by our library. This means that if we somewhere use our library and jQuery is not included, Drupal will process the dependencies and include them all, and a side-benefit of this is that dependencies are always included before your scripts, so you can also control that.

The `core/jquery` notation indicates that the extension (module or theme) that defines the `jquery` library is the Drupal core. If it had been a module or theme, `core` would have been replaced by the module or theme machine name. So, for example, to use our new library somewhere, it would be referenced as `module_name/my-library`.

Attaching libraries

Speaking of using a library, let's see what are some of the more important ways you as a module developer can make use of a library in your code.

The most common way you'll be using libraries is attaching them to your render arrays. Typically, this means that the library is needed for the rendering of that component so that if the said component is missing from the page, the library assets are no longer included.

Here is what a render array would look like with the preceding library we defined attached to it:

```
return [
  '#theme' => 'some_theme_hook',
  '#some_variable' => $some_variable,
  '#attached' => [
    'library' => [
      'my_module/my-library',
    ],
  ],
];
```

The `#attached` property is important here, and it signifies that we are essentially attaching something to the render array, which in our case happens to be a library. In Drupal 7, we could attach CSS and JS files directly, but we now have a standardized libraries API to do so in a more robust way.

However, you may have cases in which the library you need is not linked to a specific render array (a component on the page) but to the entire page itself--all pages or a subset. To attach libraries on an entire page, you can implement `hook_page_attachments()`; consider the following example:

```
function hook_page_attachments(array &$attachments) {
  $attachments['#attached']['library'][] = 'my_module/my-library';
}
```

This hook is called on each page, so you can also attach libraries contextually (for example, if the user has a specific role or something like that). Moreover, there is also the `hook_page_attachments_alter()` hook that you can use to alter any existing attachments (for example, to remove any attachment from the page).

Another way you can attach libraries is inside a preprocess function. We talked about preprocess functions earlier in this chapter; it's simple to achieve:

```
function my_module_preprocess_theme_hook(&$variables) {
  $variables['#attached']['library'][] = 'my_module/my_library';
}
```

All we have to do is add the `#attached` key (if it doesn't already exist) to the variables array.

These three methods of attaching libraries are the most common ones you'll encounter and use yourself. However, there are a few other ways and places attachments can be done--you can alter an existing render element definition and you can attach libraries straight in a Twig file. I recommend that you read the Drupal.org (`https://www.drupal.org/docs/8/creating-custom-modules/adding-stylesheets-css-and-javascript-js-to-a-drupal-8-module`) for more information on these methods.

Common theme hooks

In this section, we will look at three common theme hooks that come with Drupal core that you are likely to use quite often. The best way to understand them is, of course, referring to an example of how to use them. So, let's get to it.

Lists

One of the most common HTML constructs are lists (ordered or unordered), and any web application ends up having many of them, either for listing items or for components that do not even look like lists but for the purposes of marking up; an `ul` or `ol` fits the bill best. Luckily, Drupal has always had the `item_list` theme hook, which is flexible enough to allow us to use it in almost all cases.

The `item_list` theme hook is defined inside `drupal_common_theme()`, is preprocessed (by default) in `template_preprocess_item_list()`, uses the `item-list.html.twig` template by default, and has no default theme hook suggestions (because it's so generic and registered outside the context of any business logic). If we inspect its definition, we'll note that it takes a number of variables that build up its flexibility. Let's take a look at an example of how to use it.

Imagine that we have the following array of items:

```
$items = [
  'Item 1',
  'Item 2'
];
```

The simplest way we can render this as an `<ul>` is as follows:

```
return [
  '#theme' => 'item_list',
  '#items' => $items
];
```

Do note that the respective <ul> is wrapped in a <div class="item_list"> and that the items in our array can also be render arrays themselves.

If we want to change the list into an <ol>, we set the #list_type variable to ol. We can even have a title heading (<h3>) before the list if we set the #title variable. Moreover, we can add even more attributes on the <div> wrapper. For more information on how the other options work, I suggest that you inspect the template file and preprocessor function. However, these are the ones you'll most often use.

Links

In Chapter 2, *Creating Your First Module,* we briefly looked at how you can work with links programmatically and how to build and render them in two different ways. We also noted that it's better to use the #link render element (and we now understand what this is) if we want the link to be alterable somewhere down the line. Now, let's take a look at how we can build a list of links using the helpful links theme hook.

The links theme hook takes an array of links to be rendered, optional attributes, an optional heading, and a flag to set the active class dynamically. It then uses the links.html.twig template to construct a <ul>, much like the item_list hook.

The most important variable here is the array of links, as it needs to contain individual arrays with the following keys--title (the link text), url (a Url object), and attributes (an array of attributes to add to each link item). If you look inside the template_preprocess_links preprocessor, you'll see that it takes each of these items and transforms them into a render array with the #type => 'link' (the render element).

In addition to the array of links, you can also pass a heading (just like with item_list) and a flag for setting the active class--set_active_class. The latter will make it add an is-active class onto the <li> item in the list and the link itself if the link matches the current route. Handy stuff, isn't it? However, for more information, check out the documentation above the template_preprocess_links() implementation. Now, let's see a quick example of using this in practice:

```
$links = [
  [
    'title' => 'Link 1',
    'url' => Url::fromRoute('<front>'),
  ],
  [
    'title' => 'Link 1',
    'url' => Url::fromRoute('hello_world.hello'),
```

```
    ]
  ];

  return [
    '#theme' => 'links',
    '#links' => $links,
    '#set_active_class' => true,
  ];
```

That is all. We build an array of link data and then construct the render array using the links theme hook. We also use the set_active_class option just for kicks. This means that the is-active class will be present on the first link if this is rendered on the home page or on the second link if rendered on the Hello World page. As simple as that.

Tables

The last common theme hook we will look at now will help you build tables. It has always been a Drupal best practice to use the theme hook when building tables rather than creating the markup yourself. This is also in part because it has always been very flexible. So, let's take a look.

The table theme hook takes a bunch of variables, many of them optional. The most important, however, are the header (an array of header definitions) and rows (a multidimensional array of row definitions). It is beside the point to repeat all the possible options you have for building tables here because they are all very well documented above the template_preprocess_table() preprocessor function. So, do ensure that you check there for more information. Instead, we'll focus on a simple example of rendering a table, and we will do so via an example:

```
$header = ['Column 1', 'Column 2'];
$rows = [
  ['Row 1, Column 1', 'Row 1, Column 2'],
  ['Row 2, Column 1', 'Row 2, Column 2']
];

return [
  '#theme' => 'table',
  '#header' => $header,
  '#rows' => $rows,
];
```

So, as you can see, we have the two critical variables. We have the list of header items and the rows (whose cells are in the array in the same order as the header). Of course, you have many more options, including attributes at all levels of the table, handy sorting capability that makes it easy to integrate with a database query, and more. I strongly encourage you to explore these options in the documentation.

Attributes

In the previous three examples of theme hooks, we encountered the concept of `attributes` in the context of using them to render HTML elements. Attributes here are understood in the same way as with HTML. For example, `class`, `id`, `style`, and `href` are all HTML element attributes. Why is this important?

The reusability of theme hooks makes it so that we cannot hardcode all our HTML attributes in the Twig template files. We can have some, including classes, but there will always be the case when the business logic will need to inform the theme hook of certain classes or other attribute values to print on the HTML element, for example, an `active` class on a link. This is why, we have this concept of attributes.

Most theme hooks you'll see will have attributes in some form or another, usually the variable being called `$attributes`, `$wrapper_attributes`, or something of this nature. Also, this variable always needs to be a multidimensional array with the attribute data you want to be passed. The keys in this array are the name of the attribute, whereas the value is the attribute value. If the value can have multiple items, such as classes, it will also be an array. Consider the following example:

```
$attributes = [
    'id' => 'my-id',
    'class' => ['class-one', 'class-two'],
    'data-custom' => 'my custom data value'
];
```

As you can see, we have some common attributes, but you can also make up your own as needed (usually in the form of data attributes). However, in no way is this mandatory, and you can add only the ones you actually need. Do always, though, read the documentation on the theme hook to see how they are used and which elements are actually going to get them.

From an API point of view, Drupal handles attributes via a handy class `Attribute`. You'll note that many template preprocessors will take that array and construct a new `Attribute` object for manipulating them with more ease. Additionally, such an object is also renderable because it implements the `MarkupInterface` and Twig will know directly how to transform it into a string.

So, keep that in mind if you are writing your own theme hooks and need to handle attributes with more class (pun intended).

Theming our Hello World module

The `HelloWorldController` we built in Chapter 2, *Creating Your First Module*, currently uses a service to retrieve the string to be used as the salutation and then returns a simple markup render array with it. Let's imagine now that we want to output this message, but wrap it in our own specific markup. To make an easy thing complicated, we want to break up the salutation string into parts so that they can be styled slightly differently. Additionally, we want to allow others to override our theme using suggestions that can depend on whether or not the salutation has been overridden via the configuration form. So, let's see how we can do these things.

To get things started, this is the markup we are after:

```
<div class="salutation">
    Good morning <span class="salutation--target">world</span>
</div>
```

The first thing we need to do is to define our own theme hook capable of outputting this. To this end, we implement `hook_theme()`:

```
/**
 * Implements hook_theme().
 */
function hello_world_theme($existing, $type, $theme, $path) {
  return [
    'hello_world_salutation' => [
      'variables' => ['salutation' => NULL, 'target' => NULL, 'overridden'
=> FALSE],
    ],
  ];
}
```

For now, we only return one theme hook called `hello_world_salutation`, which takes the variables you can see. Each of them has a default value in case one is not passed from the client (render array). The first two are obvious, but we also want to have a flag on whether or not the salutation has been overridden. This will help with the theme hook suggestions.

By default, if we don't specify a template filename, this theme hook will look for a Twig template with the name `hello-world-salutation.html.twig` inside the `/templates` folder of our module. Since this is good enough for us, let's go ahead and create it:

```
<div {{ attributes }}>
  {{ salutation }}
  {% if target %}
    <span class="salutation--target">{{ target }}</span>
  {% endif %}
</div>
```

Twig notation is easy to understand. The `{{ }}` means that we are printing a variable with that name (which can be even a render array) and `{% %}` refers to control structures, such as *if statements* or *loops*. Do check out the Twig documentation (`https://twig.symfony.com/`) for more information if you are unsure.

> There are some great ways to debug what values end up being printed in the Twig template. You can use the native Twig `dump()` function, which will output things using the PHP `var_dump()` or you can install the Devel module and use the `kint()` function, which will format things in a more readable way.

We wrapped the `target` variable in an if statement so that if by any chance it's missing, we don't print an empty span tag. It's best practice to have your template mirror the possibilities of the theme hook being called with the defaults.

Finally, we also have an `attributes` array we are printing on the wrapper. We did not define this, but each theme hook comes with it. The variable is an `Attribute` object, as we discussed earlier, which gets printed into a string of the individual attributes. Instead of printing the class we want in here, we will use the preprocessor to make things more dynamic.

Let's implement the preprocessor next:

```
/**
 * Default preprocessor function for the hello_world_salutation theme hook.
 */
function template_preprocess_hello_world_salutation(&$variables) {
  $variables['attributes'] = [
    'class' => ['salutation'],
  ];
}
```

As we talked about earlier, at this stage, we are still working with an array of attributes. The theme system will turn it into the Attribute object before rendering the template, which in turn will know how to handle that.

Other modules or themes can now implement this preprocessor themselves and change the classes (or any other wrapper attributes) as they need. Had we hardcoded the class in the template file, they would have had to override the entire template--which although still a viable option is overkill if you just need to add a class.

Now, let's allow themers to have different implementations for our salutation message, depending on whether or not it is overridden by an admin. I know this particular example is quite a stretch, but it allows us to demonstrate the approach. That's what this is all about.

So, as we discussed, we can define a suggestion for our theme hook:

```
/**
 * Implements hook_theme_suggestions_HOOK().
 */
function hello_world_theme_suggestions_hello_world_salutation($variables) {
  $suggestions = [];

  if ($variables['overridden'] == TRUE) {
    $suggestions[] = 'hello_world_salutation__overridden';
  }

  return $suggestions;
}
```

If you remember, our theme hook had the overridden variable that can be used for this flag. So, in our theme hook suggestion implementation, we check for it, and if it is true, we add our suggestion. This function gets called on the fly at the moment of rendering and the most specific suggestion encountered is used if, of course, the salutation is overridden. If that is the case, it will try hello_world_salutation__overridden and if not found, it will fall back to hello_world_salutation, which exists.

Themes can now have two different templates that render the salutation in two different ways, depending on whether or not the message has been overridden:

- `hello-world-salutation.html.twig`
- `hello-world-salutation--overridden.html.twig`

Okay, our theme hook is now ready for use. Let's use it.

Since our theme template breaks our salutation message up into pieces, and can even receive the `overridden` flag, it will not be enough to just use this theme hook in the `HelloWorldController`. Instead, we will need to go back to our service and have it return the render array responsible for outputting the salutation. After all, business logic knows the structural aspects of how a certain component needs to be rendered. Theming just needs to style and alter that based on the flexibility offered by a good functional implementation.

However, let's not override the `getSalutation()` method on the service, but instead create a new one called `getSalutationComponent()`. This will then return the render array that can output the whole thing:

```
/**
 * Returns the Salutation render array.
 */
public function getSalutationComponent() {
  $render = [
    '#theme' => 'hello_world_salutation',
  ];

  $config = $this->configFactory->get('hello_world.custom_salutation');
  $salutation = $config->get('salutation');

  if ($salutation != "") {
    $render['#salutation'] = $salutation;
    $render['#overridden'] = TRUE;
    return $render;
  }

  $time = new \DateTime();
  $render['#target'] = $this->t('world');

  if ((int) $time->format('G') >= 06 && (int) $time->format('G') < 12) {
    $render['#salutation'] = $this->t('Good morning');
    return $render;
  }

  if ((int) $time->format('G') >= 12 && (int) $time->format('G') < 18) {
    $render['#salutation'] = $this->t('Good afternoon');
```

```
        return $render;
    }

    if ((int) $time->format('G') >= 18) {
      $render['#salutation'] = $this->t('Good evening');
      return $render;
    }
  }
}
```

This is how it will look. We start by creating the render array that uses our new theme hook. Then, we look in the configuration object, and if there is a message stored there, we use that, set the overridden flag to true, and return the render array. You'll note that we didn't set a target, which means that it won't get printed in the template file (as expected). If, however, it is not overridden, we proceed with our previous logic and set the message dynamically while keeping the target the same, and that's it. You can easily see how this now maps to what the theme hook and template expect for the different cases.

A couple of points to be made before going forward. First, I want to reiterate the warning that due to things such as caching, the dynamic salutation message won't actually work as expected. We'd need to set some cache metadata to prevent this render array from being cached in order for it to work. However, we will see more on that in Chapter 11, *Caching*. Second, you will have noted that the variables we defined in the theme hook show up now proceeded by a # sign as if they were properties known to the render system. As we saw earlier, they are in fact not properties, but they are known by the theme system as variables because we defined them as such. So, it's important to be able to distinguish these kinds of things when reading code that you didn't write yourself. There are, of course, many properties you don't know off the top of your head (I certainly don't know most), but with experience, you'll be able to read the code, figure out the source, and understand what it means. In this, the difference between a good developer and a great one is the ability of the latter to figure things out by reading the source code rather than relying on documentation.

Now, we have a service that can return a string representation of our message and a fully fledged renderable component. It follows that we edit our Controller and have it return this component instead of its own render array:

```
/**
 * Hello World.
 *
 * @return array
 */
public function helloWorld() {
  return $this->salutation->getSalutationComponent();
}
```

You'll note that we don't need the `#markup` property anymore, as we have our own render array. For the `salutation` token and the block we created, I choose not to use this component but rely on the string version. So, this way, we keep both options in the code for you to see.

Summary

The Drupal 8 theming system is complex and flexible, thus, it is impossible to cover it fully in one chapter of a module development book. However, we did go through the basics necessary to get you started--understanding the core tenets of the theme system, some of its most important Drupal specificities and practical use cases.

We started this chapter by discussing the abstract principle of separating business from presentation logic--a principle that is used by all modern web applications. We saw why it is critical for flexible and dynamic theming. Next, we discussed a great deal about how Drupal does this separation--the mighty theme hooks that act as a bridge between the two layers. Here, we also covered some of the highly used practices surrounding them-- preprocessor functions and theme hook suggestions for added flexibility. Then, we covered how the business logic can actually use theme hooks--the render arrays (perhaps one of the most important Drupal constructs). Also, since we were on the subject, we outlined the Drupal and Symfony render pipeline to get a better understanding of the process building up an entire page worth of render array. Next, we discussed libraries and how we can "attach" them to render arrays. We will definitely see some more examples later in the book when we talk about JavaScript. Finally, we started transitioning into the practical aspects of theming a module by exemplifying a few common theme hooks found in Drupal 8 core. In doing so, we also encountered the important topic of Attributes, an important one to understand when dealing with making theme hooks more dynamic. We ended the chapter with an overhauling of our Hello World salutation message to create a themable component. We did so by putting into practice much of what we learned about theme hooks earlier on--we defined a theme hook and template, a preprocess function, and a theme hook suggestion and built a render array dynamically to use them. All in all, not a bad day in the life of a Drupal 8 module developer.

In the next chapter, we will look at menus and the different types of menu links in Drupal 8. What kind of web application would it be without any menu links in it?

5
Menus and Menu Links

Navigation is an important part of any web application. The ability to create menus and links easily in order to connect pages together is a core aspect of any content management system. Drupal 8 is fully equipped with both the site-building capabilities and developer API to easily build and manipulate menus and links.

In this chapter, we will discuss menus and menu links from a Drupal 8 module developer perspective. In doing so, we will touch upon a few key aspects:

- The general architecture of the menu system in Drupal 8
- Manipulating and rendering menus
- Defining various types of menu links

By the end of this chapter, you should be able to understand what menus and menu links are, how to use them in your code, and how to define menu links in your module. So, let's get started.

The menu system

Before we get our hands dirty with menus and menu links, let's talk a bit about the general architecture behind the menu system. To this end, I want to describe a bit about its main components, what some of its key players are, and what classes you should be looking at. As always, no great developer has ever relied solely on a book or documentation to figure out complex systems.

Menus

Menus are configuration entities represented by the following class:
`Drupal\system\Entity\Menu`. I mentioned in `Chapter 1`, *Developing for Drupal 8*, that we have something called configuration entities in Drupal 8, which we will explore in detail later in this book. However, for now, it's enough to understand that menus can be created through the UI and become an exportable configuration. Additionally, this exported configuration can also be included inside a module so that it gets imported when the module is first installed. This way, a module can ship with its own menus that are already created. We will see how this latter aspect works when we talk about the different kinds of storage in Drupal 8. For now, we will work with either menus that come with Drupal 8 core.

Each menu can have multiple menu links, structured hierarchically in a tree with a maximum depth of 9. The ordering of the menu links can be done easily through the UI or via the weighting of the menu links, if defined in code.

Menu links

At their most basic level, menu links are plugins, but this time discoverable via a YAML discovery (instead of annotations like we are used to). To this end, the regular menu links are defined inside a `module_name.links.menu.yml` file and can be altered by other modules by implementing `hook_menu_links_discovered_alter()`. When I say regular, I mean those links that take you to menus. We will see next that there are also a few other types.

One of the reasons for the YAML discovery is that links are more definition than functionality, so they don't necessarily require classes, but can be represented through some lines inside a `YAML` file.

There are some important classes you should check out in this architecture--`MenuLinkManager` (the plugin manager) and `MenuLinkBase` (menu link plugins base class and which implements the `MenuLinkInterface`).

Menu links are, however, also content entities. The links created via the UI are stored as entities because they are considered content. The way this works is that for each created `MenuLinkContent` entity, a plugin derivative is created. We are getting dangerously close to advanced topics, which are too early to cover. However, in a nutshell, via these derivatives, it's as if a new menu link plugin is created for each `MenuLinkContent` entity, making the latter behave as any other menu link plugin. This is a very powerful system specific to Drupal 8.

Menu links have a number of properties, among which is a path or route. When created via the UI, the path can be external or internal or can reference an existing resource. When created programatically, you'll typically use a route.

Multiple types of menu links

The menu links we've been discussing so far are the links that show up in the menus. There are also a few different kinds of links that show up elsewhere but are still considered menu links and work similarly.

Local tasks

Local tasks, otherwise known as tabs, are grouped links that usually show up above the main content of a page (depending on the region where the tabs block is placed). They are usually used to group together related links that have to deal with the current page. For example, on an entity page, such as the Node Details page, you can have two tabs--one for viewing the Node and one for editing it (and maybe one for deleting it),in other words, for local tasks, as shown in the following screenshot:

Local tasks take access rules into account, so if the current user does not have access to the route of a given tab, the link is not rendered. Moreover, if that leaves only the main link, that link doesn't get rendered, as there is no point. So, for tabs, a minimum of two links are needed.

Modules can define local task links inside a `module_name.links.task.yml` file, whereas other modules can alter them by implementing `hook_menu_local_tasks_alter()`.

Local actions

Local actions are links that relate to a given route and are typically used for operations. For example, on a **list** page, you might have a local action link to create a new list item, which will take you to the relevant form page. In the following screenshot, we can see a local action link used to create a new user on the main user management page:

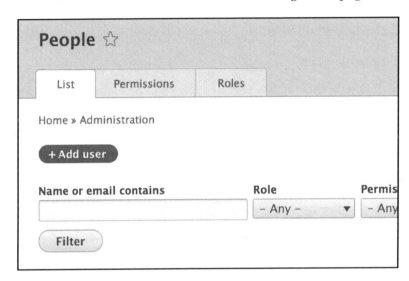

Modules can define local action links inside a `module_name.links.action.yml` file, whereas other modules can alter them by implementing `hook_menu_local_actions_alter()`.

Contextual links

Contextual links are used by the Contextual module to provide handy links next to a given component (a render array). You probably encountered this when hovering over a block, for example, and getting that little icon with a dropdown that has the **Configure block** link:

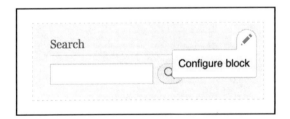

Contextual links are tied to render arrays. In fact, any render array can show a group of contextual links that are previously defined.

Modules can define contextual links inside a `module_name.links. contextual.yml` file, whereas other modules can alter them by implementing `hook_contextual_links_alter()`.

MenuLink trees

As I mentioned in the section about Menus, menu links are stored hierarchically inside a menu. This hierarchy is represented via a menu link tree. There are a number of key players here.

We have the `MenuLinkTree` service, which is the interface used to load and prepare the tree of a certain menu. The loading is deferred to the `MenuTreeStorage` service, which does so on the basis of a `MenuTreeParameters` object that contains metadata on certain restrictions to be applied on the menu links that are loaded. We will see some examples of this a bit later.

What comes out of the `MenuLinkTree` service is an array of `MenuLinkTreeElement` that is essentially a value object that wraps around the `MenuLinkInterface` plugins and that provides some extra data about its placement in the tree it finds itself in. One such important piece of information is the subtree (the array of `MenuLinkTreeElement` objects that are below it).

Menu link tree manipulators

When loading a menu link tree, you get the entire tree that fits the specified parameters. However, when using that tree, you probably want to perform some checks and remove certain items. A common example is to remove the menu links to which the user doesn't have access. This is where manipulators come into place.

The `MenuLinkTree` service has a `transform()` method, which alters a tree based on an array of manipulators. The latter take the form of callables, typically service names with specific methods. So, the actual manipulators are services that traverse the tree and make alterations to the tree items, their order, and so on.

Menu active trail

A menu trail is a list (array) of menu link plugins that are parents of a menu link. For the active trail, that specific menu link represents the current route (if there is a menu link for that route).

The Drupal 8 menu system also has a service that can be used to determine the active trail of the current route if used by a menu link. Passing a menu name to look inside of the MenuActiveTrail service returns an array of plugin IDs of the parents all the way up to the menu root, if the current route is in fact an active link. The following is a method that can be used to check that--getActiveLink().

Rendering menus

Now that we have covered some theory about the menu system, it's time to get our hands dirty with some code. The first thing we will look at is how to work with menus programmatically in view of rendering them in our module. For this, we will work with the default **Administration** menu that comes with Drupal core and has many links in it, at various levels. Note that the code we write in this section will not be included in the code repository.

Drupal core provides a block called SystemMenuBlock, which can be used to render any menu inside a block. However, let's take a look at how we can do this ourselves instead.

The first thing we will need to do is get the MenuLinkTree service. We can inject it or,if that's not possible, get it statically via the helper \Drupal class:

```
$menu_link_tree = \Drupal::menuTree();
```

Next, we will need to create a MenuTreeParameters object so that we can use it to load our menu tree. There are two ways we can do this. We can either create it ourselves and set our own options on it or we can get a default one based on the current route:

```
$parameters = $menu_link_tree->getCurrentRouteMenuTreeParameters('admin');
```

Providing the name of a menu (in our case, "admin"), this method gives us a MenuTreeParameters instance with the following options set on it:

- The links in the active trail of the current route are marked as expanded, that is, they will show up in the resulting tree that we load
- The children of the links in the active trail that have the "expanded" property set are also included in the resulting tree

Essentially, this set of parameters gives us a tree within the context of the current route we are on. In other words, it will load all the root links in the menu and all the children of the root link that is in the active trail of the current route. It will leave out the children of the other root links.

You can, of course, further customize this set of parameters or create one from scratch. For example, if we want to load only the tree of a root link inside a menu, we could do it as follows:

```
$parameters = new MenuTreeParameters();
$parameters->setRoot($plugin_id);
```

In the preceding code, `$plugin_id` is the ID of the menu link that should be at the root of the tree (defined in the YAML file or derived from a derivative).

I encourage you to look inside the `MenuTreeParameters` class and take a look at the other options that you have to load a tree.

For our example, we want to work with the entire menu tree of the Administration menu, so just instantiating a new `MenuTreeParameters` object will be enough, as we want to load all links in the menu. We can do this as follows:

```
$tree = $menu_link_tree->load('admin', $parameters);
```

Now, we have an array of `MenuLinkTreeElement` objects inside `$tree`, including the following things:

- The `link` property, which is the menu link plugin
- The `subtree` property, which is an array of `MenuLinkTreeElement` objects going down the tree
- Various metadata about the link within the tree (depth, whether in the active trail, whether it has children, access, and so on)

However, it is an important thing to note that notwithstanding any `MenuTreeParameters` we may have had, we are now sitting on top of all menu links in that menu, regardless of any access check. It is our responsibility to make sure that we don't render links to pages the user has no access to (as they will get a 403 when they get there). To do this, we use the manipulators we discussed earlier, which are simple methods on a service.

The Drupal 8 menu system comes with a few default manipulators, which can be found inside the `DefaultMenuLinkTreeManipulators` service. Most of the times, they will be enough for you:

- Access (handled by the `checkAccess()` method): Checks whether the user has access to the links in the tree. If they don't, the link becomes an instance of `InaccessibleMenuLink` and any links in its subtree are cleared out
- Node Access (handled by the `checkNodeAccess()` method): Checks whether the user has access to the Node entity linked to by the menu link. If you know that the menu has links to Nodes, you can use this before the regular access check because it's a bit more performant.
- Index and Sort (handled by the `generateIndexAndSort()` method): Creates unique indexes in the tree and sorts it by them.
- Flatten (handled by the `flatten()` method): Flattens the menu tree to one level.

If these are not enough, you can add your own manipulators as needed. All you have to do is define a service as a public method and then reference it when transforming the tree. However, speaking of transforming, let's go ahead and use the access check manipulator to ensure that the current user has access to our tree links:

```
$manipulators = [
  ['callable' => 'menu.default_tree_manipulators:checkAccess']
];
$tree = $menu_link_tree->transform($tree, $manipulators);
```

As I said earlier, we will use the `transform()` method on the service and pass an array of callables. The latter are nothing more than the service name, followed by : and the method name to be used. So, if you create your own service, you can reference it the same way.

Now, each `MenuLinkTreeElement` that remains in the tree has its `access` property filled with an instance of `AccessResultInterface` (a system of denoting access that we will talk more about in a later chapter). If the link is not accessible, it becomes an instance of `InaccessibleMenuLink`, so we know that we cannot render it, and even if we did render it, it will go to the home page rather than the 403.

Now, all we have to do is turn this tree into a render array:

```
$menu = $menu_link_tree->build($tree);
```

Inside `$menu`, we now have a render array that uses the `menu` theme hook using a theme hook suggestion based on the menu name. So, in our case, it will be `menu__admin`. Remember what these are from the theming chapter?

The `menu` theme hook will use, by default, the `menu.html.twig` (or `menu--admin.html.twig` if it exists inside a theme) to render the menu links inside a simple, albeit hierarchical, HTML list.

As a quick recap from the theming chapter, at this point you have a few options to gain full control over the output of the menu:

- Creating a new theme hook and mimicking what the `build()` method does to build the render array
- Altering the theme registry to switch out the template with your own
- Overriding the template inside a theme
- Implementing a preprocessor for the theme hook and altering variables there

So, as you can see, you have many options. The choice you make depends on what you need to achieve, how happy you are with what the default markup is, and so on.

Working with menu links

Now that we know how to load and manipulate trees of menu links, let's talk a bit more about the regular menu links. In this section, we will look at how our module can define menu links and how we can work with them programmatically once we get our hands on them from a tree or somewhere else.

Defining menu links

In our "Hello World" module, we defined a couple of routes, one of which is the `/hello` path, which shows our themed salutation component. Let's create a link to that path that goes in the main menu that comes with Drupal core.

As I mentioned, menu links are defined inside a `*.links.menu.yml` file. So, let's create that file for our module and add our menu link definition in it:

```
hello_world.hello:
  title: 'Hello'
  description: 'Get your dynamic salutation.'
  route_name: hello_world.hello
  menu_name: main
  weight: 0
```

In a typical YAML notation, we have the machine name (in this case, also the plugin ID) `hello_world.hello` followed by the relevant information below it. These are the most common things you will define for a menu link:

- The `title` is the menu link title, whereas the `description` is, by default, set as the `title` attribute on the resulting link tag
- The `route_name` indicates the route to be used behind this link
- The `menu_name` indicates the menu that it should be in; this is the machine name of the menu
- The `weight` can be used to order links within the menu

An additional common property is `parent` with which you can indicate another menu link the current one should be a child of. As such, you can build the hierarchy.

Once this is in, you should clear the cache and check out the links in the menu. You'll note that you can edit it, but some things cannot be changed through the UI due to them being defined in code.

Note that links that are created as a result of plugin derivatives, such as the ones created in the UI, have machine names (plugin IDs) in the following format:

```
main_plugin_id:plugin_derivative_id
```

The `main_plugin_id` is the ID of the menu link plugin that is responsible for deriving multiple links, whereas the `plugin_derivative_id` is the ID given to each individual derivative. For example, in the case of `MenuLinkContent` entities, the format is like this:

```
menu_link_content:867c544e-f1f7-43aa-8bf7-22fcb08a4b50
```

The UUID in the preceding code is actually the UUID of the menu link content entity, which happens to be the plugin derivative ID.

Working with menu links

I mentioned earlier that `MenuLinkTreeElement` objects wrap individual menu links, but what can we do with these programmatically if you choose to work with this data yourself and not rely on the `menu` theme hook? Let's cover a few common things you can do.

First of all, the most important thing to do is to access the menu link plugin. You can do so directly, as it is a public property on the MenuLinkTreeElement:

```
$link = $data->link;
```

Now, you can work with the $link variable, which is an instance of MenuLinkInterface, and more often than not, an actual MenuLinkDefault instance that extends the MenuLinkBase class.

So, if we inspect that interface, we can see a number of handy methods. The most common of these will be the getters for the menu link definition we saw earlier when defining the plugins. The getUrlObject() is also an important method, which transforms the route of the menu link into a Url object that we already know how to use. If the menu link is created in the UI, it could be that it has no route but only a path, in which case, this method will still be able to construct a common Url object based on that path.

If you have your hands on a menu link that is not from a tree where you have already handled access, you can ask the Url object to check access before actually using it:

```
$access = $url->access()
```

If the link is not routed, the access will always return true because it means that the link is external, or, in any case, no access check can be done. We will talk more about the access system in a separate chapter.

Defining local tasks

Let's now take a look at an example of how we can define local task links by heading back to our Hello World module. On the /hello page, let's add two local tasks--one for the regular /hello page, and the other for the configuration form where the salutation can be changed. This is a good example of using local tasks (tabs), as the configuration form is strictly related to what is on the page and is used to make changes to it.

As I mentioned, local tasks go inside a *.links.task.yml file. So, let's create one for our module with two links in it:

```
hello_world.page:
  route_name: hello_world.hello
  title: 'Hello World'
  base_route: hello_world.hello
hello_world.config:
  route_name: hello_world.greeting_form
  title: 'Configuration'
```

```
base_route: hello_world.hello
weight: 100
```

As usual, the top-most lines are the machine name (plugin IDs) of the links and we have the definitions under them. We have a `route_name` property again to specify what route these links should go to, a `title` for the link title, and a `base_route`. The latter is the route the local task should show up on. As you can see, both our links will show up on the `/hello` page. The `weight` property can be used to order the tabs.

If you clear the cache and go to that page (as a user who has access to both routes), you'll be able to see the following two tabs:

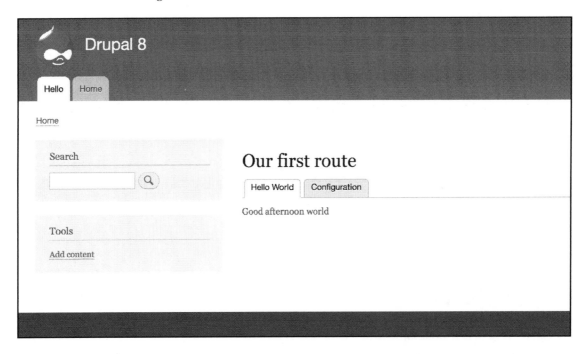

If you visit as an anonymous user, neither will show up for the reason I mentioned earlier.

Defining local actions

Nothing about our Hello World module calls for defining a local action link. So instead of doing that, let's check out one that actually makes sense. If you navigate to the `admin/content` screen, you'll see the + Add content button. It looks exactly the same as the example we saw earlier on the user management page. That is a local action link for this route. The + styling indicates that these links are primarily used to add or create new items relevant to the current route.

This particular local action link is defined in the `node` module inside the `node.links.action.yml` file, and it looks like this:

```
node.add_page:
  route_name: node.add_page
  title: 'Add content'
  appears_on:
    - system.admin_content
```

Again, we have the machine name (plugin ID) and the definition. I hope that `route_name` and `title` are, by now, clear to you. A new thing here, though, is the `appears_on` key that is used to indicate the routes (plural) on which this action link should show up. So, a key feature is that one action link can exists on multiple pages.

Defining contextual links

Contextual links are a bit more complicated than the other types of links we've seen before, but nothing is too challenging for us. So let's take a look at how we can add contextual links to our salutation component so that users can override the message via a contextual link.

First, we will need to create the `.links.contextual.yml` file and define the link:

```
hello_world.override:
  title: 'Override'
  route_name: hello_world.greeting_form
  group: hello_world
```

Nothing too complicated here. Again, we have a `title` link and a `route_name`. Additionally, we have a `group` key, which indicates the group name that this link will be a part of. We will reference this later.

Next, we will need to alter our theme hook template file because the contextual links are printed in a `title_suffix` variable that is available in all theme hooks and is used by various modules to add miscellaneous data to templates. The Contextual module is one such example. So, we will need to get that printed. This is what it will look like now:

```
<div {{ attributes }}>
  {{ title_prefix }}
  {{ salutation }}
  {% if target %}
    <span class="salutation--target">{{ target }}</span>
  {% endif %}
  {{ title_suffix }}
</div>
```

You'll note that we included the `title_prefix` variable to keep things nice and consistent. Usually, these will be empty, so no need to worry.

Finally, comes the more complex part--one that may even change in the future, but, for now, this is how we have to proceed.

Our `hello_world_salutation` theme hook defines individual variables rather than a render element. In such cases, inside a general preprocessor, the Contextual module looks at the first defined variable to check whether there are any contextual links defined. In the case of theme hooks, which use render elements, it checks that element instead.

This is what the contextual links definition looks like inside a render array and also what we need to add for our use case:

```
'#contextual_links' => [
  'hello_world' => [
    'route_parameters' => []
  ],
]
```

Here, we defined that the `hello_world` group of contextual links should be rendered here. Also, we specified an array of route parameters, which, in our case, is empty. This is because, typically, the contextual links are just that--contextual, meaning that they usually work with an entity or something that has an ID, and its route requires a parameter. So, here is where we can supply that because as we've seen, the `*.links.contextual.yml` definition is static and generic.

The `#contextual_links` property is, in fact, a render element itself that gets replaced with another render element (`contextual_links_placeholder`). The latter outputs a simple text placeholder in the HTML, which gets replaced with the right links via JavaScript.

So, now that we know how to make use of the contextual links, let's alter our Hello World salutation component to make use of this. This is what it looks like now:

```
public function getSalutationComponent() {
  $render = [
    '#theme' => 'hello_world_salutation',
    '#salutation' => [
      '#contextual_links' => [
        'hello_world' => [
          'route_parameters' => []
        ],
      ]
    ]
  ];

  $config = $this->configFactory->get('hello_world.custom_salutation');
  $salutation = $config->get('salutation');

  if ($salutation != "") {
    $render['#salutation']['#markup'] = $salutation;
    $render['#overridden'] = TRUE;
    return $render;
  }

  $time = new \DateTime();
  $render['#target'] = $this->t('world');

  if ((int) $time->format('G') >= 06 && (int) $time->format('G') < 12) {
    $render['#salutation']['#markup'] = $this->t('Good morning');
    return $render;
  }

  if ((int) $time->format('G') >= 12 && (int) $time->format('G') < 18) {
    $render['#salutation']['#markup'] = $this->t('Good afternoon');
    return $render;
  }
```

```
    if ((int) $time->format('G') >= 18) {
      $render['#salutation']['#markup'] = $this->t('Good evening');
      return $render;
    }
}
```

The main changes are as follows. First, we have already defined the #salutation variable at the top and made it into a render array. As you remember, these are highly nestable. In this render array, we added our #contextual_links render element. Second, every time we will need to set the value for the salutation string below, we do so in a #markup element this time, because, as we saw in the preceding chapter, we need a property that defines how the render array gets rendered.

So now if you clear the cache and navigate to the /hello page, you should be able to hover over the salutation and see the contextual links icon popup and contain our Override link. You should land on the salutation **configuration** form when you click on the link and also note a destination query parameter in the URL:

The destination query parameter is used by Drupal to return the user to the page they previously were on after they submitted a form on that page. This is a handy trick to keep in mind, as it is a very popular UX technique.

Summary

In this chapter, we covered a lot of ground for working with menus and menu links. We started by getting an overview of the architecture of the menu system in Drupal 8. I threw many classes and hooks at you because I am a firm believer that the best way to learn is to dig into the code.

We also saw what types of menu links there are in Drupal 8. We not only have regular links that belong to actual menus but also all sorts of other utility link systems, such as local tasks, local actions, and contextual links.

Then, we got our hands dirty and started with a practical example of how to load menu links in a tree, manipulate them, and finally turn them into a render array. Right after that, we looked at how we can define all these types of menu links Drupal 8 comes with and also how to understand the individual menu links if you need to deal with them programmatically.

In the next chapter, we will look at one of the most important aspects of any kind of content management framework--the different types of data storage we can have in Drupal 8 and how we can work with them.

6

Data Modeling and Storage

We have already gone through five chapters in this book, but we have yet to cover a topic that has to do with one of the main purposes of a CMS--data storage. Okay, we hinted at it in the preceding chapter and also saw an example of a configuration object in the second one. However, we merely scratched the surface of what is possible. It's now time to go ahead and dive into everything related to how you can store data in Drupal 8.

In this and the next chapter, we will talk about a lot of things related to storage and data manipulation and take a look at a lot of examples in the process. The focus of this chapter will, however, be more theoretical. There is a lot of ground to cover, as there are many APIs and concepts that you will need to understand. However, we will still see plenty of code examples to demonstrate in practice what we are talking about. In the next chapter, though, to make up for it, we will almost entirely work with code and build a few functionalities.

More concretely, however, this chapter will be divided into three main logical parts (not necessarily represented by headings).

First, we will talk about your options for data storage. We will talk about the State system with its Key/Value store, tempstore, user data, configuration, and finally, entities--the big one. We will leave the cache out of this, because it will be covered as a separate chapter. We will see examples of all these options and go into the architectural details necessary to understand how they work.

Second, we will dive deep into the Drupal 8 Entity API to understand the infrastructure behind it--how data is stored, and more importantly, modeled (represented in the code architecture). I am talking about the TypedData system here.

Finally, we will look at how we can manipulate entities, in other words, how we can work with them and extract data--basically, the day to day working with entities. One of the main topics here will be, of course, querying and loading entities. Moreover, here, we will also cover the validation aspect of working with entities.

By the end of this chapter, you should be able to understand a great deal about storage in Drupal 8 and make decisions on which options to choose for your requirements. You'll know the differences and the reasons for using one over another. Moreover, you'll get a good understanding of the Entity API, which, in turn will allow you to more easily navigate through Drupal core code and integrate with the entity system. Lastly, and probably, the most common thing Drupal developers do, you'll be able to work with entities: perform CRUD operations, read and write field values, and more of this good stuff.

So, let's begin.

Different types of data storage

Storing and using data are a critical part of any (web) application. Without somehow persisting data, we wouldn't be able to build much of anything. However, different uses of data warrant different systems for storing and manipulating it. For the purposes of this chapter, I will use the word *data* to mean almost anything that has to be persisted somewhere, for any given period of time.

If you've done development in Drupal 7, you already know a few ways of storing data--we had entities (primarily, the Node entity type, but others could be defined as well); the `variables` table, which was a relatively simple Key/Value store; and an API to interact with the database and do whatever we fancied. This caused many problems, such as a lack of consistency between APIs and much too heavy reliance on the database for configuration storage.

In Drupal 8, various layered APIs have been introduced to tackle common use cases for data storage. The strength of these new systems is mirrored in the fact that we rarely, if ever, need to even use the mother of all storage APIs, the database API. This is because everything has been abstracted into different layers that help us handle most of what we need. So, creating a custom table is most likely not something you should be doing for storing your data anymore, although it definitely was a common practice in Drupal 7.

State API

The State API is a Key/Value database storage and the simplest way you can store some data in Drupal 8. One of its main purposes is to allow developers to store information that relates to the *state* of the system (hence the name). Also, because the *state* of the system can be interpreted in various ways, think of this as simple information related to the current environment (Drupal installation) that is not editorial (content), for example, a timestamp of the last time they ran or any flags or markers the system sets to keep track of its tasks. It is different from caching in that it is not meant to be cleared as often and only the code that set it is responsible for updating it.

One of the main characteristics of this system is the fact that it is not for human interaction. I mean this in the sense that it is the application itself that needs to make use of it. The option for humans is the configuration system that we will talk about in detail in a later section. However, in quite a few cases, the latter falls short, and we need to (and it's perfectly acceptable) use the State system in order to store certain values input by an administrator or content editor through a form in the UI. That is because these values are of the same nature as those for which the State API is designed: they relate to only this environment, don't belong in code, and work together with the system to perform certain tasks, for example, an API key for an external service or a toggle value to enable/disable a subsystem. So, for this reason, the State API is great. There is, however, active work going on around the configuration API that would allow an easy separation between what is exportable to code and what is not. However, until then, the State API gets us covered.

So now that we know about the State API, let's jump into the technicalities and see what it's made of and how we can use it.

The State system revolves around the `StateInterface`, which provides all the methods you need to interact with it. This interface is implemented by the `State` service, which we can inject into your classes or use statically via the `\Drupal::state()` shorthand. Once we have that, things could not be any easier, as the interface tells you exactly what we can do.

We can set a value, as follows:

```
\Drupal::state()->set('my_unique_key_name', 'value');
```

Alternatively, we can get a value:

```
$value = \Drupal::state()->get('my_unique_key_name');
```

We can also set/get multiple values at once (how convenient!):

```
\Drupal::state()->setMultiple(['my_unique_key_one' => 'value',
'my_unique_key_two' => 'value']);
$values = \Drupal::state()->getMultiple(['my_unique_key_one',
'my_unique_key_two']);
```

Isn't that easy? You can also, of course, get rid of them:

```
\Drupal::state()->delete('my_unique_key_name');
\Drupal::state()->deleteMultiple(['my_unique_key_one',
'my_unique_key_two']);
```

There are a couple of things to note here. First, the key names you choose live in a single namespace, so it's recommended that you prefix them with your module name-- `my_module.my_key`. That way, you avoid collision. Second, the values you store can also be more complex than simple strings. You can store any scalar value, but also objects, as they get serialized and deserialized automatically. Be careful, though, about which objects you plan on storing. Never ever store objects that have container dependencies and do make sure that any classed objects you dump in there serialize and deserialize properly.

By now, you are probably wondering where these values end up. They go into the `key_value` table, namespaced under the `state` collection. Also, the latter is a nice segue into a talk about the underlying system that powers the State API--the Key/Value store.

Note that the State system is only one implementation of an underlying framework of Key/Value stores. If you look at the `State` service, you will note that it uses the `KeyValueFactoryInterface` (which by default is implemented by the `KeyValueDatabaseFactory`). This, in turn, creates a Key/Value storage instance (by default, the `DatabaseStorage`), which provides the public API to interact with the store. If you take a look at the `key_value` table in the database, you'll note other collections besides `state`. Those are other implementations specific to various subsystems, such as the Entity API and System schema. Guess what, you can easily write your own and customize it to your needs. However, the reason why the State API was created was so that module developers can use it. Also, valid uses of it cover much of the need for something such as a Key/Value store. So, odds are that you won't have to implement your own.

Tempstore

The next system we will look at is the tempstore (temporary store).

The tempstore is a Key/Value, session-like storage system for keeping temporary data across multiple requests. Think of a multistep form or a wizard with multiple pages which are great examples of tempstore use cases. You can even consider "work in progress", that is, not yet permanently saved somewhere but kept in the tempstore so that a certain user can keep working on it until it's finished. Another key feature of the tempstore is that entries can have an expiration date at which point they get automatically cleared so that the user rushes the work.

There are two kinds of tempstore APIs--a private and shared one. The difference between the two is that with the first one, entries strictly belong to a single user, whereas with the second one, they can be shared between users. For example, the process of filling in a multistep form is the domain of a single user, so the data related to that must be private to them. However, that form can also be open to multiple users, in which case the data can either be shared between the users (quite uncommon) or used to trigger a locking mechanism that blocks user B from making changes while user A is editing (much more common). So, there are many options, but we will see some examples soon.

First, though, let's look at some of the key players.

We will start with the `PrivateTempStore` class, which provides the API for dealing with the private tempstore. It is not a service, because in order to use it, we must instantiate it via the `PrivateTempStoreFactory`. So, that is what we now have to inject into our classes. The latter has a `get($collection)` method, which takes a collection name that we decide upon and creates a new `PrivateTempStore` object for it. If you look closely, the storage it uses is based on the `KeyValueStoreExpirableInterface`, which is very similar to the `KeyValueStoreInterface` used by the State API. The only difference is that the former has an expiration date, which allows the automatic removal of old entries, and, by default, the storage used in Drupal 8 is the `DatabaseStorageExpirable`, which uses the `key_value_expire` table to store the entries.

Up to this point, the `SharedTempStore` is strikingly similar to the private one. It is instantiated using the `SharedTempStoreFactory` service and uses the same underlying database storage by default. The main difference is the namespace occupied in the `key_value_expire` table, which is composed by `user.shared_tempstore.collection_name` as opposed to `user.private_tempstore.collection_name`.

Additionally, when asking the factory for the `SharedTempStore`, we have the option of passing an owner to retrieve it for. Otherwise, it defaults to the current user (the logged-in user ID or anonymous session ID). Also, of course, the way we interact with it and its purpose more than anything, differ slightly.

So, let's take a look at how we can work with the private and the shared tempstores.

PrivateTempStore

The following is a simple example of what we talked about in the preceding section:

```
/** @var PrivateTempStoreFactory $factory */
$factory = \Drupal::service('user.private_tempstore');
$store = $factory->get('my_module.my_collection');
$store->set('my_key', 'my_value');
$value = $store->get('my_key');
```

First, we get the `PrivateTempStoreFactory` service and ask it for the store identified by a collection name we choose. It's always a good idea to prefix it with your module name to avoid collisions. If another module names their own collection `my_collection`, it's not going to be pretty (even if the store is private).

Next, we use very simple setters and getters to set values similar to how we did with the State API.

If you run this code as user 1 (the main admin user), you'll note a new entry in the `key_value_expire` database table. The collection will be, as expected, that is, `user.private_tempstore.my_module.my_collection`, while the name will be `1:my_key`. This is the core principle of the private tempstore--each entry name is prefixed with the ID of the user who is logged in when the entry was created. Had you been an anonymous user, it would have been something like this--`-4W2kLm0ovYlBneHMKPBUPdEM8GEpjQcU3_-B3X6nLh0:my_key`, where that long string is the session ID of the user. The entry value will be a bit more complex than with the State API in that this time it's always a serialized `stdClass` object, which contains the actual value we set (which itself can be any scalar value or object that can be properly serialized), the owner (the user or session ID), and the last updated timestamp. Lastly, we have the `expire` column, which, by default, will be one week from the moment the entry was created. This is a "global" timeframe set as a parameter in the `user.services.yml` definition file and can be altered in your own services definition file if you want. However, it is still global.

We can also delete entries:

```
$store->delete('my_key');
```

We can also read the information I mentioned before about the entry (the last update, owner):

```
$metadata = $store->getMetadata('my_key');
```

This returns the `stdClass` object that wraps the entry value, but without the actual value.

A note about anonymous users

If you run that chunk of code from the preceding section as an anonymous user, you'll note that the entry gets created in the database with a session ID, as expected. However, upon the next request, if you try to retrieve the value by key, you won't find it. That is because anonymous users do not necessarily have a session started. This means a new session ID is created for each request. So, how can we solve this?

The first time you start the process or flow in which you need to interact with the private tempstore, check yourself whether the current user is anonymous. If they are, dump a variable into the `$_SESSION` super global in order to keep the session. Otherwise, it gets erased because there is no data. So, do something like this:

```
if (\Drupal::currentUser()->isAnonymous()) {
  $_SESSION['hold_session'] = true;
}
```

If you do this, the session gets preserved, and with the next request, the same user will have the same session ID and will be able to access the entries that belong to them. Of course, if you can, inject the `current_user` service instead of calling it by the static shorthand.

SharedTempStore

Now that we've seen how the private tempstore works, let's look at the shared store. The first thing we need to do in order to interact with it is, as with the private one, use the factory to create a new shared store:

```
/** @var SharedTempStoreFactory $factory */
$factory = \Drupal::service('user.shared_tempstore');
$store = $factory->get('my_module.my_collection');
```

However, unlike the private tempstore, we can pass a user identifier (ID or session ID) as a second parameter to the `get()` method to retrieve the shared store of a particular owner. If we don't, it defaults to the current user (logged in or anonymous).

Then, the simplest way we can store/read an entry is like before:

```
$store->set('my_key', 'my_value');
$value = $store->get('my_key');
```

Now, if we quickly jump to the database, we can see that the value column is the same as before, but the collection reflects that this is the shared store and the key is no longer prefixed by the owner. This is because another user should be able to retrieve the entry if they like. The original owner can still be determined by checking the metadata of the entry:

```
$metadata = $store->getMetadata('my_key');
```

Also, we can delete it exactly as with the private store:

```
$store->delete('my_key');
```

Okay. However, what else can we do with the shared store that we cannot do with the other one?

First, we have two extra ways we can set an entry. We can set it if it doesn't already exist:

```
$store->setIfNotExists('my_key', 'my_value');
```

Alternatively, we can set it if it doesn't exist or it belongs to the current user (that is, the user owns it):

```
$store->setIfOwner('my_key', 'my_value');
```

Both these methods will return a Boolean indicating whether the operation was successful or not; essentially, these are handy to check for collisions. For example, if you have like a big piece of configuration that multiple users can edit, you can create the entry which stores the work in progress only if it doesn't exist, or if it exists and the current user owns it (virtually overwriting their own previous work, which may be okay).

Then, you also have the `getIfOwner()` and `deleteIfOwner()` methods that you can use to ensure that you only use or delete the entry if it belongs to the current user.

All this fuss and for what? Why not just use the private store? This is because, in many cases, a flow can only be worked on once at the time. So, if somebody started working on it, you will need to know in order to prevent others from working on it, but even more than that, you can allow certain users to "kick out" the previous user from the flow if they "went home without finishing it". They can then continue or clear out all the changes. It all depends on your use case.

Also, as a last point, the shared tempstore also works with the same expiration system as the private one.

Tempstore conclusion

So, there we have two different, albeit similar, tempstores that you can use for various cases. If you need to store session-like data available to the user across multiple requests but which is private to them, you can use the `PrivateTempStore`. Alternatively, if this data needs to be used by either multiple users at once or the opposite, preventing multiple users from working on something at the same time, you can use the `SharedTempStore`.

Both of them have an easy-to-understand API with simple methods and you can be flexible in terms of creating your own collections for whichever use case you need.

UserData

Now, I want to briefly talk about another user-specific storage option, also provided by the User module, called *UserData*.

The purpose of the UserData API is to allow the storage of certain pieces of information related to a particular user. Its concept is similar to the State API in that the type of information stored is not configuration that should be exported. In other words, it is specific to the current environment (but belonging to a given user rather than a system or subsystem).

Users are content entities, who can have fields of various data types. These fields are typically used for structured information pertaining to the user, for example, a first and a last name. However, if you need to store something more irregular, such as user preferences or flag that a given user has done something, the UserData is a good place to do that. This is because the information is either not something structured or is not meant for the users themselves to manage. So, let's see how this works.

The UserData API is made up of two things--the `UserDataInterface`, which contains the methods we can use to interact with it (plus developer documentation), and the `UserData` service, which implements it and can be used by the client code (us):

```
/** @var UserDataInterface $userData */
$userData = \Drupal::service('user.data');
```

We are now ready to use the three methods on the interface--`get()`, `set()`, and `delete()`.

The first three arguments of all these methods are the same:

- `$module`: To store data in a namespace specific to our module name, thereby preventing collisions
- `$uid`: To tie data to a given user--it doesn't have to be the current user
- `$name`: The name of the entry being stored

Naturally, the `set()` method also has the `$value` argument, which is the data being stored, and this can be any scalar value or serializable object.

Together, all these arguments make for a very flexible storage system, a much improved one compared to the Drupal 7 option. We can essentially, for one module, store multiple entries for a given user and it doesn't stop there. Since that is possible, many of these parameters are optional. For example, we can get all the entries for a given module at once or all the entries for a given module and user combination at once. The same goes for deleting them. But where does all this data go?

The user module defines the `users_data` database table whose columns pretty much map to the arguments of these methods. The extra `serialized` column is there to indicate whether the stored data is serialized. Also, in this table, multiple records for a given user can coexist.

That is all there is to say about the UserData API. Use it wisely. Now it's time to turn to the configuration API, one of the biggest subsystems in Drupal 8.

Configuration

The configuration API is one of the most important topics a Drupal 8 developer needs to understand. There are many aspects to it that tie it into other subsystems, so it is critical to be able to both use and understand it properly.

In this subchapter, we will cover a lot about the configuration system. We start by understanding what configuration is and what it is typically used for. Then, we will go through the different options we have for managing configuration in Drupal 8, both as a site builder and a developer using the Drush commands. Next, we will talk about how configuration is stored, where it belongs, and how it is defined in the system. We will also cover a few ways that configuration can be overridden at different levels. Finally, we look at how we can interact with a simple configuration programmatically. So, let's begin with an introduction.

Introduction

Configuration is the data that the proper functioning of an application relies upon. It is those bits of information that describe how things need to behave and helps control what code does. In other words, it configures the system to behave in a certain way with the expectation that it could also configure it to behave in a different way. To this end, configuration can be as simple as a toggle (turning something on or off) or as complicated as containing hundreds of parameters that describe an entire process.

The Drupal 8 configuration system is nothing short of a revolution in the Drupal world. It is not an improvement--it is a brand new way of thinking about managing configuration. Previously, there was no configuration management to speak of. Everything was stored in the database in a way that made it impossible to properly and consistently deploy the many configuration options that Drupal is known for. Yes, there was the Features module and the Ctools exportable, but their very existence highlighted that lack of consistency and this meant many a headache for lots of Drupal developers.

In Drupal 8, the entire thing has been revamped into a well-defined and consistent subsystem, upon which any little thing that needs to be configured can depend. Far be it for me to call it perfect, it still has its shortcomings and there is work in progress on making it better and creating tools for dealing with specific configuration flows. However, it has made managing and deploying configuration so much easier, as we will see in this subchapter.

What is configuration used for?

Configuration is used in Drupal 8 for storing everything that has to be synchronized between the different environments (for example, moving from development to production). As such, it differs from the other types of data storage we saw so far in that they were specific to one environment.

Another way of looking at configuration is by examining the role of a traditional site builder. They typically navigate the UI and configure the site to behave in a certain way-- show this title on the home page, use this logo, show this type of content on the home page, and so on. As we mentioned, the result of their interactions materializes into configuration that the site builder expects would travel easily to the acceptance environment where it could be reviewed, and finally to production.

Some configuration can be actually critical to the proper functioning of the application. Certain code might break without a parameter having a value it can use. For example, if there is no site-wide email address set, what email will the system use to send its automated mails to the user? For this reason, many of these configuration parameters come with sane defaults (upon installation). However, this also shows that configuration is a part of the application and just as important as the actual code is.

Managing configuration

As we will see in a bit, Drupal stores configuration data in the database (for performance reasons), but it makes it all exportable to YAML files. So, a typical flow for managing it will have you perform changes in the UI, export the configuration, add it into Git, and deploy the code upstream to the next environment. There, it's just a matter of importing what is in code.

The import, export, and synchronization can be done both via Drush and through the UI at `admin/config/development/configuration`.

The typical flow is for the active site configuration to be synchronized with the one in the YAML files. This means importing into the database all the configurations that are different in the YAML files from those in the database. These YAML files are inside the configuration `sync` folder, which should be committed to Git (you can configure in the `settings.php` file which directory should be the `sync` folder) and the opposite is to export the active configuration to the YAML files in order to commit them into code.

The UI allows only the first option (sync what's in the YAML files with the database) but it provides you with a nice Diff interface to see what is different in YAML, as opposed to in the database:

In the preceding screenshot, we can see that the YAML files contain a small change in the site name configuration. Clicking on **Import all** will bring the database in line with the YAML files.

The first time you install a Drupal 8 site, the configuration `sync` folder will be empty. It is up to you to do a manual export of all the active configuration and put it there. You can do so via the UI manual export or through Drush:

```
drush config-export
```

You would do this step every time you make configuration changes through the UI that you want exported into YAML files.

Then, you can synchronize either in the UI as we've seen or through Drush:

```
drush config-import
```

As a Drupal developer, you will be mostly using these two Drush commands.

In addition to the entire set of configuration items, you can also import/export individual ones by copying and pasting. Be careful though, as some dependencies might not allow you to do so. However, this is useful if you want to quickly see something working in another environment, but the approach does not lend itself to a nice version-control-based flow if you abuse it.

Different types of configuration

Drupal 8 comes with two distinct types of configuration--simple and configuration entities. Let's see what the difference is.

Simple configuration is the type which stores basic data, typically represented by scalar values such as integers or strings. On the other hand, configuration entities are more complex and use the same CRUD API as the content entities.

Typically, simple configuration items are one of a kind. A module, for instance, may create and manage a configuration item that enables or disables one of its features. Most likely, this module needs this configuration to know what it should do about that feature. However, even if it doesn't, it is still a singular item that relates to that piece of functionality.

Configuration entities, on the other hand, are multiple instances of the same configuration type. For example, a view is a configuration entity and a given site can have an unlimited amount of views. It can even have none. We will talk more about configuration entities when we cover entities in general.

Configuration storage

Configuration is essentially stored in two places--the database (by default, the active configuration storage, and YAML files (the true source of the configuration).

Here is an example of a simple configuration YAML file:

```
my_string: 'Hello!'
my_int: 10
my_boolean: true
```

```
my_array:
  my_deep_string: 'Yes, hello!'
```

The name of this file is given by the ID you need to use with the configuration API to read this data.

In addition to the actual data, you can have a `dependencies` key under which you can list what this configuration item depends on:

```
dependencies:
  module:
    - views
  theme:
    - bootstrap
  config:
    - system.site
```

There are three types of dependencies--modules, themes, and other configuration items.

If you remember in `Chapter 2`, *Creating Your First Module,* we created a configuration object with the `hello_world.custom_salutation` ID in which we stored a simple value:

```
salutation: 'Whatever the user set in the form'
```

We did so programmatically through our form. This indicated that our code for displaying the salutation did not depend on this configuration item existing or having a value of some kind. Had it been mandatory for our code to work, we could have created it upon module installation. There are two ways this can be done.

The most common way is statically. Inside the `config/install` folder of a module, we can have YAML configuration files that get imported when the module is installed. However, if the values we need to set in this configuration are unknown (they need to be retrieved dynamically), we can do so in a `hook_install()` implementation (remember those from `Chapter 3`, *Logging and Mailing*?). There, we can try to get our value and create the configuration object containing it. Keep in mind that when it comes to installing modules, they will not be installed if they have configuration items in their `config/install` folder, which define some unmet dependencies.

As a bonus, you may also be able to provide configuration files with your module that should only be imported if certain dependencies are met. Otherwise, they would not be imported and the module would be installed and work just fine--in other words, optional configuration. These go inside the `config/optional` folder of the module and typically have some dependencies described in them.

Schema

In order for various systems to be able to properly interact with the configuration items, the configuration schema has been introduced. This is basically a way to define the actual configuration items, notated in the YAML format, and resides inside the `config/schema` folder of a module.

There are three main reasons why configuration needs schema definitions:

1. **Multilingual support**: As we will see later, configuration is translatable in Drupal 8. However, in order to know which parts of the configuration are needed to be, or can be, translated, the schema system has been brought in to provide this additional layer. This way, configuration items that ship with contributed modules can get their own translations on the `localize.drupal.org` website. Moreover, the schema identifies which configuration bits can be translated, and this allows users to provide translations for those in the UI.
2. **Configuration entities**: Configuration entities require schema definitions in order for the proper identification in the persistence layer of the data types that need to be exported with them.
3. Typecasting: Configuration schema ensures that the configuration API is able to always typecast properly the values to their right data types.

Let's look at a configuration example provided by Drupal core to take a look at how the schema works, namely the `system.mail` configuration provided by the `System` module. Remember in Chapter 3, *Logging and Mailing*, we talked about how this configuration item controls the mail plugin used for sending out emails? Well, by default, this is what it looks like:

```
interface:
 default: 'php_mail'
```

It's very simple; it contains only an "array" keyed by `interface` and has one item, `php_mail` (keyed by `default`). So, if we now look in the `system.schema.yml` file for the schema definition, we will find the definitions for all the configuration items that come with the System module. The top level line represents the name of the configuration item, so if we scroll down, we will find `system.mail`:

```
system.mail:
  type: config_object
  label: 'Mail system'
  mapping:
    interface:
      type: sequence
```

```
label: 'Interfaces'
sequence:
  type: string
  label: 'Interface'
```

If we look past the irony of the schema being five times bigger than the actual configuration, we can get a pretty good understanding of what this configuration item is all about and, more importantly, Drupal itself can too.

We can see that the `system.mail` configuration is of the `config_object` type. This is one of the two main types of configurations, the other being `config_entity`. The `label` key is used to indicate the human-readable name of this item, whereas the `mapping` key contains the definition of its individual elements. We can see the `interface` having the label "Interfaces" and the type `sequence`. The latter is a specific type that denotes an array in which the keys are not important. Whenever we want the keys to be taken into account, we will use `mapping` (as it's done at the top level of this schema definition) and, since we are looking at a `sequence` type, the individual items inside it are also defined as a string type with their own label.

Let's now write our own schema definition for the example configuration file we saw before:

```
my_string: 'Hello!'
my_int: 10
my_boolean: true
my_array:
  my_deep_text: 'Yes, hello, is anybody there?!'
```

If the preceding definition belonged inside a file called `my_module.settings.yml`, this would be the corresponding schema definition:

```
my_module.settings:
 type: config_object
 label: 'Module settings'
 mapping:
    my_string:
      type: string
      label: 'My string that can also be of type text if it was longer'
    my_boolean:
      type: boolean
      label: 'My boolean'
    my_array:
       type: mapping
       label: 'My array in which the keys are also important, hence not a
sequence'
        mapping:
```

```
my_deep_string:
  type: text
  label: 'My hello string'
```

As a bonus piece of information, any `config_object` typed configuration inherits the following property:

```
langcode:
  type: string
  label: 'Language code'
```

This helps with the multilingual system and invites us to add a `langcode` property to each configuration item.

Most of the properties we've seen so far have been `type`, `label`, `mapping`, and `sequence`. There are two more that you should be aware of:

- `translatable` : Very important as this indicates whether a type can be translated. By default `text` and `label` types are already set to translatable, so you don't need to do so yourself.
- `nullable` : Whether the value can be left empty. If missing, it's considered required.

Here are some types you can use to define configuration:

- Scalar types: `string`, `integer`, `boolean`, `email`, `float`, `uri`, `path`
- Lists: `mapping`, `sequence`
- Complex (extending scalar types): `label`, `path`, `text`, `date_format` and more.

Make sure you check out the `core.data_types.schema.yml` file where all these are defined.

Before we move on, let's make sure we create the configuration schema for our configuration item we created programmatically in Chapter 2, *Creating Your First Module*, namely the one storing the overridden salutation message. So, inside the `/config/schema` folder of the *Hello World* module, we can have the `hello_world.custom_salutation.yml` file with the following:

```
hello_world.custom_salutation:
  type: config_object
  label: 'Salutation settings'
  mapping:
    salutation:
      type: string
```

```
label: 'The salutation message'
```

That takes care of some technical debt we introduced back when we didn't know about configuration schemas.

Overrides

We saw that configuration exists in the database but actually belongs in neatly-organized and well-described YAML files. In order for the configuration from the YAML files to be used, they need to be imported--either via synchronization or upon module installation for those provided by modules. So, this means that the database still holds the active configuration.

To make things more dynamic, the configuration API also provides an override system by which we can, at various levels, override on the fly the active configuration. In Drupal 7, that was done via the global $conf variable, but that was also a way to unfortunately leak the overrides into the actual configuration pool. This is no longer the case in Drupal 8 and we also have three different layers at which we can override configuration.

The configuration API then takes into account these overrides in a way that prevents leaking them by accident into the active configuration. We will see examples when we talk about how to interact with the configuration API in general.

Global overrides

In Drupal 8, we still have the global override possibility via a global variable, this time called $config. This variable is available in the settings.php file for site-wide overrides, but you can also use it inside your module (if you really have to!) in order to override a specific piece of configuration:

```
global $config;
$config['system.maintenance']['message'] = 'Our own message for the site
maintenance mode';
```

In this example we changed, on the fly, the message used for the site maintenance mode. Why one would want to do that is beside the point, but you may have some other configuration which would benefit from being overridable like this. In any case, you notice the array notation we use. The first key is the name of the configuration item (of the file minus the .yml extension) and then we have the key of the individual element in the configuration file. If this were to be nested, we'd be traversing further down.

Module overrides

Although you can simply use the global $config array, that is not really the place where modules should be tinkering. First of all, because it's a global variable and it's never a good idea to change global variables, it should be mostly left to the settings.php. Second of all, because there is no way of controlling priority if multiple places try to change it in the same way. Instead, we have the module override system that we can use.

Via the module overrides, we can create a service with the config.factory.override tag (remember what tagged services are?) and in this service handle our overrides. Let's use this system to override the maintenance mode message. Inside our Hello World module, we can have the following service class:

```php
namespace Drupal\hello_world;

use Drupal\Core\Cache\CacheableMetadata;
use Drupal\Core\Config\ConfigFactoryOverrideInterface;
use Drupal\Core\Config\StorageInterface;

/**
 * Overrides configuration for the Hello World module.
 */
class HelloWorldConfigOverrides implements ConfigFactoryOverrideInterface {

  /**
   * {@inheritdoc}
   */
  public function loadOverrides($names) {
    $overrides = [];
    if (in_array('system.maintenance', $names)) {
      $overrides['system.maintenance'] = ['message' => 'Our own message for
the site maintenance mode.'];
    }

    return $overrides;
  }

  /**
   * {@inheritdoc}
   */
  public function getCacheSuffix() {
    return 'HelloWorldConfigOverrider';
  }

  /**
   * {@inheritdoc}
   */
```

```
  public function createConfigObject($name, $collection =
StorageInterface::DEFAULT_COLLECTION) {
    return NULL;
  }

  /**
   * {@inheritdoc}
   */
  public function getCacheableMetadata($name) {
    return new CacheableMetadata();
  }
}
```

Here, we have to implement the `ConfigFactoryOverrideInterface` interface which comes with four methods:

- In `loadOverrides()` we provide our overridden configuration values.
- In `getCacheSuffix()` we return a simple string to be used in the static cache identifier of our overrides.
- In `createConfigObject()` we don't actually do anything but we could create a configuration API object that would be used during installation or synchronization.
- In `getCacheableMetadata()` we return any cache metadata related to our override. We don't have any so we return an empty object.

Since this is a service, we can inject dependencies and make use of them if we want to calculate the overrides. Depending on this calculation, it can become important to set some proper cache metadata as well, but we will cover caching in another chapter.

Next, we register this as a tagged service:

```
hello_world.config_overrider:
    class: \Drupal\hello_world\HelloWorldConfigOverrides
    tags:
      - {name: config.factory.override, priority: 5}
```

We set the priority to 5 and, with this, we can control the order in which modules get their chance at overriding configuration. The higher priority will take precedence over the lower one.

And that's it. Clearing the cache will register this service and alter our configuration. If you now put the site in maintenance mode, you will notice that the message is the one we set here. However, if you go to the maintenance mode administration page at `admin/config/development/maintenance` you will still see the original message. This is so that administrators do not by accident save the override value into the configuration storage.

Language overrides

Although we will talk some more about the multilingual features of Drupal 8, let's briefly note the possibility of the language overrides.

If we enable configuration translation and add some more languages to our site, we can translate configuration items which are translatable (as described by their schema). In doing so, we are overriding the default configuration for a particular language, an override that gets stored in the configuration storage and can be exported to YAML files. So, this is an exportable type of override.

We can make use of this override programmatically, even if we are not in a specific language context. This is what the code would look like assuming we have an override in French for our maintenance mode message and we want to use that:

```
$language_manager = \Drupal::service('language_manager');
$language = $language_manager->getLanguage('fr');
$original_language = $language_manager->getConfigOverrideLanguage();
$language_manager->setConfigOverrideLanguage($language);
$config = \Drupal::config('system.maintenance');
$message = $config->get('message');
$language_manager->setConfigOverrideLanguage($original_language);
```

First, we load the language manager service and get the `Language` object for our language. Then, we keep track of the original configuration override language from the language manager but also set the French language as the one to be used going forward. Finally, we load the `system.maintenance` configuration object and read its message in French before setting back the original language on the language manager. This is a quick way to illustrate an approach by which we can temporarily switch language contexts for configuration overrides.

Priority

We have three layers for configuration overrides--global, modules, and languages. This is actually also the order of the actual priority they have. Global overrides take precedence over everything while module overrides take precedence over language ones. This is why, if we have overridden the `system.maintenance` configuration in the module, we can not use the language override in our code. So, keep this in mind.

Interacting with simple configuration

Now that we have talked about what the Drupal 8 configuration API is, what is it used for, how is it managed and stored, and what are some of the options for overriding it, it's time to talk about the API itself and how we can interact with it. In this section, we will focus only on the simple configuration as we will talk more about configuration entities when we cover all entities.

In `Chapter 2`, *Creating Your First Module*, we already became somewhat exposed to the configuration API in our `SalutationConfigurationForm` where we stored and read a simple configuration value. Now it's time to go a bit deeper to understand the API and look at some more examples of how we can use it.

The class that represents simple configuration is `Drupal\Core\Config` and it wraps around the data found in one individual configuration item. Moreover, it does all the necessaries for interacting with the underlying storage system in order to persist the configuration (by default into the database). In addition, it handles the overrides we talked about earlier automatically.

An important subclass of `Config` that we work with a lot is `ImmutableConfig`. Its purpose is to prevent changes being made to the configuration object, and as such, it is for read-only purposes.

The way we get to use instances of these classes is through the `ConfigFactory` service which has two handy methods for getting a configuration object:

```
/** @var ConfigFactoryInterface $factory */
$factory = \Drupal::service('config.factory');
$read_only_config = $factory->get('hello_world.custom_salutation');
$read_and_write_config =
$factory->getEditable('hello_world.custom_salutation');
```

The `get()` method returns an `ImmutableConfig` object which is read-only while the `getEditable()` method returns a `Config` object which can be used also for changing the configuration values. The way we do this is via the `set()` and `save()` methods:

```
$read_and_write_config->set('salutation', 'Another salutation');
$read_and_write_config->save();
```

Very simple. We also have the `setData()` method which allows us to change the entire data of the configuration item at once. As a parameter, it expects an associative array of values.

 TIP: If you cannot inject the `ConfigFactory` but have to rely on the static call, the `Drupal` class has a shortcut for loading config objects directly-- `$config = \Drupal::config('system.maintenance');`. The `config()` method takes the name of the configuration as a parameter and returns an `ImmutableConfig` object.

To read the data, we have a number of options. We can read one element from the config:

```
$value = $read_and_write_config->get('salutation');
```

This is what you would typically do. You can also get a single element even if it is nested:

```
$config = $factory->get('system.site');
$value = $config->get('page.403');
```

This will return the value set for the 403 page in the `system.site` configuration. We can also get all the values by simply not passing any parameters to the `get()` method which would return an associative array.

If you remember our discussion about the configuration overrides, by default, the `get()` method will return the values as they had been overridden through the module or globally (or as a language if the language manager has a different language set for configuration). However, if we want, we can also retrieve the original value:

```
$config = $factory->get('system.maintenance');
$value = $config->getOriginal('message', FALSE);
```

The second parameter of `getOriginal()` is whether to apply overrides and by default it is TRUE, but this way, we get the configuration value that is set in the active storage.

Finally, we can also clear configuration values or the entire objects themselves. For example, consider the following code:

```
$config->clear('message')->save();
```

It will remove the `message` key from the configuration object and save it without that value. Alternatively, we can also remove the entire thing:

```
$config->delete();
```

That is pretty much it. The power of this API also stems from its simplicity.

Entities

We have finally reached the point where we talk about the most complex, robust, and powerful system for modeling data and content in Drupal 8--the Entity API.

Entities have been around since Drupal 7, which shipped with a few types such as node, taxonomy terms, users, comments, files, and so on. However, Drupal core only provided a basic API for defining entities and loading them consistently. The *Entity API* contributed module bridged a large gap and provided a lot of functionality to make entities much more powerful. In Drupal 8, however, these principles (and more) are found in core as part of a robust data modeling system.

The Entity API integrates seamlessly with the multilingual system to bring fully translatable content and configuration entities. This means that most data you store can be translated easily into multiple languages. In Drupal 7, this was always a herculean task that involved over 10 contributed modules to achieve something not nearly as powerful as we have now.

Because there is so much to cover about entities, in this section we will start with just a general overview of the entity system. But not to worry, in the next section, and all the way to the end of this chapter, we will break it down and talk about all the important aspects.

Content versus configuration entity types

Let us start by establishing some basic terminology in order to prevent confusion down the line:

- Entities are instances of a given entity type. Thus, we can have one or more entities of a certain type, the latter being like a blueprint for the individual entities.
- Entity types can be of two kinds--content and configuration.

We talked a little bit about configuration entities in the previous section. There, we saw they are multiple instances of a certain *type* of configuration, as opposed to simple configuration, which is only one set of configuration values. Essentially, configuration entities are exportable sets of configuration values that inherit much of the same handling API as content entities.

Some examples of configuration entity types:

- View: A set of configuration values that make up a view
- ImageStyle: Defines how an image needs to be manipulated in that given style
- Role: Defines a role that can be given to a user

Content entities, on the other hand, are not exportable and are the most important way we can model and persist data in Drupal 8. These can be used for content and all sorts of other structured data used in your business logic that needs to be persisted but not deployed to the next environment.

Some examples of content entity types:

- Comment
- User
- Taxonomy Term

Apart from the exportability aspect, the main difference between the content and configuration entities is the type of fields they use. The latter uses simpler fields, the amalgamation of which gets stored as one entity "record" in the database (and exported to YAML), while the content entity fields are complex and structured both in code modeling and in the persistence layer (the database).

Moreover, configuration entities also lack bundles. Bundles are yet another categorization of entities that sits below the content entity type. That means that each content entity type can have (but they does not have to have) one or more bundles, onto which configurable fields can be attached. And not to throw more confusion at you but bundles are actually configuration entities themselves as they need to be exported and can be multiple of them.

The Entity API is very flexible in terms of the types of data that you can store. Content entity types come with a number of different field types for various forms of data, from primitive values to more complex ones such as date or entity reference. We will see some examples later on.

Content entities can also be made revisionable. This means content entity types can be configured to keep in store older versions of the same entity with some extra metadata related to the change process.

In this section and going forward, I will illustrate the most common features of entities by way of exemplifying two entity types:

- Node: The most prolific content entity type that comes with Drupal core and that is typically used as the main content modeling entity type
- NodeType: The configuration entity type that defines Node bundles

In the next chapter, we will learn how to create our own. But after everything we will learn here, it will be a breeze.

Entity type plugins

Entity types are registered with Drupal as plugins. Yes, again. The `Drupal\Core\Entity\Annotation\EntityType` class is the base annotation class for these plugins and you will mainly see two subclasses (annotations)--`ContentEntityType` and `ConfigEntityType`. These are used to register content and configuration entity types, respectively.

The annotations classes map to plugin classes used to represent the entity types. The base class for these is `Drupal\Core\Entity\EntityType`, which is then extended by another `ContentEntityType` and `ConfigEntityType`. These plugin classes are used to represent the entity types in the system and are a good resource for seeing what kind of data we can use on the annotations of these plugins. With a quick glance we can already see that the differences between the two types are not so big.

The plugin manager for entity types is the `EntityTypeManager`, a critically important service you will probably interest most with as a Drupal developer. Apart from handy things we will see a bit later, it is responsible for managing the entity type plugins using the regular annotation based discovery method.

The Node entity type is defined in `Drupal\node\Entity\Node` where you will see a huge annotation at the top of the class. The NodeType configuration entity type, on the other hand, is found in `Drupal\node\Entity\NodeType`. You can spot the difference in the annotation they use.

Identifiers

The entity type annotations start with some basic information about them, ID, label, and things like that. For example, consider the following Node entity:

```
*    id = "node",
*    label = @Translation("Content"),
*    label_singular = @Translation("content item"),
*    label_plural = @Translation("content items"),
*    label_count = @PluralTranslation(
*      singular = "@count content item",
*      plural = "@count content items"
*    ),
```

These are used in various places in the system to properly be able to reference the entity type by machine and human readable names.

Bundles

The Node entity type happens to have bundles which is the reason for which we have a `bundle_label` property as well:

```
*    bundle_label = @Translation("Content type"),
```

We can see in the following that it states "I have bundles" by defining the ID of the plugin (which maps to a configuration entity type) of its bundles:

```
bundle_entity_type = "node_type",
```

Lo and behold, that is the NodeType's `ConfigEntityType` plugin ID. On its plugin annotation, we can find the reverse `bundle_of` property which references the Node entity type. Needless to say, this is not mandatory for all configuration entity types but used for the ones that act as content entity bundles. For example, the `View` configuration entity type does not have this.

In addition, we also find on the Node plugin annotation the route to where the bundles are configured:

```
*    field_ui_base_route = "entity.node_type.edit_form",
```

This is a route defined for the NodeType configuration entity.

As I mentioned earlier, bundles do not exist for configuration entities.

Database tables

Another important bit of information for content entities is the database table name they will use for storage:

```
*    base_table = "node",
*    data_table = "node_field_data",
```

The `node` table in this case holds the primary information about the entities such as ID, uuid or bundle while the `node_field_data` table holds field data that is singular and not translatable. Otherwise, the respective fields can get their own database tables. I will explain how field data is stored a bit further on.

Entity keys

The entity API defines a set of *keys* that are consistent across all entity types and by which common entity information can be retrieved. Since not all entity types need to have the same fields for storing that data, there is a mapping that can be done in the annotation for these:

```
*    entity_keys = {
*      "id" = "nid",
*      "revision" = "vid",
*      "bundle" = "type",
*      "label" = "title",
*      "langcode" = "langcode",
*      "uuid" = "uuid",
*      "status" = "status",
*      "uid" = "uid",
*    },
```

The Node entity type has a relatively comprehensive example of entity keys. As you can see, the unique identifier field for Nodes has always been `nid`. However, the common identifier for entities across the system is `id`. So, a mapping here helps facilitate that.

Links

Each entity type has a series of links the system needs to know about. Things like the canonical URL, the edit URL, the creation URL, and so on. For the node entities we have the following:

```
*    links = {
*      "canonical" = "/node/{node}",
*      "delete-form" = "/node/{node}/delete",
*      "edit-form" = "/node/{node}/edit",
*      "version-history" = "/node/{node}/revisions",
*      "revision" = "/node/{node}/revisions/{node_revision}/view",
*    }
```

Like the entity keys, these links are common across all entity types (depending on their enabled capabilities). For example, all entity types have a canonical URL and the API allows quickly finding out which one that is from the definition.

One thing to note about these paths is that they need to be defined as routes. So, you can find them inside the `node.routing.yml` file (where you also find the routes used by the NodeType configuration entity type). Alternatively, though, these routes can be defined dynamically in order to prevent duplication. This can be done using a route provider handler. We will talk about handlers soon but also see a concrete example in the next chapter. In case you were wondering where the missing routes for the Node links are, check the `NodeRouteProvider` which registers them.

Entity translation

Entities are translatable in Drupal 8--like most of everything else--across the board. To mark an entity type as such, all we need is the following in the plugin annotation:

```
*    translatable = TRUE,
```

This exposes the entity type to all the multilingual goodness. However, as we will see a bit later, the individual fields need to also be declared translatable.

Entity revisions

In Drupal 8, all content entity types are easily revisionable with only a few settings on the plugin annotation. Since Node is such an example, we can check out its definition which has two main options to make it so.

First, we have the database table information where revisions are stored. This mirrors exactly the original tables we saw before:

```
 *    revision_table = "node_revision",
 *    revision_data_table = "node_field_revision",
```

Second, we have the entity key for the revision ID we saw earlier:

```
 *    entity_keys = {
 *      ...
 *      "revision" = "vid",
 *      ...
 *    },
```

The entity fields are not automatically revisioned so a flag needs to also be set on them.

Configuration export

Configuration entity types have a few extra options on their plugin definitions that relate to the exportability of the entities. By default, a number of configuration entity fields are persisted and exported. However, the `config_export` property needs be used to declare which other fields should be included in the export. For example, the NodeType configuration entity type defines the following:

```
 *    config_export = {
 *      "name",
 *      "type",
 *      "description",
 *      "help",
 *      "new_revision",
 *      "preview_mode",
 *      "display_submitted",
 *    }
```

Keep in mind that, without this definition, the configuration schema is used as a fallback to determine which fields to persist. If the configuration entity type doesn't have a schema (which it should though), no extra fields will get persisted.

Additionally, configuration entity types have a prefix that is used for the namespace in the configuration system. This is also defined in the plugin annotation:

```
 *    config_prefix = "type",
```

Handlers

The last main group of settings on the entity type plugins are the handlers. Handlers are the objects used by the entity API to manage various tasks related to entities. The Node entity type is a good example to look at, because it defines quite a lot of them, giving us an opportunity to learn:

```
*    handlers = {
*       "storage" = "Drupal\node\NodeStorage",
*       "storage_schema" = "Drupal\node\NodeStorageSchema",
*       "view_builder" = "Drupal\node\NodeViewBuilder",
*       "access" = "Drupal\node\NodeAccessControlHandler",
*       "views_data" = "Drupal\node\NodeViewsData",
*       "form" = {
*         "default" = "Drupal\node\NodeForm",
*         "delete" = "Drupal\node\Form\NodeDeleteForm",
*         "edit" = "Drupal\node\NodeForm"
*       },
*       "route_provider" = {
*         "html" = "Drupal\node\Entity\NodeRouteProvider",
*       },
*       "list_builder" = "Drupal\node\NodeListBuilder",
*       "translation" = "Drupal\node\NodeTranslationHandler"
*    },
```

As we can immediately notice, these are all simple references to class namespaces. So, when in doubt, it's always a good idea to go and see what they do and how they work. But let's briefly talk about all of them and see what their main responsibility is.

The `storage` handler is one of the most important. It does all that has to do with CRUD operations and interacting with the underlying storage system. It is always an implementation of `EntityStorageInterface` and sometimes a parent of the `ContentEntityStorageBase` or `ConfigEntityStorage` classes. If the entity type does not declare one, it will default to `SqlContentEntityStorage` (since we are using a SQL database most of the time) or `ConfigEntityStorage` for configuration entities.

The `storage_schema` handler is not something you will deal with too much. Its purpose is to handle the schema preparations for the storage handler. It will default to the `SqlContentEntityStorageSchema` if one is not provided and it will take care of the database tables needed for the entity type definition.

The `view_builder` handler is an `EntityViewBuilderInterface` implementation responsible for creating a render array out of an entity in view of preparing it for display. If one is not specified, it defaults to `EntityViewBuilder`.

The `access` handler is an `EntityAccessControlHandlerInterface` implementation responsible for checking the access for any of the CRUD operations on a given entity of the respective type. If one is not provided, the default `EntityAccessControlHandler` is use; it will trigger the access hooks modules can implement to have a say in the access rules of a given entity. We will talk a lot more about access in a dedicated chapter later on.

The `views_data` handler is an `EntityViewsDataInterface` implementation responsible for exposing the respective entity type to the Views API. This is used so that Views is able to properly understand the entity and fields. By default, it uses the generic `EntityViewsData` if one is not provided.

The `form` handlers are `EntityFormInterface` implementations used for various types of entity manipulations such as create, edit and delete. The referenced classes are forms that are used for managing the entities.

The `route_provider` handlers are `EntityRouteProviderInterface` implementations responsible for dynamically providing routes necessary for the respective entity type. The Node entity type defines one for HTML pages but others can be defined for other kinds of HTTP formats as well.

The `list_builder` handler is an `EntityListBuilderInterface` implementation responsible for building a listing of entities of the respective type. This listing is typically used on the administration screen for managing the entities. This is an important one to have as without it the admin listing won't work.

The `translation` handler is a `ContentTranslationHandlerInterface` implementation responsible for exposing the entities of this type to the translation API.

Fields

The principle way data is modeled by entities is through fields. Entities themselves are essentially just a collection of different types of fields which hold various types of data.

Drupal 7 developers will remember that in D7, entities had two types of fields, usually referred to as properties and Field UI fields. The former were essentially simple properties on the entity class and were stored in the entity table itself. The latter were fields that were attached to bundles through the UI and had separate database tables.

Things are somewhat similar in Drupal 8 but also very different. First of all, we make a big difference between the fields that belong to content versus configuration entities. Then, as in D7, we still make a distinction between two types of content entity fields--base fields and configurable fields. However, this is not as big as it used to be in D7 as they both have the same foundation.

Configuration entity fields

Configuration entities have relatively simple fields, due to their storage handling. We can store complex configuration but there is no complex database schema to reflect that. Instead, we have the configuration schema layer that describes configuration entities so the Entity API can understand the types of data they store and represent. We talked about this earlier in the chapter when we looked at the configuration system. But let's examine the NodeType configuration entity type to better understand its fields.

The fields on configuration entities are essentially declared as class properties. So, we can see that NodeType has fields such as $description, $help and others. As I mentioned a bit earlier, the plugin annotation includes a reference to which of these class properties are actually to be persisted and exported. As you can imagine, a class should be allowed to also have some properties that are not actually field values that need to be exported.

The configuration entity class can also have some specific getter and setter methods for its field, but can also rely on the ConfigEntityBase parent class set() and get() methods for setting and accessing field values. Things are relatively simple to understand.

Now, let's check out the NodeType configuration schema found in node.schema.yml and see what that is all about:

```
node.type.*:
  type: config_entity
  label: 'Content type'
  mapping:
    name:
      type: label
      label: 'Name'
    type:
      type: string
      label: 'Machine-readable name'
    ....
    new_revision:
      type: boolean
      label: 'Whether a new revision should be created by default'
    ...
```

This is just a sample of the schema definition without some of the fields because we already know how to read those. However, there are some things which are new though.

We can see the wildcard notation which indicates that this schema should apply to all configuration items that start with that prefix. So, essentially, to all entities of a certain type. In this case, the entity type name is `type` as denoted in the NodeType annotation `config_prefix` property. Of course, the namespace is prefixed by the module name.

Next, we see that the type is `config_entity`, which as we know is the other major complex type besides `config_object` used to denote simple configuration. These are basically extensions of the `mapping` type with some extra information. In the case of configuration entities, these are the definitions for the fields that automatically get exported--`uuid`, `langcode`, `status`, `depedencies` and `third_party_settings`. That is to say, these fields exist on all configuration entities of any type and are always persisted/exported.

Lastly, we have the schema definitions for each individual fields such as `name`, `type`, and more. So, now the system knows that the `new_revision` field should be treated as a Boolean or that the `name` field is translatable (since it is of a type label which extends the simple `string` type with the translation flag on).

So, as you can see, the field matrix of a configuration entity type is not so complex to understand. Content entities are much more complex and we will talk about that next.

Content entity fields

As in Drupal 7, content entities in D8 have two types of fields--base fields and configurable fields. For Drupal 7 developers, the former are essentially the old "property" fields while the latter are the "field UI" fields. However, as we will see in a moment, they are now very different implementations in that they are very similar to each other.

First and foremost, content entity fields in Drupal 8 are built on top of the low-level TypedData API. The latter is a complex system for modeling data in code and it is widely used in Drupal 8. Unfortunately, it is also one of the APIs least understood by developers. Not to worry, in the next section I will break it down for you. Since we still don't know anything about it, we will now talk about fields from a higher-level perspective.

Base fields

Base fields are the fields most close to a given entity type, things like the title, creation/modification date, publication status, and so on. They are defined in the entity type class as `BaseFieldDefinition` implementations and are installed in the database based on these definitions. Once installed, they are no longer configurable from a storage point of view from the UI (except in some cases, in which certain aspects can be overridden). Additionally, some display and form widget configuration changes can still be made (also depending on whether the individual definitions allow this).

Let's check out the Node entity type's `baseFieldDefinitions()` method and see an example of a base field definition:

```
$fields['title'] = BaseFieldDefinition::create('string')
    ->setLabel(t('Title'))
    ->setRequired(TRUE)
    ->setTranslatable(TRUE)
    ->setRevisionable(TRUE)
    ->setSetting('max_length', 255)
    ->setDisplayOptions('view', array(
      'label' => 'hidden',
      'type' => 'string',
      'weight' => -5,
    ))
    ->setDisplayOptions('form', array(
      'type' => 'string_textfield',
      'weight' => -5,
    ))
    ->setDisplayConfigurable('form', TRUE);
```

This is the definition of the Node `title` field. We can deduce it's of the type `string` due to the argument passed to the `create()` method of the `BaseFieldDefinition` class. The latter is a complex data definition class on top of the TypedData API.

Other common types of fields that can be defined are `boolean`, `integer`, `float`, `timestamp`, `datetime`, `entity_reference`, `text_long`, and many others. You can find out what field types you can use by checking the available `FieldType` plugins provided by Drupal core and any other modules. These are the same types of fields that can be used by configurable fields in the UI. In a later chapter, we will see how we can write our own custom field type.

The field definition can get a number of options that may also differ depending on the type of field being defined. I will skip the obvious ones here and jump to the `setTranslatable()` and `setRevisionable()` methods and ask you to remember when we saw earlier how the Node entity type plugin annotation indicated that Nodes will be translatable and revisionable. This is where the fields themselves are configured to that effect. Without these settings, they'd be left out of the translation capability and revisions.

The `setSetting()` method is used to provide various options to the field. In this case, it's used to indicate the maximum length for the field, which is also mirrored in the table column in the database. Then we have the display options which configure the view formatter and form widget the field should use. They reference plugin IDs of the type `FieldFormatter` (`string`) and `FieldWidget` (`string_textfield`) plugins, respectively. In a later chapter, we will see how we can define our field plugins that can be used both for base fields and also configuration fields in the UI.

Lastly, we have the `setDisplayConfigurable()` method, which is used to enable/disable configuration changes on the form widget or display through the UI. In this case, only the form widget is exposed for changes.

Not all these options and configurations are always used or mandatory. It depends on what type of field we are defining, how we want the field to be configured, and whether defaults are okay for us. An important option that can be used is cardinality--whether the field can have more than one value of the same type. This allows a field to store multiple values that follow the same data definition on that entity field.

If we create our own entity type and want to later add or modify a base field, we can do just that. However, for entities that do not "belong" to us, we need to implement some hooks in order to contribute with our own changes. To provide a new base field definition to an exiting entity type, we can implement `hook_entity_base_field_info()` in our module and return an array of `BaseFieldDefinition` items just as we saw before in the Node entity type. Alternatively, we can implement `hook_entity_base_field_info_alter()` and alter existing base field definitions to our liking. Do keep in mind that this latter hook might be changed in the future, although at the time of writing, not a great priority has been set on that.

Configurable fields

Configurable fields are typically created through the UI, attached to an entity type bundle, and exported to code. The part highlighted with bold is a critical difference between these and base fields in that base fields exist on all bundles of the entity type:

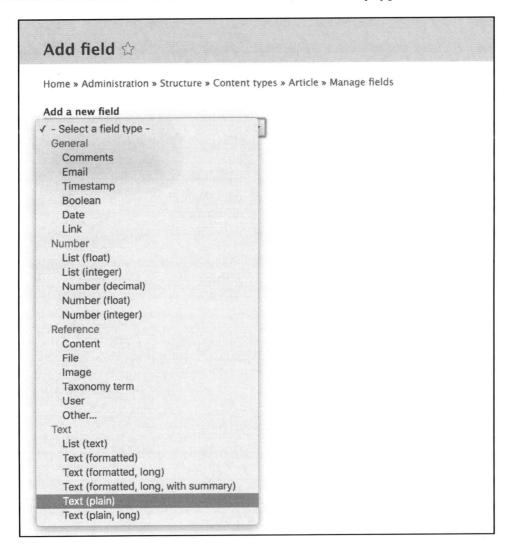

They also use the TypedData API for their definitions, as well as the same field type, widget, and formatter plugins we talked about earlier. Architecturally speaking, the main difference between base and configurable fields is that the latter are made up of two parts-- storage configuration (`FieldStorageConfig`) and field configuration (`FieldConfig`). These are both configuration entity types, whose entities, together, make up a configurable field. The former defines the field settings that relate to how the field is stored. These are options that apply to that particular field across all the bundles of an entity type it may be attached to (such as cardinality, the field type, and so on). The latter defines options for the field specific to a bundle it is attached to. These can, in some case, be overrides of the storage config but also new settings (such as the field description, whether it is required, and more).

The easiest way to create configurable fields is through the UI. Just as easily, you get them exported into code. You could alternatively write the field storage configuration and field configuration yourself and add it to your module's `config/install` folder, but you can achieve the same if you just export them through the UI.

Moreover, you can use a couple of hooks to make alterations to existing fields. For example, implementing `hook_entity_field_storage_info_alter()` you can alter field storage configurations while with `hook_entity_bundle_field_info_alter()` you can alter field configurations as they are attached to an entity type bundle.

Field storage

We earlier saw how configuration entities are persisted and exported based on the configuration schema and plugin definition. Let's quickly talk about how the fields used on content entities are stored in the database.

Base fields, by default, end up in the entity base table (the one defined in the plugin annotation as `base_table`). This makes things more performant than having them in individual tables. However, there are some exceptions to this.

If the entity type is translatable, a "data" table gets created where records of the same entity base field values in different languages can be stored. This is the table the Node entity type plugin annotation declared with the property `data_table`. If this property is missing, the table name will be by default `[base_table]_field_data`.

Moreover, if the field cardinality of a given field is higher than 1, a new table is created for the field with the name `[entity_type_name]__[field_name]` where multiple records for the same field can be stored.

If the entity and field have translation enabled and the respective field cardinality is higher than 1, the "data" table holds the records for an entity in all languages it is translated into while the `[entity_type_name]__[field_name]` table holds the all value records in all language for a given field.

Configurable fields, on the other hand, always get a separate field data table named `[entity_type_name]__[field_name]`, where the multiple values for the same field and in multiple language can be stored.

Entity types summary

The Entity API is quite complex. We have only begun our journey to understanding the different kinds of entity types, bundles, fields, and so on. We have so far talked about the differences between configuration and content entity types and what exactly makes them up. To this end, we also touched upon the different types of fields they can use and how the data in these fields is stored.

However, there is still a lot to understand about entities, especially content entities, which will be our focus in the next sections. We are going to first look at the TypedData API to better understand how content entity field data is modeled. As of now, that is still a black box, am I right? Next, we'll look at how to actually work with the API to query, create, and manipulate entities (both content and configuration). Finally, we'll talk a bit about the validation API the content entities and fields use consistently to ensure they hold proper data. So, let's get to it.

TypedData

In order to really understand how entity data is modeled, we need to understand the TypedData API. Unfortunately, this API, at the time of writing, still remains quite a mystery for many. But you're in luck because in this section we're gonna get to the bottom of it.

Why?

It helps to understand things better if we first talk about why there was the need for this API. It all has to do with the way PHP as a language *is*, compared to others, and that is loosely typed. This means that in PHP it is very difficult to use native language constructs to rely on the type of certain data or understand more about that data, as opposed to languages like Java or Python.

The difference between the string `"1"` and integer 1 is a very common example. We are often afraid of using the `===` sign to compare them because we never know what they actually come back as from the database or wherever. So, we either use `==` (which is not really good) or forcefully cast them to the same type and hope PHP will be able to get it right.

In PHP 7, we have type hinting for scalar values in function parameters which is good, but still not enough. Scalar values alone are not gonna cut it if you think of the difference between `1495875076` and `2495877076`. The first is a timestamp while the second is an integer. Even more importantly, the first has meaning while the second one does not. At least seemingly. Maybe I want it to have some meaning because it is the specific formatting for the tracking IDs in my package tracking app.

Drupal was not exempt from the problems this loosely typed nature of PHP can create. Drupal 7 developers know very well what it meant to deal with field values in this way, but not anymore because we now have the TypedData API in Drupal 8.

What?

The TypedData API is a low-level and generic API that essentially does two things from which a lot of power and flexibility is derived.

First, it wraps "values" of any kind of complexity. More importantly, it forms "values". This can be a simple scalar value to a multidimensional map of related values of different type that together are considered one value. Let's take for example a New York license plate--`405-307`. This is a simple string but we "wrap" it with TypedData to give it meaning. In other words, we know programmatically that it is a license plate and not just a random PHP string. But wait, that plate number can be found in other states as well (possibly, I have no idea). So, in order to better define a plate, we need also a state code--`NY`. This is another simple string wrapped with TypedData to give it meaning--a state code. Together, they can become a slightly more complex piece of TypedData--US license plate, which has its own meaning.

Second, as you can probably infer, it gives meaning to the data that it wraps. If we continue our previous example, the US license plate TypedData now has plenty of meaning. So, we can programmatically ask it what it is and all sorts of other things about it, such as what is the state code for that plate and the API facilitates this interaction with the data.

As I mentioned, from this flexibility, a lot of power can be built on top. Things like data validation are very important in Drupal 8 and rely on TypedData. As we will see later in this chapter, validation happens at the TypedData level using constraints on the underlying data.

The low-level API

Now that we have a basic understanding of the principles behind TypedData and why we need it, let's start exploring the API, starting from the smallest pieces and going up.

There are two main pillars of this API--DataType plugins and data definitions.

DataType plugins

DataType plugins are responsible for defining the available types of data that can be used in the system. For example, the StringData plugin is used to model a simple primitive string. Moreover, they are responsible for interacting with the data itself; things like setting and accessing the respective values.

The DataType plugins are managed by the TypedDataManager and are annotated by the DataType annotation class. They implement the TypedDataInterface and typically extend the TypedData base class or one of its subclasses.

There are three main types of DataType plugins out there, depending on the interface they implement. First, there is the TypedDataInterface I mentioned before; this is typically used for simple primitive values such as strings or integers. Second, there is the ListInterface which is used to form a collection of other TypedData elements. It comes with methods specific to interacting with lists of elements. Third, there is ComplexDataInterface which is used for more complex data formed of multiple properties that have names and can be accessed accordingly. Going forward, we will see examples of all these types.

The best way to understand how these plugins are used is to first talk about data definitions as well.

Data definitions

Data definitions are the objects used to store all that meaning about the underlying data we talked about. They define the type of data they can hold (using an existing DataType plugin) and any kind of other meaningful information about that data. So, together with the plugins, the data definitions are one mean data modeling machine.

At the lowest level, they implement the `DataDefinitionInterface` and typically extend the `DataDefinition` class (or one of its subclasses). Important subclasses of `DataDefinition` are the `ListDefinition` and `ComplexDefinitionBase` which are used to define more complex data types. And as you might expect, they correlate to the `ListInterface` and `ComplexDataInterface` plugins I mentioned earlier.

Let us see an example of a simple usage of data definitions and DataType plugins by modeling a simple string--`my_value`.

It all starts with the definition:

```
$definition = DataDefinition::create('string');
```

The argument we pass to the `create()` method is the DataType plugin ID we want to be defining our data as. In this case, it is the `StringData` plugin.

We already have some options out of the box to define our string data. For example, we can set a label:

```
$definition->setLabel('Defines a simple string');
```

We can also mark it as read only or set whatever "settings" we want onto the definition. However, one thing we don't do is deal with the actual value. This is where the DataType plugin comes into play. The way this happens is that we have to create a new plugin instance, based on our definition and a value:

```
/** @var TypedDataInterface $data */
$data = \Drupal::typedDataManager()->create($definition, 'my_value');
```

We used the `TypedDataManager` to create a new instance of our definition with our actual string value. What we get is a plugin that we can use to interact with our data, understand it better, change its value, and so on:

```
$value = $data->getValue();
$data->setValue('another string')
$type = $data->getDataDefinition()->getDataType();
$label = $data->getDataDefinition()->getLabel();
```

We can see what kind of data we are dealing with, its label, and other things.

Let's take a look at a slightly more complex example and model our license plate use case we talked about earlier.

We first define the number:

```
$plate_number_definition = DataDefinition::create('string');
$plate_number_definition->setLabel('A license plate number.');
```

Then, we define the state code:

```
$state_code_definition = DataDefinition::create('string');
$state_code_definition->setLabel('A state code');
```

We are keeping these generic because nobody says we cannot reuse these elsewhere; we might need to deal with state codes.

Next, we create our full plate definition:

```
$plate_definition = MapDataDefinition::create();
$plate_definition->setLabel('A US license plate');
```

We use the `MapDataDefinition` here which uses by default the `Map` DataType plugin. Essentially, this is a well defined associative array of properties. So, let's add our definitions to it:

```
$plate_definition->setPropertyDefinition('number',
$plate_number_definition);
$plate_definition->setPropertyDefinition('state', $state_code_definition);
```

This map definition gets two named property definitions--number and state. You can see now the hierarchical aspect of the TypedData API.

Finally, we instantiate the plugin:

```
/** @var Map $plate */
$plate = \Drupal::typedDataManager()->create($plate_definition, ['state' =>
'NY', 'number' => '405-307']);
```

The value we pass to this type of data is an array whose keys should map to the property names and values to the individual property definitions (which in this case are strings).

Now, we can benefit from all the goodness:

```
$label = $plate->getDataDefinition()->getLabel();
$number = $plate->get('number');
$state = $plate->get('state');
```

The `$number` and `$state` variables are `StringData` plugins which can then be used to access the individual values inside:

```
$state_code = $state->getValue();
```

Their respective definitions can be accessed the same way we did before. So, we managed in these few lines to properly define a US license plate construct and make it intelligible by the rest of our code. Next, we will look at even more complex examples and inspect how content entity data is modeled using TypedData. Configuration entities, as we saw, rely on configuration schemas to define the data types. Under the hood, the schema types themselves reference TypedData API data type plugins themselves. So, behind the scenes, the same low level API is used. To keep things a bit simpler, we will look at content entities where this API is much more explicit and you will actually have to deal with it.

Content entities

Let's now examine entities and fields and see how they make use of the TypedData API for modeling the data they store and manage. This will also help you better understand how data is organised when you are debugging entities and their fields.

The main place data is stored and modeled are fields. As we saw, we have two types--base fields and configurable fields. However, when it comes to TypedData, they do not differ very much. They both use the `FieldItemList` DataType plugin (either directly or a subclass). In terms of definitions, base fields use `BaseFieldDefinition` instances while configurable fields use `FieldConfig` instances. The latter are slightly more complicated because they are actually configuration entities themselves (to store the field configuration) but that implement down the line the `DataDefinitionInterface`. So, they combine the two tasks. Moreover, base fields can also use `BaseFieldOverride` definition instances which are essentially also configuration entities and that are used for storing alterations made through the UI to the fields defined as base fields. Just as the `FieldConfig` definitions, these extend the `FieldConfigBase` class, because they share the same exportable characteristics.

In addition to fields, entities themselves have a TypedData plugin that can be used to wrap entities and expose them to the API directly--the `EntityAdapter`. These use an `EntityDataDefinition`, instance which basically includes all the individual field definitions. Using plugin derivatives, each entity types get dynamically an `EntityAdapter` plugin instance.

Let's now examine a simple base field and understand the usage of the TypedData API in the context of fields. The `BaseFieldDefinition` class extends `ListDataDefinition` which is responsible for defining multiple items of data in a list. Each item in the list is an instance of `DataDefinitionInterface` as well, so you can see the same kind of hierarchy as we had with our license plate example. But why is one field a list of items?

You probably know that when you create a field in the UI, you can choose how many items this one field can hold--its cardinality. You typically choose one, but can choose many. The same is true with all types of fields. Regardless of the cardinality you choose, the data is modeled as a list. If the field has a cardinality of one, the list will only have one item. It is as simple as that. So, if base field definitions are lists of definitions, what are the individual item definitions? The answer is implementations of `FieldItemDataDefinition`.

In terms of DataType plugins, as I mentioned, we have the `FieldItemList` class which implements the `ListInterface` I mentioned earlier as one of the more complex data types. The individual items inside are subclasses of `FieldItemBase` (which extends the `Map` DataType we encountered earlier). So, we have the same kind of data structure. But just to make matters slightly more complicated, another plugin type comes into play here--`FieldType`. These individual field items are actually instances of these plugins (which as I said extend `FieldItemBase` and down the line a `DataType` plugin of some kind). So, for instance, a text field will use the `StringItem` `FieldType` plugin which inherits a bunch of functionality from the `Map` DataType. So, you can see how the TypedData API is at a very low level and things can be built on top of it.

So now, if we combine what we learned and look at a base field, we see the following--a `FieldItemList` data type using a `BaseFieldDefinition` (or `BaseFieldOverride`) data definition. Inside, each item is a `FieldItemBase` implementation (a `FieldType` plugin extending some sort of `DataType` plugin) using a `FieldItemDataDefinition`. So, not that complicated after all. We will put this knowledge to good use in the final section of this chapter when we see how we can interact with entities and field data. I am not throwing all these notions at you just for the sake of it.

The configurable fields work almost exactly the same except that the definition corresponding to the `FieldItemList` is an instance of `FieldConfig` (a configuration entity that stores the settings for this field and which is similar to the `BaseFieldOverride`). However, it is also a type of list definition with the individual list items being the same as with the base fields.

TypedData summary

So, as we've seen, the scope of understanding the TypedData API in Drupal 8 is quite broad. We can make things very simple, like with our first example, but then hit some really complicated territory with its use in the Entity system. The point of this section has been to make you aware of this API, understand its reasoning, see a couple of simple examples, and breakdown all the components that are used in the Entity API.

However, I admit, it must have been quite a difficult section to follow. All this terminology and theory can be pretty daunting. But don't worry, if you didn't fully understand everything, that's fine. It's there for you to reference as we go through the next section because we will apply all that knowledge and you will see why it's useful to be aware of it. In other words, we will now focus on interacting with entities (both content and configuration) and in doing so make heavy use of the functionality made possible by the TypedData API.

Interacting with the Entity API

In this final section of the chapter, we're going to cover the most common things you will be doing with content and configuration entities. These are the main topics we discuss going forward:

- Querying and loading entities
- Reading entities
- Manipulating entities (update/save)
- Creating entities
- Rendering entities
- Validating entity data

So, let's hit it.

Querying and loading entities

One of the most common things you will do as a programmer is query for stuff, such as data in the database. This is what we were doing a lot in Drupal 7 to get our data. A lot. We'd either use the database API or simple query strings and load our data. However, in Drupal 8 the entity API has become much more robust and offers a layer that reduces the need to query the database directly. In a later chapter, we will see how to do that still for when things become more complex. For now, since most of our structured data belongs in entities, we will use the entity query system for retrieving entities.

The service we use for querying entities is the `entity.query` service (`QueryFactory`). So, we can inject this into our class or use it statically:

```
$query = \Drupal::entityQuery('node')
```

Here, `node` is the entity type for which we want to query.

However, we also have the option of using the `entity_type.manager` service (`EntityTypeManager`) and get the query factory from it:

```
\Drupal::entityTypeManager()->getStorage('node')->getQuery();
```

We request the storage handler (remember what that is from when we talked about entity type handlers?) which then can give us the query factory for that entity type.

The reason we might want to do that is that the entity query will always return IDs of the entities found. So, if we want to actually load them, we still need the `EntityTypeManager` to do so. So, why would we want to always inject both of these services into our class? In the preceding examples, I used static calls but, as always, you should inject the services where you can.

Building queries

Now that we have an entity query factory on our hands, we can build a query that is made up of conditions and all sorts of typical query elements. Here's a simple example of querying for the last 10 published article nodes:

```
$query
      ->condition('type', 'article')
      ->condition('status', TRUE)
      ->range(0, 10)
      ->sort('created', 'DESC');
$ids = $query->execute();
```

The first thing you can see is that the methods on the factory are chainable. We have some expected methods to set conditions, range, sorting, and so on. I strongly recommend you check out the `QueryInterface` class for some documentation about these methods, especially the `condition()` method which is the most complex. As you can already deduce, the first parameter is the field name and the second is the value. An optional third parameter can also be the operator for the condition. Here is a slightly more complex condition that would returns nodes of two different types:

```
->condition('type', ['article', 'page'], 'IN')
```

Additionally, you can also use condition groups, with OR or AND conjunctions:

```
$query
  ->condition('status', TRUE);
$or = $query->orConditionGroup()
  ->condition('title', 'Drupal', 'CONTAINS')
  ->condition('field_tags.entity.name', 'Drupal', 'CONTAINS');
$query->condition($or);
$ids = $query->execute();
```

In the preceding query, we see a few new things. First, we create a condition group of the type OR in which we add two conditions. One of them checks whether the node title field contains the string "Drupal". The other checks whether any of the entities referenced by the `field_tags` field (in this case taxonomy terms) has the string "Drupal" in their name. So, you can see the power we have in traversing into referenced entities. Finally, we use this condition group as the first parameter to the `condition()` method of the query (instead of field name and value).

 Entity queries for the Node entity type take access restrictions into account as they are run from the context of the current user. This means that, for example, a query for unpublished nodes triggered on a page hit by an anonymous user is not going to return results, but it will if triggered by an administrator. You can disable this by adding the `->accessCheck(FALSE)` instruction to the query IF you are sure the results are not going to expose unwanted content to users. We will talk more about node access in a later chapter.

Configuration entities work in the same way. We get the query factory for that entity type and build a query. Under the hood, the query is of course run differently due to the flat nature of the storage.

Each entity gets one record in the database so they need to be loaded and then examined. Moreover, the conditions can be written to also match the nested nature of configuration entity field data. For example:

```
$query = \Drupal::entityTypeManager()->getStorage('view')->getQuery();
$query
    ->condition('display.*.display_plugin', 'page');
$ids = $query->execute();
```

This query searches for all the View configuration entities which have the display plugin of the type "page". The condition essentially looks inside the display array for any of the elements (hence the * wildcard). If any of these elements has a display_plugin key with the value "page", it's a match. This is what an example view entity looks like in YAML format:

```
. . .
base_field: nid
core: 8.x
display:
  default:
    display_options:
      . . .
    display_plugin: default
    display_title: Master
  . . .
  page_1:
    display_options:
      . . .
    display_plugin: page
    display_title: Page
```

I removed a bunch of data from this entity just to keep it short. But as you can see, we have the display array, with the default and page_1 elements and each has a display_plugin key with a plugin ID.

Loading entities

Now that we have our entity IDs found by the query, it's time to load them. It couldn't be simpler to do so. We just use the storage handler for that entity type (and we get that from the entity type manager):

```
$nodes =
\Drupal::entityTypeManager()->getStorage('node')->loadMultiple($ids);
```

This will return an array of `EntityInterface` objects (in this case `NodeInterface`) or if we have only one ID to load:

```
$nodes = \Drupal::entityTypeManager()->getStorage('node')->load($id);
```

These will return a single `NodeInterface` object.

The Entity type storage handler also has a shortcut method that allows you to perform simple queries and load the resulting entities in one go. For example, if we wanted to load all article nodes:

```
$nodes =
\Drupal::entityTypeManager()->getStorage('node')->loadByProperties(['type'
=> 'article']);
```

The `loadByProperties()` method takes one parameter--an associative array that contains simple field value conditions that need to match. Behind the scenes, it builds a query based on these and loads the returning entities. Do keep in mind that you cannot have complex queries here and access checks will be taken into account in the query being built under the hood. So, for full control, just build the query yourself.

Reading entities

So, we have our entity loaded and we can now read its data. For content entities, this is where the TypedData knowledge comes into play. Before we look at that, let's see quickly how we can get the data from configuration entities. Let's inspect the Article `NodeType` for this purpose:

```
/** @var NodeType $type */
$type =
\Drupal::entityTypeManager()->getStorage('node_type')->load('article');
```

The first and simplest thing we can do is inspect the individual methods on the entity type class. For example, `NodeType` has a `getDescription()` method which is a handy helper to get the description field:

```
$description = $type->getDescription();
```

This is always the best way to try to get the field values of configuration entities, because you potentially get return type documentation which can come in handy with your IDE. Alternatively, the `ConfigEntityBase` class has the `get()` method that can be used to access any of the fields:

```
$description = $type->get('description');
```

This is going to do the same thing and it is the common way any field can be accessed across the different configuration entity types. The resulting value is the raw field value, in this case a string. So, this is pretty simple.

Apart from the typical field data, we have the entity keys (if you remember from the entity type plugin definitions). These are common for both configuration and content entities and the relevant accessor methods are found on the `EntityInterface`. Here are the ones you will typically see and use yourself:

```
$id = $type->id();
$label = $type->label();
$uuid = $type->uuid();
$bundle = $type->bundle();
$language = $type->language();
```

The resulting information depends on the entity type of course. For example, configuration entities don't have bundles or some content entity types either. So, the `bundle()` method will return the name of the entity type if there are no bundles. By far the most important one is `id()` but you will often use `label()` as well as a shortcut to the primitive field value of the field used as the label for the entity type. There are other entity keys as well that individual entity types can declare. For example, the Node entity has a `status` entity key and a corresponding method `status()`. This is used for the publishing state. So, for any other entity keys, do check the respective entity type if you can use them.

Some extra methods you can use to inspect entities of any type:

- `isNew()` checks if the entity has been persisted already or not.
- `getEntityTypeId()` returns the machine name of the entity type of the entity.
- `getEntityType()` returns the `EntityTypeInterface` plugin of the given entity.
- `getTypedData()` returns the `EntityAdapter` DataType plugin instance that wraps the entity. It can be used for further inspection; it is most useful for content entities.

Moreover, we can also check whether they are a content or a configuration entity:

```
$entity instanceof ContentEntityInterface
$entity instanceof ConfigEntityInterface
```

Similarly, we can also check whether they are a specific type of entity:

```
$entity instanceof NodeInterface
```

This is similar to using `$entity->getEntityTypeId === 'node'` but is much more explicit and clear, plus the IDE can benefit from the information in many cases.

Now, let's turn to content entities and see how we can read their field data.

Similar to configuration entity types, many content entity types can have helper methods on their class to make accessing certain fields easier. For example, the Node entity type has the `getTitle()` method that gets the first primitive value of its title field. However, let's see how we can apply what we learned in the TypedData section and navigate through the field values like a pro. To exemplify, we will examine a simple article node.

Content entities also have the `get()` method, but unlike configuration entities, it doesn't return the raw field value. Instead, it returns an instance of `FieldItemList`:

```
/** @var NodeInterface $node */
$node = Node::load(1);
/** @var FieldItemListInterface $title */
$title = $node->get('title');
```

For quick prototyping, in the preceding example I used the static `load()` method on the content entity class to load an entity by ID. Under the hood, this will delegate to the relevant storage class. This is a quick alternative to using the entity manager, but you should only rely on it wherever you cannot inject dependencies.

Here are some of the things we can learn about the title `FieldItemList`:

```
$parent = $title->getParent();
```

This is its parent (the DataType plugin it belongs in - in this case the `EntityAdapter`).

```
$definition = $title->getFieldDefinition();
```

This is the `DataDefinitionInterface` of the list. In this case it's a `BaseFieldOverride` instance but can be a `BaseFieldDefinition` (for example for the `nid` field) or a `FieldConfig` for fully configurable fields:

```
$item_definition = $title->getItemDefinition();
```

This is the `DataDefinitionInterface` for the individual items in the list, typically a `FieldItemDataDefinition`:

```
$total = $title->count();
$empty = $title->isEmpty();
$exists = $title->offsetExists(1);
```

These are some handy methods for inspecting the list. We can see how many items there are in it, whether it's empty, and whether there are any values at a given offset. Do keep in mind that value keys start at 0, so if the cardinality of the field is 1, the value will be at the key 0.

To retrieve values from the list, we have a number of options. The most common thing you'll end up doing is the following:

```
$value = $title->value;
```

This is a magic property pointing to the first primitive value in the list. However, it's very important to note that although most fields use the property `value`, some fields have a different property name. For example, entity reference fields use `target_id`:

```
$id = $field->target_id;
```

This returns the ID of the referenced entity. As an added bonus, if you use the magic `entity` property, you get the fully loaded entity object:

```
$entity = $field->entity;
```

But enough of this magic way of doing things and let's see what other options we have:

```
$value = $title->getValue();
```

The `getValue()` method is present on all `TypedData` objects and returns the raw values that it stores. In our case, it will return an array with one item (since we only have one item in the list) that contains the individual item raw values. In this case, Which in this case is an array with one element keyed `value` and the title string as its value. We will see in a moment why this is keyed by `value`.

In some cases, we might want this to be returned and can find it useful. In other cases though, we might just want the one field value. For this, we can ask for a given item in the list:

```
$item = $title->get(0);
$item = $title->offsetGet(0);
```

Both of these do the same thing and return a `FieldType` plugin which, as we saw, extends `FieldItemBase` which is nothing more than a fancy `Map` DataType plugin. Once we have this, we again have a few choices:

```
$value = $item->getValue();
```

This again returns an array of the raw values, in this case with one key called `value` and the string title as the array element. So, just as we called `getValue()` on the list, but this time returning the raw values of only one item instead of an array of raw values of multiple items.

The reason why we have the actual title string keyed by `value` is because we are requesting the raw value from the `StringItem` field type plugin, which in this case happens to define the value columns as `value`. Others might differ (for example the entity reference field which stores a `target_id` named value).

Alternatively, again, we can navigate a bit further down:

```
$data = $item->get('value');
```

We know that this field uses the name `value` for its property so we can use the `get()` method from the `Map` DataType (which if you remember is subclassed by the `StringItem` field type) to retrieve its own property by name. This is exactly the same as we did with the license plate map and when we requested the number or state code. In the case of `StringItem` field types, this is going to be a `StringData` DataType plugin.

As we did before, we can ask this final plugin for its value:

```
$value = $data->getValue();
```

Now we have the final string for the title. Of course, all the way down from the top, we have the opportunity to inspect the definitions of each of these plugins and learn more information about them.

Typically, on the day-to-day, you will use two methods for retrieving values from fields, depending on the cardinality. If the field has only one value, you will end up using something like this:

```
$title = $node->get('title')->value;
$id = $node->get('field_referencing_some_entity')->target_id;
$entity = $node->get('field_referencing_some_entity')->entity;
```

If the field can have multiple values, you will end up using something like this:

```
$names = $node->get('field_names')->getValue();
$tags = $node->get('field_tags')->referencedEntities();
```

The `referencedEntities()` is a helper method provided by the `EntityReferenceFieldItemList` (which is a subclass of `FieldItemList`) that loads all the referenced entities and returns them in an array keyed by the position in the field (the delta).

Manipulating entities

Now that we know how we can read field data programmatically, let's see how we can change this data and persist it to the storage. So, let's look at the same Node title field and update its value programmatically.

The most common way you can change a field value on a content entity is this:

```
$node->set('title', 'new title');
```

This works well with fields that have only one value (cardinality = 1) and behind the scenes essentially this happens:

```
$node->get('title')->setValue('new title');
```

This one value gets transformed into a raw array of one value because we are dealing with a list of items and the first item receives the changed value. If the field has a higher cardinality and we pass only one value as such, we essentially remove both of them and replace them with only one. So, if we want to make sure we are not deleting items but instead adding to the list, we can do this:

```
$values = $node->get('field_multiple')->getValue();
$values[] = ['value' => 'extra value'];
$node->set('field_multiple', $values);
```

If we want to change a specific item in the list, we can do this:

```
$node->get('field_multiple')->get(1)->setValue('changed value');
```

This will change the value of the second item in the list. You just have to make sure it is set first before chaining:

```
$node->get('field_test')->offsetExists(1);
```

All these modifications we make to field values are, however, kept in memory (they are not persisted). To save them to a database we have to do something extremely complicated:

```
$node->save();
```

That's it. Under the hood, Drupal still uses some deprecated ways to do the saving using the old `EntityManager`, which is no longer recommended but is essentially responsible for saving the storage handler; of the entity type. So, we can achieve the same thing via the entity type manager:

```
\Drupal::entityTypeManager()->getStorage('node')->save($node);
```

But nobody is going to look down on you if you just use the `save()` helper method on the entity object. Since we are talking about saving, deleting entities can be done in the exact same way, except by using the `delete()` method on the entity object. We also have this method on the storage handler, however, it accepts an array of entities to delete, so you can use that to delete more entities at once.

Configuration entities have it a bit easier since their fields do not deal with TypedData. This is how we can easily change the value of a configuration entity field:

```
/** @var NodeType $type */
$type =
\Drupal::entityTypeManager()->getStorage('node_type')->load('article');
$type->set('name', 'News');
$type->save();
```

Nothing to complex going on here. We load the entity, set a property value and save it using the same API.

Creating entities

Programmatically creating new entities is also not rocket science and, again, we use the entity type storage handler to do so:

```
$values = [
  'type' => 'article',
  'title' => 'My title'
];
/** @var NodeInterface $node */
$node = \Drupal::entityTypeManager()->getStorage('node')->create($values);
$node->set('field_custom', 'some text');
$node->save();
```

The storage handler has the `create()` method, which takes one argument in the form of an associative array of field values. The keys represent the field name and the values the value. This is where you can set initially some simpler values, and for more complex fields you still have the API we covered earlier.

If the entity type has bundles, such as the Node example given before, the bundle needs to be specified in the `create()` method. The key it corresponds to is the entity key for the bundle. If you remember the Node entity type plugin, that is `type`.

That is pretty much it. Again, we need to save it in order to persist it in our storage.

Rendering content entities

Now, let's see what we can do with an entity to render it on the page. In doing so, we will stick to the existing view modes and try not to break it up into pieces for rendering in a custom template through our own theme hook. If you want to do that, you can. You should have all the knowledge for that already:

- Defining a theme hook with variables
- Querying and loading entities
- Reading the values of an entity
- Creating a render array that uses the theme hook

Instead, we will rely on the entity's default building methodology that allows us to render it according to the display mode configured in the UI, so, for example, as a teaser or as the full display mode. As always, we will continue with the Node as an example.

The first thing we need to do is get our hands on the *view builder* handler of the entity type. Remember it from the entity type plugin definition? Just like the storage handler, we can request it from the `EntityTypeManager`:

```
/** @var NodeViewBuilder $builder */
$builder = \Drupal::entityTypeManager()->getViewBuilder('node');
```

Now that we have that, the simplest way of turning our entity into a render array is using the `view()` method:

```
$build = $builder->view($node);
```

By default, this will use the full view mode, but we can pass a second parameter and specify another, such as teaser or whatever we have configured. A third optional parameter is the langcode of the translation (if we have it) we want to render in. We will talk more about translations in the multilingual chapter.

The `$build` variable is now a render array that uses the `node` theme hook defined by the Node module. You will notice also a `#pre_render` theme property which specifies a callable to be run before the rendering of this array. That is actually a reference back to the `NodeViewBuilder` (the node entity type view builder) which is responsible for preparing all the field values and all sorts of other processing we are not going to cover now. But the `node.twig.html` template file preprocessed by the `*_preprocess_node()` preprocessors also plays a big role in providing some extra variables to be used or rendered in the template.

If we want, we can also build render arrays for multiple entities at once:

```
$build = $builder->viewMultiple($node);
```

This will still return a render array which contains multiple children for each entity being rendered. The `#pre_render` property I mentioned earlier, however, will stay at the top level and this time be responsible for building multiple entities.

Essentially it is that simple to get from loading an entity to turning it into a render array. You have many different places where you can take control over the output. As I said, you can write your own theme hook and break up the entity into variables. You can also implement the preprocessor for its default theme functions and change some variables in there. You can even change the theme hook used and append a suggestion to it and then take it from there, as we saw in the chapter on theming:

```
$build = $builder->view($node);
$build['#theme'] = $build['#theme'] . '__my_suggestion';
```

Another important way we can control the output is by implementing a hook that gets fired when the entity is being built for rendering--`hook_entity_view()` or `hook_ENTITY_TYPE_view()`. So, let's see an example by which we want to append a disclaimer message at the bottom of all our Node entities when they are displayed in their `full` view mode. We can do something like this:

```
function module_name_entity_view(array &$build, EntityInterface $entity,
EntityViewDisplayInterface $display, $view_mode) {
  if ($entity->getEntityTypeId() == 'node' && $view_mode == 'full') {
    $build['disclaimer'] = [
      '#markup' => t('The content provided is for general information
purposes only.'),
      '#weight' => 100
    ];
  }
}
```

The three important arguments we work with are the `$build` array passed by reference and which contains the render array for the entire entity, the `$entity` object itself, and the `$view_mode` the latter is being rendered in. So, all we have to do is add our own render bits inside the `$build` array. As a bonus, we try to ensure that the message gets printed at the bottom by using the `#weight` property.

Pseudo-fields

Drawing from our example on implementing `hook_entity_view()`, there's a neat little technique we can use to empower our site builders further with respect to that disclaimer message. This is by turning it into a *pseudo field*. By doing this, site builders will be able to choose the bundles it should show on, as well as the position relative to the other fields, all through the UI in the Manage Display section:

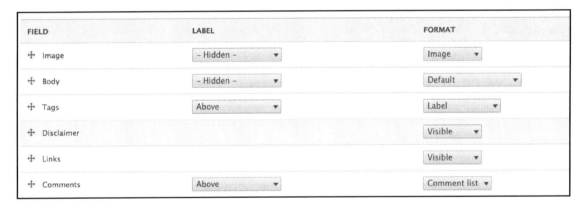

So, there are two things we need to do for this. First, we need to implement `hook_entity_extra_field_info()` and define our *pseudo field*:

```
/**
 * Implements hook_entity_extra_field_info().
 */
function module_name_entity_extra_field_info() {
  $extra = [];

  foreach (NodeType::loadMultiple() as $bundle) {
    $extra['node'][$bundle->Id()]['display']['disclaimer'] = [
      'label' => t('Disclaimer'),
      'description' => t('A general disclaimer'),
      'weight' => 100,
      'visible' => TRUE,
    ];
```

```
    }

    return $extra;
  }
```

As you can see, we loop through all the available node types and for the `node` entity display list, we add our `disclaimer` definition with some defaults to use. The weight and visibility will, of course, be overridable by the user, per node bundle.

Next, we need to go back to our `hook_entity_view()` implementation and make some changes. Because we know we want this applied to Node entities only, we can implement the more specific hook instead:

```
/**
 * Implements hook_ENTITY_TYPE_view().
 */
function module_name_node_view(array &$build, EntityInterface $entity,
EntityViewDisplayInterface $display, $view_mode) {
  if ($display->getComponent('disclaimer')) {
    $build['disclaimer'] = [
      '#markup' => t('The content provided is for general information
purposes only.'),
    ];
  }
}
```

In this case we don't need to check for view modes or entity types, but rather use the entity view display configuration object to check for the existence of this extra `disclaimer` field (technically called a *component*). If found, we simply add our markup to the `$build` array. Drupal will take care things like weight and visibility to match whatever the user has set through the UI, and that's it. Clearing the cache, we should still see our disclaimer message, but we can now control it a bit from the UI.

Content entity validation

The last thing we are going to talk about in this chapter is entity validation and how we can make sure that field and entity data as a whole contains valid data. When I say valid, I don't mean whether it complies with the strict TypedData definition but whether, within that, it complies with certain restrictions (constraints) we impose on it.

Drupal 8 uses the Symfony Validator component for applying constraints and then validating entities, fields and any other data against those constraints. I do recommend that you check out the Symfony documentation page on this component to better understand its principles. For now, let's quickly see how it is applied in Drupal 8.

There are three main parts to a validation--a constraint plugin, a validator class and potential violations. The first is mainly responsible for defining what kind of data it can be applied to, the error message it should show, and which validator class is responsible for validating it. If it omits the latter, the validator class name defaults to the name of the constraint class with the word `Validator` appended to it. The validator, on the other hand, is called by the validation service to validate the constraint and build a list of violations. Finally, the violations are data objects which provide helpful information about what went wrong in the validation things like the error message from the constraint, the offending value, the path to the property that failed. To better understand things, we have to go back to the TypedData and see some simple examples because that is the level at which the validation happens.

So, let's look at the same example I introduced TypedData with:

```
$definition = DataDefinition::create('string');
$definition->addConstraint('Length', ['max' => 20]);
```

The data definitions have methods for applying and reading constraints. If you remember, one of the reasons why we need this API is to be able to enrich data with meta information. Constraints are such information. In the preceding example, we are applying a constraint called `Length` (the plugin ID) with some arbitrary parameters expected by that constraint (in this case a maximum length but also a minimum would work). Having applied this constraint,we are essentially saying that this piece of string data is only valid if it's shorter than 20 characters. We can use this, like so:

```
/** @var TypedDataInterface $data */
$data = \Drupal::typedDataManager()->create($definition, 'my value that is
too long');
$violations = $data->validate();
```

DataType plugins have a `validate()` method on them which uses the validation service to validate their underlying data definition against any of the constraints applied to it. The result is an instance of `ConstraintViolationList` iterator that contains a `ConstraintViolationInterface` instance for each validation failure. In the preceding example, we should have a violation from which we can get some information like so:

```
/** @var ConstraintViolationInterface $violation */
foreach ($violations as $violation) {
  $message = $violation->getMessage();
  $value = $violation->getInvalidValue();
  $path = $violation->getPropertyPath();
}
```

The $message is the error message that comes from the failing constraint, the $value is the actual incorrect value, and the $path is a string representation of the hierarchical path down to the value that has failed. If you remember our license plate example or the content entity fields, TypedData can be nested, which means you can have all sorts of values at different levels. In our previous example, the $path is, however, going to be "" (an empty string) because the data definition has only one level.

Let's revisit our license plate example and see how such a constraint would work there. Imagine we wanted to add a similar constraint to the state code definition:

```
$state_code_definition = DataDefinition::create('string');
$state_code_definition->addConstraint('Length', array('max' => 2));
// The rest of the set up code we saw earlier.

/** @var Map $plate */
$plate = \Drupal::typedDataManager()->create($plate_definition, ['state' =>
'NYC', 'number' => '405-307']);
$violations = $plate->validate();
```

If you look closely, I instantiated the plate with a state code longer than two characters. Now, if we ask our individual violations for the property path, we get state, because that is what we called the state definition property within the bigger map definition.

Finally, let's see an example of validating constraints on entities. First of all, we can run the validate() method on an entire entity which will then use its TypedData wrapper (EntityAdapter) to run a validation on all the fields on the entity + any of the entity level constraints. The latter can be added via the EntityType plugin definition. For example, the Comment entity type has this bit:

```
*      constraints = {
*        "CommentName" = {}
*      }
```

This means that the constraint plugin ID is CommentName and it takes no parameters (since the braces are empty). We can even add constraints to entity types that do not belong to us by implementing hook_entity_type_alter(), for example:

```
function my_module_entity_type_alter(array &$entity_types) {
  /** @var ContentEntityType $node */
  $node = $entity_types['node'];
  $node->addConstraint('ConstraintPluginID', ['option']);
}
```

Going one level below and knowing that content entity fields are built on top of the TypedData API, it follows that all those levels can have constraints. We can add the constraints regularly to the field definitions or in the case of either fields that are not "ours" or configurable fields, we can use hooks to add constraints. Using `hook_entity_base_field_info_alter()` , we can add constraints to base fields while with `hook_entity_bundle_field_info_alter()`, we can add constraints to configurable fields (and overridden base fields). Let's see an example of how we can add constraints to the Node ID field:

```
function my_module_entity_base_field_info_alter(&$fields,
EntityTypeInterface $entity_type) {
  if ($entity_type->id() === 'node') {
    /** @var BaseFieldDefinition $nid */
    $nid = $fields['nid'];
    $nid->addPropertyConstraints('value', ['Range' => ['mn' => 5, 'max' =>
10]]);
  }
}
```

As you can see, we are still just working with data definitions. One thing to note, however, is that when it comes to base fields and configurable fields (which are lists of items), we also have the `addPropertyConstraints()` method available. This simply makes sure that whatever constraint you are adding is targeted towards the actual items in the list (specifying which property), rather than the entire list as it would have happened we had used the main `addConstraint()` API. Another difference with this method is that constraints get wrapped into a `ComplexDataConstraint` plugin. However, you don't have to worry too much about that, just be aware when you see it.

We can even inspect the constraints found on a data definition object. For example, this is how we can read the constraints found on the Node ID field:

```
$nid = $node->get('nid');
$constraints = $nid->getConstraints();
$item_constraints = $nid->getItemDefinition()->getConstraints();
```

Where the `getConstraints()` method returns an array of constraint plugin instances. Now let's see, though, how we can validate entities:

```
$nid = $node->get('nid');
$node_violations = $node->validate();
$nid_list_violations = $nid->validate();
$nid_item_violations = $nid->get(0)->validate();
```

The entity level `validate()` method returns an instance of `EntityConstraintViolationList` which is a more specific version of the `ConstraintViolationList` we talked about earlier. The latter is, however, returned by the `validate()` method of the other cases given in the following. But for all, inside we have a collection of `ConstraintViolationInterface` instances from which we can learn some things.

The entity level validation goes through all the fields and validates them; this means that is where we will get most violations (if that's the case). Next, the list will contain violations of any of the items in the list while the item will contain only the violation on that individual item in the list. The property path is something interesting to observe the following is the result of calling `getPropertyPath()` on a violation found in all three of the resulting violation lists preceding:

```
nid.0.value
0.value
value
```

As you can see, this reflects the TypedData hierarchy. When we validate the entire entity, it gives us a property path all the way down to the value--field name -> delta (position in the list) -> property name. Once we validate the field, we already know what field we are validating so that is omitted. And the same goes for the individual item (we know also the delta of the item).

A word of warning about base fields that can be overridden per bundle such as the Node title field. As I mentioned earlier, the base definition for these fields use an instance of `BaseFieldOverride`, which allows certain changes to be made to the definition via the UI. In this respect, they are very close to configurable fields. The "problem" with this is that, if we tried to apply a constraint like we just did with the `nid` to, say, the Node `title` field, we wouldn't have gotten any violations when validating. This is because the validator performs the validation on the `BaseFieldOverride` definition rather than the `BaseFieldDefinition`.

This is no problem, though, as we can use `hook_entity_bundle_field_info_alter()` and do the same thing as done before which will then apply the constraint to the overridden definition. In doing so, we can also account for the bundle we want this applied to. This is the same way to apply constraints to a configurable field you create in the UI.

Validation summary

As we've seen, Drupal 8 applies the Symfony validation component to its very own TypedData and plugin API both for discoverability and data validation handling. In doing so, we get a low level API for applying constraints to any kind of data, ranging from simple primitive data definitions all the way to complex entities and fields. We have not covered this here, but we can also easily create our own constraints and validators if the ones provided are not enough.

Summary

You didn't think you we are ever going to see this heading did you? This chapter has been very long and highly theoretical. We haven't built anything fun and the only code we saw was to exemplify most of the things we talked about. It was a difficult chapter as it covered many complex aspects of data storage and handling. But trust me, these things are important to know and this chapter can serve both as a starting point to dig deeper into the code and a reference to get back to when unsure of certain aspects.

We saw what the main options for storing data in Drupal 8 are. Ranging from the State API all the way to entities, you have a host of alternatives. After covering the more simple ways, such as the State API, the private and shared tempstores and the UserData API, we dove a bit more into the configuration system which is a very important one to understand. There, we saw what kinds of configuration types we have, how to work with simple configuration, how it's managed and stored, and so on. Finally, in what is arguably the most complex part of the chapter, we looked at entities, both content and configuration. Just as you were recovering from reading all about how entity types are plugins with so many options, I hit you with the TypedData API. But right after that we put it to good use and saw how we can interact with entities--query, load, manipulate and validate data based on TypedData.

In the next chapter, we will apply in a very practical way a lot of the knowledge we learned in this one, especially related to content and configuration entities, but also plugin types and so on. So, that should be much more enjoyable, as we are going to create a new module that actually does something useful.

7
Your Own Custom Entity and Plugin Types

I am sure that you are looking forward to applying some of the knowledge gained from the previous chapters and do something practical and fun. As promised, in this chapter, we will do just that. Also, apart from implementing our own entity types, we will cover some new things as well. So, here's the game plan.

The premise is that we want to have products on our site that hold some basic product information, such as an ID, a name, and a product number. However, these products need to somehow get into our site. One way will be manual entry. Another, more important way will be through an import from multiple external sources (such as a JSON endpoint). Now, things will be kept simple. For all intents and purposes, these products aren't going to do much, so don't expect an e-commerce solution being laid out for you. Instead, we will practice modeling data and functionality in Drupal 8.

First, we will create a simple content entity type to represent our products. In doing so, we will make sure that we can use the UI to create, edit, and delete these products with ease by taking advantage of many Entity API benefits available out of the box.

Second, we will model our importing functionality. One side of the coin will be creating a simple configuration entity type to represent the configuration needed for our various importers. Again, we will make use of the Entity API for quick scaffolding and entity management. The other side will be creating a custom plugin type that will actually perform the import based on the configuration found in the entities. As such, these will be linked from the direction of the config entities, which will choose to use one plugin or another.

So, these are the highlights. In building all this, we will see much of what is needed to define a content and configuration entity type with fields to hold data and configuration, as well as a plugin type to encapsulate logic. When defining these things, we will go through the manual, more tedious, route to make sure that we understand what each component does and we are comfortable with what we are doing. Once you know all that, you'll be able to greatly speed up these processes using the Drupal Console to automatically generate much of the boilerplate code.

The code we write in this chapter will go inside a new module called products. Since we have learned how to create a module from scratch, I will not cover the initial steps needed for getting started with it.

Custom content entity type

As we saw in the preceding chapter, when looking at the Node and NodeType entity types, entity type definitions belong inside the `Entity` folder of our module's namespace. In there, we will create a class called `Product`, which will have an annotation at the top to tell Drupal this is a content entity type. This is the most important part in defining a new entity type:

```
namespace Drupal\products\Entity;

use Drupal\Core\Entity\ContentEntityBase;
use Drupal\Core\Entity\EntityChangedTrait;
use Drupal\Core\Entity\EntityTypeInterface;
use Drupal\Core\Field\BaseFieldDefinition;

/**
 * Defines the Product entity.
 *
 * @ContentEntityType(
 *   id = "product",
 *   label = @Translation("Product"),
 *   handlers = {
 *     "view_builder" = "Drupal\Core\Entity\EntityViewBuilder",
 *     "list_builder" = "Drupal\products\ProductListBuilder",
 *
 *     "form" = {
 *       "default" = "Drupal\products\Form\ProductForm",
 *       "add" = "Drupal\products\Form\ProductForm",
 *       "edit" = "Drupal\products\Form\ProductForm",
 *       "delete" = "Drupal\Core\Entity\ContentEntityDeleteForm",
 *     },
 *     "route_provider" = {
```

```
 *        "html" = "Drupal\Core\Entity\Routing\AdminHtmlRouteProvider"
 *      }
 *    },
 *    base_table = "product",
 *    admin_permission = "administer site configuration",
 *    entity_keys = {
 *      "id" = "id",
 *      "label" = "name",
 *      "uuid" = "uuid",
 *    },
 *    links = {
 *      "canonical" = "/admin/structure/product/{product}",
 *      "add-form" = "/admin/structure/product/add",
 *      "edit-form" = "/admin/structure/product/{product}/edit",
 *      "delete-form" = "/admin/structure/product/{product}/delete",
 *      "collection" = "/admin/structure/product",
 *    }
 *  )
 */
class Product extends ContentEntityBase implements ProductInterface {}
```

In the preceding code block, I omitted the actual contents of the class to first focus on the annotation and some other aspects. We will see the rest of it shortly. However, the entire working code can be found in the accompanying repository.

If you remember from the preceding chapter, we have the ContentEntityType annotation with the entity type plugin definition. Our example is relatively barebones compared to Node, for example, because I wanted to keep things simple. It has no bundles and is not revisionable, nor translatable. Also, for some of its handlers, we fall back to Entity API defaults.

The entity type ID and label are immediately visible, so no need to explain that; however, we can instead skip to the handlers section.

For the view builder handler, we choose to default to the basic EntityViewBuilder because there is nothing our products especially need for being rendered. Many times, this will be enough, but you can also extend this class and create your own.

For the list builder, although still keeping things simple, we needed our own implementation in order to take care of things such as the list headers. We will see this class soon. The form handler to create and edit products is our own implementation found inside the Form namespace of our module, and we will see it soon to get a better understanding. We rely on Drupal 8 to help us out with the delete form, though.

Finally, for the route provider, we used the default `AdminHtmlRouteProvider`, which takes care of all the routes necessary for an entity type to be managed in the admin UI. This means that we no longer need to do anything for routing the links referenced in the `links` section of the annotation. Speaking of links, it makes sense to place them under the `admin/structure` section of our administration for our example, but you can choose another place if you want.

The database table our products will be stored in is `products`, and the permission needed for users to manage them is `administer site configuration`. I have purposefully omitted creating permissions specific to this entity type because we will cover this topic in a chapter dedicated to access.

Finally, we also have some basic entity keys to map to the respective fields.

Our `Product` class extends the `ContentEntityBase` class to inherit all the necessary stuff from the API and implements our very own `ProductInterface`, which will contain all the methods used to access relevant field values. Let's create that one real quick in the same `Entity` folder:

```
namespace Drupal\products\Entity;

use Drupal\Core\Entity\ContentEntityInterface;
use Drupal\Core\Entity\EntityChangedInterface;

/**
 * Represents a Product entity.
 */
interface ProductInterface extends ContentEntityInterface,
EntityChangedInterface {

  /**
   * Gets the Product name.
   *
   * @return string
   */
  public function getName();

  /**
   * Sets the Product name.
   *
   * @param string $name
   *
   * @return \Drupal\products\Entity\ProductInterface
   *    The called Product entity.
   */
  public function setName($name);
```

```
/**
 * Gets the Product number.
 *
 * @return int
 */
public function getProductNumber();

/**
 * Sets the Product number.
 *
 * @param int $number
 *
 * @return \Drupal\products\Entity\ProductInterface
 *   The called Product entity.
 */
public function setProductNumber($number);

/**
 * Gets the Product remote ID.
 *
 * @return string
 */
public function getRemoteId();

/**
 * Sets the Product remote ID.
 *
 * @param string $id
 *
 * @return \Drupal\products\Entity\ProductInterface
 *   The called Product entity.
 */
public function setRemoteId($id);

/**
 * Gets the Product source.
 *
 * @return string
 */
public function getSource();

/**
 * Sets the Product source.
 *
 * @param string $source
 *
 * @return \Drupal\products\Entity\ProductInterface
 *   The called Product entity.
```

```
  */
  public function setSource($source);

  /**
   * Gets the Product creation timestamp.
   *
   * @return int
   */
  public function getCreatedTime();

  /**
   * Sets the Product creation timestamp.
   *
   * @param int $timestamp
   *
   * @return \Drupal\products\Entity\ProductInterface
   *   The called Product entity.
   */
  public function setCreatedTime($timestamp);
}
```

As you can see, we are extending the obligatory `ContentEntityInterface` but also the `EntityChangedInterface`, which provides some handy methods to manage the last changed date of the entities. Those method implementations will be added to our `Product` class via the `EntityChangedTrait`:

```
use EntityChangedTrait;
```

The methods on the `ProductInterface` are relatively self-explanatory. We will have a product name, number, remote ID, and source field, so it's nice to have getters and setters for those. If you remember, the Entity API provides the `get()` and `set()` methods using which we can consistently access and store field values across all entity types. However, I find that using an interface with well-defined methods makes code much clearer, not to mention that IDE autocompletion is a great time-saver. We also have a getter and setter for the created date field, which is a typical field content entities have.

Now, we can take a look at the `baseFieldDefinitions()` method of our `Product` entity type and see how we actually defined these fields:

```
public static function baseFieldDefinitions(EntityTypeInterface
$entity_type) {
    $fields = parent::baseFieldDefinitions($entity_type);

    $fields['name'] = BaseFieldDefinition::create('string')
      ->setLabel(t('Name'))
      ->setDescription(t('The name of the Product.'))
```

```
  ->setSettings([
    'max_length' => 255,
    'text_processing' => 0,
  ])
  ->setDefaultValue('')
  ->setDisplayOptions('view', [
    'label' => 'hidden',
    'type' => 'string',
    'weight' => -4,
  ])
  ->setDisplayOptions('form', [
    'type' => 'string_textfield',
    'weight' => -4,
  ])
  ->setDisplayConfigurable('form', TRUE)
  ->setDisplayConfigurable('view', TRUE);

$fields['number'] = BaseFieldDefinition::create('integer')
  ->setLabel(t('Number'))
  ->setDescription(t('The Product number.'))
  ->setSettings([
    'min' => 1,
    'max' => 10000
  ])
  ->setDefaultValue(NULL)
  ->setDisplayOptions('view', [
    'label' => 'above',
    'type' => 'number_unformatted',
    'weight' => -4,
  ])
  ->setDisplayOptions('form', [
    'type' => 'number',
    'weight' => -4,
  ])
  ->setDisplayConfigurable('form', TRUE)
  ->setDisplayConfigurable('view', TRUE);

$fields['remote_id'] = BaseFieldDefinition::create('string')
  ->setLabel(t('Remote ID'))
  ->setDescription(t('The remote ID of the Product.'))
  ->setSettings([
    'max_length' => 255,
    'text_processing' => 0,
  ])
  ->setDefaultValue('');

$fields['source'] = BaseFieldDefinition::create('string')
  ->setLabel(t('Source'))
```

```
      ->setDescription(t('The source of the Product.'))
      ->setSettings([
        'max_length' => 255,
        'text_processing' => 0,
      ])
      ->setDefaultValue('');

  $fields['created'] = BaseFieldDefinition::create('created')
      ->setLabel(t('Created'))
      ->setDescription(t('The time that the entity was created.'));

  $fields['changed'] = BaseFieldDefinition::create('changed')
      ->setLabel(t('Changed'))
      ->setDescription(t('The time that the entity was last edited.'));

  return $fields;
}
```

First and foremost, we will need to inherit the base fields of the parent class. This includes things such as the ID and UUID fields.

Second, we define our own fields, starting with the product name field, which is of the `string` type. This `string` type is nothing more than a `FieldType` plugin I mentioned in the preceding chapter. If you remember, this plugin extends a `TypedData` class itself. Apart from the obvious label and description, it has some settings, most notably a maximum length for the value, which is 255 characters. The `view` and `form` display options reference `FieldFormatter` and `FieldWidget` plugins, respectively, which together with the `FieldType` make up a field. Lastly, with the `setDisplayConfigurable()`, we state that some of the options on this field should be configurable through the UI. For example, we can change the label in the UI.

Then, we have the `number` field that is of the `integer` type and for this example is restricted to a number between 1 and 10,000. This restriction setting turns into a constraint under the hood. The rest of the options are similar to the name field.

Next, we have the `remote_id` string field, but it doesn't have any widget or display settings because we don't necessarily want to display or edit this value. It is mostly for internal use to keep track of the product ID of the remote source it came from. Similarly, the `source` string field is also not displayed or configurable because we want to use it to store the source of the product, where it has been imported from and also to keep track programmatically.

Finally, the `created` and `changed` fields are special fields that store the timestamps for when the entity is created and modified. Not much more than that is needed to do because these fields automatically set the current timestamps as necessary as the field values.

By now, we can also see the rest of the class contents, which is mostly made up of the methods required by the `ProductInterface`:

```
use EntityChangedTrait;

  /**
   * {@inheritdoc}
   */
  public function getName() {
    return $this->get('name')->value;
  }

  /**
   * {@inheritdoc}
   */
  public function setName($name) {
    $this->set('name', $name);
    return $this;
  }

  /**
   * {@inheritdoc}
   */
  public function getProductNumber() {
    return $this->get('number')->value;
  }

  /**
   * {@inheritdoc}
   */
  public function setProductNumber($number) {
    $this->set('number', $number);
    return $this;
  }

  /**
   * {@inheritdoc}
   */
  public function getRemoteId() {
    return $this->get('remote_id')->value;
  }

  /**
```

```
 *  {@inheritdoc}
 */
public function setRemoteId($id) {
  $this->set('remote_id', $id);
  return $this;
}

/**
 *  {@inheritdoc}
 */
public function getSource() {
  return $this->get('source')->value;
}

/**
 *  {@inheritdoc}
 */
public function setSource($source) {
  $this->set('source', $source);
  return $this;
}

/**
 *  {@inheritdoc}
 */
public function getCreatedTime() {
  return $this->get('created')->value;
}

/**
 *  {@inheritdoc}
 */
public function setCreatedTime($timestamp) {
  $this->set('created', $timestamp);
  return $this;
}
```

As promised, we are making use of the `EntityChangedTrait` to handle the `changed` field and implement simple getters and setters for the values found in the fields we defined as base fields. If you remember the `TypedData` section, the way we access a value (since the cardinality is always 1 for these fields) is by running the following command:

```
$this->get('field_name')->value
```

Let's now move through the Entity type plugin annotation and create the handlers we've been referencing there. Also, we can start with the list builder, which we can place at the root of our namespace:

```
namespace Drupal\products;

use Drupal\Core\Entity\EntityInterface;
use Drupal\Core\Entity\EntityListBuilder;
use Drupal\Core\Link;
use Drupal\Core\;Url;

/**
 * EntityListBuilderInterface implementation responsible for the Product
entities.
 */
class ProductListBuilder extends EntityListBuilder {

  /**
   * {@inheritdoc}
   */
  public function buildHeader() {
    $header['id'] = $this->t('Product ID');
    $header['name'] = $this->t('Name');
    return $header + parent::buildHeader();
  }

  /**
   * {@inheritdoc}
   */
  public function buildRow(EntityInterface $entity) {
    /* @var $entity \Drupal\products\Entity\Product */
    $row['id'] = $entity->id();
    $row['name'] = Link::fromTextAndUrl(
      $entity->label(),
      new Url(
        'entity.product.canonical', [
          'product' => $entity->id(),
        ]
      )
    );
    return $row + parent::buildRow($entity);
  }

}
```

The purpose of this handler is to build the administration page that lists the available entities. On this page, we will then have some info about the entities and operation links to edit and delete and whatever else we might need. For our products, we will simply extend from the default `EntityListBuilder` class, but override the `buildHeader()` and `builderRow()` methods to add some information specific to our products. The names of these methods are self-explanatory, but one thing to keep in mind is that keys from the `$header` array we return need to match the keys from the `$row` array we return. Also, of course, the arrays need to have the same number of records so that the table header matches the individual rows. If you look inside `EntityListBuilder`, you note some other handy methods you might want to override, such as the one that builds the query and the one that loads the entities. For us, this is enough.

Our Products list builder will have, for now, only two columns--the ID and the name. For the latter, each row will be actually a link to the Product canonical URL (the main URL for this entity in Drupal). The construct for this route is in the `entity.[entity_type].canonical` format. Other useful entity links can be built by replacing the word `canonical` with the keys from the `links` definition of the Entity type plugin annotation. Finally, you remember, from `Chapter 2`, *Creating Your First Module*, how to build links with the `Link` class, right?

That is pretty much it for the list builder, and we can move on to the form handler. Since creating and editing an entity share so much in terms of what we need in the form, we use the same `ProductForm` for both those operations. Let's create that form class now:

```
namespace Drupal\products\Form;

use Drupal\Core\Entity\ContentEntityForm;
use Drupal\Core\Form\FormStateInterface;

/**
 * Form for creating/editing Product entities.
 */
class ProductForm extends ContentEntityForm {

  /**
   * {@inheritdoc}
   */
  public function buildForm(array $form, FormStateInterface $form_state) {
    /* @var $entity \Drupal\products\Entity\Product */
    $form = parent::buildForm($form, $form_state);
    return $form;
  }

  /**
   * {@inheritdoc}
```

```
    */
  public function save(array $form, FormStateInterface $form_state) {
    $entity = &$this->entity;

    $status = parent::save($form, $form_state);

    switch ($status) {
      case SAVED_NEW:
        drupal_set_message($this->t('Created the %label Product.', [
          '%label' => $entity->label(),
        ]));
        break;

      default:
        drupal_set_message($this->t('Saved the %label Product.', [
          '%label' => $entity->label(),
        ]));
    }
    $form_state->setRedirect('entity.product.canonical', ['product' =>
$entity->id()]);
  }

}
```

We extend `ContentEntityForm`, which is a specialized form class for content entities. It itself extends `EntityForm`, which then subclasses the `FormBase` we've already encountered in `Chapter 2`, *Creating Your First Module*. However, the former two give us a lot of functionalities needed to manage our entities without writing much code ourselves.

First, inside the `buildForm()` method, we will do nothing--not a thing. We might if we wanted to, but the parent classes are smart enough to read our Product entity and prepare all the necessary form elements with the right widgets (`FieldWidget` plugins) to build our form. Second, we skip the submit and validate handlers because there is nothing we need to do in them for our products. The only thing we actually want to do is override the `save()` method in order to write a message to the user informing them that the product has either been created or updated. This we can deduce because the `EntityInterface::save()` method returns a specific constant to denote the type of saving that happened. Lastly, we also want to redirect to the canonical URL of the product entity. This we do with a very handy method on the `FormStateInterface` by which we can specify a route (and any necessary parameters), and it will make sure that when the form is submitted, the user will be redirected to that route. Neat, isn't it?

As I mentioned, for the delete operation, we just use the `ContentEntityDeleteForm`, which does all we need--it presents a confirmation form where we submit and trigger the delete. This is a typical flow for deleting resources in Drupal. As we will see a bit later, for configuration entities, there will be some methods we will need to write ourselves for this same process to happen.

All our handlers are done now, and our product entity type is operational. However, in order to be able to work with it, let's create some links in the admin menu for being able to easily manage them. First, create the `products.links.menu.yml` file:

```yaml
# Product entity menu items
entity.product.collection:
  title: 'Product list'
  route_name: entity.product.collection
  description: 'List Product entities'
  parent: system.admin_structure
  weight: 100
```

This defines a menu link under the Structure link for the product list (the page built with our list builder handler).

Next, let's create some local tasks (tabs) so that we get handy links on the product page to edit and delete the product entity. So, inside the `products.links.task.yml` file:

```yaml
# Product entity task items
entity.product.canonical:
  route_name: entity.product.canonical
  base_route: entity.product.canonical
  title: 'View'

entity.product.edit_form:
  route_name: entity.product.edit_form
  base_route: entity.product.canonical
  title: 'Edit'

entity.product.delete_form:
  route_name:  entity.product.delete_form
  base_route:  entity.product.canonical
  title: Delete
  weight: 10
```

You remember this from Chapter 5, *Menus and Menu Links*, don't you? The base route is always the canonical route for the entity, which essentially groups the tabs together. Then, the routes we use for the other two tasks are the edit_form and delete_form links of the entity type. You can refer to the links section of the Entity type plugin annotation to understand where these come from. The reason we don't need to specify any parameters here (since those routes do require a product ID) is because the base route has that parameter already in the URL. So, the tasks will use that one.

Finally, we also want an action link to create a new product entity, which will be on the product list page. So, inside the products.links.action.yml file:

```
entity.product.add_form:
  route_name: entity.product.add_form
  title: 'Add Product'
  appears_on:
    - entity.product.collection
```

Again, none of this should be new, as we covered it in detail in Chapter 5, *Menus and Menu Links*.

We are finally done. If the products module was enabled on your site before writing all the entity code, you will need to run the drush entity-updates command in order for all the necessary tables to be created in the database. Otherwise, installing the module will do that automatically. However, keep the first point in mind for when you add new content entity types and fields or even change existing fields on an entity type. The underlying storage might need to be changed to accommodate your modifications. Moreover, another thing to keep in mind is that changing fields that already have data in them will not be okay with Drupal and will prevent you from making those changes. So, you might need to delete existing entities.

Now that we've done that, we can go to admin/structure/product and take a look at our (empty) product entity list:

We can now create new products, edit them, and finally delete them. Remember, due to our field configuration, the manual product creation/edit does not permit the `remote_id` and `source` fields to be managed. For our purpose, we want those to be only programmatically available since any manual products will be considered as not needing that data. For example, if we want to make the source field show up as a form widget, all we have to do is change its base field definition to this:

```
$fields['source'] = BaseFieldDefinition::create('string')
  ->setLabel(t('Source'))
  ->setDescription(t('The source of the Product.'))
  ->setSettings([
    'max_length' => 255,
    'text_processing' => 0,
  ])
  ->setDefaultValue('')
  ->setDisplayOptions('form', [
    'type' => 'string_textfield',
    'weight' => -4,
  ]);
```

Also, we need to clear the cache. This will make the form element for the source field show up, but the value will still not be displayed on the canonical page of the entity because we have not set any `view` display options. In other words, we have not chosen a formatter.

However, in any case, our product entity is ready to store data, and all the TypedData APIs we practiced in the preceding chapter with the Node entity type will work just as well with this one. So, we can now turn to writing our importer logic to get some remote products into our website.

Custom plugin type

Since pretty much the second page of this book, you've been reading about how important plugins are and how widely they are used in Drupal 8. I have backed that claim with references to "this or that" being a plugin in basically every chapter. However, I have not really explained how you can create your own custom plugin type. However, since our importer logic is a perfect candidate for plugins, I will do so here, and to exemplify the theory, we will implement an `Importer` plugin type.

The very first thing a plugin type needs is a manager service. This is responsible for bringing together two critical aspects of plugins (but not only)--discovery and factory (instantiation). For these two tasks, it delegates to specialized objects. The most common way of discovery is through annotations (`AnnotatedClassDiscovery`), and the most common factory is the container-aware one--`ContainerFactory`. So, essentially, the manager is the central player that finds and processes all the plugin definitions and instantiates plugins. Also, it does so with the help of those other guys.

Many plugin types in Drupal 8, since they follow the defaults I mentioned before, use the `DefaultPluginManager`, or should I say, they extend this class. It provides them with the annotated discovery and container-aware factory. So, that is what we will do as well and see how simple it is to create a plugin type manager.

Typically, it lives in the `Plugin` namespace of the module, so ours can look like this:

```
namespace Drupal\products\Plugin;

use Drupal\Core\Plugin\DefaultPluginManager;
use Drupal\Core\Cache\CacheBackendInterface;
use Drupal\Core\Extension\ModuleHandlerInterface;

/**
 * Provides the Importer plugin manager.
 */
class ImporterManager extends DefaultPluginManager {

  /**
   * ImporterManager constructor.
   *
   * @param \Traversable $namespaces
   *   An object that implements \Traversable which contains the root paths
   *   keyed by the corresponding namespace to look for plugin
implementations.
   * @param \Drupal\Core\Cache\CacheBackendInterface $cache_backend
   *   Cache backend instance to use.
   * @param \Drupal\Core\Extension\ModuleHandlerInterface $module_handler
   *   The module handler to invoke the alter hook with.
   */
  public function __construct(\Traversable $namespaces,
CacheBackendInterface $cache_backend, ModuleHandlerInterface
$module_handler) {
    parent::__construct('Plugin/Importer', $namespaces, $module_handler,
'Drupal\products\Plugin\ImporterInterface',
'Drupal\products\Annotation\Importer');

    $this->alterInfo('products_importer_info');
```

```
        $this->setCacheBackend($cache_backend, 'products_importer_plugins');
    }
}
```

Aside from extending the `DefaultPluginManager`, we will need to override the constructor and re-call the parent constructor with some parameters specific to our plugins. This is the most important part, and in order, these are the following (omitting the ones that are simply passed through):

- The relative namespace where plugins of this type will be found--in this case, in the `Plugin/Importer` folder
- The interface each plugin of this type needs to implement--in our case, the `Drupal\products\Plugin\ImporterInterface` (which we have to create)
- The `annotation` class used by our plugin type (the one whose class properties map to the possible annotation properties found in the docblock about the plugin class)--in our case, `Drupal\products\Annotation\Importer` (which we have to create)

In addition to calling the parent constructor with these options, we will need to provide the "alter" hook for the available definitions. This will make it possible for other modules to implement this hook and alter the found plugin definitions. The resulting hook in our case is `hook_products_importer_info_alter`.

Lastly, we also provide a specific cache key for the backend responsible for caching the plugin definitions. This is for increased performance as you already should know by now, creating a new plugin requires clearing the cache.

That's it with our manager. However, since this is a service, we will need to register it as such inside the `products.service.yml` file:

```
services:
  products.importer_manager:
    class: Drupal\products\Plugin\ImporterManager
    parent: default_plugin_manager
```

As you noted, we inherit the dependencies (arguments) from the `default_plugin_manager` service instead of duplicating them here again. If you remember from Chapter 3, *Logging and Mailing*, this is a neat little trick in Drupal 8.

Now, since we referenced some classes in the manager, we will need to create them. Let's start with the annotation class:

```
namespace Drupal\products\Annotation;
```

```
use Drupal\Component\Annotation\Plugin;

/**
 * Defines a Importer item annotation object.
 *
 * @see \Drupal\products\Plugin\ImporterManager
 *
 * @Annotation
 */
class Importer extends Plugin {

  /**
   * The plugin ID.
   *
   * @var string
   */
  public $id;

  /**
   * The label of the plugin.
   *
   * @var \Drupal\Core\Annotation\Translation
   *
   * @ingroup plugin_translatable
   */
  public $label;
}
```

This class needs to extend `Drupal\Component\Annotation\Plugin`, which is the base class for annotations and implements `AnnotationInterface`.

For our purpose, we keep it simple. All we need is a plugin ID and a label. If we wanted to, we could add more properties to this class and describe them. It's a standard practice to do so because otherwise there is no way to know which properties a plugin annotation can contain.

Next, let's also write the interface the plugins are required to implement:

```
namespace Drupal\products\Plugin;

use Drupal\Component\Plugin\PluginInspectionInterface;

/**
 * Defines an interface for Importer plugins.
 */
interface ImporterInterface extends PluginInspectionInterface {
```

```
  /**
   * Performs the import. Returns TRUE if the import was successful or
FALSE otherwise.
   *
   * @return bool
   */
  public function import();
}
```

Again, we keep it simple. For now, our importer will have only one method specific to it: import(). However, it will have other methods specific to plugins, which can be found in the PluginInspectionInterface we are extending. These are getPluginId() and getPluginDefinition() and are also quite important as the system expects to be able to get this info from the plugins.

Then, plugins of any type need to extend PluginBase because it contains a host of mandatory implemented methods (such as the ones I mentioned before). However, it is also a best practice for the module that introduces a plugin type to also provide a base plugin class that plugins can extend. Its goal is to extend PluginBase and also provide all the necessary logic needed by all the plugins of this type. For example, when we create a new Block, we extend BlockBase, which somewhere down the line extends PluginBase.

In our case, this base (abstract) class can look something like this:

```
namespace Drupal\products\Plugin;

use Drupal\Component\Plugin\Exception\PluginException;
use Drupal\Component\Plugin\PluginBase;
use Drupal\Core\Entity\EntityTypeManager;
use Drupal\Core\Plugin\ContainerFactoryPluginInterface;
use Drupal\products\Entity\ImporterInterface;
use Drupal\products\Plugin\ImporterInterface as ImporterPluginInterface;
use GuzzleHttp\Client;
use Symfony\Component\DependencyInjection\ContainerInterface;

/**
 * Base class for Importer plugins.
 */
abstract class ImporterBase extends PluginBase implements
ImporterPluginInterface, ContainerFactoryPluginInterface {

  /**
   * @var \Drupal\Core\Entity\EntityTypeManager
   */
  protected $entityTypeManager;
```

```
/**
 * @var \GuzzleHttp\Client
 */
protected $httpClient;

/**
 * {@inheritdoc}
 */
public function __construct(array $configuration, $plugin_id,
$plugin_definition, EntityTypeManager $entityTypeManager, Client
$httpClient) {
    parent::__construct($configuration, $plugin_id, $plugin_definition);
    $this->entityTypeManager = $entityTypeManager;
    $this->httpClient = $httpClient;

    if (!isset($configuration['config'])) {
      throw new PluginException('Missing Importer configuration.');
    }

    if (!$configuration['config'] instanceof ImporterInterface) {
      throw new PluginException('Wrong Importer configuration.');
    }
}

/**
 * {@inheritdoc}
 */
public static function create(ContainerInterface $container, array
$configuration, $plugin_id, $plugin_definition) {
    return new static(
      $configuration,
      $plugin_id,
      $plugin_definition,
      $container->get('entity_type.manager'),
      $container->get('http_client')
    );
}
}
```

We implement `ImporterInterface` (renamed to prevent collision) to require subclasses to have the `import()` method. However, we also make the plugins container aware and has already injected some helpful services. One is the `EntityTypeManager` because we expect all importers to need it. The other is the Guzzle HTTP Client that we use in Drupal 8 to make PSR-7 requests to external resources.

Adding this here is a judgment call. We can imagine more than one plugin needing external requests, but if it turns out they don't, we should surely remove it and add it only in that specific plugin. The opposite also holds true. If in the third plugin implementation, we identify another common service, we can remove it from the plugins and inject it here.

Before talking about those exceptions we're throwing in the constructor, it's important to know how the plugin manager creates a new instance of a plugin. It uses its `createInstance()` method, which takes a plugin ID as a first parameter and an option array of plugin configuration as a second parameter. The relevant factory then passes that array of configuration as a first parameter of the plugin constructor itself. Many times, this is empty. However, for our plugin type, we will need configuration to be passed to the plugin in the form of a configuration Entity (which we have to create next). Without such an entity, we want the plugins to fail because they cannot work without the instructions found in this entity. So, in the constructor, we check whether the `$configuration['config']` is an instance of `Drupal\products\Entity\ImporterInterface`, which will be the interface our configuration entity will implement.

Our plugin type is for now complete. Obviously, we don't have any plugins yet, and before we create one, let's create the configuration entity type first.

Custom configuration entity type

Remember `NodeType` from the preceding chapter, and, by now, you know the essentials of creating custom entity types. So, let's create our `Importer` type now. Like before, we start with the annotation part, which is this time a `ConfigEntityType`:

```
namespace Drupal\products\Entity;

use Drupal\Core\Config\Entity\ConfigEntityBase;
use Drupal\Core\Url;

/**
 * Defines the Importer entity.
 *
 * @ConfigEntityType(
 *   id = "importer",
 *   label = @Translation("Importer"),
 *   handlers = {
 *     "list_builder" = "Drupal\products\ImporterListBuilder",
 *     "form" = {
 *       "add" = "Drupal\products\Form\ImporterForm",
 *       "edit" = "Drupal\products\Form\ImporterForm",
 *       "delete" = "Drupal\products\Form\ImporterDeleteForm"
```

```
 *        },
 *        "route_provider" = {
 *          "html" = "Drupal\Core\Entity\Routing\AdminHtmlRouteProvider",
 *        },
 *      },
 *    config_prefix = "importer",
 *    admin_permission = "administer site configuration",
 *    entity_keys = {
 *      "id" = "id",
 *      "label" = "label",
 *      "uuid" = "uuid"
 *    },
 *    links = {
 *      "add-form" = "/admin/structure/importer/add",
 *      "edit-form" = "/admin/structure/importer/{importer}/edit",
 *      "delete-form" = "/admin/structure/importer/{importer}/delete",
 *      "collection" = "/admin/structure/importer"
 *    }
 *  )
 */
class Importer extends ConfigEntityBase implements ImporterInterface {}
```

Similar to the `Product` entity, we will need to create a list builder handler, as well as form handlers. In this case, though, we also need to create a form handler for the `delete` operation as we will soon see why. Finally, since we have a configuration entity, we also specify a `config_prefix` to be used in the exporting. One thing you'll note is that we don't have a canonical link because we don't really need one--our entities don't need a details page.

Now, it's time to create the `ImporterInterface` that the entities need to implement. It is named the same as the plugin interface we created earlier, but it resides in a different namespace:

```
namespace Drupal\products\Entity;

use Drupal\Core\Config\Entity\ConfigEntityInterface;
use Drupal\Core\Url;

/**
 * Importer configuration entity.
 */
interface ImporterInterface extends ConfigEntityInterface {

  /**
   * Returns the Url where the import can get the data from.
   *
   * @return Url
```

```
    */
    public function getUrl();

    /**
     * Returns the Importer plugin ID to be used by this importer.
     *
     * @return string
     */
    public function getPluginId();

    /**
     * Whether or not to update existing products if they have already been
  imported.
     *
     * @return bool
     */
    public function updateExisting();

    /**
     * Returns the source of the products.
     *
     * @return string
     */
    public function getSource();
}
```

In these configuration entities, we want to store, for now, a URL to the resource where the products can be retrieved from, the ID of the Importer plugin to use, whether we want existing products to be updated if they had already been imported, and the source of the products. For all these fields, we create some getter methods. You'll note that getUrl() needs to return a Url instance. Again, we create a well-defined interface for the public API of the entity type as we did with the product entity type.

This is what the Importer class that implements this interface looks like:

```
    /**
     * The Importer ID.
     *
     * @var string
     */
    protected $id;

    /**
     * The Importer label.
     *
     * @var string
     */
```

```
  protected $label;

  /**
   * The URL from where the import file can be retrieved.
   *
   * @var string
   */
  protected $url;

  /**
   * The plugin ID of the plugin to be used for processing this import.
   *
   * @var string
   */
  protected $plugin;

  /**
   * Whether or not to update existing products if they have already been
imported.
   *
   * @var bool
   */
  protected $update_existing = TRUE;

  /**
   * The source of the products.
   *
   * @var string
   */
  protected $source;

  /**
   * {@inheritdoc}
   */
  public function getUrl() {
    return $this->url ? Url::fromUri($this->url) : NULL;
  }

  /**
   * {@inheritdoc}
   */
  public function getPluginId() {
    return $this->plugin;
  }

  /**
   * {@inheritdoc}
   */
```

```
public function updateExisting() {
    return $this->update_existing;
}

/**
 * {@inheritdoc}
 */
public function getSource() {
    return $this->source;
}
```

If you remember from the preceding chapter, defining fields on a configuration entity type is as simple as defining properties on the class itself. Moreover, you may recall the `config_export` key on the annotation, that lists which of these properties need to be exported and persisted. We omitted that because we will simply rely on the configuration schema (which we will create soon). Lastly, the interface methods are implemented next, and there is no rocket science involved in that. The `getUrl()`, as expected, will try to create an instance of `Url` from the value.

Since we talked about the configuration schema, let's define that as well. If you remember, it goes inside the `config/schema` folder of our module in a `*.schema.yml` file. This can be named after the module and contain the schema definitions of all configurations of the module or after the individual configuration entity type, so, in our case, `importer.schema.yml` (to keep things neatly organized):

```
products.importer.*:
  type: config_entity
  label: 'Importer config'
  mapping:
    id:
      type: string
      label: 'ID'
    label:
      type: label
      label: 'Label'
    uuid:
      type: string
    url:
      type: uri
      label: Uri
    plugin:
      type: string
      label: Plugin ID
    update_existing:
      type: boolean
      label: Whether to update existing products
```

```
    source:
      type: string
      label: The source of the products
```

If you recall, the wildcard is used to apply the schema to all configuration items that match the prefix. So, in our case, it will match all `importer` configuration entities. Next, we have the `config_entity` schema with a mapping of the fields we defined. Apart from the default fields each entity type comes with, we are using a `uri`, `string`, and `boolean` schema type (which under the hood maps to the corresponding TypedData data type plugins). This schema now helps the system understand our entities (for example, know which fields need to be exported).

Now, let's go ahead and create the list builder handler that will take care of the admin entity listing:

```
namespace Drupal\products;

use Drupal\Core\Config\Entity\ConfigEntityListBuilder;
use Drupal\Core\Entity\EntityInterface;

/**
 * Provides a listing of Importer entities.
 */
class ImporterListBuilder extends ConfigEntityListBuilder {

  /**
   * {@inheritdoc}
   */
  public function buildHeader() {
    $header['label'] = $this->t('Importer');
    $header['id'] = $this->t('Machine name');
    return $header + parent::buildHeader();
  }

  /**
   * {@inheritdoc}
   */
  public function buildRow(EntityInterface $entity) {
    $row['label'] = $entity->label();
    $row['id'] = $entity->id();
    return $row + parent::buildRow($entity);
  }
}
```

This time we are extending the ConfigEntityListBuilder, which provides some potential functionalities specific to configuration entities. However, we are essentially doing the same as with the products listing--setting up the table header and the individual row data, nothing major. I recommend that you inspect ConfigEntityListBuilder and see what else you can do in the subclass.

Now, we can finally take care of the form handler and start with the default create/edit form:

```
namespace Drupal\products\Form;

use Drupal\Core\Entity\EntityForm;
use Drupal\Core\Form\FormStateInterface;
use Drupal\products\Entity\Importer;
use Drupal\products\Plugin\ImporterManager;
use Symfony\Component\DependencyInjection\ContainerInterface;

/**
 * Form for creating/editing Importer entities.
 */
class ImporterForm extends EntityForm {

  /**
   * @var \Drupal\products\Plugin\ImporterManager
   */
  protected $importerManager;

  /**
   * ImporterForm constructor.
   *
   * @param \Drupal\products\Plugin\ImporterManager $importerManager
   */
  public function __construct(ImporterManager $importerManager) {
    $this->importerManager = $importerManager;
  }

  /**
   * {@inheritdoc}
   */
  public static function create(ContainerInterface $container) {
    return new static(
      $container->get('products.importer_manager')
    );
  }

  /**
   * {@inheritdoc}
```

```php
     */
    public function form(array $form, FormStateInterface $form_state) {
      $form = parent::form($form, $form_state);

      /** @var Importer $importer */
      $importer = $this->entity;

      $form['label'] = [
        '#type' => 'textfield',
        '#title' => $this->t('Name'),
        '#maxlength' => 255,
        '#default_value' => $importer->label(),
        '#description' => $this->t('Name of the Importer.'),
        '#required' => TRUE,
      ];

      $form['id'] = [
        '#type' => 'machine_name',
        '#default_value' => $importer->id(),
        '#machine_name' => [
          'exists' => '\Drupal\products\Entity\Importer::load',
        ],
        '#disabled' => !$importer->isNew(),
      ];

      $form['url'] = [
        '#type' => 'url',
        '#default_value' => $importer->getUrl() instanceof Url ?
$importer->getUrl()->toString() : '',
        '#title' => $this->t('Url'),
        '#description' => $this->t('The URL to the import resource'),
        '#required' => TRUE,
      ];

      $definitions = $this->importerManager->getDefinitions();
      $options = [];
      foreach ($definitions as $id => $definition) {
        $options[$id] = $definition['label'];
      }

      $form['plugin'] = [
        '#type' => 'select',
        '#title' => $this->t('Plugin'),
        '#default_value' => $importer->getPluginId(),
        '#options' => $options,
        '#description' => $this->t('The plugin to be used with this
importer.'),
        '#required' => TRUE,
```

```
    ];

    $form['update_existing'] = [
      '#type' => 'checkbox',
      '#title' => $this->t('Update existing'),
      '#description' => $this->t('Whether to update existing products if
already imported.'),
      '#default_value' => $importer->updateExisting(),
    ];

    $form['source'] = [
      '#type' => 'textfield',
      '#title' => $this->t('Source'),
      '#description' => $this->t('The source of the products.'),
      '#default_value' => $importer->getSource(),
    ];

    return $form;
  }

  /**
   * {@inheritdoc}
   */
  public function save(array $form, FormStateInterface $form_state) {
    /** @var Importer $importer */
    $importer = $this->entity;
    $status = $importer->save();

    switch ($status) {
      case SAVED_NEW:
        drupal_set_message($this->t('Created the %label Importer.', [
          '%label' => $importer->label(),
        ]));
        break;

      default:
        drupal_set_message($this->t('Saved the %label Importer.', [
          '%label' => $importer->label(),
        ]));
    }
    $form_state->setRedirectUrl($importer->toUrl('collection'));
  }

}
```

We are extending directly `EntityForm` in this case because configuration entities don't have a specific form class like content entities do. For this reason, we also have to implement the form elements for all our fields inside the `form()` method, but first things first.

We know we want the configuration entity to select a plugin to use, so, for this reason, we inject the `ImporterManager` we created earlier. We will use it to get all the existing definitions.

Inside the `form()` method, we will define all the form elements for the fields. We use a `textfield` for the label and a `machine_name` field for the ID of the entity. The latter is a special JavaScript-powered field that derives its value from a "source" field (which defaults to the field `label` if one is not specified). It is also disabled if we are editing the form and is using a dynamic callback to try to load an entity by the provided ID and will fail validation if it exists. This is useful to ensure that IDs do not repeat. Next, we have a `url` form element, which does some URL-specific validation and handling to ensure that a proper URL is added. Then, we create an array of `select` element options of all the available Importer plugin definitions. For this, we use the plugin manager `getDefinitions()` from which we can get the IDs and labels. A plugin definition is an array that contains primarily the data found in the annotation and some other data processed and added by the manager (in our case, only defaults). This is performant because we don't even have to instantiate plugins to get this information. We use those options on the select list. Finally, we have the simple `checkbox` and `textfield` elements for the last two fields, as we want to store the `update_existing` field as a Boolean and the `source` as a string.

The `save()` method is pretty much like with the Product entity form; we are simply displaying a message and redirecting the user to the entity listing page. Since we named the form elements exactly as the fields, we don't need to do any mapping of the form values to the fields. That is taken care of for us.

Let's now take care of the delete form handler:

```
namespace Drupal\products\Form;

use Drupal\Core\Entity\EntityConfirmFormBase;
use Drupal\Core\Form\FormStateInterface;
use Drupal\Core\Url;

/**
 * Form for deleting Importer entities.
 */
class ImporterDeleteForm extends EntityConfirmFormBase {

  /**
```

```
    *  {@inheritdoc}
    */
  public function getQuestion() {
     return $this->t('Are you sure you want to delete %name?', ['%name' =>
$this->entity->label()]);
  }

  /**
    *  {@inheritdoc}
    */
  public function getCancelUrl() {
     return new Url('entity.importer.collection');
  }

  /**
    *  {@inheritdoc}
    */
  public function getConfirmText() {
     return $this->t('Delete');
  }

  /**
    *  {@inheritdoc}
    */
  public function submitForm(array &$form, FormStateInterface $form_state)
{
     $this->entity->delete();

     drupal_set_message($this->t('Deleted @entity importer.', ['@entity' =>
$this->entity->label()]));

     $form_state->setRedirectUrl($this->getCancelUrl());
  }
}
```

As I mentioned earlier, for configuration entities, we will need to implement this form handler ourselves. However, it's not a big deal because we can extend EntityConfirmFormBase and just implement some simple methods--in getQuestion(), we return the string to be used as the question for the confirmation form, whereas in getConfirmText(), the same goes for the label of the delete button; the route in getCancelUrl() will be used to redirect it after either a cancellation or a successful delete; and finally, in the submitForm() method, we simply delete the entity, print a success message, and redirect it to the URL we set in the getCancelUrl().

That should take care of our configuration entity type. The last thing we might want to do is create some menu links to be able to navigate to the relevant pages (same as we did for the Product entity type). For the entity list page, we can have this in our `products.links.menu.yml` file:

```
# Importer entity menu items
entity.importer.collection:
  title: 'Importer'
  route_name: entity.importer.collection
  description: 'List Importer entities'
  parent: system.admin_structure
  weight: 99
```

There's nothing new here. We can also create the action link to add a new entity inside the `products.links.action.yml` file:

```
entity.importer.add_form:
  route_name: 'entity.importer.add_form'
  title: 'Add Importer'
  appears_on:
    - entity.importer.collection
```

Same thing here as we did with the Products. However, we won't create local tasks because we don't have a canonical route for the configuration entities, so we don't really need it.

Now, if we clear our cache and go to `admin/structure/importer`, we should see the empty Importer entity listing:

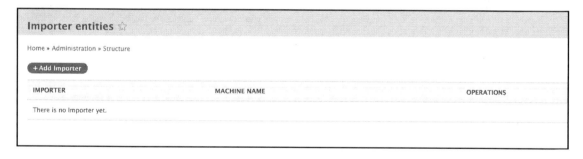

The Importer plugin

Alright, since all of our setup is in place, we can now go ahead and create our first Importer plugin. As we defined it in the manager, these need to go in the `Plugin/Importer` namespace of modules. So, let's start with a simple `JsonImporter` that will use a remote URL resource to import products. This is an example JSON file that will be processed by this plugin, just for testing purposes:

```
{
  "products" : [
    {
      "id" : 1,
      "name": "TV",
      "number": 341
    },
    {
      "id" : 2,
      "name": "VCR",
      "number": 123
    },
    {
      "id" : 3,
      "name": "Stereo",
      "number": 234
    }
  ]
}
```

I know, VCR right? We have an ID, a name, and a product number. This is all totally made up information about products just to illustrate the process. So, let's create our `JsonImporter`:

```
namespace Drupal\products\Plugin\Importer;

use Drupal\products\Entity\ImporterInterface;
use Drupal\products\Entity\ProductInterface;
use Drupal\products\Plugin\ImporterBase;

/**
 * Product importer from a JSON format.
 *
 * @Importer(
 *   id = "json",
 *   label = @Translation("JSON Importer")
 * )
 */
class JsonImporter extends ImporterBase {
```

```php
/**
 * {@inheritdoc}
 */
public function import() {
  $data = $this->getData();
  if (!$data) {
    return FALSE;
  }

  if (!isset($data->products)) {
    return FALSE;
  }

  $products = $data->products;
  foreach ($products as $product) {
    $this->persistProduct($product);
  }
  return TRUE;
}

/**
 * Loads the product data from the remote URL.
 *
 * @return \stdClass
 */
private function getData() {
  /** @var ImporterInterface $config */
  $config = $this->configuration['config'];
  $request = $this->httpClient->get($config->getUrl()->toString());
  $string = $request->getBody()->getContents();
  return json_decode($string);
}

/**
 * Saves a Product entity from the remote data.
 *
 * @param \stdClass $data
 */
private function persistProduct($data) {
  /** @var ImporterInterface $config */
  $config = $this->configuration['config'];

  $existing =
$this->entityTypeManager->getStorage('product')->loadByProperties(['remote_
id' => $data->id, 'source' => $config->getSource()]);
  if (!$existing) {
    $values = [
      'remote_id' => $data->id,
```

```
            'source' => $config->getSource()
        ];
        /** @var ProductInterface $product */
        $product =
$this->entityTypeManager->getStorage('product')->create($values);
        $product->setName($data->name);
        $product->setProductNumber($data->number);
        $product->save();
        return;
    }

    if (!$config->updateExisting()) {
        return;
    }

    /** @var ProductInterface $product */
    $product = reset($existing);
    $product->setName($data->name);
    $product->setProductNumber($data->number);
    $product->save();
  }
}
```

You can immediately spot the Plugin annotation where we specify an ID and a label. We don't have any other data there we need. Next, by extending `ImporterBase`, we inherit the dependent services and ensure that the required interface is implemented. Speaking of which, we basically just implement the `import()` method. So, let's break down what we are doing:

1. Inside the `getData()` method, we retrieve the product information from the remote resource. We do so by getting the URL from the `Importer` configuration entity and using Guzzle to make a request to that URL. We expect that to be JSON, so we just decode it as such. Of course, error handling is virtually nonexistent in this example, and that is not good.

2. We loop through the resulting product data and call the `persistProduct()` method on it. In there, we first check whether we already have the product entity. We do so using the simple `loadByProperties()` method on the product entity storage and try to find products that have the specific source and remote ID. If one doesn't exist, we create it. This should all be familiar from the preceding chapter when we looked at manipulating entities. If the product aready exists, we first check whether according to configuration, we can update it and only do so if that allows us to. The `loadByProperties()` method always returns an array of entities, but since we only expect to have a single product with the same remote ID and source combination, we simply `reset()` this array to get to that one entity. Then, we just set the name and product number on the entity.

As you can see, instead of using the Entity API/TypedData `set()` method to update the entity field values, we use our own interface methods. I find that this is much cleaner, more modern, and an IDE-friendly way because everything is very explicit.

One thing you might notice is the error handling in this import process or more precisely, a lack thereof. This is because I kept things simple for the purpose of focusing on the current topic. Normally, you would want to maybe throw and catch some exceptions and definitely log some messages (both error and success). You know how to do the latter from Chapter 3, *Logging and Mailing*.

That is pretty much it. We can now create our first `Importer` entity and make it use this Importer plugin (after clearing the cache of course):

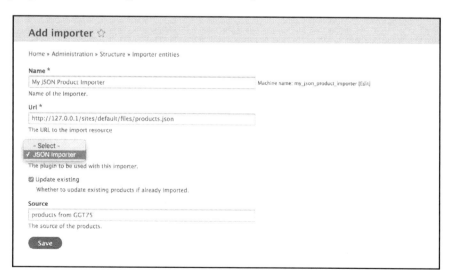

The URL in the preceding screenshot is just some local URL where an example JSON file is found, and we can see the only plugin available to choose, as well as the other entity fields we created form elements for. By saving this new entity, we can make use of it programmatically (assuming that the products.json file referenced in the URL exists):

```
/** @var Importer $config */
$config =
\Drupal::entityTypeManager()->getStorage('importer')->load('my_json_product
_importer');
$plugin =
\Drupal::service('products.importer_manager')->createInstance($config->getP
luginId(), ['config' => $config]);
$plugin->import();
```

This is it. We first load the importer entity by ID. Then, we use the ImporterManager service to create a new instance of a plugin using the createInstance() method. Only one parameter is required for it--the ID of the plugin--but as I said earlier, we want to pass the configuration entity to it because it depends on it. So we do just that. Then, we call the import() method on the plugin. After running this code, the product entity listing will show some shiny new products.

Let's, however, improve things a bit. Since the configuration entities and plugins are so tightly connected, let's use the plugin manager to do this entire thing rather than having to first load an entity and request the plugin from it. So, have a method on the plugin manager where we can pass the configuration entity ID, and it returns an instance of the relevant plugin; something like this:

```
/**
 * Creates an instance of ImporterInterface plugin based on the ID of a
 * configuration entity.
 *
 * @param $id
 *    Configuration entity ID
 *
 * @return null|ImporterPluginInterface
 */
public function createInstanceFromConfig($id) {
  $config = $this->entityTypeManager->getStorage('importer')->load($id);
  if (!$config instanceof ImporterInterface) {
    return NULL;
  }

  return $this->createInstance($config->getPluginId(), ['config' =>
$config]);
  }
```

The preceding code block uses two extra use statements at the top:

```
use Drupal\products\Entity\ImporterInterface;
use Drupal\products\Plugin\ImporterInterface as ImporterPluginInterface;
```

Here, we essentially do the same thing as before, but we return NULL if there is no configuration entity found. You can choose to throw an exception if you want instead. However, as you may have noticed correctly, we also need to inject the EntityTypeManager into this class, so our constructor changes as well to take it as a last parameter and set it as a class property. Finally, we will need to alter the service definition for the plugin manager to add the EntityTypeManager as a dependency:

```
products.importer_manager:
  class: Drupal\products\Plugin\ImporterManager
  parent: default_plugin_manager
  arguments: ['@entity_type.manager']
```

As you can see, we keep the parent inheritance key so that all the parent arguments are taken in. On top, however, we add our own regular arguments key, that will add them after the ones that come from the parent. So, we will need to ensure that the EntityTypeManager is the last constructor parameter.

Now, we have simplified things for the client code:

```
$plugin =
\Drupal::service('products.importer_manager')->createInstanceFromConfig('my
_json_product_importer');
$plugin->import();
```

All we have to interact with is the plugin manager, and we can directly run the import. This is in some ways better because our configuration entities are not something we designed for being used by anyone else. They are simple configuration storage used only by our Importer plugins.

Content entity bundles

We have written a neat little piece of functionality. There are still improvements that we can, and will make but those are for later chapters when we cover other topics that we will need to learn about. Now, however, let's take a step back to our content entity type and extend our products a bit by enabling bundles. We want to have more than one type of product that can be imported, bundled, which will be an option to choose when creating an Importer configuration. However, first, let's make the Product entity type "bundlelable".

We start by adjusting our Product entity plugin annotation:

```
/**
 * Defines the Product entity.
 *
 * @ContentEntityType(
 *   ...
 *   label = @Translation("Product"),
 *   bundle_label = @Translation("Product type"),
 *   handlers = {
 *   ...
 *   entity_keys = {
 *     ...
 *     "bundle" = "type",
 *   },
 *   ...
 *   bundle_entity_type = "product_type",
 *   field_ui_base_route = "entity.product_type.edit_form"
 * )
 */
```

We add a `bundle_label` for our bundle, an entity key for it that will map to the `type` field, the `bundle_entity_type` that will act as a bundle for the products, and a `field_ui_base_route`. This latter option is something we could have added before but was not necessary. Now, we can (and should) add it because we need a route where we can configure our Product entities from the point of view of managing UI fields and the bundles. We'll see these a bit later on.

Moreover, we also need to change something about the links. First, we will need to alter the `add-form` link:

```
"add-form" = "/admin/structure/product/add/{product_type}",
```

This will now take a product type in the URL to know which bundle we are creating. If you remember from the preceding chapter when we were creating entities programmatically, the bundle is a required value from the beginning if the entity type has bundles.

Then, we add a new link, as follows:

```
"add-page" = "/admin/structure/product/add",
```

This will go to the initial `add-form` path, but will list options of available bundles to select for creating a new Product. Clicking on one of those will take us to the `add-form` link.

Since we made these changes, we will also need to make a quick alteration to the product entity action link to use the `add-page` instead of `add-form` route:

```
entity.product.add_page:
  route_name: entity.product.add_page
  title: 'Add Product'
  appears_on:
    - entity.product.collection
```

This is required because on the product entity list page (collection URL) we don't have a product type in context, so we cannot build a path to `add-form`, nor would it be logical to do so as we don't know what type of product the user wants to create. As a quick bonus, if there is only one bundle, Drupal will redirect them to the `add-form` link of that particular bundle.

The good thing is that since we specified an entity key for the bundle, we don't have to define the field that will reference the bundle configuration entity. It will be done for us by the parent `ContentEntityType::baseFieldDefinitions()`. So, what is left to do is to create the `ProductType` configuration entity type that will serve as product bundles. We already know more or less how this works. Inside our `Entity` namespace we start our class like so:

```
namespace Drupal\products\Entity;

use Drupal\Core\Config\Entity\ConfigEntityBundleBase;

/**
 * Product type configuration entity type.
 *
 * @ConfigEntityType(
 *   id = "product_type",
 *   label = @Translation("Product type"),
 *   handlers = {
 *     "list_builder" = "Drupal\products\ProductTypeListBuilder",
 *     "form" = {
 *       "add" = "Drupal\products\Form\ProductTypeForm",
 *       "edit" = "Drupal\products\Form\ProductTypeForm",
 *       "delete" = "Drupal\products\Form\ProductTypeDeleteForm"
 *     },
 *     "route_provider" = {
 *       "html" = "Drupal\Core\Entity\Routing\AdminHtmlRouteProvider",
 *     },
 *   },
 *   config_prefix = "product_type",
 *   admin_permission = "administer site configuration",
 *   bundle_of = "product",
```

```
 *    entity_keys = {
 *      "id" = "id",
 *      "label" = "label",
 *      "uuid" = "uuid"
 *    },
 *    links = {
 *      "canonical" = "/admin/structure/product_type/{product_type}",
 *      "add-form" = "/admin/structure/product_type/add",
 *      "edit-form" = "/admin/structure/product_type/{product_type}/edit",
 *      "delete-form" =
"/admin/structure/product_type/{product_type}/delete",
 *      "collection" = "/admin/structure/product_type"
 *    }
 * )
 */
class ProductType extends ConfigEntityBundleBase implements
ProductTypeInterface  {

  /**
   * The Product type ID.
   *
   * @var string
   */
  protected $id;

  /**
   * The Product type label.
   *
   * @var string
   */
  protected $label;
}
```

Much of this is exactly the same as when we created the Importer configuration entity type. The only difference is that we have the `bundle_of` key in the annotation, which denotes the content entity type this serves as a bundle for. Also, we don't really need any other fields. Because of that, the `ProductTypeInterface` can look as simple as this:

```
namespace Drupal\products\Entity;

use Drupal\Core\Config\Entity\ConfigEntityInterface;

/**
 * Product bundle interface.
 */
interface ProductTypeInterface extends ConfigEntityInterface {}
```

Let's quickly take a look at the individual handlers, which will seem very familiar by now as well. The list builder looks almost the same as for the Importer:

```
namespace Drupal\products;

use Drupal\Core\Config\Entity\ConfigEntityListBuilder;
use Drupal\Core\Entity\EntityInterface;

/**
 * List builder for ProductType entities.
 */
class ProductTypeListBuilder extends ConfigEntityListBuilder {

  /**
   * {@inheritdoc}
   */
  public function buildHeader() {
    $header['label'] = $this->t('Product type');
    $header['id'] = $this->t('Machine name');
    return $header + parent::buildHeader();
  }

  /**
   * {@inheritdoc}
   */
  public function buildRow(EntityInterface $entity) {
    $row['label'] = $entity->label();
    $row['id'] = $entity->id();
    return $row + parent::buildRow($entity);
  }
}
```

The create/edit form handler also looks very similar, albeit much simpler due to not having many fields on the configuration entity type:

```
namespace Drupal\products\Form;

use Drupal\Core\Entity\EntityForm;
use Drupal\Core\Form\FormStateInterface;
use Drupal\products\Entity\ProductTypeInterface;

/**
 * Form handler for creating/editing ProductType entities
 */
class ProductTypeForm extends EntityForm {

  /**
   * {@inheritdoc}
```

```
   */
  public function form(array $form, FormStateInterface $form_state) {
    $form = parent::form($form, $form_state);

    /** @var ProductTypeInterface $product_type */
    $product_type = $this->entity;
    $form['label'] = [
      '#type' => 'textfield',
      '#title' => $this->t('Label'),
      '#maxlength' => 255,
      '#default_value' => $product_type->label(),
      '#description' => $this->t('Label for the Product type.'),
      '#required' => TRUE,
    ];

    $form['id'] = [
      '#type' => 'machine_name',
      '#default_value' => $product_type->id(),
      '#machine_name' => [
        'exists' => '\Drupal\products\Entity\ProductType::load',
      ],
      '#disabled' => !$product_type->isNew(),
    ];

    return $form;
  }

  /**
   * {@inheritdoc}
   */
  public function save(array $form, FormStateInterface $form_state) {
    $product_type = $this->entity;
    $status = $product_type->save();

    switch ($status) {
      case SAVED_NEW:
        drupal_set_message($this->t('Created the %label Product type.', [
          '%label' => $product_type->label(),
        ]));
        break;

      default:
        drupal_set_message($this->t('Saved the %label Product type.', [
          '%label' => $product_type->label(),
        ]));
    }
    $form_state->setRedirectUrl($product_type->toUrl('collection'));
  }
```

```
  }
```

Speaking of fields, we mustn't forget about the configuration schema:

```
products.product_type.*:
  type: config_entity
  label: 'Product type config'
  mapping:
    id:
      type: string
      label: 'ID'
    label:
      type: label
      label: 'Label'
    uuid:
      type: string
```

Lastly, we should remember the form handler for deleting product types:

```
namespace Drupal\products\Form;

use Drupal\Core\Entity\EntityConfirmFormBase;
use Drupal\Core\Form\FormStateInterface;
use Drupal\Core\Url;

/**
 * Form handler for deleting ProductType entities.
 */
class ProductTypeDeleteForm extends EntityConfirmFormBase {

  /**
   * {@inheritdoc}
   */
  public function getQuestion() {
    return $this->t('Are you sure you want to delete %name?', ['%name' =>
$this->entity->label()]);
  }

  /**
   * {@inheritdoc}
   */
  public function getCancelUrl() {
    return new Url('entity.product_type.collection');
  }

  /**
   * {@inheritdoc}
   */
```

```
  public function getConfirmText() {
    return $this->t('Delete');
  }

  /**
   * {@inheritdoc}
   */
  public function submitForm(array &$form, FormStateInterface $form_state)
{
    $this->entity->delete();

    drupal_set_message($this->t('Deleted @entity product type.', ['@entity'
=> $this->entity->label()]));

    $form_state->setRedirectUrl($this->getCancelUrl());
  }

}
```

You should already be familiar with what we're doing here.

Now, we are done. We can clear the caches and run the `drush entity-updates` command because Drupal needs to create the `type` field on the product entities. Once that is done, we can go the UI and see our changes.

We now have a Product type entity listing where we can create Product bundles. Moreover, we also have some extra operations since this entity type is used as a bundle--we can manage fields and displays (both for viewing and for the forms) for each individual bundle:

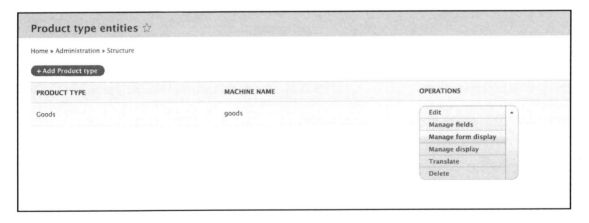

Managing fields and displays would have been possible before creating the bundle, had we provided the `field_ui_base_route` to the Product entity type and created a menu link for it.

Now we can add fields to our individual bundles and can distinguish between our product types--for example, we can have a bundle for goods and one for services. We can well imagine that the two types might require a different set of fields and/or they are being pulled from different external resources. So, let's just update our importing logic to allow the selection of a bundle because now it is actually mandatory to specify one when we attempt to create a Product.

We start by adding a new field to the Importer entity type, first, for the interface change:

```
/**
 * Returns the Product type that needs to be created.
 *
 * @return string
 */
public function getBundle();
```

Then, we will take a look at the implementation in the class:

```
/**
 * The product bundle.
 *
 * @var string
 */
protected $bundle;
...
/**
 * {@inheritdoc}
 */
public function getBundle() {
  return $this->bundle;
}
```

Next, we must include the new field in the configuration schema:

```
...
bundle:
  type: string
  label: The product bundle
```

The last thing we will need to do on the Importer entity type is add the form element for choosing a bundle:

```
$form['bundle'] = [
  '#type' => 'entity_autocomplete',
  '#target_type' => 'product_type',
  '#title' => $this->t('Product type'),
  '#default_value' => $importer->getBundle() ?
$this->entityTypeManager->getStorage('product_type')->load($importer->getBu
ndle()) : NULL,
  '#description' => $this->t('The type of products that need to be
created.'),
];
```

Here, we use an `entity_autocomplete` form element that gives us the possibility to use an autocomplete text field to look up an existing entity and select one of the found ones. The ID of the selected entity will then be submitted in the form as the value. This field definition requires choosing a `#target_type`, which is the entity type we want to autocomplete. One thing to note is that even if the submitted value is only the ID (in our case, a string as expected and which is what we also want to store), the `#default_value` requires the full entity object itself (or an array of entity objects). This is because the field shows more information about the referenced entity than just the ID.

In order to load the referenced entity for the default value, we will need to inject the `EntityTypeManger`. You should already know how to do this injection, so I'm not gonna show it here again. We simply tack on the dependency to the `ImporterManager`, which is already being injected.

That should be it for the Importer entity type alterations. The one last thing we need to do is handle the bundle inside the `JsonImporter` plugin we wrote. However, this is as simple as adding the `type` value when creating the product entity:

```
if (!$existing) {
  $values = [
    'remote_id' => $data->id,
    'source' => $config->getSource(),
    'type' => $config->getBundle(),
  ];
  /** @var ProductInterface $product */
  $product =
$this->entityTypeManager->getStorage('product')->create($values);
...
```

Here we are. Running the import code will now create products of the bundle specified in the Importer configuration.

Drush command

So our logic is in place, but we will need to create a handy way we can trigger the imports. One option is to create an administration form where we go and press a button. However, a more typical example is a command that can be added to the crontab and that can be run at specific intervals automatically. So that's what we are going to do now, and we will do so using Drush.

The Drush command we are going to write will take an optional parameter for the ID of the importer configuration entity we want to process. This will allow the use of the command for more than one just importer. Alternatively, passing no options will process each importer (in case this is something we want to do later on). One thing to note is that we won't focus on performance in this example. This means the command will work just fine for smaller sets of data (as big as one request can process) but will be probably better to use a queue and/or batch processing for larger sets. Also, we will have a chapter dedicated for these subsystems later on, but, for now, let's get on with our example.

Before we actually write our new Drush command, let's make some alterations to our logic as they will make sense in the context of what we want to do. First, let's add a getter method to the Importer plugins to retrieve the corresponding configuration entities. We start with the interface like so:

```
/**
 * Returns the Importer configuration entity.
 *
 * @return \Drupal\products\Entity\ImporterInterface
 */
public function getConfig();
```

Then, on the `ImporterBase` class, we can add the implementation (it will be the same for all individual plugin instances):

```
/**
 * {@inheritdoc}
 */
public function getConfig() {
  return $this->configuration['config'];
}
```

As you can see, it's not rocket science.

Second, let's add a `createInstanceFromAllConfigs()` method to the `ImporterManager` that will return an array of plugin instances for each existing Importer configuration entities:

```
/**
 * Creates an array of ImporterInterface from all the existing Importer
 * configuration entities.
 *
 * @return ImporterPluginInterface[]
 */
public function createInstanceFromAllConfigs() {
  $configs =
$this->entityTypeManager->getStorage('importer')->loadMultiple();
    if (!$configs) {
      return [];
    }
    $plugins = [];
    /** @var ImporterInterface $config */
    foreach ($configs as $config) {
      $plugin = $this->createInstanceFromConfig($config->id());
      if (!$plugin) {
        continue;
      }

      $plugins[] = $plugin;
    }

    return $plugins;
  }
```

Here, we use the `loadMultiple()` method on the entity storage handler, which if we use without any arguments will load all existing entities, and if we have any, we use our existing `createInstanceFromConfig()` method to instantiate the plugins based on each configuration entity. That's it; we can now go ahead and create our Drush command.

Drush commands are still being written using procedural code and are defined inside the `my_module.drush.inc` file of our module, so in our case, it will be `products.drush.inc`. The definition of a Drush command is made up of two parts--the implementation of `hook_drush_command()` and of a callback for each defined commands. Both of these go inside the same `*.drush.inc` file. So let's define our command:

```
/**
 * Implements hook_drush_command().
 */
function products_drush_command() {
  $items = [];

  $items['products-import-run'] = [
    'description' => 'Run the product importers',
    'options' => [
      'importer' => 'The Importer configuration entity to run.',
    ],
    'aliases' => ['pir'],
    'callback' => 'products_products_import_run'
  ];

  return $items;
}
```

This hook returns an array of command definitions, keyed by the actual command name. Also, a command can have certain definition options. In our case, we have a description, a list of options, a list of aliases for the command name, and a callback function to be run. If we omit the callback, the function name defaults to `drush_[command_name_with_underscores_instead_of_dashes]`. In our case, it would have been `drush_products_import_run`. The aliases are an array of typically shorter command names by which we can refer to this command.

We also have a named option to this command, which as you may have guessed, is optional. When running the command, it will be used like this:

```
drush command --option-name=option_value
```

However, the command should run just as well with the option omitted from the call. This is unlike "arguments" that a Drush command can also have and are mandatory. In our case, we don't need any arguments, though.

Let's now write the callback function that will be called when this command runs:

```
/**
 * Callback for the products-import-run Drush command.
 */
function products_products_import_run() {
  $importer = drush_get_option('importer', NULL);
  /** @var \Drupal\products\Plugin\ImporterManager $manager */
  $manager = \Drupal::service('products.importer_manager');
  if (!is_null($importer)) {
    $plugin = $manager->createInstanceFromConfig($importer);
    if (is_null($plugin)) {
      drush_log(t('The specified importer does not exist'), 'error');
      return;
    }

    _products_products_import_run_plugin($plugin);
    return;
  }

  $plugins = $manager->createInstanceFromAllConfigs();
  if (!$plugins) {
    drush_log(t('There are no importers to run'), 'error');
    return;
  }

  foreach ($plugins as $plugin) {
    _products_products_import_run_plugin($plugin);
  }
}
```

The way we retrieve the value of an option within a Drush command is using `drush_get_option()`, whose second parameter sets a default value in case one is not found in the command. So what we did in the preceding code then is get the option (the Importer ID), and if one is found, we do what we did before--get a plugin instance based on that ID and run the import using the `_products_products_import_run_plugin()` function:

```
/**
 * Runs an individual Importer plugin.
 *
 * @see products_products_import_run().
 *
 * @param \Drupal\products\Plugin\ImporterInterface $plugin
 */
function
_products_products_import_run_plugin(\Drupal\products\Plugin\ImporterInterf
```

```
ace $plugin) {
  $result = $plugin->import();
  $message_values = ['@importer' => $plugin->getConfig()->label()];
  $message = $result ? t('The "@importer" importer has been run.',
$message_values) : t('There was a problem running the "@importer"
importer.', $message_values);
  $message_status = $result ? 'success' : 'error';
  drush_log($message, $message_status);
}
```

We are also setting a success or error message depending on the results we are getting from the importer. In this message, we use the actual Importer entity label rather than the ID, which is nicer.

Instead of the regular `drupal_set_message()` that we normally use to print out messages to the user, in this case--since we are in the Drush command-line environment--we use the special Drush function for logging messages--`drush_log()`.

One other thing to note is that the name of this function starts with an underscore. This is to denote that it is private and not supposed to be used by anyone else, except our command callback. It's of course not enforceable, but rather a standard naming convention to denote this (used also in other programming languages).

Going back to our command callback, we use our new `createInstanceFromAllConfigs()` method to get our hands on all the available Importers to run. Then, we simply defer back to our helpful function that runs the import and prints the relevant message. That's pretty much it.

Going to our terminal, we first have to clear the Drush cache in order to pick this command up using the following command:

```
drush cc drush
```

Then, we can run either of these command variations for processing all the available importers:

```
drush products-import-run
drush pir
```

Alternatively, we can run a specific importer:

```
drush products-import-run --importer=my_json_product_importer
drush pir --importer=my_json_product_importer
```

Better yet, we can now add these commands to our crontab and have them run at specific intervals, once a day, for example.

Summary

In this chapter, we got to implement some fun stuff. We created our very own content and configuration entity types as well as a custom plugin type to handle our logic.

What we built was a Product entity type that holds some product-like data in various types of fields. We even created a bundle configuration entity type so that we can have multiple types of products with the possibility of different fields per bundle, a great data model.

We wanted to be able to import products from all sorts of external resources. For this reason, we created the Importer plugin type that is responsible for doing the actual imports--a great functional model. However, these only work based on a set of configurations, which we represented via a configuration entity type. These can then be created in the UI and exported into YAML files like any other configuration.

Finally, to use the importers, we created a Drush command, that can process either a single Importer or all the existing ones. This can be used inside a crontab for automatic imports.

There are still some shortcomings to the way we constructed the importing functionality, though. For example, we added the URL field on the Importer configuration entity as if all imports need to happen from an external resource. What if we want an import to be from a CSV file? The URL field would be superfluous, and we'd need a file upload field on the configuration entity. This very much points to the difference between generic Importer configuration values and the plugin-specific ones. In future chapters, we'll come back to our module and make some adjustments in this respect.

In the next chapter, we will look at the Database API and how we can directly interact with the underlying storage engine.

8

The Database API

In the previous two chapters, we discussed and our options as Drupal 8 module developers for modeling and storing data in Drupal 8. We also saw some examples of how to use things such as the State, Configuration, and Entity APIs, going to greater lengths with the latter by using it to build something useful. One of the key takeaways from these chapters is that--compared to Drupal 7, at least--the need for custom database tables and/or direct queries against these and the database has become minimal.

The Entity system is much more flexible and robust, the combination of configuration and content entities providing much of the needs for storing data. Moreover, the Entity query and loading mechanisms have also made finding them easy.Odds are, this is enough for most of your cases.

Furthermore, storage subsystems such as the State API (key value) and UserData have also removed much of the need for creating custom tables to store that kind of "one-off" data. Also, the configuration API provides a unified way to model exportable data, leaving no need for something else.

However, apart from these features, Drupal also has a strong database API that actually powers them under the hood. This API is made available to us in case we need it. For example, we can create our own database tables and then run queries against them however we want, all through a secure layer that can work on top of multiple types of databases.

Creating custom database tables is not something you will do very often, maybe never, but in this chapter, you will still learn how the API works in order to do so. There are contributed modules out there that have legitimate uses for them, and who knows you might also use them. So, it is still important to understand. However, even more pertinent is the API for running queries (particularly select queries), because you may need to run these, even against entities. There are times in which the Entity Query does not provide all you need, so looking up entities based on complex queries can, in fact, be more common. Hence, we will cover how to do that in this chapter, as well.

More concretely, in this chapter, we will start by creating a couple of database tables so that we can see how the Schema API works in Drupal 8. For D7 developers, this will look strikingly familiar. Then, we will see the various ways we can perform queries against these tables by using the database abstraction layer. We can make two different types of select queries, and we will practice both. For the others (INSERT, UPDATE, and DELETE), there is a standard way of doing it. Next, we will take a look at how queries can be altered and how we can tag them for targeting. Finally, we will look at the database update hooks, which were one of the principle ways configuration was being deployed in previous versions of Drupal. In reality, the purpose of these hooks is to make database updates once the tables have already been created.

The Schema API

The purpose of the Schema API is to allow the definition of database table structures in PHP and to have Drupal interact with the database engine and turn these definitions into a reality. Apart from the fact that we don't ever have to see things such as CREATE TABLE, we ensure that our table structures can be applied to multiple types of databases. If you remember, in Chapter 1, *Developing for Drupal 8*, it was mentioned that Drupal can work with MySQL, PostgreSQL, SQLite, and others, if they support PDO, so the Schema API ensures this cross-compatibility.

The central component of the Schema API is hook_schema(). This is used to provide the initial table definitions of a given module. Implementations of this hook belong in the *.install file of the module and are fired when the module is first installed. If alterations need to be made to the existing database tables, there are a number of methods that can be used inside update hooks to make these changes.

In this section, we will create a new module called sports in which we want to define two tables--players and teams. The records in the former can reference records in the latter, as each player can be part of only one team at a time. This is a simple example, and one which could, and should, be implemented using entities. However, for the purpose of demonstrating the database API, we will stick with the manual setup.

So, in our sports.install file, we can implement hook_schema() as follows:

```
/**
 * Implements hook_schema().
 */
function sports_schema() {
  $schema = [];

  $schema['teams'] = [
```

```
    'description' => 'The table that holds team data.',
    'fields' => [
      'id' => [
        'description' => 'The primary identifier.',
        'type' => 'serial',
        'unsigned' => TRUE,
        'not null' => TRUE,
      ],
      'name' => [
        'description' => 'The team name.',
        'type' => 'varchar',
        'length' => 255,
        'not null' => TRUE,
      ],
      'description' => [
        'description' => 'The team description.',
        'type' => 'text',
        'size' => 'normal',
      ],
    ],
    'primary key' => ['id'],
];

$schema['players'] = [
    'description' => 'The table that holds player data.',
    'fields' => [
      'id' => [
        'description' => 'The primary identifier.',
        'type' => 'serial',
        'unsigned' => TRUE,
        'not null' => TRUE,
      ],
      'team_id' => [
        'description' => 'The ID of the team it belongs to.',
        'type' => 'int',
        'unsigned' => TRUE,
      ],
      'name' => [
        'description' => 'The player name.',
        'type' => 'varchar',
        'length' => 255,
        'not null' => TRUE,
      ],
      'data' => [
        'description' => 'Arbitrary data about the player.',
        'type' => 'blob',
        'size' => 'big',
      ],
```

```
    ],
    'primary key' => ['id'],
  ];

  return $schema;
}
```

Implementations of this hook need to return an associative array keyed by the table name whose values are an array that defines the respective table. The table definition consists of various types of information, particularly the individual column definitions (fields), and also things such as which fields represent the primary key, foreign keys (strictly for documentation purposes), unique keys, and indexes. For a full reference of all the available options, check out the Drupal.org (https://www.drupal.org/) documentation pages for the Schema API.

In our preceding example, we defined the two tables we mentioned and defined their fields inside the fields array. The primary key indicates which of the tables will be used for that purpose, opting for the standard id field for both. Speaking of which, the latter is a field of the type serial, which means that it is an integer that has an auto-increment option to it. For number fields such as integer, float, and numeric, the unsigned option means that numbers cannot go below 0. Also, the not null is pretty easy to understand--it prevents the column from ever being empty.

For the team and player name, we opted for a simple varchar field that takes a maximum of 255 characters (a pretty standard table column definition), and these, too, cannot be null. The description field, on the other hand, is of the text type with the normal size (as opposed to tiny, small, medium, or big). In here, we want to store strings that are longer than 255 characters. At the time of writing this book, there is no full documentation for the available data types (and their options) for Drupal 8; however, the D7 version (https://www.drupal.org/docs/7/api/schema-api/data-types) is a good indicator and will pretty much work exactly the same.

Lastly, for the player, we also have a team_id, which is a simple integer field, and a data column, in which we want to store some arbitrary serialized data. This is a blob type, which can also be big or normal.

That is pretty much all for our schema definitions. Installing the `sports` module will create these tables for us automatically, according to these definitions. Also, just as important, uninstalling the module will delete these tables, so we don't need to do any kind of handling. However, if our module is already enabled and we have added this implementation afterward, it won't get fired. Instead, we will need to implement an update hook and use the `drupal_install_schema()` function, which will trigger it, as follows:

```
drupal_install_schema('sports');
```

We will see more about update hooks soon.

Running queries

Now that we have some tables to work with, let's take a look at how we can run queries against them. If you are following along, for testing purposes, feel free to add some dummy data into the tables via the database management tool of your choice. We will look at `INSERT` statements soon, but before that, we will need to talk about the more common types of queries you'll run--`SELECT`.

Queries using the Drupal 8 database abstraction layer are run using a central database connection service--`database`. Statically, this can be accessed via a shortcut:

```
$database = \Drupal::database();
```

This service is a special one compared to the ones we saw before, because it is actually created using a factory:

```
database:
    class: Drupal\Core\Database\Connection
    factory: Drupal\Core\Database\Database::getConnection
    arguments: [default]
```

This is a definition by which the responsibility for the instantiation is delegated to the factory mentioned, instead of the container as we've seen before. So, the resulting class does not necessarily need to match the one specified for the `class` key. However, in this case, the `Drupal\Core\Database\Connection` is an abstract base class that the resulting service extends. Again, in this case, the `arguments` are responsible for specifying the type of connection that it has to create. The site-default type is used (MySQL, usually), which means that the resulting service will be an instance of `Drupal\Core\Database\Driver\mysql\Connection`.

From this connection service, we can then request the relevant object with which we can build queries. So, let's see how these work.

Select queries

There are two ways we can run select queries in Drupal 8, and they both work similarly to the way they did in Drupal 7. We have the D8 equivalents of db_query() and db_query_range() and the equivalent of db_select(). This will look familiar to D7 developers. In Drupal 8, these procedural functions still exist, but, in a deprecated state. This only means that instead of using the old functions, we should use the connection service I mention next.

The first type of select queries are typically more performant because we construct them by writing the SQL statements ourselves (with placeholders, of course), whereas the db_select() type of query is an OOP query builder that still needs to transform a chained object construct into an SQL statement. However, don't let this performance be a real deciding factor, because as you can imagine, the impact is minimal. Also, the query builder is the more proper way of running queries, because they are alterable (can be deconstructed).

Also, the first type of select query is typically used for simpler queries, but if you are an SQL guru, it can actually be faster and easier to write a complex query using that method. Moreover, they rely on developers, ensuring that the SQL statement is compatible with the underlying database. So, it is up to you which of the two types you choose, considering all of these factors.

Let's first take a look at how we can run a basic query against our tables using the db_query()-like method. We'll then see how the same query can be run using the other way:

```
$database = \Drupal::database();
$result = $database->query("SELECT * FROM {players} WHERE id = :id", [':id'
=> 1]);
```

This is a simple SQL statement, albeit a bit funky if you have not done any D7 development. We passed the query to the first parameter of the `query()` method of the connection object as a string whereas we would pass an array of placeholder values for the second parameter. These are found throughout the SQL string proceeded by a colon (`:id`) and are later replaced with the value that maps to the same key in the placeholder values array. Another thing to note is that the table name in the query is surrounded by curly braces. This is because in reality, table names can be prefixed when the site is installed, and our code should not concern itself with that prefix. Drupal will prepend it automatically.

Now, let's take a look at how we can run the same query using the query builder:

```
$result = $database->select('players', 'p')
  ->fields('p')
  ->condition('id', 1)
  ->execute();
```

This time, we will use the `select()` method on the connection object to get our hands on a `SelectInterface` instance with which we can build our query. We need to pass the table we want to query to it, as well as an alias for that table. This is particularly important when performing joins. Then, we use the `fields()` method to specify which of the table columns we want to retrieve. The first parameter is the table alias, whereas the second (optional) is an array of column names. Ll columns will be included (`*`). Next, we have a single condition being applied to the query for the column `id` and value 1. The third optional parameter is the operator that defaults to `=`. Lastly, we execute the query and get the same result as with the preceding example.

You will immediately note, if you remember, that the structure of this query builder is very similar to the Entity Query, and the components are also chainable to a certain extent, as we will see.

Handling the result

Both of the preceding queries return a `StatementInterface`, which is traversable. So, to access its data, we can do this:

```
foreach ($result as $record) {
  $id = $record->id;
  $team_id = $record->team_id;
  $name = $record->name;
  $data = $record->data;
}
```

Each item in the loop is a `stdClass`, and their property names are the actual names of the columns returned, while their values are the column values.

Alternatively, the `StatementInterface` also has some fetcher methods that can prepare the results for us in different ways. These mostly come from the parent `\PDOStatement` class, which is native PHP. The simplest is `fetchAll()`:

```
$records = $result->fetchAll();
```

This returns an array of `stdClass` objects as we saw before, so it does all the looping to extract the records for us. If we want this array keyed by the value of a field in the record, we can perform the following:

```
$records = $result->fetchAllAssoc('id');
```

This will use the value in the `id` field to key the array.

If we're expecting single records, we can also use the `fetch()` method, which returns only one such object (the next one in the result set); `fetchObject()` does the same thing.

More complex select queries

Let's create a more complex query now, to join our team table and retrieve the team information in the same record as the player:

```
$result = $database->query("SELECT * FROM {players} p JOIN {teams} t ON
t.id = p.team_id WHERE p.id = :id", [':id' => 1]);
```

This will return the same record as before, but inclusive of the values from the matching team record. Note that since we have a join, we had to use table aliases here as well. There is one problem with this query, though--since both tables have the `name` column, we cannot use the `*` to include all of the fields, as they will get overridden. Instead, we need to include them manually:

```
$result = $database->query("SELECT p.id, p.name as player_name, t.name as
team_name, t.description as team_description, p.data FROM {players} p JOIN
{teams} t ON t.id = p.team_id WHERE p.id = :id", [':id' => 1]);
```

As you can see, we specified the fields from both tables we wanted to include, and we indicated different names as aliases where there was a name conflict. Now, let's write the same query using the query builder:

```
$query = $database->select('players', 'p');
$query->join('teams', 't');
$query->addField('p', 'name', 'player_name');
$query->addField('t', 'name', 'team_name');
$query->addField('t', 'description', 'team_description');
$result = $query
  ->fields('p', ['id', 'data'])
  ->condition('p.id', 1)
  ->execute();

$records = $result->fetchAll();
```

First of all, not all methods on the query builder are chainable. The `join()` method (and the other types of join methods, such as `innerJoin()`, `leftJoin()`, and `rightJoin()`) and the `addField()` method are prominent examples. The latter is a way we can add fields to the query by specifying an alias (we cannot do it via the `fields()` method). Moreover, the `condition()` field is also prefixed with the table alias it needs to be in (which was not necessary before, when we didn't use a join).

For all the other methods useful for building queries, go to `SelectInterface` and `ConditionInterface`. They are typically well documented in there.

Range queries

Since limiting queries to a certain range depends on the underlying database engine, we also have the `queryRange()` method on our database connection service, which we can use to write queries that include ranges:

```
$result = $database->queryRange("SELECT * FROM {players}", 0, 10);
```

In this example, we query for all the players and limit the result set to the first ten records (from 0 to 10). So, with this method, the placeholder value array is the fourth parameter after `$from` and `$count`.

Alternatively, using the SELECT query builder, we have a method on the SelectInterface whereby we can specify a range. So, in that format, the preceding query would look like this:

```
$result = $database->select('players', 'p')
  ->fields('p')
  ->range(0, 10)
  ->execute();
```

As you can see, we have the range() method, which takes those arguments and limits the query.

A note on running select queries on Entity tables: if you can do so using the Entity Query, use that. If not, feel free to use the database API. However, stick to using the query to figure out the IDs of the entities you need, but then use the entity storage handler to load those entities properly. This is unlike the many times in Drupal 7 where we simply used field values from such queries directly. In Drupal 8, that is highly discouraged.

Pagers

Now that we saw how to make SELECT queries of all kinds, let's take a look at how we can use Drupal's built-in pagination capabilities and how pagers work in Drupal 8. We will illustrate these by running some queries and rendering the results inside a table. Refer to Chapter 4, *Theming*, if you don't remember the theming aspects of outputting a table.

Our playground will be inside a new controller method (SportsController::players()) that maps to the route with the /players path. Refer to Chapter 2, *Creating Your First Module*, for a refresher on how to create routes if you don't remember.

The first thing we'll do is create a simple query that loads all the players and outputs them inside a table. We'll stick to only showing the player names for simplicity:

```
/**
 * Renders a table of players.
 */
public function players() {
  $query = $this->database->select('players', 'p')
    ->fields('p');
  $result = $query->execute()->fetchAll();
  $header = [$this->t('Name')];
```

```
$rows = [];

foreach ($result as $row) {
  $rows[] = [
    $row->name
  ];
}

$build = [];
$build[] = [
  '#theme' => 'table',
  '#header' => $header,
  '#rows' => $rows,
];

  return $build;
}
```

All of this should already be familiar to you. We are running the query and preparing the data for a table, using the `table` theme hook to render it. You'll note that we are creating a `$build` array so that we can include more things in the final output. This will be our baseline to explore pagers.

Pagers work by storing some information regarding a query in the global state, namely the total number of items to be paged, the limit of items per page, and an identifier for the respective pager (so we can potentially have multiple pagers at once). All of this information is set using the following code:

```
pager_default_initialize($total, $limit, $element = 0);
```

Moreover, the current page is determined by the query parameter in the URL, named `page`.

Once the pager is initialized, we have a `pager` render element we can use to easily render a themed pager that uses this information and builds all the necessary links to move across the pages. As query builders, we then have to read the current page and use that inside our query.

However, there is a much simpler way to work with pagers, and that is using *select extenders*. These are *decorator* classes for the SELECT query class we've seen before, and they allow us to decorate it with an extra functionality, such as pagers or sorting; they encapsulate the necessary functionality for handling pagers in the query. So, let's see it in action.

Here is how our player query would look using the `PagerSelectExtender`:

```
$limit = 5; // The number of items per page.
$query = $this->database->select('players', 'p')
  ->fields('p')
  ->extend('\Drupal\Core\Database\Query\PagerSelectExtender')
  ->limit($limit);
$result = $query->execute()->fetchAll();
```

As you can see, we have an `extend()` method on the SELECT query builder, which allows us to pass the name of the class that will decorate the resulting SELECT query class. This also provides us with a new method called `limit()`, through which we specify the number of records to load per page. Under the hood, it uses the `range()` method we saw earlier. Moreover, when running the query, it initializes the pager for us using `pager_default_initialize()`, and even determines the current page all on its own.

 The *Decorator Pattern* is an object-oriented programming design pattern that allows us to statically or dynamically add behavior to an existing object without altering how it, or other objects of the same class, behaves inside. A decorator essentially wraps an existing object to provide an extra functionality from the outside.

So, all we need to do now is render the following pager (below the table):

```
$build[] = [
  '#type' => 'pager'
];
```

Positively rocket science, right? Not really. If we refresh the page, we should now see only five players in the table, and also a pager below it.

The Pager render element (`https://api.drupal.org/api/drupal/core%21lib%21Drupal%21Core%21Render%21Element%21Pager.php/class/Pager/8.2.x`) has some interesting properties to customize it further. We can append query elements to the resulting links, or even specify another route for the links if we want to. We can, of course, control the label of the pager links, and even the number of links being output. Check out the documentation of this element for more information.

Moreover, for full customization, we also have the option of preprocessing these variables by implementing our own preprocessor for the `pager` hook (such as `template_preprocess_page`) and/or overriding the `pager.twig.html` template file. How to do the things that we covered in Chapter 4, *Theming*.

Insert queries

In order to get data into our custom database tables, we have an INSERT query builder that we can use. For this, and, the other types of queries, it is highly discouraged to use the db_query() approach because Drupal cannot ensure that it works across the different types of database engines. Instead, we can use the insert() method on the connection service and build our query using the Insert object that gets returned. So, let's see how we can add a record to our players table:

```
$database->insert('players');
$fields = ['name' => 'Diego M', 'data' => serialize(['known for' => 'Hand
of God'])];
$id = $database->insert('players')
  ->fields($fields)
  ->execute();
```

The main thing about an insert query is the fields() method. It expects an array of key/value pairs, where the keys are the column names and the values are the data that needs to be added to the respective columns. Alternatively, the first argument can be an array of the column names and the second an array of the values in the same order as the column names from the first array.

We can also run an INSERT query with multiple sets of values (records):

```
$values = [
  ['name' => 'Novak D.', 'data' => serialize(['sport' => 'tennis'])],
  ['name' => 'Micheal P.', 'data' => serialize(['sport' => 'swimming'])]
];
$fields = ['name', 'data'];
$query =  $database->insert('players')
  ->fields($fields);
foreach ($values as $value) {
  $query->values($value);
}
$result = $query->execute();
```

In the preceding example, the fields() method receives only an array of column names that need to be inserted, and we use subsequent values() method calls to add the individual values.

The `execute()` method typically returns the ID (primary key) of the last record to be inserted. This is handy, especially if you insert only one record however, for multiple inserts, it can also be misleading. So, do experiment for yourself with different use cases.

Update queries

Now that we've seen `INSERT` queries, let's take a look at how we can update existing records. Say we wanted to update one of our player records; we will do so as follows:

```
$result = $database->update('players')
    ->fields(['data' => serialize(['sport' => 'swimming', 'feature' => 'This
guy can swim'])])
    ->condition('name', 'Micheal P.')
    ->execute();
```

`UPDATE` queries are like `INSERT` ones, except that they take a `condition()` to figure out which records to update (all that match the condition). Leaving this out will update all records, naturally. Using the `fields()` method, we will simply specify which columns are getting updated, and with what. If we leave out a column, it will stay untouched. Lastly, the result of this query is the total number of records affected.

Delete queries

Lastly, we can also get rid of our records using the `DELETE` query:

```
$result = $database->delete('players')
    ->condition('name', 'Micheal P.')
    ->execute();
```

All the records that match the condition will get removed. Be careful with this because as with update queries, leaving out a condition will basically truncate your table, and the query will return the number of records affected, that is, deleted.

 Although you can make `SELECT` queries against entity and field tables to find the IDs of the entities you want to load, you should never perform `INSERT`, `UPDATE`, or `DELETE` queries against these tables. You run a very high risk of corrupting your data.

Transactions

The Drupal database API also provides a way to represent and handle database transactions (for the database types which support them). Transactions are ways in which database operations can be wrapped and grouped together in view of committing them, all or none. For example, if you have multiple records that are related, it's possible you will want only some of them written if one fails its INSERT operation for some reason. This could leave you with a corrupt or incomplete data that could throw your application into a spin.

Performing multiple database-changing operations after a transaction has been opened only finalizes (commits) those changes to the database when that transaction closes. If something goes wrong, it can also be rolled back, which will prevent the data from being committed.

In Drupal 8, a transaction is represented by a Transaction object (a specific subclass for each database type). As soon as the object is destroyed (is no longer in scope), the operations get committed to the database. However, if we get an indication that something went wrong in our operations (usually via catching an exception), we can roll back the transaction, which will stop those operations from being committed. Moreover, transactions can be nested, so Drupal keeps track of transactions that have been opened within the scope of other transactions.

Let's see an example of how to use transactions:

```
$transaction = $database->startTransaction();
try {
  $database->update('players')
    ->fields(['data' => serialize(['sport' => 'tennis', 'feature' => 'This
guy can play tennis'])])
    ->condition('name', 'Novak D.')
    ->execute();
}
catch (\Exception $e) {
  $transaction->rollback();
  watchdog_exception('my_type', $e);
}
```

The first thing we did was start a transaction using our connection service. Then, we wrapped our operation in a try/catch block to catch any exceptions that might be thrown in performing them. If one does get thrown, we roll back the transaction, because we don't want to commit anything to the database, as we don't know what failed and what shape our data is in. Finally, we used the `watchdog_exception()` helper to log the exception to the database log. Do note that logging this before the rollback would prevent the exception from being written to the database as well.

If there is no exception, the operation gets committed as soon as the `$transaction` variable gets removed and is no longer in scope (usually at the end of the function). It is also interesting to note that if within this transaction we call another function in which we perform database operations, those operations will be part of this same transaction by default. So, they also get rolled back, if we roll back or get committed if we don't. This is why the database watchdog log will not be saved if called before the rollback.

Query alters

Lots of things in Drupal are alterable using various hooks; queries are no different. This means that if a module writes a query such as we've seen before, other modules can alter it by implementing `hook_query_alter()`. So let's consider an example of how this may work.

Let's assume the following query, which simply returns all player records:

```
$result = $database->select('players', 'p')
  ->fields('p')
  ->execute();
```

Imagine that another module wants to alter this query and limit the results to find only the players in a specific team. There is one problem. Our query has no markers that can indicate to another module that this is the one that needs to be altered. As you can imagine, there are a bunch of queries run in any given request, so identifying queries becomes impossible. In such a situation, enter *query tags*.

The preceding query would not be alterable because it's not recognizable, and therefore, `hook_query_alter()` is not even fired on it. In order to make it alterable, we will need to add a query tag and make it identifiable. There is a simple method on the query builder for doing just that--`addTag()`:

```
$result = $database->select('players', 'p')
  ->fields('p')
  ->addTag('player_query')
  ->execute();
```

Query tags are simple strings that can be read from inside a `hook_query_alter()` implementation. So, we could alter the query like this:

```
/**
 * Implements hook_query_alter().
 */
function
hello_world_query_alter(Drupal\Core\Database\Query\AlterableInterface
$query) {
  if (!$query->hasTag('player_query')) {
    return;
  }

  // Alter query
}
```

The only parameter of this hook is the query object onto which we can apply our changes. It also has methods for reading the tags, such as `hasTag()`, `hasAnyTag()`, or `hasAllTags()`. In the preceding example, we took a defensive approach and simply exited if the query was not about our `player_query` tagged query. I'll come back to this later on.

Now, let's see how we can alter this query to achieve what we set out to do:

```
$query->join('teams', 't', 't.id = p.team_id');
$query->addField('t', 'name', 'team_name');
$query->condition('t.name', 'My Team');
```

As you can see in the preceding example, we are doing a similar thing to what we did before when we built our joined query. We join the team table, add its name field (as a bonus), and set a condition to only return the players in a certain team. Easy peasy.

Let's now return for a second to my remark about the defensive approach we took with this hook implementation. I personally prefer to keep methods short and return early, rather than have a bunch of unintelligible nested conditions. This is typically easy to do in an object-oriented setting. However, with procedural code, it becomes a bit more tedious, as you need many private functions that are tricky to name, and even more so with hook implementations into which you might need to add more than one block of code. For example, in our `hook_query_alter()` implementation, we might need to add an alteration for another query later on. Also, since we return early, we need to add another condition for checking for two tags, and then some more conditions and if statements, and even more conditions (rant over). From a PHP point of view, in this case, you'd delegate the actual logic to another function based on the tag of the query, either using a simple switch block or if conditionals. This way, if a new tag comes, a new function can be created for it specifically and called from the switch block. However, we can do one better in this case.

There are a few hooks, particularly alter ones, which have a general targeting but also a more specific one. In this example, we also have a `hook_query_TAG_alter()` hook, which is specific to a given tag. So, instead of us delegating to other functions, we could implement the hook for this and any of our other, future queries we need altered in this module:

```
/**
 * Implements hook_query_TAG_alter().
 */
function
hello_world_query_player_query_alter(Drupal\Core\Database\Query\AlterableIn
terface $query) {
  // Sure to alter only the "player_query" tagged queries.
}
```

So, essentially, the tag itself becomes part of the query name, and we don't need any extra functions.

Update hooks

At the beginning of this chapter, we defined two tables using `hook_schema()`, which got installed together with the module. To reiterate, if the module had already been installed, we could have triggered the schema installation using the `drupal_install_schema()` function. However, what if we needed to add another column later on, say to the `teams` table? Our module is installed, and so is the schema; so, we cannot exactly uninstall it on production just for triggering the schema creation again, not to mention losing the data. Luckily, there is a system in place for this, in the name of *update* hooks--`hook_update_N()`--where N represents the schema version. These are sequentially named hook implementations that go inside the module `*.install` file and which are triggered when running the updates, either via going to `/update.php` or by using the `drush updatedb` command.

The main purpose of these update hooks is making schema alterations to existing database tables. However, partly due to the weak configuration management system in earlier versions of Drupal, they have evolved--through developer creativity--into a mechanism for updating various types of configuration or performing tasks (even content related) upon a deployment to the next environment. Helping out with this is the `$sandbox` argument passed to the hook implementations, which can be used for batching these operations (to prevent an execution timeout). We will not cover this aspect here, but will instead talk about the standalone Batch API in a future chapter, lessons from which you'll be able to apply here as well. Instead, we will see how to implement such a hook to perform schema updates.

As mentioned, these hook implementations go into the `*.install` file. Let's see an example:

```
/**
 * Update hook for performing an update task.
 */
function my_module_update_8001(&$sandbox) {
  // Do stuff
}
```

The DocBlock of this hook implementation needs to contain a description of what it does. It is used when running the updates (either via the UI or using Drush).

The name of the function is one of its most important aspects. It starts with the module name, followed by `update`, and finally, by the module's schema version (the next one if we want this update hook to actually run); but what is a module's schema version?

When installed, Drupal sets each module a schema version--8000. In Drupal 7, it was 7000, and in 6, it was 6000. You get the difference between the major versions of Drupal. When an update hook runs, Drupal sets that module's schema version to the number found in the update hook. So, in the preceding example, it will be 8001. This is to keep track of all the update hooks and to not run them more than once. By convention, but not necessity, the second from left digit in the schema version represents the major version number of the module itself. For example, for an `8.x-1.x` version, it would be 8101.

Let's now see how we can alter our `teams` database table with an update hook and add a column to store a `location` string field. The first thing we want to do is update our `hook_schema()` implementation and add this information there as well. This won't do anything in our case; however, due to the way update hooks work, we need to do it. What I mean by this is that if a module is first installed and it has update hooks in it already, those update hooks do not run, but the module's schema version gets set as the number of the last update hook found in it. So, if we do not add our new column inside the `hook_schema()`, installing this module on another site (or even on the current one after an uninstall) will not get our new column in. So, we need to account for both situations.

In the field definition of our `teams` table schema, we can add the following column definition:

```
'location' => [
  'description' => 'The team location.',
  'type' => 'varchar',
  'length' => 255,
],
```

It's as simple as that. Next, we can implement an update hook and add this field to the table:

```
/**
 * Adds a the "location" field to the teams table.
 */
function sports_update_8001(&$sandbox) {
  $field = [
    'description' => 'The team location.',
    'type' => 'varchar',
    'length' => 255,
  ];
  $schema = $database = \Drupal::database()->schema();
  $schema->addField('teams', 'location', $field);
}
```

Here, we used the same field definition, loaded the database connection service, and used its schema object to add that field to the table. The code itself is pretty self-explanatory, but it's also worth mentioning that this is an example in which we cannot inject the service, and we have to use it statically. So, don't feel bad for situations like this.

Next, we can use Drush to run the updates:

```
vagrant@vagrant:/var/www$ drush updb -y
The following updates are pending:

sports module :
  8001 -   Adds a the "location" field to the teams table.

Do you wish to run all pending updates? (y/n): y
Performing sports_update_8001
Cache rebuild complete.
Finished performing updates.
vagrant@vagrant:/var/www$ ▉
```

Sure enough, the `teams` table now has a new column. If you try to run the updates again, you'll note that there are none to be run because Drupal has set the schema version of the `sports` module to 8001. So, the next one in line to be run has to have 8002 at the end (or, something greater than 8001 and lower than 9000, in any case).

In the preceding example, we added a new field to an existing table. However, we might need to create a new table entirely, or even delete one. The schema object on the database connection service has the relevant methods to do so. The following are a few examples, but I recommend that you check out the base `Drupal\Core\Database\Schema` class for the available methods:

```
$schema->createTable('new_table', $table_definition);
$schema->addField('teams', 'location', $field);
$schema->dropTable('table_name');
$schema->dropField('table_name', 'field_to_delete');
$schema->changeField('table_name', 'field_name_to_change',
'new_field_name', $new_field_definition);
```

There are a few cautionary aspects you need to consider when using update hooks. For example, you cannot be sure of the state of the environment before the hooks actually run, so ensure that you account for this. I recommend you check out the documentation (`https://api.drupal.org/api/drupal/core%21lib%21Drupal%21Core%21Extension%21module.api.php/function/hook_update_N/8.2.x`) about `hook_update_N()` and carefully read the section about the function body.

Summary

In this chapter, we looked at the basics of interacting with the database API. Although it's something that has taken a significant step back in importance in day-to-day Drupal module development, it's important to understand and be able work with.

We started the chapter by creating our very own database tables to hold player and team information in a relational way. We've done so using an API that transforms definitions into actual tables without us having to even understand much of MySQL. The SQL terminology and basic operations are, however, something that every developer should be familiar with, notwithstanding their actual day to day application in Drupal.

Then, we looked at some examples of how we can run SELECT, INSERT, UPDATE, and DELETE queries using both the more SQL-oriented way of writing statements and the query builder approach, which uses an OO representation of the queries. We've also seen how these queries can be wrapped into transactions (where supported) so that we can commit data changes while minimizing the potential for incomplete or corrupt data. Finally, we've seen how these queries can be altered using query tags, allowing for yet another small extension point that other modules can contribute through. Regardless of how we build our queries, however, a key takeaway is that using this API is crucial for a secure interaction with the database. Moreover, it accounts for cross-compatibility with the different database types Drupal can work with.

Lastly, we looked at update hooks and how they can be used to perform changes to our database tables. More than that, they can be employed to perform some other tasks that might need to be coded and then deployed to the next environment to be run once. However, due to the Drupal 8 configuration API, the need for this has gone down significantly.

In the next chapter, we will look at custom Drupal 8 entity fields and see how we can define our own; yes, we'll be playing with some more plugins.

9
Custom Fields

In Chapter 6, *Data Modeling and Storage*, and Chapter 7, *Your Own Custom Entities and Plugin Types*, we talked quite extensively about content entities and how they use fields to store the actual data that they are supposed to represent. Then, we saw how these fields, apart from interacting with the storage layer for persisting it, extend TypedData API classes in order to organize this data better at the code level. For example, we saw that the `BaseFieldDefinition` instances used on entities are actually data definitions (and so are the `FieldConfig` ones). Moreover, we also saw the Datatype plugins at play there, namely the `FieldItemList` with their individual items, which down the line extend a basic DataType plugin (`Map` in most cases). Also, if you remember, when we were talking about these items, I mentioned how they are actually instances of yet another plugin--`FieldType`. So, essentially, they are a plugin type whose plugins extend plugins of another type. I recommend that you revisit that section if you are fuzzy on the matter.

Most of these concepts are buried inside the Entity API and are only seen and understood by developers. However, the `FieldType` plugins (together with their corresponding `FieldWidget` and `FieldFormatter` plugins) break out and are one of the principle things site builders and content editors actually work with in the UI. They allow users to input structured data and save it to the database. If you recall, I had mentioned them a few times in Chapters 6 and 7, and I promised you a chapter in which we will see how we can create field types that a site builder can then add to an entity type and use for inputting data. Well, this is that chapter, but first, let's do a quick recap on what we know about them.

Field type plugins extend the lower-level TypedData API to create a unique way of not only representing data (within the context of entities), but also storing it to the database (and other stuff as well). They are primarily known as the type of fields site builders can add to an entity type bundle, for example, a plain text field or a select list with multiple options. Nothing can be more common than that in a CMS.

However, they are also used as entity base field types. If you remember our product entity type's name field definition, we actually did use these plugin types:

```
$fields['name'] = BaseFieldDefinition::create('string')
  ->setLabel(t('Name'))
  ->setDescription(t('The name of the Product.'))
  ->setSettings([
    'max_length' => 255,
    'text_processing' => 0,
  ])
  ->setDefaultValue('')
  ->setDisplayOptions('view', [
    'label' => 'hidden',
    'type' => 'string',
    'weight' => -4,
  ])
  ->setDisplayOptions('form', [
    'type' => 'string_textfield',
    'weight' => -4,
  ])
  ->setDisplayConfigurable('form', TRUE)
  ->setDisplayConfigurable('view', TRUE);
```

The create() method of the definition class accepts a FieldType plugin ID. Also, the type of the view display option provided a bit below in the code is a FieldFormatter plugin ID, whereas the type of the form display option provided even lower in the code is a FieldWidget plugin ID.

So, although Drupal has its fair share of complexities, when it comes to fields, things are quite consistent. However, in order to figure out the similarities between base fields and configurable ones, we had to dig a little into the code. The former are not as hip as the ones that you can click together in the UI and which everybody knows are FieldType plugins with corresponding widget and formatter plugins.

A crucial lesson from this introduction that I insist you retain--when defining your custom entities, think about the type of fields you need. If there are bundles that need to have different sets of fields, configurable fields are your choice. Otherwise, base fields are perhaps more appropriate. They sit tightly with your Entity type class, appear on all bundles (if that's something you need), and encourage you to explore the Drupal code base and understand the existing field types, widgets, and formatters better (as well as relevant settings they come with).

Also, when you define base fields, think the same way as you would if adding them through the UI--which field type do I want (find a `FieldType` plugin), how do I want users to interact with it (find a `FieldWidget` plugin), and how do I want its values to be shown (find a `FieldFormatter` plugin). Then, inspect the relevant classes to determine the right settings that will go with them.

In this chapter, we will take a look at how we can create our own custom field type with its own default widget and formatter. To provide a bit of continuity, I am going to ask you to think back to the more complex example employed when talking about the TypedData API--the license plate. We will create a field type designed specifically to store license plates in the following format--*CODE NUMBER* (just as we saw with the example New York plate). Why?

At the moment, there is no field type that can represent this accurately. Of course, we have the simple text field, but that implies having to add both pieces of data that make up a license plate into the same field, stripping them off its meaning. When we were discussing the TypedData API, we saw that one of its core principles is the ability to apply meaning to a piece of data so as to understand that `$license_plate` (for example) is actually a license plate from which we can ask its code and its number (as well as some general description if we want to). Similar to this (or actually building on top of this), fields are also about storing this data. So, apart from understanding it in code, we also need to persist it in the same way. That is, placing the individual pieces of data in separate meaningful table columns as to also persist that meaning.

An example from Drupal core that does the same thing is the `Text (formatted)` field. Apart from its string value, this field also stores a format for each value, which is used upon rendering. Without that format, the string value loses its meaning, and Drupal is no longer able to reliably render it in the way it was intended upon creation. So, you can now see that fields take the idea of meaning from TypedData and also apply it to storage as needed. So, in this chapter, you will learn how these three types of plugins work, by creating your own license plate type field. Let's get started.

Field type

The primary plugin type for creating a field is, as we discussed, the `FieldType`. It is responsible for defining the field structure, how it is stored in the database, and various other settings. Moreover, it also defines a default widget and formatter plugin that will be autoselected when we create the field in the UI. You see, a single field type can work with more than one widget and formatter. If more exist, the site builder can choose one when creating the field and adding it to an entity type bundle.

Otherwise, it will be the default; each field needs one because without a widget, users can't add data, and without a formatter, they can't see it. Also, as you'd expect, widgets and formatters can also work with more than one field type.

The field we will create in this section is for the license plate data, which, as we saw, needs two individual pieces of information--a code (such as the state code) and the number. License plates around the world are more complex than this, but I chose this example to keep things simple.

Our new `FieldType` plugin needs to go inside the `Plugin/Field/FieldType` namespace of a new module we will create called `license_plate`. Although not mandatory, the class name should end with the word `Item`. It's a pretty standard thing done in Drupal core, and we will follow suit. So, let's take a look at our `LicensePlateItem` plugin implementation and then talk about its code:

```
namespace Drupal\license_plate\Plugin\Field\FieldType;

use Drupal\Component\Utility\Random;
use Drupal\Core\Field\FieldDefinitionInterface;
use Drupal\Core\Field\FieldItemBase;
use Drupal\Core\Field\FieldStorageDefinitionInterface;
use Drupal\Core\Form\FormStateInterface;
use Drupal\Core\TypedData\DataDefinition;

/**
 * Plugin implementation of the 'license_plate_type' field type.
 *
 * @FieldType(
 *   id = "license_plate",
 *   label = @Translation("License plate"),
 *   description = @Translation("Field for creating license plates"),
 *   default_widget = "default_license_plate_widget",
 *   default_formatter = "default_license_plate_formatter"
 * )
 */
class LicensePlateItem extends FieldItemBase {}
```

I omitted the class contents, as we will be adding the methods one by one and discussing them individually. However, first, we have the plugin annotation, which is very important. We have the typical plugin metadata such as the ID, label, and description and also will indicate the plugin IDs for the widget and formatter that will be used by default with this field type. Make a note of those, because we will create them soon.

Speaking from experience, often, when creating a field type, you'll extend the class of an already existing field type plugin, such as a text field or an entity reference. This is because Drupal core already comes with a great set of available types, and, usually, all you need is either to make some tweaks to an existing one or maybe combine them or add an extra functionality.

This makes things easier, and you don't have to copy and paste code or come up with it again yourself. Naturally, though, at some point, you'll be extending from `FieldItemBase` because that is the base class all field types need to extend from.

In our example, however, we will extend straight from the `FieldItemBase` abstract class because we want our field to stand on its own. Also, it's not super practical to extend from any existing ones in this case. That is not to say, though, that it doesn't have commonalities with other field types, such as `TextItem`, for example.

Let's now take a look at the first method:

```
/**
 * {@inheritdoc}
 */
public static function defaultStorageSettings() {
  return [
    'number_max_length' => 255,
    'code_max_length' => 5,
  ] + parent::defaultStorageSettings();
}
```

The first thing we do in our class is override the `defaultStorageSettings()` method. The parent class method returns an empty array; however, it's still a good idea to include whatever it returns to our own array. If the parent method changes and returns something later on, we are a bit more robust.

The purpose of this method is two-fold--specify what storage settings this field has and set some defaults for them. Also, note that it is a static method, which means that we are not inside the plugin instance. However, what are storage settings, you may ask?

Storage settings are the configuration that applies to the field everywhere it's used. As you may know, a field can be added to multiple bundles of an entity type. In Drupal 7, you could reuse a field even across entity types, but this is no longer possible, so fields are now reusable only on the bundles of a single entity type. You'll need to create another field of that type if you need it on some other content entity type. So, the storage settings are those that apply to this field across each bundle it is attached to.

They usually deal with things related to the schema--how the database table columns are constructed for this field but they also deal with a lot of other things. Also, even more important to know is that once there is data in the field tables, they cannot be changed. It makes sense, as you cannot easily change database tables when there is data in them. This restriction is something we enforce, as we will see in a bit.

In our example, we only have two storage settings--number_max_length and code_max_length. These will be used when defining the schema for the two-table columns, where the license plate data will be stored (as the maximum length that can be stored in those table fields). By default, we will go with the ever-so-used 255 maximum length on the number column and 5 for the code column, but these are just defaults. The user will be able to change them when creating the field or when editing, as long as there is no data yet.

Next, we can write our storage settings form, which allows users to provide the actual settings when creating a field:

```
/**
 * {@inheritdoc}
 */
public function storageSettingsForm(array &$form, FormStateInterface
$form_state, $has_data) {
  $elements = [];

  $elements['number_max_length'] = [
    '#type' => 'number',
    '#title' => t('Plate number maximum length'),
    '#default_value' => $this->getSetting('number_max_length'),
    '#required' => TRUE,
    '#description' => t('Maximum length for the plate number in
characters.'),
    '#min' => 1,
    '#disabled' => $has_data,
  ];

  $elements['code_max_length'] = [
    '#type' => 'number',
    '#title' => t('Plate code maximum length'),
    '#default_value' => $this->getSetting('code_max_length'),
    '#required' => TRUE,
    '#description' => t('Maximum length for the plate code in
characters.'),
    '#min' => 1,
    '#disabled' => $has_data,
  ];
```

```
        return $elements + parent::storageSettingsForm($form, $form_state,
    $has_data);
    }
```

The preceding method is called by the main field configuration form, and we need to return an array of form elements from it that can be used to set values to the storage settings we defined earlier. We have access to the main `$form` and `$form_state` of the form where this is embedded, as well as a handy Boolean `$has_data`, which tells us whether there is already any data in this field. We use this to disable the elements we don't want to be changed if there is data in the field (in our case, both).

So, basically, our form consists of two number form elements (both required), whose values default to the lengths we specified earlier. The `number` form element also comes with `#min` and `#max` properties, which we can use to restrict the number to a range. Also, we obviously want our minimum lengths to be a positive number, that is, above 1. This method is relatively straightforward to understand if you get the basics of the Form API, which you should by now.

Finally, for our storage handling, we will need to implement the schema method and define our table columns:

```
/**
 * {@inheritdoc}
 */
public static function schema(FieldStorageDefinitionInterface
$field_definition) {
  $schema = [
    'columns' => [
      'number' => [
        'type' => 'varchar',
        'length' => (int)
$field_definition->getSetting('number_max_length'),
      ],
      'code' => [
        'type' => 'varchar',
        'length' => (int) $field_definition->getSetting('code_max_length'),
      ],
    ],
  ];

  return $schema;
}
```

This is another static method, but one that receives the current fields's `FieldStorageDefinitionInterface` instance. From there, we can access the settings the user has saved when creating the field, and based on those, we define our schema. If you've been paying attention in the preceding chapter, when we discussed `hook_schema()`, this should already be very clear to you. What we need to return is an array of column definitions keyed by their name. So, we define two columns of the `varchar` type with the maximum lengths the user has configured--no rocket science involved. Of course, we could have had more storage settings and had this schema definition even more configurable if we'd wanted to.

With these three methods, our storage handling is complete; however, our field type is not quite. We still have a couple more things to take care of.

Apart from storage, as we discussed, fields also deal with data representation at the code level with TypedData structures. So, our field type needs to define its individual properties for which we create storage. For this, we have two main methods--first, to actually define the properties, and then, to set some potential constraints on them:

```
/**
 * {@inheritdoc}
 */
public static function propertyDefinitions(FieldStorageDefinitionInterface
$field_definition) {
  $properties['number'] = DataDefinition::create('string')
    ->setLabel(t('Plate number'));

  $properties['code'] = DataDefinition::create('string')
    ->setLabel(t('Plate code'));

  return $properties;
}
```

The preceding code will look very familiar to the one in Chapter 6, *Data Modeling and Storage*, when we talked about TypedData. Again, this is a static method, which needs to return the `DataDefinitionInterface` instance for the individual properties. We choose to call them `number` and `code`, respectively, and set some sensible labels--nothing too complicated.

The preceding code is actually enough to define the properties, but if you remember, our storage has some maximum lengths in places-meaning that the table columns are only so long. So, if the data that gets into our field is longer, the database engine will throw a fit in a not so graceful way. In other words, it will throw a big exception, and we can't have that. So, there are two things we can do to prevent that--put the same maximum length on the form widget to prevent users from inputting more than they should and add a constraint on our data definitions. The second one is more important because it ensures that the data is valid in any case, whereas the first one only deals with forms. However, since Drupal 8 is so much more API oriented, if we create an entity programmatically and set its field values, we bypass forms completely. However, not to worry; we will also take care of the form, so our users can have a nicer experience and are aware of the maximum size of the values they need to input.

So, let's add the following constraints:

```
/**
 * {@inheritdoc}
 */
public function getConstraints() {
  $constraints = parent::getConstraints();
  $constraint_manager =
\Drupal::typedDataManager()->getValidationConstraintManager();
  $number_max_length = $this->getSetting('number_max_length');
  $code_max_length = $this->getSetting('code_max_length');
  $constraints[] = $constraint_manager->create('ComplexData', [
    'number' => [
      'Length' => [
        'max' => $number_max_length,
        'maxMessage' => t('%name: may not be longer than @max characters.',
[
          '%name' => $this->getFieldDefinition()->getLabel() . ' (number)',
          '@max' => $number_max_length
        ]),
      ],
    ],
    'code' => [
      'Length' => [
        'max' => $code_max_length,
        'maxMessage' => t('%name: may not be longer than @max characters.',
[
          '%name' => $this->getFieldDefinition()->getLabel() . ' (code)',
          '@max' => $code_max_length
        ]),
      ],
    ],
  ]);
```

```
    return $constraints;
  }
```

Since our field class actually implements the `TypedDataInterface`, it also has to implement the `getConstraints()` method (which the `TypedData` parent already starts up). However, we can override it and provide our own constraints based on our field values.

We are taking a slightly different approach here of adding constraints than what we've seen in Chapter 6, *Data Modeling and Storage*. Instead of adding them straight to the data definitions, we will create them manually using the validation constraint manager (which is the plugin manager of the `Constraint` plugin type we saw in Chapter 6, *Data Modeling and Storage*). This is because fields use a specific `ComplexDataConstraint` plugin, which can combine the constraints of multiple properties (data definitions). Do note that even if we had only one property in this field, we'd still be using this constraint plugin.

> There aren't many type of classes in Drupal 8 in which you cannot inject dependencies, but `FieldType` plugins are one of them. So, for this reason, we have to request the services we need statically in this case. This is because these plugins are actually built on top of the `Map` TypedData plugin, and their manager doesn't use a container-aware factory for instantiation but instead delegates it to the `TypedDataManger` service, which, as we saw, is not container aware either.

The data needed to create this constraint plugin is a multidimensional array keyed by the property name, which contains constraint definitions (as we saw in Chapter 6, *Data Modeling and Storage*) for each of them. So, we have a `Length` constraint for both properties, whose options denote a maximum length and a corresponding message if exceeded. If we wanted, we could have had a minimum length in the same way also--`min` and `minMessage`. As for the actual length, we will use the values chosen by the user when creating the field (the storage maximum). Now, regardless of the form widget, our field will not validate unless the maximum lengths are respected.

It's time to finish this class with the following last two methods:

```
/**
 * {@inheritdoc}
 */
public static function generateSampleValue(FieldDefinitionInterface
$field_definition) {
  $random = new Random();
  $values['number'] = $random->word(mt_rand(1,
$field_definition->getSetting('number_max_length')));
  $values['code'] = $random->word(mt_rand(1,
```

```
$field_definition->getSetting('code_max_length')));
    return $values;
}

/**
 * {@inheritdoc}
 */
public function isEmpty() {
    // We consider the field empty if either of the properties is left empty.
    $number = $this->get('number')->getValue();
    $code = $this->get('code')->getValue();
    return $number === NULL || $number === '' || $code === NULL || $code ===
'';
}
```

With `generateSampleValue()`, we create some random words that fit within our field--that's it. This can be used when profiling or site building for populating the field with values. Arguably, this is not going to be your top priority, but it is good to know.

Finally, we have the `isEmpty()` method, which is used to determine whether the field has values or not. It may seem pretty obvious, but it's an important method, especially for us, and you can probably deduce from the implementation why. When creating the field in the UI, the user can specify whether it's required or not. However, typically, that applies (or should apply) to the entire set of values within the field. Also, if the field is not required, and the user only inputs a license plate code without a number, what kind of useful value is that to save? So, we want to make sure that both of them have something before even considering this field as having a value (not being empty), and that is what we are checking in this method.

Now that we are finished with the actual plugin class, there is one last thing that we need to take care of, something that we tend to forget, myself included--configuration schema. Our new field is a configurable field whose settings are stored--guess where?--in configuration. Also, as you remember, all configuration needs to be defined by a schema. Drupal already takes care of those storage settings that come from the parent. However, we need to include ours. So, let's create the typical `license_plate.schema.yml` (inside `config/schema`), where we will put the definitions for the field type and any others that we will need in this module.

Then, we can have the following code inside it:

```
field.storage_settings.license_plate_type:
  type: mapping
  label: 'License plate storage settings'
  mapping:
    number_max_length:
      type: integer
      label: 'Max length for the number'
    code_max_length:
      type: integer
      label: 'Max length for the code'
```

The actual definition will already be familiar, so the only thing that is interesting to explain is its actual naming. The pattern is `field.storage_settings.[field_type_plugin_id]`. Drupal will dynamically read the schema and apply it to the settings of the actual `FieldStorageConfig` entity being exported.

That's it for our `FieldType` plugin. When creating a new field of this type, we have the two storage settings we can configure (which will be disabled when editing if there is actual field data already in the database):

Unless we work only programmatically or via an API to manage the entities that use this field, it won't really be useful, as there are no widgets or formatters it can work with. So, we will need to create those as well.

Field widget

Our new license plate field type could be added to an entity type, but there would be no way users can use it. For this, we will need at least a widget. A given field type can work, however, with multiple widgets. So, let's create that default license plate widget plugin we referenced in the annotation of the field type, which belongs in the `Plugin/Field/FieldWidget` namespace of our module:

```
namespace Drupal\license_plate\Plugin\Field\FieldWidget;

use Drupal\Core\Field\FieldItemListInterface;
use Drupal\Core\Field\WidgetBase;
use Drupal\Core\Form\FormStateInterface;

/**
 * Plugin implementation of the 'default_license_plate_widget' widget.
 *
 * @FieldWidget(
 *   id = "default_license_plate_widget",
 *   label = @Translation("Default license plate widget"),
 *   field_types = {
 *     "license_plate"
 *   }
 * )
 */
class DefaultLicensePlateWidget extends WidgetBase {}
```

Again, we started by examining the annotation and class parents for just a bit. We will notice nothing particularly complicated, except maybe the `field_types` key, which specifies the `FieldType` plugin IDs this widget can work with. Just as a field type can have more than one widget, a widget can work with more than one field type. Also, it's important that we specify it here, otherwise we site builders won't be able to use this widget with our field type.

We extended `WidgetBase`, which implements the obligatory `WidgetInterface` and provides some common defaults for all its subclasses.

The first thing we can do inside the class is handle our settings. First, we will define what settings this widget has and set the default values for these settings:

```
/**
 * {@inheritdoc}
 */
public static function defaultSettings() {
  return [
    'number_size' => 60,
    'code_size' => 5,
    'fieldset_state' => 'open',
    'placeholder' => [
      'number' => '',
      'code' => '',
    ],
  ] + parent::defaultSettings();
}
```

Here, we have some settings specific to how the form widget would be configured for our field. We will use the first two settings mentioned in the preceding code to limit the size of the form element. It will not actually prevent users from filling in longer values, but will be a good indication for them as to how long the values should be. Then, we have the `fieldset_state` setting, which we will use to indicate whether the form fieldset we use to group the two license place textfields is by default open or closed. We will see that in a minute. Lastly, each of these textfields can have a placeholder value (potentially). So, we have that setting as well. Do note that these are all settings we make up and that make sense for our field. You can add your own if you want.

Next, we have the form used to configure these settings (as part of the widget configuration):

```
/**
 * {@inheritdoc}
 */
public function settingsForm(array $form, FormStateInterface $form_state) {
  $elements = [];

  $elements['number_size'] = [
    '#type' => 'number',
    '#title' => t('Size of plate number textfield'),
    '#default_value' => $this->getSetting('number_size'),
    '#required' => TRUE,
    '#min' => 1,
    '#max' => $this->getFieldSetting('number_max_length'),
  ];
```

```
    $elements['code_size'] = [
      '#type' => 'number',
      '#title' => t('Size of plate code textfield'),
      '#default_value' => $this->getSetting('code_size'),
      '#required' => TRUE,
      '#min' => 1,
      '#max' => $this->getFieldSetting('code_max_length'),
    ];

    $elements['fieldset_state'] = [
      '#type' => 'select',
      '#title' => t('Fieldset default state'),
      '#options' => [
        'open' => t('Open'),
        'closed' => t('Closed')
      ],
      '#default_value' => $this->getSetting('fieldset_state'),
      '#description' => t('The default state of the fieldset which contains
the two plate fields: open or closed')
    ];

    $elements['placeholder'] = [
      '#type' => 'details',
      '#title' => t('Placeholder'),
      '#description' => t('Text that will be shown inside the field until a
value is entered. This hint is usually a sample value or a brief
description of the expected format.'),
    ];

    $placeholder_settings = $this->getSetting('placeholder');
    $elements['placeholder']['number'] = [
      '#type' => 'textfield',
      '#title' => t('Number field'),
      '#default_value' => $placeholder_settings['number'],
    ];
    $elements['placeholder']['code'] = [
      '#type' => 'textfield',
      '#title' => t('Code field'),
      '#default_value' => $placeholder_settings['code'],
    ];

    return $elements;
}
```

We have to return the elements for our widget settings, which will then be added to a bigger form (passed as an argument). There is nothing special about the first three form elements. We have two `number` fields and a `select` list to control the first three settings we saw in our defaults. For the first two settings, we want the numbers to be positive and max out at the same maximum length we have set in the storage. We don't want the widget exceeding that length. However, if we want, we can shorten the size of the element.

The textfields for the two placeholder values are wrapped inside a `details` form element. The latter is a fieldset that can be open or closed and can contain other form elements. We will use the same to wrap the actual textfields with which users will input license plate data.

The preceding form will look like this when users configure the widget:

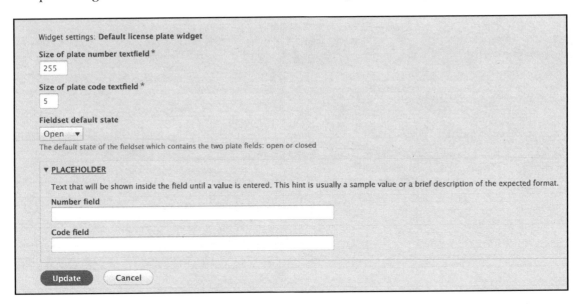

Lastly, we have the summary of the settings the widget, which will be displayed in the "Manage form display" page for our field:

```php
/**
 * {@inheritdoc}
 */
public function settingsSummary() {
  $summary = [];

  $summary[] = t('License plate size: @number (for number) and @code (for
code)', ['@number' => $this->getSetting('number_size'), '@code' =>
$this->getSetting('code_size')]);
```

```
  $placeholder_settings = $this->getSetting('placeholder');
  if (!empty($placeholder_settings['number']) &&
!empty($placeholder_settings['code'])) {
    $placeholder = $placeholder_settings['number'] . ' ' .
$placeholder_settings['code'];
    $summary[] = t('Placeholder: @placeholder', ['@placeholder' =>
$placeholder]);
  }
  $summary[] = t('Fieldset state: @state', ['@state' =>
$this->getSetting('fieldset_state')]);

  return $summary;
}
```

This method needs to return an array of strings that will make up the settings summary. That is what we will do now--reading all of our settings values and listing them out in a human-friendly way. The end result will look something like this:

Default license plate widget ▾

License plate size: 255 (for number) and 5 (for code)
Placeholder: NY 543345
Fieldset state: open

Next, we will have to implement the core of the field widget plugins--the actual form used for inputting the field data:

```
/**
 * {@inheritdoc}
 */
public function formElement(FieldItemListInterface $items, $delta, array
$element, array &$form, FormStateInterface $form_state) {
  $element['details'] = [
    '#type' => 'details',
    '#title' => $element['#title'],
    '#open' => $this->getSetting('fieldset_state') == 'open' ? TRUE :
FALSE,
    '#description' => $element['#description'],
  ] + $element;

  $placeholder_settings = $this->getSetting('placeholder');
  $element['details']['code'] = [
    '#type' => 'textfield',
    '#title' => t('Plate code'),
    '#default_value' => isset($items[$delta]->code) ? $items[$delta]->code
: NULL,
    '#size' => $this->getSetting('code_size'),
    '#placeholder' => $placeholder_settings['code'],
    '#maxlength' => $this->getFieldSetting('code_max_length'),
```

```
      '#description' => '',
      '#required' => $element['#required'],
    ];

    $element['details']['number'] = [
      '#type' => 'textfield',
      '#title' => t('Plate number'),
      '#default_value' => isset($items[$delta]->number) ?
$items[$delta]->number : NULL,
      '#size' => $this->getSetting('number_size'),
      '#placeholder' => $placeholder_settings['number'],
      '#maxlength' => $this->getFieldSetting('number_max_length'),
      '#description' => '',
      '#required' => $element['#required'],
    ];

    return $element;
  }
```

This is a bit more complicated at first glance, but we'll break it down, and you'll see that it actually makes sense with what you've been learning in the previous chapters.

The first argument passed to this method is the entire list of values for this field. Remember that each field can have multiple values, hence the usage of the `FieldItemListInterface` instance to hold them. So, from there, we can get the values of any of the items in the list. The second argument is the actual delta of the item in the list, which we can use to pinpoint the one for which the form is being built (in order to retrieve the default value). Then, we have an `$element` array, which we should actually return, but which contains some pieces of data already prepared for us based on the field configuration. For example, when creating a field, if we set it to be required, then this `$element` already contains the form property `#required` => TRUE. Likewise, it contains the weight of the field (compared to the others on the entity type), the `#title` property, and many others. I recommend that you debug that array and see what's in it. Also, you can look inside `WidgetBase::formMultipleElments()` and `WidgetBase::formSingleElement()` and see how this array is prepared. Lastly, we get the form definition and form state information of the larger form our field element gets embedded in.

So, what we are doing inside the method is getting a bit creative with the data that we have. One value fields would typically just extend the `$element` array, and then the method would simply return that. However, we have two values we want to wrap inside a nice collapsible fieldset, so we create a `details` element for that.

It is on this element that we copy over the field title and description the user has specified when creating the field, which is prepared for us in the $element array. This is because those relate to the entire field, not just one of the values. Moreover, we also set the default #open state to whatever was stored in the widget settings. Lastly, to all this, we add the rest of the values found in the $elements array because we want to inherit them as well.

 Note that I could have left the #title and #description to be also inherited, but overtly added it to make it more visible for you.

Next, within our details element, we can add the two textfields for the license plate code and number. For both of these, we use the widget settings to set the element size and placeholder value, as well as a maximum length value equal to the field item storage. This is what will prevent users from providing values that are longer than what the database columns can handle. The default value for the two form elements will be set to the actual field values of these properties, retrieved from the list of items using the current delta key. Finally, we set the #required property to whatever the user has configured for this field. This property would be useless on the parent details element, so we have to move it down to the actual text fields, and that's pretty much it.

The last method we can implement, and in our case, have to, is one that prepares the field values a bit when submitting:

```
/**
 * {@inheritdoc}
 */
public function massageFormValues(array $values, array $form,
FormStateInterface $form_state) {
  foreach ($values as &$value) {
    $value['number'] = $value['details']['number'];
    $value['code'] = $value['details']['code'];
    unset($value['details']);
  }

  return $values;
}
```

Here's what happens. From our property definitions, our field expects two properties--number and code. However, submitting this form will present only one property called "details" because that is what we arbitrarily named our fieldset form element, which contains the properties inside. Also, since we made this choice, we will need to now massage the submitted values a bit to match the expected properties. In other words, we have to bring the number and code properties to the top level of the $values array and unset the details element, as it's no longer needed upon submission. So, now, the field receives the array in the following format:

```
$values = [
  'number' => 'My number',
  'code' => 'My code'
];
```

If you remember, this is incidentally also what we would pass to the set() method of the field if we wanted to set this value on the field. Take a look at the following example:

```
$node->set('field_license_plate', ['code' => 'NY', 'number' => '63676']);
```

With that, our widget is done; well, not quite. We again forgot about the configuration schema. Let's not do that again. In the same file as we did the field storage schema, we can add the definition for the widget settings:

```
field.widget.settings.default_license_plate_widget:
  type: mapping
  label: 'Default license plate widget settings'
  mapping:
    number_size:
      type: integer
      label: 'Number size'
    code_size:
      type: integer
      label: 'Code size'
    fieldset_state:
      type: string
      label: 'The state of the fieldset which contains the two fields:
open/closed'
    placeholder:
      type: mapping
      label: 'The placeholders for the two fields'
      mapping:
        number:
          type: string
          label: 'The placeholder for the number field'
        code:
          type: string
          label: 'The placeholder for the code field'
```

It works just like before--a dynamic schema name that starts with `field.widget.settings.` and has the actual plugin ID at the end, and inside, we have a property mapping as we've seen before. With this, we are really done.

Field formatter

Alright, so our field now also has a widget that users can input data with. We can already use this field if we want, but when viewing the nodes, we have no way of displaying the field data, unless we do some custom preprocessing and retrieve it manually as we've seen earlier in the book. So, let's instead create the default field formatter because even if we don't need one, it's still a good practice to have one in place to make the field whole.

Before actually coding it, let's establish what we want our formatter to look and behave like. By default, we want the license plate data to be rendered like this:

```
<span class="license-plate--code">{{ code }}</span> <span class="license-plate--number">{{ number }}</span>
```

So, each component is wrapped inside its own span tag, and some handy classes are applied to them. Alternatively, we may want to concatenate the two values together into one single span tag:

```
<span class="license-plate">{{ code }} {{ number }}</span>
```

This could be a setting on the formatter, allowing the user to choose the preferred output. So, let's do it then.

Field formatters go inside the `Plugin/Field/FieldFormatter` namespace of our module, so let's go ahead and create our own:

```
namespace Drupal\license_plate\Plugin\Field\FieldFormatter;

use Drupal\Component\Utility\Html;
use Drupal\Core\Field\FieldItemInterface;
use Drupal\Core\Field\FieldItemListInterface;
use Drupal\Core\Field\FormatterBase;
use Drupal\Core\Form\FormStateInterface;

/**
 * Plugin implementation of the 'default_license_plate_formatter'
 * formatter.
 *
 * @FieldFormatter(
 *   id = "default_license_plate_formatter",
```

```
 *      label = @Translation("Default license plate formatter"),
 *      field_types = {
 *        "license_plate"
 *      }
 *  )
 */
class DefaultLicensePlateFormatter extends FormatterBase {}
```

Again, we start by inspecting the annotation, which looks very unsurprising. It looks almost like the one for our widget earlier, as formatters can also be used on multiple field types.

The class extends `FormatterBase`, which itself implements the obligatory `FormatterInterface`. By now, you recognize the pattern used with plugins--they all have to implement an interface and typically extend a base class, which provides some helpful functionalities common to all plugins of those types. Fields are no different.

The first thing we do inside this formatter class is, again, deal with its own settings (if we need any)- and as it happens, we have a configurable setting for our formatter, so let's define it and provide a default value:

```
/**
 * {@inheritdoc}
 */
public static function defaultSettings() {
  return [
    'concatenated' => 1,
  ] + parent::defaultSettings();
}
```

This is just like with the previous plugins. The `concatenated` setting will be used to determine the output of this field according to the two options we talked about earlier.

Next, predictably, we will need the form to manage this setting:

```
/**
 * {@inheritdoc}
 */
public function settingsForm(array $form, FormStateInterface $form_state) {
  return [
    'concatenated' => [
      '#type' => 'checkbox',
      '#title' => t('Concatenated'),
      '#description' => t('Whether to concatenate the code and number into
a single string separated by a space. Otherwise the two are broken up into
separate span tags.'),
      '#default_value' => $this->getSetting('concatenated'),
    ]
```

```
    ] + parent::settingsForm($form, $form_state);
}
```

Again, nothing special; we have a checkbox, which we use to manage a Boolean value (represented by 1 or 0). Lastly, just like with the widget, we have a summary display for formatters as well that we can define:

```
/**
 * {@inheritdoc}
 */
public function settingsSummary() {
    $summary = [];
    $summary[] = t('Concatenated: @value', ['@value' => (bool)
$this->getSetting('concatenated') ? 'Yes' : 'No']);
    return $summary;
}
```

Here, we just print in a human-readable name of whatever has been configured, and this will be displayed when managing the field display in the UI and will look just like it did with the widget. Consistency is nice.

Now, we've reached the most critical aspect of any field formatter--the actual display:

```
/**
 * {@inheritdoc}
 */
public function viewElements(FieldItemListInterface $items, $langcode) {
    $elements = [];

    foreach ($items as $delta => $item) {
        $elements[$delta] = $this->viewValue($item);
    }

    return $elements;
}

/**
 * Generate the output appropriate for one field item.
 *
 * @param \Drupal\Core\Field\FieldItemInterface $item
 *    One field item.
 *
 * @return array
 */
protected function viewValue(FieldItemInterface $item) {
    $code = $item->get('code')->getValue();
    $number = $item->get('number')->getValue();
    return [
```

```
      '#theme' => 'license_plate',
      '#code' => $code,
      '#number' => $number,
      '#concatenated' => $this->getSetting('concatenated')
   ];
 }
```

The method used for this is `viewElements()`, but for each element in the list, we simply delegate the processing to a helper method, because as you remember, the field is itself a list of value items (depending on the field cardinality), even if there is only one value in the field. These are keyed by a delta, which we also use to key the array of `$elements` that we return from the method.

For each individual item in the list, we then retrieve the value of the license plate code and number using the TypedData accessors we've seen earlier. Remember that at this point we are working with a `FieldItemInterface` whose `get()` method returns the DataType plugin that represents the actual value, which, in our case, is `StringData`, because that is what our field property definitions were:

```
$properties['number'] = DataDefinition::create('string')
      ->setLabel(t('Plate number'));
```

Also, the actual value inside these plugins are the string representations the user actually provided. We use these values together with the setting on whether to concatenate and pass them to a custom theme function (we have yet to define this). The important thing to keep in mind is that what we need to return, for each item, is a render array. This can be anything; consider the following example:

```
return [
   '#markup' => $code . ' ' . $number,
];
```

However, that doesn't look nice, nor is configurable or overridable. So, we opt for a clean new theme function that takes those three arguments:

```
/**
 * Implements hook_theme().
 */
function license_plate_theme($existing, $type, $theme, $path) {
  return [
    'license_plate' => [
      'variables' => ['code' => NULL, 'number' => NULL, 'concatenated' =>
TRUE],
    ],
  ];
}
```

We default the value for `concatenated` to TRUE because that is what we set the default value to be inside `defaultSettings()`. So, we have to be consistent. The template file that goes with this, `license-plate.html.twig`, is also very simple:

```
{% if concatenated %}
  <span class="license-plate">{{ code }} {{ number }}</span>
{% else %}
  <span class="license-plate--code">{{ code }}</span> <span class="license-
plate--number">{{ number }}</span>
{% endif %}
```

Depending on our setting, we output the markup differently. Other modules and themes now have a host of options to alter this output:

- They can create a new formatter plugin altogether
- They can override the template inside a theme
- They can alter the template to be used by this theme hook

That's it for the formatter plugin itself, but this time we're not forgetting about the configuration schema. Although we have a measly little Boolean value to define, it still needs to be done:

```
field.formatter.settings.default_license_plate_formatter:
  type: mapping
  label: 'Default license plate formatter settings'
  mapping:
    concatenated:
      type: boolean
      label: 'Whether to concatenate the two fields into one single span
tag'
```

This works the same way as the other ones but with a different prefix-- `field.formatter.settings`.

With that, we have our field formatter in the bag. The only thing left is for site builders to create fields of this type and start using it.

However, I still think we can do one better. Since we are working with license plates that deal with certain known formats, what if we make our field configurable to provide a list of license plate codes that can be used when inputting the data? This will have the added benefit of us learning something new about fields--field settings.

Field settings

When we created our field type, we specified some storage settings, and we saw that these are typically linked to underlying storage and cannot be changed once the field has data in it. This is because databases have a hard time making table column changes when there is data present in them. However, apart from storage settings, we also have something called field settings, which are specific to the field instance on a certain entity bundle. Even more, they can (or should) be changeable even after the field has been created and has data in it. An example of such a field setting, which is available from Drupal core on all field types, is the "required" option that marks a field as required or not. So, let's see how we can add our own field settings to configure what we said we want to do.

Back in our `LicensePlateItem` plugin class, we start by adding the default field settings:

```
/**
 * {@inheritdoc}
 */
public static function defaultFieldSettings() {
  return [
      'codes' => '',
    ] + parent::defaultFieldSettings();
}
```

This is the same pattern we've been seeing by which we specify what are the settings and what are their relevant defaults. Then, as expected, we need the form, where users can specify the setting values for each field instance:

```
/**
  * {@inheritdoc}
  */
  public function fieldSettingsForm(array $form, FormStateInterface
$form_state) {
    $element = [];

    $element['codes'] = [
      '#title' => $this->t('License plate codes'),
      '#type' => 'textarea',
      '#default_value' => $this->getSetting('codes'),
      '#description' => t('If you want the field to be have a select list
with license plate codes instead of a textfield, please provide the
available codes. Each code on a new line.')
    ];

    return $element;
  }
```

So what we provide here is a `textarea` form element by which the administrator can add multiple license plate codes, one per each line. In our widget, we will use these and turn them into a select list. However, before we do that, we need to provide the configuration schema for this new setting:

```
field.field_settings.license_plate_type:
  type: mapping
  label: 'License plate field settings'
  mapping:
    codes:
      type: string
      label: 'Codes'
```

With this in place, we can turn to our field widget and make the necessary changes.

Inside the `formElement()` method, let's replace the block where we defined the code form element with this:

```
$this->addCodeField($element, $items, $delta, $placeholder_settings);
```

Since the logic for determining that element depends on configuration, it's a bit more complicated, so it's best to refactor to its own method. Now, let's take a look at it:

```
/**
 * Adds the license plate code field to the form element.
 *
 * @param $element
 * @param \Drupal\Core\Field\FieldItemListInterface $items
 * @param $delta
 * @param $placeholder_settings
 */
protected function addCodeField(&$element, FieldItemListInterface $items,
$delta, $placeholder_settings) {
  $element['details']['code'] = [
    '#title' => t('Plate code'),
    '#default_value' => isset($items[$delta]->code) ? $items[$delta]->code
: NULL,
    '#description' => '',
    '#required' => $element['#required'],
  ];

  $codes = $this->getFieldSetting('codes');
  if (!$codes) {
    $element['details']['code'] += [
      '#type' => 'textfield',
      '#placeholder' => $placeholder_settings['code'],
      '#maxlength' => $this->getFieldSetting('code_max_length'),
```

```
        '#size' => $this->getSetting('code_size'),
    ];
    return;
  }

  $codes = explode("\r\n", $codes);
  $element['details']['code'] += [
    '#type' => 'select',
    '#options' => array_combine($codes, $codes),
  ];
}
```

We start by defining the code form element defaults, such as title, default, and value. Then, we get the field settings for the codes setting we just created. Note that getFieldSetting() and getFieldSettings() delegate to the actual field type and return both storage and field settings combined. So, we don't need to use separate methods. However, an implication is that you should probably stick to different setting names for the two categories.

Then, if we don't have any codes configured in this particular field instance, we build up our textfield form element as we did before. Otherwise, we break them up into an array and use them into a select list form element. Also, note that in this latter case, we no longer need to put any length limits because of the validation inherent to select lists. Values not present in the original options list will be considered invalid.

That's pretty much it. The field can now be configured to either default to the open textfield for adding a license plate code or to a select list of predefined ones. Also, the same field can be used in these two ways on two different bundles, which is neat.

Using as a base field

In the beginning of this chapter, I stressed the importance of understanding the makeup of a field (type, widget, and formatter) for being able to easily define base fields on custom entity types. This understanding allows you to navigate through Drupal core code and discover their settings and use them on base fields. So, let's cement this understanding by seeing how our new field could be defined as a base field on a custom entity type.

Here is an example where we actually use all the available settings we defined for each of the three plugins. Note that any settings that are left out default to the values we specified in the relevant defaults method, as follows:

```
$fields['plate'] = BaseFieldDefinition::create('license_plate')
  ->setLabel(t('License plate'))
```

```
->setDescription(t('Please provide your license plate number.'))
->setSettings([
  'number_max_length' => 255,
  'code_max_length' => 5,
  'codes' => implode("\r\n", ['NY', 'FL', 'IL']),
])
->setDisplayOptions('view', [
  'label' => 'above',
  'type' => 'default_license_plate_formatter',
  'weight' => 5,
  'settings' => [
    'concatenated' => 0,
  ]
])
->setDisplayOptions('form', [
  'type' => 'default_license_plate_widget',
  'weight' => 5,
  'settings' => [
    'number_size' => 60,
    'code_size' => 5,
    'fieldset_state' => 'open',
    'placeholder' => [
      'number' => '',
      'code' => '',
    ],
  ]
])
->setDisplayConfigurable('form', TRUE)
->setDisplayConfigurable('view', TRUE);
```

This is very similar to what we've been seeing. For the create() method, we use the FieldType plugin ID ,and inside the setSettings(), we pass both storage and field settings. They will then be used appropriately. Note that since the codes setting is stored as a string with codes separated by line breaks, we will need to add it accordingly.

Similarly, for the view and form display options, we use the formatter and widget plugin IDs, respectively, and inside a settings array, we pass any of the settings we have defined. Lastly, the setDisplayConfigurable() indicates that all these settings for the formatter and widget are also configurable through the UI. Doing so will turn the BaseFieldDefinition into a BaseFieldOverride, as it needs to store the configured overrides.

This should be a recap for you, as we covered all these concepts in earlier chapters.

Summary

In this chapter, we covered how to create custom fields that site builders (and developers) can add to entity types. This has implied defining three plugin types--`FieldType`, `FieldWidget`, and `FieldFormatter`, each with its own responsibility. The first defined the actual field and its storage and individual data properties, using the TypedData API. The second defined the form through which users can input field data when creating or editing entities that use the field. The third defined how the values inside this field can be displayed when viewing the entity.

We also saw that each of these plugins can have arbitrary sets of configurable settings that can be used to make the field dynamic--both in how the widget works and in how the values are displayed. Moreover, these settings are parts of exported field configuration, so we saw how we can define their respective configuration schemas.

Lastly, we also saw how--aside from creating our new field through the UI--developers can add it to an entity type as a base field, making it available on all bundles of that entity type.

In the next chapter, we will talk about access control, a very important topic, as we need to ensure that our data and functionality is only exposed to the users we want, when we want.

10

Access Control

We've already talked about quite a few topics in the previous chapters, but we have been purposefully omitting an important aspect in many of them--access control. Much of what we covered deals in some way or another with access, but we have kept it out of our discussions to keep things more to the point. However, access control is an immensely important topic for Drupal development because it has implications in almost everything we do. So, for this purpose, we have a chapter dedicated to it in which we will cover the most important things you need to know in order to keep your application secure.

When I say secure I don't mean writing code in a secure way to avoid your site getting hacked. For that, we have an appendix at the end of the book to give you some pointers. Instead, I mean handling access control programmatically to ensure that your pages and any other resources are only accessible to the right users.

In this chapter, aside from introducing new concepts that stand on their own, we'll be revisiting some of the previous topics and seeing how we can apply access control in that context. We will start by talking about how Drupal sees access restrictions at a high level, but then dive deep into more specific and complex examples. Also, as usual, we will see code in order to better understand what we talk about.

However, what exactly are we going to learn in this chapter?

First, we will introduce the Drupal access system of roles and permissions and see how we can create them in our code. Even more important for us as module developers, we will see how we can check whether users have permissions programmatically. This is still while keeping things general.

Next, we will dive into more exciting things by looking at route permissions. We have an enormous flexibility here and will explore a number of approaches we can use to restrict access to custom and existing routes--ranging from simply permission-based access control to dynamic service-oriented access handlers.

After covering routes, we will look at entities and how access control works with them. In doing so, we will work a bit on the Product entity we created in Chapter 7, *Your Own Custom Entity and Plugin Types*. Moreover, we will also talk about the *Node Access Grants* system, which is a powerful way to control access specific to the Node entity type.

Finally, we will also look at Block plugins and see how we can control access and ensure that they are rendered on the page. Blocks can have certain contextual rules that determine whether they are displayed on a certain page in the region they have been added to. So, we will talk about that a bit as well.

The purpose of this chapter is to bring together all aspects related to access control that you need to get started as a Drupal 8 module developer. However, you can expect even more than that, and for this reason, it can also serve as a resource for coming back and reading up on certain approaches to access control you may want to use in your own project, rather than having them scattered across the book.

Introduction to the Drupal access system

If you've been doing some site building in Drupal 8 or have experience with previous versions of Drupal, you may already know a thing or two about roles and permissions. If not, no need to worry, as we will talk a bit about how these work.

Essentially, one of the things that makes Drupal special is the flexible access system it has out of the box, based on user roles and permissions. Roles are attributes that can be given to a user. The latter can have multiple roles assigned, but always has at least the default "Authenticated User" role. Permissions are the individual access indicators that can be assigned to roles. By the transitive property, users have all the permissions assigned to the roles they have been assigned. So, the end result is a matrix of permissions by role, and that's actually how it is visualized in the UI at admin/people/permissions:

PERMISSION	ANONYMOUS USER	AUTHENTICATED USER	ADMINISTRATOR
Block			
Administer blocks	☐	☐	☑
Comment			
Administer comment types and settings *Warning: Give to trusted roles only; this permission has security implications.*	☐	☐	☑
Administer comments and comment settings	☐		☑
Edit own comments	☐		☑
Post comments	☐	☑	☑
Skip comment approval	☐	☑	☑
View comments	☑	☑	☑

Drupal core, by default, comes with three roles--**ANONYMOUS USER,
AUTHENTICATED USER**, and **ADMINISTRATOR**. Also, by default, there are a large
number of permissions already defined by Drupal core (and contributed) modules, ready to
be assigned to various roles.

The anonymous user role is pretty self-explanatory and can be used as a bucket for the
permissions all anonymous users should have - that is, users who are not authenticated.
Similarly, the authenticated user role is automatically assigned to all users upon logging in
(and cannot be removed). So, it can be used as a bucket of permissions that all authenticated
users should have.

The super admin user (the one with the ID = 1) actually has all the permissions on the site
without having to explicitly assign roles or permissions. Most of the time, it bypasses most
of the access control in any given subsystem.

Roles and permissions under the hood

Roles are configuration entities (`user_role`) represented by the `Role` entity type class. So,
they can be created through the UI and exported as configuration to be available on all the
environments. As such, there is not much you need to do in your code to define a role, but
simply create them as needed in the UI and export them to configuration. As you
remember, if you want your role to be provided by your module, add the exported YAML
file to the `config/install` folder (and remove the UUID). Refer to `Chapter 6`, *Data
Modeling and Storage*, for more information.

Permissions, on the other hand, are a custom construct. They used to be defined by implementing `hook_permissions()`, but are created using a YAML file (very similar to how we define menu links) in Drupal 8. However, they are not plugins, but a custom construct created by the core User module. The `PermissionHandler` service is responsible for reading all the YAML files and figuring out all the existing permissions on the site. This is not something you need to worry about, as you won't be interacting with this service. You'll be mostly interested in defining new permissions and checking whether a user has them, or setting those permissions in various access contexts.

Defining permissions

The way to create permissions in a custom module is by creating a `*.permissions.yml` file and adding the definitions in there. Consider the following example:

```
administer my feature:
  title: 'Administer my feature'
  restrict access: true
```

In this example, `administer my feature` is the machine name of the permission and actually the most important part. This is what you will use in your code to reference it. Then, we have a title that shows up on the permissions management page we saw earlier. Finally, we have a `restrict access` key by which we can specify whether we need a warning to be output on the permissions management page regarding the security implications, as follows--*Warning: Give to trusted roles only; this permission has security implications.* This is to indicate that our permission is more sensitive, and administrators should pay attention to who they assign it to. This option, can however, be left out (as you will in most cases actually).

You may have noted the static nature of this way of defining permissions. In other words, we hardcoded the permission name and only have one permission. In most cases, this will be fine. However, there can be times where you will need multiple permissions defined dynamically based on some other factors in your application. For this, we can use a permission callback.

For example, the Node module defines individual permissions to manage each of its bundles, and this makes sense. Some roles should have access to some bundles while other roles should have access to other bundles. However, there is no way it can know which bundles it will have at any given point. So, it uses a permission callback:

```
permission_callbacks:
  - \Drupal\node\NodePermissions::nodeTypePermissions
```

This is found in the `node.permissions.yml` file just like the statically defined ones, but it delegates the responsibility of getting the permissions to the `nodeTypePermissions` method of the `NodePermissions` class. This is the same notation we use to define Controllers in the route. As a matter of fact, the same class resolver is used to instantiate it.

Checking the user credentials

You can easily check whether a given user should access a certain resource as long as you have that user account at hand. Here, you can encounter two scenarios:

- You want to interrogate the current user
- You want to interrogate a given user, not necessarily the current one

As we saw in Chapter 2, *Creating Your First Module*, the current user is represented by a service, which implements the `AccountProxyInterface` interface. This service can be accessed by the `current_user` key or statically with this shorthand:

```
/** @var AccountProxyInterface $accountProxy */
$accountProxy = \Drupal::currentUser();
```

From this account proxy, we can request the `AccountInterface`, which represents the actual logged-in user account (the `UserSession` object). It holds a reference to the User entity, with a few of its "account" related data, but that is pretty much it. If we need to access its entity fields, we need to load the entity as we normally do:

```
/** @var UserInterface $user */
$user =
\Drupal::entityTypeManager()->getStorage('user')->load($accountProxy->id())
;
```

The resulting UserInterface, by the way, also implements the same AccountInterface, so these common methods can be used on both objects. So, the User entity type is essentially the storage facility for the AccountInterface that represents an user who is browsing the pages. However, for the moment, the User entity is not so relevant, so we will get back to the account, which we can retrieve from the proxy, like so:

```
/** @var AccountInterface $account */
$account = $accountProxy->getAccount();
```

The methods on this interface allow us to interrogate the account (either the current user account or the one represented by a given User entity) as to its credentials. Also, many of them are also present in the AccountProxy, meaning that you can ask it directly for these.

Two very general but often helpful methods are the following:

```
$account->isAnonymous();
$account->isAuthenticated();
```

These check whether the account is anonymous or not, without taking any roles or permissions into account. Sometimes, your access control is solely based on this distinction.

We can also get a list of roles the account has, as follows:

```
$account->getRoles();
```

Even more important, check whether the user has a given permission:

```
$account->hasPermission($permission)
```

Where $permission is a string (the machine name of the permission as we saw it defined earlier). This method is very helpful because it checks all the roles the user has for the specified permission.

So, you can use these methods anywhere in your code when you need to check whether a user should be accessing certain parts of your functionality.

Route access

Now that we saw how the access system works in Drupal 8 at a basic level, and how we can define permissions and check user credentials, it's time to talk about routes.

As we've seen from the very first time we wrote code in this book, routes are the entry points into your application. Also, as a developer, it is one of the main things you'll be dealing with, and controlling who exactly can access these routes falls under the purview of the access system.

There are a number of ways we can ensure that routes are only accessible to the right users, so let's see what these are.

The simplest way is by checking for a permission. We've actually done that in Chapter 2, *Creating Your First module*, when we defined our `hello_world.hello` route:

```
hello_world.hello:
  path: '/hello'
  defaults:
    _controller:
'\Drupal\hello_world\Controller\HelloWorldController::helloWorld'
    _title: 'Our first route'
  requirements:
    _permission: 'access content'
```

The `requirements` key in a route definition contains all the data that the request trying to reach this route must have. This can contain mostly access-like information, and also things such as the request format.

The requirement in the preceding example is `_permission` (all these options typically start with an underscore).It is used to specify that the user accessing this route needs to have that permission, similar to how we checked whether a user has it earlier:

```
$account->hasPermission($permission).
```

The `access content` permission is something defined by Drupal core and is basically the one you'd use when the restrictions are very lax, meaning that all users should be able to access the resource because, by default, this permission is also present on the Anonymous user role.

Speaking of lax restrictions, there is one option that is even more open, fully open:

```
_access: "TRUE"
```

This essentially opens up the route to basically everybody under any circumstance--not something you'll probably use often, but it's very handy in some cases.

Returning to permissions, we can also include multiple permissions in this requirement. For example, to check whether a user has either of two permissions, we separate them by a comma:

```
_permission: "my custom permission,administer site configuration"
```

For checking whether the user has all the given permissions, we separate them by a plus (+) sign:

```
_permission: "my custom permission+my other permission"
```

So, we can already see quite some flexibility. The `administer site configuration` is another staple permission from Drupal core, which we can use to ensure that the user is an administrator; it is typically a sensitive permission given only to these users.

Next, we also have a requirement by which we can check whether the user has a given role. In a similar manner, we can include multiple roles to check, depending on whether we want to do AND or OR checking:

```
_role: "administrator"
_role: "editor,administrator"
_role: "editor+administrator"
```

This approach is not as flexible as using permissions and is a little "hardcody". By this I mean that you are hardcoding an access rule based on site configuration (as roles are configuration entities). So, if that configuration is removed, you may have broken code. Permissions, on the other hand, are also code, as they are defined in a module (or Drupal core). However, the option is there if you need it.

The next type of requirement we should be covering here is `_entity_access`. However, understanding this requires us to first know a bit about entity level access, so we will skip it now; we'll definitely come back to it later in the chapter. Instead, we will talk about the mother of all route access approaches--the custom one.

Route access requirements can also be stacked, which means that we can add more than one access requirement to a route and the access will be given if all of them grant access. If one denies it, access is denied to the route. This is done by simply adding multiple requirements to the route.

Custom route access

The previous ways of controlling routes are powerful and relatively flexible, but static. We are hardcoding the rules into a file and expect the incoming user to abide by them. However, what if things are more complicated than that, and we need a more dynamic approach? Trust me, things get complicated, fast. We can use the _custom_access option of the route requirements.

In this subsection, we will see how these work and how we can create our custom access checkers. Just something simple to demonstrate the process. Then, we will see a more advanced implementation that will have us work a bit with routes programmatically.

There are two ways custom access checkers can be created and used with a route, and they both involve creating a class. Also, the way this class is used makes the distinction--we can either reference it directly (statically) or make it into a service and reference it like so. We will see an example of both later in this chapter.

To demonstrate, let's say that we want to make sure that our Hello World route is only accessible to users who don't have a specific role--editor. Doesn't make much sense, but it's a simple example we can run with.

Static approach

The static approach involves creating a method on our Controller (or somewhere else), usually called access(), and reference it from the route definition. So, inside our controller we can have this:

```
/**
 * Handles the access checking.
 *
 * @param AccountInterface $account
 *
 * @return AccessResultInterface
 */
public function access(AccountInterface $account) {
  return in_array('editor', $account->getRoles()) ?
AccessResult::forbidden() : AccessResult::allowed();
}
```

This method receives the current user's `AccountInterface`, which we can use to determine the roles. Moreover, if we type hint some extra parameters, Drupal will pass them to the method as well:

- `\Symfony\Component\Routing\Route $route`
- `\Drupal\Core\Routing\RouteMatch $route_match`

We've already discussed the `CurrentRouteMatch` service in Chapter 2, *Creating Your First Module*, and we saw that we can use it to find out things about the route that has just been accessed. In reality, that service simply uses `RouteMatch` objects underneath. So, in case our access rules for this route depend on something that relates to the route, this argument can be very important. Soon, I will demonstrate why that is in further detail.

Similarly, we can also type hint the actual `Route` object that contains data about the route. This plays to the same point I made in the preceding paragraph, and we can also use it in our logic, but alas, for our use case, these won't be necessary, so we will stick with the `AccountInterface`.

What we are returning in this method is very important, as it needs to be an instance of `AccessResultInterface`. This is the standard interface the access system in Drupal 8 works with. The following are the three main implementations of this interface you will often encounter:

- `AccessResultAllowed`
- `AccessResultNeutral`
- `AccessResultForbidden`

The gateway to these objects, however, is typically the `AccessResult` abstract base class (which all the preceding mentioned implementations extend as well) and its static methods. As you saw in the preceding example, we used the `allowed()` and `forbidden()` methods to instantiate these objects. Of course, there is also the corresponding `neutral()` method we can use to indicate that we don't have a say in the matter. Typically, this is used when there are multiple actors involved in deciding access to a certain resource, and one such actor encounters a resource for which they don't need to control access.

Some other built-in capabilities of the `AccessResult` base class are related to cacheability, but it also has convenience methods to achieve a bit more complex access logic. For example, the following methods can prove handy:

- `allowedIf($condition)`
- `forbiddenIf($condition)`

You simply pass a Boolean to these methods, and they return the right access object--so, a Boolean-to-`AccessResultInterface` converter, if you will. Do keep in mind that these methods return an `AccessResultNeutral` object in case the condition evaluates to FALSE. So, you cannot use these methods if you need to map a Boolean to an explicitly allowed or explicitly denied result.

Additionally, we have methods like the following:

- `allowedIfHasPermission()`
- `allowedIfHasPermissions()`

This will check whether a given account has one or more permissions and returns the right access object depending on the case.

Finally, we also have the `orIf()` and `andIf()` methods, with which we can build more complex access structures that combine multiple `AccessResultInterface` results.

Closing the parenthesis on the `AccessResultInterface`, let's reference this method in our route in order to actually make use of it. This is what the route definition looks like now:

```
hello_world.hello:
  path: '/hello'
  defaults:
    _controller:
'\Drupal\hello_world\Controller\HelloWorldController::helloWorld'
    _title: 'Our first route'
  requirements:
    _custom_access:
'\Drupal\hello_world\Controller\HelloWorldController::access'
```

Instead of the `_permission` requirement, we use `_custom_access` with a reference to our Controller method--easy peasy. While clearing the cache, our new access checker will kick in to kick out those pesky `editor` users.

This static approach, as you can imagine, is slightly more powerful than using permission or roles-based access checking, because it allows you to write PHP logic in order to determine the access. However, it falls short in a number of respects, and this is where the service-based approach can be used.

Service approach

The service approach involves creating a tagged service and referencing that in the route definition as a requirement. There are a number of advantages to this method compared to the one we've just seen:

- Allows you to encapsulate complex access logic in its own class
- Allows you to inject dependencies and make use of them in calculating the access
- Allows you to reuse the access checker on multiple routes

So, let's take a look at how we can implement this for our Hello World route. We will replace the preceding approach, but keep the goal of denying access to editors. However, to increase a bit, complexity, editors will be allowed if the Hello World salutation has not been overridden via the configuration form. If you recall, in Chapter 2, *Creating Your First Module*, we created a form where the salutation message can be overridden and stored in a configuration object.

First, let's create our class. Typically, access-related classes go inside the Access folder of the module namespace--it's not necessarily so, but it makes sense to put them there. Then, we can have something like this:

```
namespace Drupal\hello_world\Access;

use Drupal\Core\Access\AccessResult;
use Drupal\Core\Config\ConfigFactoryInterface;
use Drupal\Core\Routing\Access\AccessInterface;
use Drupal\Core\Session\AccountInterface;

/**
 * Access handler for the Hello World route.
 */
class HelloWorldAccess implements AccessInterface {

  /**
   * @var \Drupal\Core\Config\ConfigFactoryInterface
   */
  protected $configFactory;

  /**
   * HelloWorldAccess constructor.
   *
   * @param \Drupal\Core\Config\ConfigFactoryInterface $configFactory
   */
  public function __construct(ConfigFactoryInterface $configFactory) {
    $this->configFactory = $configFactory;
```

```
    }

    /**
     * Handles the access checking.
     *
     * @param AccountInterface $account
     *
     * @return AccessResult
     */
    public function access(AccountInterface $account) {
        $salutation =
$this->configFactory->get('hello_world.custom_salutation')->get('salutation
');
        return in_array('editor', $account->getRoles()) && $salutation != "" ?
AccessResult::forbidden() : AccessResult::allowed();
    }
}
```

Right off the bat, I would like to mention that the `AccessInterface` we're implementing is at this point a bit up in the air. If you look inside, you'll see that it has no methods. This is because of the dynamic argument resolving we talked about earlier, by which we can get the route and route match if we type hint them. There was an ongoing discussion at the time of writing this book on marking it deprecated and maybe eventually removing it completely (or finding another solution). So, it's something worth paying attention to in the long run.

Also, since there is no interface, the `access()` method naming is not enforced. However, we will need it because that is the name being looked for by the access system when using the service. As before, we get the user making the request from which we can get the roles. Moreover, we injected the configuration factory and checked whether the salutation text had been overridden. Only if that is the case, will editors be denied access. It's nothing too complicated for us at this point.

Now, let's take a look at how we define this as a service to be used by our route as an access checker:

```
hello_world.access_checker:
    class: \Drupal\hello_world\Access\HelloWorldAccess
    arguments: ['@config.factory']
    tags:
        - { name: access_check, applies_to: _hello_world_access_check }
```

As you can see, tagged services are very important in Drupal 8 and are a great example of an extension point with which we can contribute our own code to an existing set of functionality. In this example, apart from tagging it for access checking, we also see another option to this tag--`applies_to`. The corresponding string is what we can now use in our route definition to target this particular access checker. So instead of the following line:

```
_custom_access:
'\Drupal\hello_world\Controller\HelloWorldController::access'
```

We have this one:

```
_hello_world_access_check: 'TRUE'
```

The TRUE value we set doesn't make much of a difference. If we wanted, we could add a string value that could actually be used by the access checker internally. However, we'll use a different approach for that later. So, for now, the standard thing to do is just use TRUE.

After clearing the cache, our new access checker will kick in, and that is pretty much it.

Programmatically checking access on routes

If we defined routes and users go to those routes, Drupal will check access for us automatically (according to the requirements set forth in the route definition). However, we may often need to check access to a given route programmatically, for example, to know whether we should show a link to it to the current user. Drupal is of the opinion that if a user doesn't have access to a route, they should never see a link to it anywhere. So, we should follow suit in our custom code.

In `Chapter 2`, *Creating Your First Module*, we saw how to work with the `Url` objects to create links, and we can use these very `Url` objects to check access on a given route; consider the following example:

```
$url = Url::fromRoute('hello_world.hello');
if ($url->access()) {
  // Do something.
}
```

The `access()` method on the `Url` object works only with *routed* URLs, those which have been determined to have a route behind them. It will obviously not work with things such as external URLs, so, in these cases, it will always return TRUE. Also, we can pass an `AccountInterface` to this method in case we want to check whether a specific user has access to that route. Without an argument, it defaults to the current user.

Under the hood, the `Url` class uses the `AccessManager` service statically to check the access of the route. This is done statically, so if you want, you can inject the service yourself (`access_manager`) and check the route access:

```
$access = $accessManager()->checkNamedRoute('hello_world.hello', [],
$account)
```

The empty array we pass as a second argument is an array of parameters that the route needs. You remember how route parameters work from Chapter 2, *Creating Your First Module*, right?

I mentioned earlier that it's very important to use the account, route, and route match that are being passed to the access checker as dynamic arguments if you need them for calculating the access logic, as opposed to injecting the current user or current route match services and using those. Maybe, now, you can start to understand why. Let me break it down.

One of my earlier points was that an advantage of the service-based access checking approach is that it allows us to use the same service on multiple routes. This means that we can have highly dynamic access rules by which we can check route options within the access checker and calculate access based on those, and this is quite powerful.

However, if you inject the current route match service and make use of that, your access rules will work only when that route is being requested in the browser, so, basically, when the user is trying to go to that path. This is because the current route just happens to be the same as the route the access checker is using (the injected one). However, if you programmatically check access on that route from another page (as we just saw), the current route match will be of that other page instead of the one you actually want to check access to.

You'll see this happen even if you don't manually check access on routes with menu links. If a given route is used in a menu link and printed on a page, Drupal will do the access checking automatically to ensure that users have access to that link. Moreover, if you remember from Chapter 5, *Menu and Menu Links*, you will note that if you want to render menu links programmatically, one of the things you'll typically do is run the menu tree through a set of manipulators. An important manipulator is that which checks whether the current user has access to that route.

In these cases, you have the same problem. So, do remember to type hint your access checker with the route and/or route match objects and do not inject them. Of course, do not inject the current user service either (unless you have a very specific reason for doing so).

Bonus - dynamic route options for access control

We've seen how to create a service-based access checker that we can use on our routes. Using this technique, I want to demonstrate the flexibility of using the service on multiple routes. Imagine that we have multiple routes, which display some user information. However, these routes are specific to a user type, and hence accessible only for that user type. In this example, a user type will be defined based on the value of a simple text field on the user entity, and we want to specify in the route definition for which user type it should be accessible to. The code we write for this demonstration will go inside a new user_types module.

An alternative approach to checking the access inside a route for this example is to simply verify inside the Controller that the current user should access it. If not, throwing an AccessDeniedHttpException inside a Controller method will turn the request into a 403 (access denied). However, this is almost always the wrong approach because the route can no longer be verified for access, and we'll end up with links on our site that potentially lead to 403 pages, and we don't want that. So, for this reason, if the page has access rules, they belong in the access system and not in the Controller.

We'll go into this example with the assumption that the user entity has a field called field_user_type already on it; that we have users of three types--board_member, manager, and employee; and that we have the following four route definitions:

```
user_types.board_members:
  path: '/board-member'
  defaults:
    _controller:
'\Drupal\user_types\Controller\UserTypesController::boardMember'
    _title: 'Board member'
user_types.manager:
  path: '/manager'
  defaults:
    _controller:
'\Drupal\user_types\Controller\UserTypesController::manager'
    _title: 'Manager'
user_types.employee:
  path: '/employee'
  defaults:
    _controller:
'\Drupal\user_types\Controller\UserTypesController::employee'
    _title: 'Employee'
user_types.leadership:
  path: '/leadership'
  defaults:
    _controller:
```

```
'\Drupal\user_types\Controller\UserTypesController::leadership'
    _title: 'Leadership'
```

The preceding routes don't have any access requirements yet, as it is our job to create those now. However, you can already understand what kind of users should be able to access these routes. The `user_types.board_members` route is for board members, `user_types.manager` is for managers, `user_types.employee` is for both employees and managers (since both are actual employees), and `user_types.leadership` is for the board members and managers. So, a bit of mix and match to highlight the need for flexibility in our access checker.

Obviously, we don't want to write a service for each combination of user types to handle the access here. Also, using the static approach is not suitable either because we need to inject a dependency, and we also don't want to duplicate the logic using different callables.

So, let's define our service definition for this access checker:

```
user_types.access_checker:
  class: \Drupal\user_types\Access\UserTypesAccess
  arguments: ['@entity_type.manager']
  tags:
    - { name: access_check, applies_to: _user_types_access_check }
```

We inject the entity type manager service so that we can load the user entity corresponding to the user whose access is being checked. As you remember, the `AccountInterface` is not enough to read field data from that user.

Now, we can update our route requirements (for all four routes) to make use of this access checker:

```
requirements:
  _user_types_access_check: 'TRUE'
```

 Earlier we saw the static access checker being referenced using the `_custom_access` requirement. This is the same as the one we are creating now, but provided by Drupal core and which maps to the `CustomAccessCheck` service (instead of our custom one we are now writing). This in turn delegates the responsibility to the class method set in the definition.

Now, it's time to make the distinction between our four routes in terms of the types of users that should have access to them, and we can use route options for this. Options are a set of arbitrary pieces of data that we can put on a route definition and retrieve later programmatically. If you remember, in Chapter 2, *Creating Your First Module*, parameter converters are such an example that can be defined as an option in the route.

Let's take a look at just one of the routes as an example in full, and you'll extrapolate what the other routes will have to look like:

```
hello_world.employee:
  path: '/employee'
  defaults:
    _controller:
'\Drupal\hello_world\Controller\UserTypesController::employee'
    _title: 'Employee'
  requirements:
    _user_types_access_check: 'TRUE'
  options:
    _user_types:
      - manager
      - employee
```

Route options are placed under the options key and are conventionally named with an underscore at the beginning (however, this is not mandatory). In a standard YAML notation, we have a sequence of string values underneath our _user_types option, which will be turned into a PHP array when read into the Route object.

Now, we can create our access checker service and make use of all this for controlling access:

```
namespace Drupal\user_types\Access;

use Drupal\Core\Access\AccessResult;
use Drupal\Core\Entity\EntityTypeManager;
use Drupal\Core\Routing\Access\AccessInterface;
use Drupal\Core\Session\AccountInterface;
use Symfony\Component\Routing\Route;

/**
 * Access handler for the User Types routes.
 */
class UserTypesAccess implements AccessInterface {

  /**
   * @var \Drupal\Core\Entity\EntityTypeManager
   */
  protected $entityTypeManager;
```

```
/**
 * UserTypesAccess constructor.
 *
 * @param \Drupal\Core\Entity\EntityTypeManager $entityTypeManager
 */
public function __construct(EntityTypeManager $entityTypeManager) {
  $this->entityTypeManager = $entityTypeManager;
}

/**
 * Handles the access checking.
 *
 * @param AccountInterface $account
 * @param \Symfony\Component\Routing\Route $route
 *
 * @return \Drupal\Core\Access\AccessResult
 */
public function access(AccountInterface $account, Route $route) {
  $user_types = $route->getOption('_user_types');
  if (!$user_types) {
    return AccessResult::forbidden();
  }
  if ($account->isAnonymous()) {
    return AccessResult::forbidden();
  }
  $user =
$this->entityTypeManager->getStorage('user')->load($account->id());
  $type = $user->get('field_user_type')->value;
  return in_array($type, $user_types) ? AccessResult::allowed() :
AccessResult::forbidden();
  }
}
```

As per the service definition, we inject the entity type manager as a dependency. This is something we could not have done using the static approach. Then, in our `access()` method, we also type hint the route on which this service is used for evaluating access. Now comes the fun part.

We inspect the route and try to retrieve our option by name. Just as a fail safe, we deny access if the option is missing. This should never be the case, as we only use this access checker on routes that do have the option, but you never know. Additionally, we also deny access if the user is anonymous. Anonymous users are sure to not have any user type field value.

Then, we load the user entity of the current account and simply check that field value and return access according to whether it is within the allowed ones for the route. I recommend that you inspect the Route class and see what other handy data you can make use of.

This is it. Now, we have a flexible access checking service that we can use on any number of routes that need this *user type* access control.

A key takeaway from this bonus technique is that you can build incredibly flexible architectures using options on routes. In this example, we used them for access, but you can also use them for other functionalities that tie to, and can be controlled from, the route.

CSRF protection on routes

Drupal comes equipped with various tools for handling CSRF protection.

> *Cross Site Request Forgery (CSRF) is an attack that forces an end user to execute unwanted actions on a web application in which they're currently authenticated.*
>
> *-(OWASP)*

One such tool is for handling the addition of a CSRF token to a route built using the Drupal API automatically. Let's take a look at an example.

Imagine that you have a route that is used as some sort of a callback. Hitting this route triggers a process (typically for logged-in users), so you need to make sure that users only end up on this route from the place they should come (part of the flow that needs to trigger that process). Tokens can be used for this, and Drupal 8 has this covered.

There are two things we need to do--add a requirement to the route for CSRF protection and then build that link using the regular Drupal API we saw in Chapter 2, *Creating your First Module*. Here's the requirement:

```
_csrf_token: 'TRUE'
```

Also, note that this can go together with other access-based requirements such as the ones we've been talking about in this section.

Adding the CSRF token requirement now makes the route inaccessible, if simply accessed by navigating to the path in the browser. To make it accessible, we will need to print a link to it somewhere using the Drupal API:

```
$url = Url::fromRoute('my_module.my_route');
$link = [
```

```
    '#type' => 'link',
    '#url' => $url,
    '#title' => 'Protected callback'
];
```

What is mentioned in the preceding paragraph is one way, but we can also use the
LinkGenerator service or the Link class, as we've seen in Chapter 2, *Creating Your First
Module*. They will all render the link with a token appended to the URL as a query
parameter. Drupal will then evaluate that token as part of the access control and make sure
that it is valid. As a matter of fact, the link building actually plays no role. It is the URL
generator that handles it. So, getting the string URL will contain the token:

```
$path = $url->toString();
```

Under the hood, to manage the creation and validation of the tokens, Drupal uses the
CsrfTokenGenerator service, which we can also use if we need to. For example, after
getting our hands on the service (csrf_token), we can create a token:

```
$token = $generator->get('my_value');
```

Here, my_value is an optional string that the generator can use to make the token unique. It
also uses the current user session and the private site key. Keep in mind that if the user is
anonymous and no session has been started, the token will be unique on each request. So, if
that's a problem, make sure that you start the session manually as we did in Chapter 6,
Data Modeling and Storage.

We can then validate this token as follows:

```
$valid = $generator->validate($token, 'my_value');
```

Here, $generator is the same service we used for creating it.

Using the token generator manually can be handy, but as we saw, it is very easy to just put
a requirement on the route, and let Drupal do the rest. Moreover, CSRF protection is
embedded in the Form API, so we don't have to do absolutely anything when it comes to
forms for additional protection.

Altering routes

We've seen so far how to create access rules on our own routes. However, it would not be
Drupal if it wasn't also easy to alter existing routes and change their access rules to
whatever we want. This is yet another small extension point with which our custom
modules can contribute to an existing functionality.

Altering route access is done by altering the routes themselves. Of course, access is not the only reason why routes may be altered, as you can change just about anything else on the definition. So, with this occasion, we will see how you can alter routes for any purpose you might need.

Routes can be altered by subscribing to an event, just as we've seen in Chapter 2, *Creating Your First Module*, when we subscribed to the `kernel.request` event. This event is dispatched at the moment all the routes are being built and before they get cached. So, the alteration will not happen dynamically (upon someone accessing the route), but only when they all get rebuilt. So, let's take a look at how we can subscribe to that event.

Unlike most other subscribers, the `EventSubscriberInterface` class for routes typically goes in the `Routing` namespace of the module so that's where we'll put it. Moreover, the event we're listening to is `RoutingEvents::ALTER`. However, the routing system provides us with a base subscriber class we can extend and which contains all this boilerplate code, leaving us to do only the alterations themselves.

And these alterations can look like this:

```
namespace Drupal\hello_world\Routing;

use Drupal\Core\Routing\RouteSubscriberBase;
use Symfony\Component\Routing\RouteCollection;

/**
 * Subscribes to route events for the Hello World module.
 */
class HelloWorldRouteSubscriber extends RouteSubscriberBase {

  /**
   * {@inheritdoc}
   */
  protected function alterRoutes(RouteCollection $collection) {
    $route = $collection->get('user.register');
    if (!$route) {
      return;
    }

    // Example 1:
    // We deny access to the Register page in all cases. With this requirement,
    // it doesn't matter anymore what other access requirements exist or if they
    // evaluate positively.
    $route->setRequirement('_access', 'FALSE');
```

```
    // Example 2:
    // We check for the presence of a specific access requirement and if it
exists,
    // we clear all the access requirements on the route and set our own.
    if ($route->hasRequirement('_access_user_register')) {
      $route->setRequirements([]);
      $route->setRequirement('_user_types_access_check', 'TRUE');
    }
  }
}
```

We extended `RouteSubscriberBase`, which subscribes to the event and provides us with the `alterRoutes()` method and a collection of all the routes on the site. I encourage you to look into the `RouteCollection` class, as it's a very handy one to know when working with routes. One important feature is that we can retrieve routes based on their name, which we did in the preceding example.

Then, we will work with `Route` objects like we did a bit earlier. We can see two examples, all with comments I will not repeat here. The second example does not make any sense in a real-world scenario, as we cannot have logged-in users register for new accounts anyway. However, it serves to illustrate how we can add our own access checker to an existing route.

Similar to how we manipulate access requirements, we can change a lot of other things: options, parameters, controller, and even the actual route path. For this, I encourage you to familiarize yourself with the `Route` class methods and see what you can set on the new route. Couple this information with the documentation (https://www.drupal.org/docs/8/api/routing-system/structure-of-routes) on all the things you can add to routes for a better understanding.

The only thing left for this to work is to register the subscriber as a tagged service, just like we did in Chapter 2, *Creating Your First Module*:

```
hello_world.route_subscriber:
  class: Drupal\hello_world\Routing\HelloWorldRouteSubscriber
  tags:
    - { name: event_subscriber }
```

Now, we are done with altering our routes.

Entity access

Now that we've covered how access control works on routes, let's dive into the entity access system and see how we can ensure that only the right users interact with our entities. To demonstrate these, we will work with the Product entity type we created in Chapter 7, *Your Own Custom Entity and Plugin Types*.

When we created the Product entity type, the annotation we wrote had an admin_permission property, where we referenced the general permission to be used for any interaction with the entities of this type. Since we didn't reference and implement an access control handler, this is the only access checking done on products. In many cases, this is enough. After all, entity types can be created for the sole purpose of structuring some data that nobody even needs to interact with in the UI. However, many other cases require more granular access control on operating with the entities, especially the content-oriented ones, such as Node.

There are four operations for which we can control access when it comes to entities--view, create, update, and delete. The first one is clearly the most common one, but we always need to account for the rest as well. Let's first define permissions for all these operations:

```
view product entities:
  title: 'View Product entities'
edit product entities:
  title: 'Edit Product entities'
delete product entities:
  title: 'Delete Product entities'
add product entities:
  title: 'Create new Product entities'
```

These are four simple permissions that map to the operations that can be performed on Product entities.

Now, let's go ahead and create an access control handler for our Product entity type. You remember what these handlers are from Chapter 6, *Data Modeling and Storage*, don't you?

First, we will reference the class we will build on the product annotation:

```
"access" = "Drupal\products\Access\ProductAccessControlHandler",
```

I choose to put this handler in the Access namespace of the module, but feel free to put it where you want.

Second, we will need the actual class:

```
namespace Drupal\products\Access;

use Drupal\Core\Entity\EntityAccessControlHandler;
use Drupal\Core\Entity\EntityInterface;
use Drupal\Core\Session\AccountInterface;
use Drupal\Core\Access\AccessResult;
use Drupal\products\Entity\ProductInterface;

/**
 * Access controller for the Product entity type.
 */
class ProductAccessControlHandler extends EntityAccessControlHandler {

  /**
   * {@inheritdoc}
   */
  protected function checkAccess(EntityInterface $entity, $operation,
AccountInterface $account) {
    /** @var ProductInterface $entity */
    switch ($operation) {
      case 'view':
        return AccessResult::allowedIfHasPermission($account, 'view product
entities');

      case 'update':
        return AccessResult::allowedIfHasPermission($account, 'edit product
entities');

      case 'delete':
        return AccessResult::allowedIfHasPermission($account, 'delete
product entities');
    }

    return AccessResult::neutral();
  }

  /**
   * {@inheritdoc}
   */
  protected function checkCreateAccess(AccountInterface $account, array
$context, $entity_bundle = NULL) {
    return AccessResult::allowedIfHasPermission($account, 'add product
entities');
  }
}
```

As I mentioned in Chapter 6, *Data Modeling and Storage*, entity access control handlers need to extend the EntityAccessControlHandler base class. If one is not specifically provided, that is actually the handler the entity type defaults to. Also, there are two methods we will need to implement here (override):

- checkAccess(), which is used to control access on the view and update and delete operations
- checkCreateAccess(), which is used to control access on the create operation

The reason why these are separate is because for the create operation we don't have an entity we can inspect in the process.

Our access rules for the Product entity type are very simple. For each operation, we allow access if the user has the relevant permission; otherwise, access is neutral. However, what happens in this case?

It's worth looking into the EntityAccessControlHandler base class and understanding what is going on. The main access entry points are the access() and createAccess() methods. We should never override these because the logic happening in there is quite standardized and is expected behavior by everyone. Instead, our rules go inside the two methods we saw in our own handler subclass.

The access() and createAccess() methods invoke entity access hooks (we'll talk about those in a minute). If those do not come back with an access denied message, they call their respective access methods we are overriding in our own subclass, and the results of these are combined with the ones from the access hooks inside an orIf() access result. Remember earlier when we talked about the AccessResult base class and its handy orIf() and andIf() methods?

It's important to note how access is determined with all these factors. If at least one of the hook implementations grants access and none deny it, the user will have access, unless we deny access in our access handler. Neutral access plays no role in this equation, except if all hook implementations and the access handler return neutral access (so no specific access being granted), then the access will be denied.

In our example, we defined permissions, and the handler simply checks for these. Already, this is pretty flexible because administrators can now assign these permissions to roles and control using which users can perform any of these operations. However, there is nothing stopping us from adding more logic to these methods. For example, we can even inspect the entities (and/or the user account) and determine access based on some values. Moreover, we can inject services into the access handler and make use of them in these calculations.

Injecting services into Entity handlers

One of the powers of using the access handler is that we can make it aware of the service container and inject whatever services we might need to determine access. However, it's not immediately clear how you can do this, so we'll break it down here.

The first thing we will need is to have our access handler implement the `EntityHandlerInterface`. Note that this applies in the same way to the other types of handlers, not just access related. This interface has one method, which will receive the container and the entity type definition--`createInstance()`.

Knowing this, the rest is very similar to how we injected services into Controllers and Forms using the `create()` method, which only takes the container as argument, or into plugins, which also takes some plugin information:

```
/**
 * @var \Drupal\Core\Entity\EntityTypeManager
 */
protected $entityTypeManager;

/**
 * ProductAccessControlHandler constructor.
 *
 * @param EntityTypeInterface $entity_type
 * @param \Drupal\Core\Entity\EntityTypeManager $entityTypeManager
 */
public function __construct(EntityTypeInterface $entity_type,
EntityTypeManager $entityTypeManager) {
  parent::__construct($entity_type);
  $this->entityTypeManager = $entityTypeManager;
}

/**
 * {@inheritdoc}
 */
public static function createInstance(ContainerInterface $container,
EntityTypeInterface $entity_type) {
  return new static(
    $entity_type,
    $container->get('entity_type.manager')
  );
}
```

With this, we have injected the entity type manager into the access handler, and if we want, we can use it. Of course, if we don't need it, we should not inject it in the first place.

Entity access hooks

As I mentioned, the entity access handler invokes access hooks that modules that don't own the entity type can implement in order to have their say in the access to an entity. There are two sets of access hooks to speak of. The first set covers *create* operations, as follows:

- hook_entity_create_access()
- hook_[entity_type]_create_access()

The second set covers view, update, and delete operations:

- hook_entity_access()
- hook_[entity_type]_access()

For each set, we have two hooks invoked at the same time that go from generic to entity type specific. For example, when trying to view a node, the second hook that is invoked is hook_node_access().

The entity access hook implementations, as you remember from our earlier discussion, also have to return an AccessResultInterface. This is because the result is used inside the orIf() combination with the access result of the access handler.

So, let's take a look at how we can implement these access hooks, especially their signatures. Hence, we begin with the first set:

```
/**
 * Implements hook_entity_create_access().
 */
function
my_module_entity_create_access(\Drupal\Core\Session\AccountInterface
$account, array $context, $entity_bundle) {
  // Perform access check and return an AccessResultInterface instance.
}
```

This is the generic entity create access hook. To make it specific to an entity type, we replace the word entity from the function name with the actual ID of the entity type. The parameters, however, remain the same--the user account being checked for access, a context (an array containing the entity type ID and the langcode of the entity being created), and the bundle of the entity being created.

The second set looks like this:

```
function my_module_entity_access (\Drupal\Core\Entity\EntityInterface
$entity, $operation, \Drupal\Core\Session\AccountInterface $account) {
  // Perform access check and return an AccessResultInterface instance.
}
```

Again, to make it specific to an entity type, we can just replace the word `entity` with the ID of the entity type we want. Once again, the parameters remain, in essence, consistent--the entity being accessed (type hinted with the relevant entity interface if implementing the more specific hook), the operation being attempted (one of three strings--`view`, `update`, and `delete`), and the user account being checked for access.

That's pretty much it. These hooks are invoked dynamically whenever access is being checked on an entity for the given operation. Let's talk about some examples of this.

First, the entity routes that come out of the box are checking access against these operations, so no need to worry there. So, if we navigate to the canonical, form, or delete URL, access will be checked.

Secondly, if we programmatically load an entity and render it as we saw in Chapter 6, *Data Modeling and Storage*, using the view builder handler, the entity access with the `view` operation gets invoked. However, if we load the entity and simply retrieve some data from it and print it within our own template, we bypass access control. So, if we are doing this, we will need to make sure that we always check access manually:

```
$access = $entity->access('view', $account);
```

This will return a Boolean, unless you specify a third argument as TRUE, which will return an `AccessResultInterface` object; your call, depending on the circumstances.

Thirdly, if we load an entity programmatically that we use inside a form builder and want to render the form, we again bypass access check. So, we should perform it manually again using the `update` operation instead.

When it comes to programmatically dealing with URLs and menu links to pages that have CRUD connotations with regards to entities, we will need to perform access checking ourselves, but we will discuss entity access in routes in a minute; first, a word of caution.

Earlier, I stated a note about extracting entity data and simply rendering field values. The same problem occurs when running entity queries--the results will contain entities that the current user may not have access to. So, we must be aware of this and handle it appropriately. This problem becomes even more prominent with Views, which makes custom database queries and will include potentially inaccessible entities in the result set. Compounded by the possibility of rendering field values with Views, this can cause quite unexpected behavior. So, keep in mind that for cases like this, the entity access hooks and access control handler do not fire. The Node module, however, has a complex grant system that takes care of all this, but, unfortunately, this is available only for node entities. We will talk about these soon as well.

Field access

We've seen so far how the entity level access works. However, a very similar system also exists for the fields inside entities. If you look inside the `EntityAccessControlHandler`, you'll note that there is a `fieldAccess()` method. This is called whenever access needs to be checked on a given field. For example, the `FieldItemList::access()` method does just that and delegates to the entity handler. Inside that, a call is made to `checkFieldAccess()`, which is what we can implement in our access handler subclass to customize access rules if we need to.

In a similar way, we have multiple operations that access can be checked for, but `view` will be your most common one. For example, when manually rendering an entity using the entity builder handler, as we've seen before, each field is being checked for access to the `view` operation. The same goes, this time, when an entity form is being built for the entity to edit it. Each field that is being rendered in the form gets checked for access first using the `edit` operation.

Again, we also have access hooks other modules can implement to have a say in whether or not fields should be accessible:

- `hook_entity_field_access()`
- `hook_entity_field_access_alter()`

In this case, we don't have an entity type or a field type-specific hook that we can implement. However, we have an alter hook that we can use to alter the access rules proposed by other modules.

Similar to the entity-level access handler, the field level one takes its input from multiple sources--subclass and hook implementations. However, the order and combination of these are different. First, the access handler subclass is called (via the `checkFieldAccess()` method). Then, all the `hook_entity_field_access()` hooks are invoked to provide their input. Both of these in turn are then alterable by implementing `hook_entity_field_access_alter()`. Finally, the resulting access rules are combined into an `orIf()` and returned. So, the same principles are available as we saw at the entity level, but in a different order.

Entity access in routes

Now that we understand how entity level access control works, let's return to routes for a moment. If you remember, I mentioned the `_entity_access` route requirement and how we would talk about it once we had covered entity access.

The `_entity_access` route requirement is nothing more than a service-based access checker, much like the one we wrote ourselves. However, it is created by the entity system in order to control access to routes based on dynamic entity parameters in those routes. Let's see a quick example of a route definition that can use the `_entity_access` requirement:

```
products.view_product:
  path: '/our-products/{product}'
  defaults:
    _controller:
 '\Drupal\products\Controller\ProductsController::showProduct'
  requirements:
    _entity_access: 'product.view'
  options:
    parameters:
      product:
        type: 'entity:product'
```

This route has a dynamic parameter called `Product`. In the options, we map this parameter to the Product entity type, so that our Controller method (`showProduct()`) already receives the loaded product entity instead of just the ID. An added benefit of this is that if the product is not found, a 404 is thrown for us. Since this route is clearly dependent on that particular product, we also want to make sure that it can be accessible only if the user has access to view that product.

One way we can ensure access is to add a permission requirement that matches the one for viewing the Product entities. However, this is not a good idea for two reasons:

- If we change the permission used by the Product entity, we have to change it in this definition as well
- Even more importantly, if the entity access logic depends on something more, such as dynamic data from the user or entity, this won't work anymore

An alternative way to counter these problems is to implement an access checker service and check for the access on the entity inside that service:

```
$access = $entity->access('view', $account);
```

However, there's a lot of boilerplate setup involved for just this line of code. We'd have to do so for all entity types and operations.

Instead we use the built-in _entity_access access checker as in the example route definition. Instead of TRUE (what we've been using for our access checker), this one actually expects a value it will make use of, and that is a string with two parts separated by a period (.). The first part is the entity type, whereas the second is the operation. Under the hood, EntityAccessCheck will look in the route parameters and check for the found entity's access using the provided operation. Easy peasy.

Node access grants

Earlier I warned about the entity access controls we've been talking about not being taken into account during queries (either written by us or Views). This is something to pay attention to. For example, if you make a listing of entities, you will need to ensure that users have access to these entities before printing the results out. The problem here occurs when using the built-in paging capabilities of either the entity query or database API. That's because the pager information will reflect all the query results. So, if you don't print the inaccessible entities, there will be a mismatch between the pager information and visible results.

If you remember, in Chapter 6, *Data Modeling and Storage,* I mentioned that when it comes to nodes, the entity query takes access into account. If you want to avoid that, you should use the accessCheck(FALSE) method on the query builder. Let's elaborate a bit on this.

First, this method is available on all entity types, not just nodes. However, it is really useful only for those which have defined a `status` field to denote that entities can be either published or unpublished (or/off, enabled/disabled however you prefer). The query will simply add a condition to that field and only return the ones with the status that equals 1. Also, passing FALSE to this method simply removes that condition.

Second, the Node entity type has a much more powerful built-in access system called *access grants*. These have been there from previous versions of Drupal, and this is why we have it available in D8 as well. Unfortunately, it is not there for other entity types. However, if you really need it, you could technically write it yourself now that you know how the entity access system works in general, and can look into how the node access grants are built. But what is this system about?

The node access grants system is a granular way by which we can control access to any of the operations on a node. This is done using a combination of *realms* and *grants*. When a node is saved, we have the opportunity to create *access records* for that node that contain the following information:

- *realm* (string): A category for our access records. Typically, this is used to denote specific functionality under which the access control happens.
- *gid (grant ID)* (int): The ID of the grant by which we can verify the user trying to access the node. Typically, this will map to either a role or a custom-defined "group" that users belong to. For example, a *manager* user type (from the earlier example) can map to the grant ID 1. You'll understand this in a moment.
- *grant_view, grant_update, grant_delete* (int): Boolean indicating whether this access record is for this operation.
- *langcode* (string): The language of the node this access record should apply to.

Then, we can return grant records for a given user when they try to access the node. For a given user, we can return multiple grants as part of multiple realms.

The node access records get stored inside the `node_access` table, and it's a good idea to keep checking that table while you are developing and preparing your access records. By default, if there are no modules that provide access records, there will be only one row in that table referencing the Node ID "0" and the realm `all`. This means that basically the node access grants system is not used, and all nodes are accessible for viewing in all realms. That is to say, default access rules apply. Once a module creates records, as we will see, this row is deleted.

To better understand how this system works, let's see a practical code example. For this, we'll get back to our User Types module and create some node access restrictions based on these user types. We'll start with an easy example and then expand on it to make it more complex (and more useful).

To begin with, we want to make sure that Article nodes are only viewable by users of all three types (so there are still some restrictions, as users need to have a type). Page nodes, on the other hand, are restricted to managers and board members. So let's get it done.

All the work we do now takes place inside the .module file of the module. First, let's create a rudimentary mapping function to which we can provide a user type string (as we've seen before) and which returns a corresponding grant ID. We will then use this consistently to get the grant ID of a given user type:

```
/**
 * Returns the access grant ID for a given user type.
 *
 * @param $type
 *
 * @return int
 */
function user_types_grant_mapping($type) {
  $map = [
    'employee' => 1,
    'manager' => 2,
    'board_member' => 3
  ];

  if (!isset($map[$type])) {
    throw new InvalidArgumentException('Wrong user type provided');
  }

  return $map[$type];
}
```

It's nothing too complicated. We have our three user types that map to simple integers. Also, we throw an exception if a wrong user type is passed--now comes the fun part.

Working with node access grants restrictions involves the implementation of two hooks-- one for creating the access records of the nodes, and the other to provide the grants of the current user. Let's first implement hook_node_access_records():

```
/**
 * Implements hook_node_access_records().
 */
function user_types_node_access_records(\Drupal\node\NodeInterface $node) {
```

```
    $bundles = ['article', 'page'];
    if (!in_array($node->bundle(), $bundles)) {
      return [];
    }

    $map = [
      'article' => [
        'employee',
        'manager',
        'board_member',
      ],
      'page' => [
        'manager',
        'board_member'
      ]
    ];

    $user_types = $map[$node->bundle()];
    $grants = [];

    foreach ($user_types as $user_type) {
      $grants[] = [
        'realm' => 'user_type',
        'gid' => user_types_grant_mapping($user_type),
        'grant_view' => 1,
        'grant_update' => 0,
        'grant_delete' => 0,
      ];
    }

    return $grants;
}
```

This hook is invoked whenever a node is being saved, and it needs to return an array of access records for that node. As expected, the parameter is the node entity.

The first thing we do is simply return an empty array if the node is not one of the ones we are interested in. If we return no access records, this node will be given one single record for the realm `all` with the grant ID of 1 for the `view` operation. This means that it is accessible in accordance to the default node access rules.

Then, we will create a simple map of the user types we want viewing our node bundles. Also, for each user type that corresponds to the current bundle, we create an access record for the `user_type` realm with the grant ID that maps to that user type, and with permission to view this node.

There are two ways we can trigger this hook and persist the access records. We can edit and save a node, which will create the records for that node, or we can rebuild the permissions that will do so for all the nodes on the site. The link to do so can be found on the status report page:

Image toolkit	gd
	GD2 image manipulation toolkit
Node Access Permissions	27 permissions in use
	If the site is experiencing problems with permissions to content, you may have to rebuild the permissions c
	replace them with permissions based on the current modules and settings. Rebuilding may take some time
	After rebuilding has completed, content will automatically use the new permissions. Rebuild permissions
PHP	5.6.9-0+deb8u1 (more information)
PHP extensions	Enabled
PHP memory limit	512M
PHP OPcode caching	Enabled

It's a good idea to rebuild the permissions while developing to make sure that your changes get applied to all the nodes. Once we do this, our nodes now become inaccessible to basically anyone (except the super user with the ID of 1). That's because we now need to specify the grants a given user should have by implementing hook_node_grants():

```
/**
 * Implements hook_node_grants().
 */
function user_types_node_grants(\Drupal\Core\Session\AccountInterface
$account, $op) {
  if ($account->isAnonymous()) {
    return [];
  }

  if ($op !== 'view') {
    return [];
  }

  $user =
\Drupal::entityTypeManager()->getStorage('user')->load($account->id());
  $user_type = $user->get('field_user_type')->value;
  if (!$user_type) {
    return [];
  }

  try {
```

```
    $gid = user_types_grant_mapping($user_type);
  }
  catch (InvalidArgumentException $e) {
    return [];
  }

  return ['user_type' => [$gid]];
}
```

This hook is invoked by the node access system every time access is being checked on a given node (for a given operation). Moreover, it is also invoked when running entity queries against the node entity type and the access check has not been disabled. Finally, it is also invoked in database API queries when the `node_access` tag is used. Remember the query alters based on tags that we talked about in Chapter 8, *The Database API*?

As an argument, it receives the user account for which access needs to be checked--the grants that it has within the node access grants system of the given operation. So, what we do here is start by returning an empty array (no grants) if the user is anonymous or the operation they are attempting to do is not `view`--you have not been granted access. The same thing happens if the user entity does not have any value in the `field_user_type` field. If they do, however, we get the corresponding grant ID and return an array of access grants keyed by the realm. For each realm, we can include more than one grant ID. In this case, though, it is only once since the user can only be of one type. We can also return multiple realms if needed, and, of course, other modules may do so as well, the results being centralized and used in the access logic.

With this in place, all our page nodes are now available for viewing only to board member and manager users, whereas articles are available for viewing to employees as well. If users don't have any type, they don't have access. The great thing is that these restrictions are now being taken into account also when running queries. So, we can automatically exclude from query results the nodes to which users don't have access. This works with Views as well.

Let's now enhance this solution with the following changes:

- Unpublished article nodes are only available to managers and board members
- Managers also have access to update and delete articles and pages

The first one is easy. After we define our internal map inside
`user_types_node_access_records()`, we can unset the `employee` from the array in
case the node is unpublished:

```
if (!$node->isPublished()) {
  unset($map['article'][0]);
}
```

This was a very simple example, but one meant to draw your attention to an important but
often forgotten point. If you create access records for a node, you will need to account for
the node status yourself. This means that if you grant access to someone to view a node,
they will have access to view that node, regardless of the status (publishing state). Also,
more often than not, this is not something you want. So, just make sure that you consider
this point when implementing access grants.

Now, let's see how we can alter our logic to allow managers to update and delete nodes
(both articles and pages). This is how `user_types_node_access_records()` looks like
now:

```
$bundles = ['article', 'page'];
if (!in_array($node->bundle(), $bundles)) {
  return [];
}

$view_map = [
  'article' => [
    'employee',
    'manager',
    'board_member',
  ],
  'page' => [
    'manager',
    'board_member'
  ]
];

if (!$node->isPublished()) {
  unset($view_map['article'][0]);
}

$manage_map = [
  'article' => [
    'manager',
  ],
  'page' => [
    'manager',
  ]
```

```
];

$user_types = $view_map[$node->bundle()];
$manage_user_types = $manage_map[$node->bundle()];
$grants = [];

foreach ($user_types as $user_type) {
  $grants[] = [
    'realm' => 'user_type',
    'gid' => user_types_grant_mapping($user_type),
    'grant_view' => 1,
    'grant_update' => in_array($user_type, $manage_user_types) ? 1 : 0,
    'grant_delete' => in_array($user_type, $manage_user_types) ? 1 : 0,
  ];
}

return $grants;
```

What we are doing different is, first, we rename the $map variable to $view_map in order to reflect the actual grant associations. Then, we create a $manage_map to hold the user types that can edit and delete the nodes. Based on this map, we can then set the grant_update and grant_delete values to 1 for the user types that are allowed. Otherwise, they stay as they were.

All we need to do now is go back to the hook_node_grants() implementation and remove the following:

```
if ($op !== 'view') {
  return [];
}
```

We are now interested in all operations, so users should be provided all the possible grants. After rebuilding the permissions, manager user types will be able to update and delete articles and pages, while the other user types won't have these permissions. This does have many implications for queries because those use the view operation.

Before closing the topic on the node access grants, you should also know that there is an alter hook available that can be used to modify the access records created by other modules--hook_node_access_records_alter(). This is invoked after all the modules provide their records for a given node, and you can use it to alter whatever they provided before being stored.

The access grants system, as mentioned, is limited to the node entity type. It has been there from previous versions of Drupal, and it didn't quite make it to become standard across the entity system. There is talk, however, of doing this, but it's quite incipient.

To better understand how it works under the hood in case you want to write your own such system, I encourage you to explore the NodeAccessControlHandler. You'll note that its checkAccess() method delegates to the NodeGrantDatabaseStorage service responsible for invoking the grant hooks we've seen before. Moreover, you can also check out the node_query_node_access_alter implementation of hook_query_QUERY_TAG_alter() in which the Node module uses the same grant service to alter the query in order to take into account the access records. It's not the easiest system to dissect, especially if you are a beginner, but well worth going through and to learn more.

Block access

Another major area where you will deal with access is when trying to control access to a custom block. If you remember in Chapter 2, *Creating Your First Module*, we created the HelloWorldSalutationBlock plugin so that our salutation can also be rendered using a block. Now, that block can be placed in a region and even configured to show up only on certain pages, for certain user roles, or even on node pages restricted by bundle. This is all done in the UI:

Block description: Hello world salutation

Title *

Hello world salutation   Machine name:

helloworldsalutation [Edit]

☑ Display title

Visibility

Language Not restricted	**Pages**
Content types Not restricted	[text area]
Pages Not restricted	Specify pages by using their paths. Enter one path per line. The '*' character is a wildcard. An example path is */user/* for every user page. *<front>* is the front page.
Roles Not restricted	◉ Show for the listed pages ◯ Hide for the listed pages

However, this is oftentimes not enough, and you will want to have a block placed in a region and control yourself under what circumstances it should show up--enter block access.

Inside the `BlockBase` plugin base class, there is the `blockAccess()` method, which always returns positively. This is because, by default, all blocks will be rendered--once they are placed in a region. Unless, of course, they are configured to only show in certain cases, in which case a system of visibility based on the available contexts kicks in to control that. However, if we override this method in our block plugin class, we can control whether or not the block is shown. So, we can leave the visibility options empty when placing the block in a region and then handle everything we want regarding its visibility inside the `blockAccess()` method. Neat, isn't it?

Also, as expected, the method has one parameter, namely the account being checked, and needs to return an `AccessResultInterface`. Since we can inject services into our block plugin (by implementing the `ContainerFactoryPluginInterface` as we saw in Chapter 2, *Creating Your First Module*), we can use what we want to check whether the given user should see the block. If we deny access, the block is simply not rendered.

That is pretty much all there is to the block access control.

Summary

In this chapter, we talked about many access-related topics and techniques. In doing so, we covered what you need to know when starting Drupal 8 module development. Of course, as you progress, you'll dive deeper into the code and learn more subtle aspects and advanced concepts that you can employ in your modules. However, what we covered should set you well on your way. So, what exactly did we talk about?

We started by introducing the high-level Drupal 8 access system that is made up of the matrix between roles and permissions. In doing so, we've seen how we can define permissions in code and also how we can check whether a user has those permissions. Of course, we looked at other ways we can check a user's credentials and saw how we can use the `AccountInterface` for this.

Then, we moved on to routes and saw all the various ways we can ensure access control there. In doing so, we covered simple checks such as permissions and roles, but also went into more advanced examples of using custom access checkers. We saw that these can be both static and service based to make access checking fully dynamic. To demonstrate these concepts, we also looked at a case study of using route options to basically configure the access checker used on a group of similar routes.

Another major topic we covered was access on entities. We saw how we can create our own access control handler and check access for all the operations specific to entities. The access hooks invoked by the base access handler also go hand in hand with this, which allow other modules to have a say in the access to a given entity. Moreover, we also saw how we can use entity access checks on routes which have entity parameters.

Finally, we briefly covered the block access by which we can control the visibility of blocks based on whatever rules we want, including user credentials.

Apply these lessons in your code, and do not take access issues lightly. If there is one thing you should know a great deal about from the beginning, it is access. So, this chapter also serves as a reference point for when you are doing development; feel free to come back to it as many times as you need.

In the next chapter, we will look at caching and how to ensure that our application is performant.

11
Caching

Application performance has always been one of the pain points when performing development with Drupal, and there are many reasons for this. For example, PHP is not the fastest language out there. Many beginner Drupal developers fell pray to the multitude of modules available and go a bit overboard with enabling more than needed. Indeed, the Drupal architecture is simply not the most performant. In its defense though, it is a very complex architecture that does a lot out of the box will have some speed trade-offs.

One critical component in this game, however, is caching. For those of you not familiar with this term, caching is the application strategy of storing copies of processed code (or anything that results from it) in view of delivering it faster to the user when requested subsequent times. For example, when you go to a website, you browser is most likely going to *cache* (store) certain assets locally on your computer so that when you visit the site the next time, it can show them to you faster.

Although caching has been steadily improving with recent versions of Drupal, it was still lacking significantly. Particularly when it comes to serving registered users. Drupal 8, however, is a completely different ball game. The system has been totally revamped and has all aspects of the Drupal architecture. Unfortunately, though, this has put yet another big new thing on the plate of things Drupal 7 developers need to learn. Because it's a complex system, we simply cannot (and should not) get around it. But you're in luck, because in this chapter we will break it all down and see what we're dealing with. So when you are doing module development in Drupal 8, your code will be more performant, your site will run faster, and ultimately your users will be happier.

So, what exactly are we going to talk about in this chapter?

First, we are going to cover some introductory notions about the caching system in Drupal 8 and look at the main types of caching available. Here, we will also see how, during development, we can disable caching to increase our productivity.

Next, we are going to talk about cacheability metadata. This is one of the most important things you'll need to know as a Drupal 8 module developer when it comes to caching. It has to do with declaring render arrays (and other objects) in a way in which Drupal can cache them properly (and invalidate the caches accordingly). We will talk about things such as cache tags, contexts, and max-age, but also see how to apply them to render arrays, block plugins, and access results.

After that, we will look at how we can tackle highly dynamic components (render arrays), which cannot or should not be cached. Drupal 8 has a powerful *auto-placeholdering* system that uses lazy builders to postpone rendering until a later stage, which can greatly improve both cacheability and perceived performance.

Lastly, we are going to look at how we can interact with the Cache API ourselves in order to create, read, and invalidate our own cache entries. Sometimes we need to perform expensive calculations or show external data on our site, which can benefit from being cached.

So let's get to it.

Introduction

The first thing I would like to mention before getting into the meat of the Cache API is that this subsystem is one of the best documented ones (at the time of writing). You can check out the main entry page (`https://www.drupal.org/docs/8/api/cache-api/cache-api`), and I recommend keeping it close by when carrying out Drupal 8 development.

The Cache system in Drupal 8 provides the API needed to handle the creation, storage, and invalidation of cached data. From a storage perspective, it is extensible, allowing us to write our own custom cache *backends* (`CacheBackendInterface`). By default, however, cache data gets stored in the database and hence the default backend is `DatabaseBackend`. Going forward, we will focus only on this implementation, since it is the most commonly used one, especially when starting a new project. Quite often though, once the site becomes more complex, alternative caching backends can be employed for better performance--such as Memecache or Redis.

The simplest type of cache in Drupal 8 is the so called *Internal Page Cache*, whose functionality resides inside the *Page Cache* core module. The goal of this cache layer is to serve anonymous users with responses that are cached in their entirety. The primary assumption is that certain pages can be cached once and served to all anonymous users just the same--an approach similar to what we had in Drupal 7. Unlike the previous version though, this one is much smarter when it comes to (not) serving stale content as it makes use of the so called *cache tags* to invalidate the cached pages when something on that page changes. We will talk about cache tags in more detail soon.

This module is enabled by default when installing Drupal 8 and can be configured more or less the same as in Drupal 7 by going to `admin/config/development/performance`:

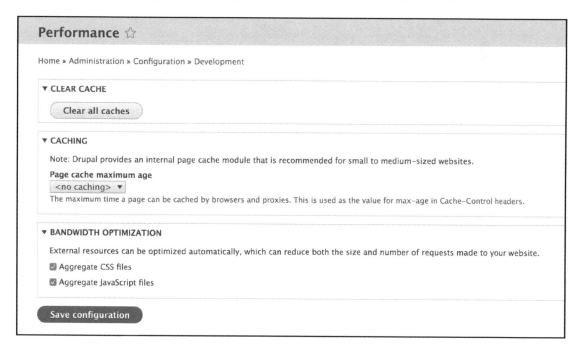

Although serving anonymous users in not-so-complex websites was not that bad in Drupal 7, when it came to authenticated users it was quite the opposite. The contributed *Authcache* module was the best solution for dynamic and granular caching, but it was extremely difficult to use and implement. Some of its core tenets, however, have been used in the development of the `Dynamic Page Cache` module in Drupal 8, which makes things much simpler (and robust).

This core module also comes enabled by default and provides all the necessaries for caching pages for all kinds of users, that is, pages that can depend on certain *cache contexts*. In a nutshell, the approach of this module is to cache together the bits of the page, which can be served for all users and handle the dynamic content that depends on a context separately. It can do so because of the standardization of those *bits* into render arrays and other components which can provide *cacheability metadata*. The latter is collected and used to cache and invalidate the final result. We will talk about cache contexts and all this metadata in this chapter and get a better understanding of it.

Before continuing, I recommend you look back to the *Developer settings* of Chapter 1, *Developing for Drupal 8*, where I recommended you to use the developer settings when doing development. One of the reasons is caching, primarily the dynamic page cache, which you can disable inside the settings.php file:

```
$settings['cache']['bins']['dynamic_page_cache'] = 'cache.backend.null';
```

It is very difficult to do actual development with caching enabled, but at the same time, it's important to often enable it and make sure your code still runs correctly. It is very easy to forget about certain bits of code which depend on a context or should be invalidated upon an action, and sometimes you will only spot these if you test with caching enabled.

That being said, let's talk about cacheability metadata and how this works with render arrays.

Cacheability metadata

Cacheability metadata is used to describe the *thing* which is rendered with respect to its *dynamism*. Most of the time, as Drupal 8 module developers, we will be using this metadata when working with render arrays. We will see a bit later where else these come into play, but for now, let's see what the actual properties are and what they are used for in the context of render arrays.

When creating render arrays, there are a few things we need to think about when it comes to caching. We always need to think about these things.

Cache tags

The first thing we need to think about is what our render array depends on. Are we rendering some entity data? Are we using some configuration values? Or anything that might be changed elsewhere impacting what we have to render? If the answer is yes, we need to use *cache tags*. If we don't use them, our render array gets cached as it is, and if the underlying data changes, we end up showing our users stale content or data.

To look at this an other way, imagine a simple Article node. This content can be shown on its main detail page, in a listing of article teasers or even a listing of article titles (and many other places potentially). And since there is no way of knowing where it will be used, it is the responsibility of the render array that displays this content to mark this node entity as a dependency using cache tags. This way, when the node gets updated, all the render arrays that depend on it get invalidated as well.

Cache tags are simple strings and we can declare many cache tags for a single render array. They do have a special form in the following pattern--`thing:identifier`, or in some cases, just simply `thing` (if there is only one single element of that "thing"). For example, the cache tag for a given node would be in the format `node:1`, where the identifier is the actual node ID. Or for a configuration object it would be `config:hello_world.custom_salutation`.

I hinted before how, for example, some node content can be present in a list and therefore, using the cache tags, we can ensure that the render array for that node gets updated when the node does. Since render arrays are highly granular, this can present a small extra problem as the list itself can be a render array that may not even know which nodes it renders. Or even more, it does not know when new nodes are created and should be included in it. To solve this issue, we have a special "list" cache tag we can use when rendering entities. For example, the `node_list` cache tag can be used for node entities, while the `product_list` cache tag can be used for the product entities. These are automatically understood by the Drupal caching system, so all we have to do is use them appropriately.

To make life easier, however, all entities and configuration objects can be "interrogated" to provide their respective cache tags. For example:

```
$tags = $node->getCacheTags();
```

Where `$tags` will be an array containing one tag--`node:[nid]`.

The same applies to configuration objects and this is handy because it prevents typos and errors. This is due to the generic `CacheableDependencyInterface` they implement and which defines the methods for retrieving the cache metadata properties. In fact, any value that needs to be a cache dependency can and should implement this interface. As you'll find, there are a quite a few classes in Drupal core that do so.

 You will also encounter `RefinableCacheableDependencyInterface`, which is used in cases in which the cacheability of the underlying object can change at runtime. For example, an entity translation is added, which means that a new cache context needs to be added for that language.

We can also figure out the "list" cache tag specific to a given entity type. For example, instead of hardcoding the `product_list` tag, we can use the `getListCacheTags()` method and ask for the `EntityTypeInterface` for it.

If your render array depends on something custom, you can use custom cache tags, but it will be your responsibility to also invalidate them when the underlying data is changed. We will see how this is done when we interact with the Cache API directly. It's always good to consistently use the `CacheableDependencyInterface` for any custom value objects.

Cache contexts

Once we thought about the dependencies of the render array, the second most important thing to consider is what it differs by. In other words, is there any reason why this render array should be shown one way sometimes but another way some other time?

Let's take a simple example of a render array that prints out the name of the current user. Nothing could be less complicated. Ignoring the cache tags for now, we immediately realize that we cannot show the same username to all users, right? So, the user *Danny* should see "Hi Danny" while user *John* should see "Hi John". We are talking about the same render array but one that differs by context. In other words, a variation of this render array needs to get cached separately for each encountered context. This is where we use the aforementioned *cache contexts*.

Similar to cache tags, cache contexts are simple strings, and a render array can be defined with more than just one. For example, the `user` context will cache a variation of a given render array for each user.

Moreover, they are hierarchical in nature in the sense that some contexts can include others. For example, let's continue with our previous example. Let's assume that users with `editor` role should see the greeting message but the ones with the `contributor` role should see a different, more complicated one. In this case, the cache context would be on the roles the user has. But since it already depends on the actual user due to the need to show its username, it doesn't make sense to even bother with the roles context, because the former encompasses the latter. Moreover, Drupal is smart enough to remove the superfluous one when combining the cache contexts from all the render arrays that make up a page. But if our render array differs, for example, only on the user roles and not necessarily the user itself, we should use the specific context--`user.roles`. As you may notice, the hierarchical nature is reflected in the dot (`.`) separation of the contexts.

There are a number of cache contexts already defined by Drupal core. Although you probably won't have to, at least in the beginning, other contexts can also be defined. I recommend you check out the documentation page (`https://www.drupal.org/docs/8/api/cache-api/cache-contexts`) for the available cache contexts that come out of the box.

Max-age

The last main thing we need to think about when creating render arrays is how long they should be stored in the cache barring no changes in the underlying data that might invalidate them. This is something that you will probably rarely set and by default it will be cached permanently. More often, however, you will set this cache property to "0" in order to denote that this render array should never be cached. This is when you are rendering something highly dynamic that doesn't make sense to be cached at all.

Using the cache metadata

Now that we have looked at the three main cache properties, we need to consider creating render arrays, so let's revisit some of our previous work and apply this in practice as needed.

Quite often you'll see the `CacheableMetadata` object being used and passed around in Drupal 8 core code. This is simply used to represent cache metadata and also provides some handy methods to apply that metadata to a render array, statically instantiate itself from one, or from a `CacheableDependencyInterface` object, as well as merge itself with another `CacheableMetadata` object.

The render array we will look at is inside the
`HelloWorldSalutation::getSalutationComponent()` service and is used to render
the salutation message. We are building it quite dynamically, but a simplified version looks
like this (omitting some things):

```
$render = [
  '#theme' => 'hello_world_salutation',
  '#salutation' => [
    '#markup' => $salutation
  ]
];
```

`$salutation` is either the message from the configuration object or generated based on the
time of day.

Right off the bat, I will mention that this is one of those cases in which we cannot really
cache the render array due to its highly dynamic nature. This is caused by the dependency
of the time of day. Sure, we could set a maximum age of a few seconds or an hour, but is it
even worth it? And we also run the risk of showing the wrong salutation.

So in this case, what we can do is add a maximum age of zero:

```
$render = [
  '#theme' => 'hello_world_salutation',
  '#salutation' => [
    '#markup' => $salutation
  ],
  '#cache' => [
    'max-age' => 0
  ]
];
```

The cache metadata goes under a #cache render array property as in the preceding
example.

Specifying the max-age basically tells Drupal not to ever cache this render array. Something
important to know about this is that this declaration will bubble up to the top level render
array that makes the Controller response, preventing the entire thing from being cached. So,
do not make the decision to prevent caching lightly. In our example, this is basically the
entire Controller response and it is actually a very simple calculation, so we are good. Later
in the chapter, we will talk about the ways this can be mitigated.

There is still a problem with us setting the `max-age` to zero in this example. Although it will work with dynamic page caching (the `max-age` will bubble up), the internal page cache serving anonymous users does not get this information. So, anonymous users will see the same thing every time. Possibly in future Drupal 8 releases, this will be fixed. We won't account for this issue yet because it's a great example of a bug that becomes apparent using automated tests, and we will see that in the final chapter of the book--as well as the solution of course.

Let's, for a minute, assume that our salutation component is simply rendering the message stored in the configuration object and does not show time specific content. If you remember:

```
$config = $this->configFactory->get('hello_world.custom_salutation');
$salutation = $config->get('salutation');
```

In this case, we could cache the render array, but as we discussed earlier, we'd need to think about the dependencies as well as the potential variations it can have. It is already pretty obvious what the dependencies are--the configuration object. So, we would do the following:

```
$render = [
  '#theme' => 'hello_world_salutation',
  '#salutation' => [
    '#markup' => $salutation
  ],
  '#cache' => [
    'tags' => $config->getCacheTags()
  ]
];
```

Basically, we are requesting this particular configuration object's cache tags and setting those onto the render array. If we had more sets of cache tags to set from multiple objects, we would have to merge them. There is a tool we can use to ensure we do it right. For example:

```
$tags = Cache::mergeTags($config_one->getCacheTags(),
$config_two->getCacheTags());
```

This will merge two arrays of cache tags, pure and simple. The `Drupal\Core\Cache\Cache` class also has helper static methods for merging cache contexts and max-ages (among other things, I encourage you to check this out as you progress).

Thankfully, our render array is simple and does not vary, and we hence we don't need cache contexts. If, however, we had appended the current username to the salutation, we would have had to add the `user` context to the render array as follows:

```
'#cache' => [
  'tags' => $config->getCacheTags(),
  'contexts' => ['user']
]
```

This would have cached the render array differently for each user who visits the page and would serve them accordingly at subsequent visits.

Caching in block plugins

The render array we saw earlier was used as part of a Controller response. The latter is also known as the *main content* as it is the primary output of the page. On a normal Drupal installation, which uses the block module, this is included inside the `Main page content` block. We also said that setting a max-age of zero will bubble up to the top level render array causing the entire page to not be cached. This is true so far as the Controller response is concerned. Other blocks are still cached independently according to their own metadata.

In this book, you have already learned how we can create custom blocks, and we saw that they are also built using render arrays. Since this is the case, cache metadata can also be applied to those arrays for caching them properly. However, since we are extending from the `BlockBase` class when creating block plugins, we are essentially implementing the `CacheableDependencyInterface` due to `BlockPluginInterface` extending it.

So instead of setting the metadata on the render array, we should, whenever possible, use the methods on that interface by overriding the default parent implementations. For example:

```
/**
 * {@inheritdoc}
 */
public function getCacheContexts() {
  return Cache::mergeContexts(parent::getCacheContexts(), ['user']);
}
```

We should always merge our own values with the ones from the parent.

In some cases, though, especially when declaring cache tags, it makes more sense to set them inside the render array of the `build()` method. That is because you may have already done some work to get your hand on the dependent objects, and it doesn't make sense to repeat that inside another method. That is totally fine.

Caching access results

Another important place where access metadata needs to be considered is `AccessResultInterface`. If you remember from the previous chapter, objects implementing this interface are used consistently to represent access to a certain resource. On top of that, they can also contain cacheability metadata. This is because access may depend on certain data that can change with an impact on the access result itself. Since Drupal tries to cache access as well, we need to inform it of these dependencies.

A good example to see this in action is our `HelloWorldAccess` service where we dynamically check access to our `hello_world.hello` route. So instead of simply returning the `AccessResultInterface`, we add cacheable dependencies to it before doing so:

```
$access = in_array('editor', $account->getRoles()) && $salutation != "" ?
AccessResult::forbidden() : AccessResult::allowed();
$access->addCacheableDependency($salutation);
$access->addCacheableDependency($account);
return $access;
```

The `addCacheableDependency()` method usually takes `CacheableDependencyInterface` objects to read their cache metadata. If something else is passed, the access result is deemed un-cacheable. So in our preceding example, since the access depends on both the salutation configuration object and the user account, we add them both as cache dependencies.

Placeholders and lazy building

Now that we've seen a bit how the cacheability metadata can be used in the more common scenarios, let's shift gears and talk about those page components, which have highly dynamic data.

When we set the maximum age of our Hello World salutation to zero seconds (don't cache), I mentioned that there are ways this can be improved in order to help performance. This takes the form of postponing the rendering of the respective bit to the very last moment with the help of placeholders. But first, a bit of background.

Each of the cache properties we talked about can have values that make caching the render array pointless. We've already talked about the maximum age being set to zero, but you can also argue very low expiration times to have the same effect. Additionally, certain cache tags can be invalidated too frequently, again making the render arrays that depend on what they represent pointless to cache. Finally, certain cache contexts can provide many variations that significantly limit the effectiveness of the cache to the point it may even be counterproductive (high storage cost).

Cache tags are something very specific to the application we are building, so there are no general assumptions that can be made as to which have a high invalidation rate. However, there are two cache contexts that by default are considered to have much too high cardinality for being effective--`session` and `user`. Yes, we talked about the `user` context earlier as a good example but in reality--by default--adding this context to a render array has pretty much the same effect as setting the max-age to zero--it will not be cached. The same goes for the `session` context because there can be so many sessions and users on the site, you probably won't want to have cache records for each individual one.

Since these are not rules that have to necessarily apply to all applications, Drupal configures these values as service parameters, making them changeable if needed. Inside the `core.services.yml` file (which lists most of the core services), we can find some parameter definitions as well, including this one:

```
renderer.config:
  auto_placeholder_conditions:
    max-age: 0
    contexts: ['session', 'user']
    tags: []
```

As you can see, the max-age value of zero and the previously mentioned cache contexts are included, but no tags. We can also change these values. So, for example, if in our application we know that we won't have too many users and it does, in fact, make sense to cache by user context, or we know of certain cache tags with high invalidation frequency, it makes sense to do so. There are two ways we can do it--either we use our site-wide `services.yml` file and copy these declarations (while making the appropriate changes) or we can use the services file of a given module in the same way. Both ways have the effect of overriding the default parameters set by Drupal core.

Now that we are clear on why certain things are not cacheable, let's see how this can be addressed using *auto-placeholdering*.

Auto-placeholdering is the process by which Drupal identifies the render arrays that cannot or should not be cached, due to reasons we mentioned before, and replaces them with a placeholder. The latter is then replaced at the very last possible moment while allowing the rest of the page components to be cached. This is also called *lazy building*.

Drupal identifies the bits which need to be lazy built by the cache metadata that fits the conditions we saw before and the presence of the `#lazy_builder` property (mapping to a callback) on the render array. The former does not necessarily have to be on the render array containing the `#lazy_builder`property, it can also be on the resulting one from the callback.

Lazy builders

Lazy builders are nothing more than callbacks on a render array that Drupal can use to build the render array at a later stage. The callbacks can be static (a reference to a class and method) or dynamic (a reference to a service and method). Using the latter approach is more flexible as we can inject dependencies from the container as we do regularly with services. Moreover, the callback can take parameters, which means it can build the render array already, having at least part of the needed data.

The best way to understand this is to see an example. Since we decided that our salutation component should have a cache lifetime of zero seconds, it's a good opportunity to build it using a lazy builder.

The first thing we need to do is replace our `helloWorld` Controller method in which we directly call the salutation service with this:

```
return [
  '#lazy_builder' => ['hello_world.lazy_builder:renderSalutation', []],
  '#create_placeholder' => TRUE,
];
```

Back in `Chapter 4`, *Theming*, when I said a render array needs to have at least one of the four properties (#type, #theme, #markup, or #plain_text), I lied. We can also use a lazy builder like this to defer the building of the render array to a later stage.

The `#lazy_builder` needs to be an array whose first item is the callback and the second is an array of parameters to pass to it. In our case, we don't need any of the latter. We could pass the salutation service, but instead, we will inject it into the new `hello_world.lazy_builder` service we will create in a minute. The callback reference is in the format of `service_name:method` (one colon used for separation) or for static calls `class_name::method` (two colons). We also explicitly declare `#create_placeholder` to make it clear that this render array should be replaced with a placeholder. Lastly, as I mentioned earlier, the cache metadata can be applied to this render array or it can also be in the resulting one from the lazy builder. So, we'll opt for the latter approach in this case.

Let's now define our service:

```
hello_world.lazy_builder:
  class: Drupal\hello_world\HelloWorldLazyBuilder
  arguments: ['@hello_world.salutation']
```

Nothing out of the ordinary here, but we are injecting the `HelloWorldSalutation` service as a dependency so that we can ask it for our salutation component. The actual service class looks like this:

```
namespace Drupal\hello_world;

/**
 * Lazy builder for the Hello World salutation.
 */
class HelloWorldLazyBuilder {

  /**
   * @var \Drupal\hello_world\HelloWorldSalutation
   */
  protected $salutation;

  /**
   * HelloWorldLazyBuilder constructor.
   *
   * @param \Drupal\hello_world\HelloWorldSalutation $salutation
   */
  public function __construct(HelloWorldSalutation $salutation) {
    $this->salutation = $salutation;
  }

  /**
   * Renders the Hello World salutation message.
   */
  public function renderSalutation() {
    return $this->salutation->getSalutationComponent();
```

```
        }
    }
```

All very simple. The `renderSalutation()` method is required as we referenced it from our lazy builder. That is all we have to do. But, what exactly happens with this?

When Drupal renders our Controller, it finds the lazy builder and registers it with a placeholder which is then used instead of the actual final render array. Then, at a much later stage in the page building process, the lazy builder is invoked and the actual output is rendered to replace the placeholder. There are a couple of advantages and implications with this. First, it allows Drupal to bypass this highly dynamic bit of output and cache the rest of the components in the dynamic page cache. This is to prevent the lack of cacheability from infecting the entire page. Second, there are two different strategies (so far) with which placeholders can be processed. By default, in using the so-called *Single Flush* method, the placeholder replacement is postponed until the last minute, but the response is not sent back to the browser before this is done. So, the dynamic page cache does improve things (caches what it can), but the response still depends on the placeholder processing finishing. Depending on how long that takes, the page load, in general, can suffer. This is the traditional way of building responses and is the default in Drupal 8. However, when using the **BigPipe** (`https://www.facebook.com/notes/facebook-engineering/bigpipe-pipelining-web-pages-for-high-performance/389414033919`) approach, the response is sent back to the browser before the placeholders are replaced. And as the latter finishes as well, the replacements are streamed to the browser. This greatly improves the perceived performance of the site as users can already see most parts of the page before the slower bits appear.

The *BigPipe* technique was invented by Facebook as a way to deal with highly dynamic pages and was gradually brought into Drupal 8 as an experimental core module. With version 8.3, it is expected to be a stable module and ready for use in production sites.

Using the Cache API

So far in this chapter, we mostly preoccupied ourselves with render arrays and how we can expose them to the Cache API for better performance. It's now time to talk a bit about how cache entries are stored by default in Drupal and how we can interact with them ourselves in our code.

As mentioned earlier, a central interface for the cache system is the `CacheBackendInterface`, which is the interface any caching system needs to implement. It basically provides the methods for creating, reading, and invalidating cache entries.

As we might expect, when we want to interact with the Cache API, we use a service to retrieve an instance of the CacheBackendInterface. However, the service name we use depends on the cache *bin* we want to work with. Cache bins are repositories that group together cache entries based on their type. So, the aforementioned implementation wraps a single cache bin, and each bin has a machine name, so the service name will be in the following format--cache.[bin]. This means that for each cache bin, we have a separate service.

The static shorthand for getting this service looks like this:

```
$cache = \Drupal::cache();
```

This will return the default bin represented by a CacheBackendInterface implementation. If we want to request a specific bin, we pass the name as an argument:

```
$cache = \Drupal::cache('render');
```

This will return the render cache bin.

And of course, if we need to inject a cache bin wrapper somewhere, we simply use the service machine name in the format I mentioned before.

Even though we have a separate service for each cache bin, they all basically do the same thing, and that is use the CacheFactory to instantiate the right type of cache backend for that bin. Individual cache backends can be registered and set as default either globally or for specific bins.

As I mentioned at the beginning of the chapter, the default cache backend in Drupal--the one this factory will instantiate for all the bins--is the DatabaseBackend. Each bin is represented by a database table. This is similar in concept to what we had in Drupal 7.

Now that we know how to load the cache backend service, lets see how we can use it to read and cache things. When it comes to this, your number one reference is the CacheBackendInterface, which documents all the methods. However, since it does not reinforce return values, the examples we will see next are done with the database cache backend. They might differ from other cache backend implementations.

The first method we'll talk about is get(), which takes the ID of the cache entry we want to retrieve ($cid) and an optional $allow_invalidparameter. The first one is clear enough, but the second one is used in case we want to retrieve the entry even if it has expired or has been invalidated. This can be useful in those cases in which *stale* data is preferred over the recalculation costs of multiple concurrent requests.

```
$data = $cache->get('my_cache_entry_cid');
```

The resulting `$data` variable is a PHP standard class, which contains the `data` key (the data that has been cached) and all sorts of metadata about the cache entry-- expiration, creation timestamp, tags, valid status, and so on.

Of course, there is also a `getMultiple()` method, which you can use to retrieve multiple entries at once. More fun, though, is the `set()` method, which allows us to store something in the cache. There are four parameters to this method:

- `$cid` : The cache ID that can be used to retrieve the entry.
- `$data` : A serializable data structure like an array or object (or simple scalar value).
- `$expire` : The UNIX timestamp after which this entry is considered invalid, or `CacheBackendInterface::CACHE_PERMANENT` to indicate that this entry is never invalid unless specifically invalidated. The latter is the default.
- `$tags` : An array of cache tags that will be used to invalidate this entry if it depends on something else (cache metadata, basically).

So to use it, we would do something like this:

```
$cache->set('my_cache_entry_cid', 'my_value');
```

With this statement, we are creating a simple non-serialized cache entry into our chosen bin and which does not expire unless specifically invalidated (or deleted). Subsequent calls with the same cache ID will simply override the entry. If the cache value is an array or object, it will get serialized.

When it comes to deleting, there are two easy methods--`delete()` and `deleteMultiple()`, which take the `$cid` (or array of cache IDs, respectively) as arguments and remove the entries from the bin completely. If we want to delete all the items in the bin, we can use the `deleteAll()` method.

Instead of deleting, quite often it's a good idea to invalidate the entries. We'll still be able to retrieve the data using the `$allow_invalid` parameter and can use the entry while the new one is being recalculated. This can be done almost exactly as deleting but using the following methods instead--`invalidate()`, `invalidateMultiple()`, and `invalidateAll()`.

Okay, but what about those cache tags we can store with the entry? We already kind of know their purpose and that is to *tag* cache entries across multiple bins with certain data markers that can make them easy to invalidate when the data changes. Just like with render arrays. So, how can we do this?

Lets assume that we store the following cache entry as follows:

```
$cache->set('my_cache_entry_cid', 'my_value',
CacheBackendInterface::CACHE_PERMANENT, ['node:10']);
```

We essentially make it dependent on changes to the Node with the ID of 10. This means that when that node changes, our entry (together with all other entries in all other bins that depend on it) becomes invalid. Simple as that.

But we can also have our own tags that make it depend on something custom of ours like a data value (which, as we discussed earlier in the chapter, should implement the `CacheableDependencyInterface`) or a process of some kind. In that case, we would also have to take care of invalidating all the cache entries that have our tag. The simplest way we can do this is statically, using the `Cache` class we've encountered earlier when merging metadata together:

```
Cache::invalidateTags(['my_custom_tag']);
```

This will invalidate all cache entries that are *tagged* with any of the tags passed in the array. Under the hood, this method uses a static call to the cache invalidator service, so whenever possible, it's best to actually inject that service--`cache_tags.invalidator`.

Creating our own cache bin

Usually, the existing cache bins, particularly the default one, will be enough to store our own cache entries. However, there are times in which we need to create multiple entries for the same functionality, in which case it would help to have a special bin for that. So, let's see how that can be created.

It's quite easy because all we have to do is define a service:

```
cache.my_bin:
  class: Drupal\Core\Cache\CacheBackendInterface
  tags:
    - { name: cache.bin }
  factory: cache_factory:get
  arguments: [my_bin]
```

The class used in this service definition is actually an interface. This is because we are using a factory to instantiate the service rather than the container directly. This means we don't know what class will be instantiated. In this case, the factory in question is the service with the name `cache_factory` and its `get()` method. In Chapter 3, *Logging and Mailing*, we saw an example in which something like this happened when we talked about logger channels.

The `cache.bin` tag is used so that Drupal can understand the function of this service, namely, that it is a cache bin. The responsibility of making sure this bin gets its storage belongs to the actual backend. So in our example, the `DatabaseBackend` creates and removes the cache table as needed.

Lastly, the static argument is the name of the bin that gets passed to the factory and which is used to create the cache backend for this particular bin. That is pretty much it. If we clear the cache, we can already see in the database a new cache table for our bin.

Summary

In this chapter, we covered the main aspects related to caching in Drupal 8, any module developer needs to be familiar with. We introduced some key concepts and talked about the two main types of caching--Internal Page Cache (used for anonymous users) and Dynamic Page Cache (used for any kind of user).

We dug deeper into cacheability metadata, which is probably the most important and common thing we need to understand. It's imperative to use this properly so that all the render arrays we build are cached and invalidated correctly. We've also seen how block plugins have specific methods we can use to define their cacheability metadata and how access results should also receive cacheability dependencies as needed. Stemming from this, we also explored lazy builders and the *auto-placeholdering* strategies that allow us to handle highly dynamic components while maintaining good cacheability overall.

Lastly, we looked into using the Cache API ourselves in order to store, read, and invalidate our own cache entries. We even saw how to create our own custom cache bin.

Caching is a very important aspect of Drupal 8 module development. In previous versions, it didn't even come close and we were able to get away quite often with not even paying attention to it. Now, we have a powerful system in place to make rendering more performant, and we should make use of it.

In the next chapter, we are going to talk about JavaScript and how we can use it in a Drupal context, as well as the powerful Ajax API.

12
JavaScript and the Ajax API

So far in this book, we've only talked about topics that can be considered to relate to *backend development*. This means heavy PHP, working with the APIs and the database, and so on. This is because this book is oriented toward module developers rather than themers. Also, the author of this book is admittedly not a JavaScript, or any kind of frontend, developer.

Nevertheless, in this chapter we'll switch gears and talk a bit about *frontend development*, namely, how to work with JavaScript in a Drupal 8 application. This is because there are many things developers can and should be doing in their modules that require frontend technologies. There are a few approaches and techniques specific to Drupal when it comes to adding and using JavaScript files and we will talk about those here. Moreover, we will also prove how powerful Drupal 8 is in allowing us to do quite a bit of "JavaScript" work without actually writing a single line of JavaScript code.

So, there are a few things we will cover in this chapter.

First, we will talk about the approach of writing JavaScript in Drupal. You already learned in `Chapter 4`, *Theming*, how you can create libraries and attach them to render arrays, elements, or pages. Basically, using libraries, we can get our JavaScript files loaded when we need. I recommend you check out the section Assets and libraries from `Chapter 4`, *Theming*, if you don't remember exactly how libraries work. Because in this chapter, we will continue from there and talk a bit about what actually goes inside those JavaScript files.

 A good resource to keep handy is the documentation page (`https://www.drupal.org/node/172169`) that lists the coding standards for JavaScript in Drupal 8 that we should abide by.

We won't actually write a lot of JavaScript code in the first part--enough to get you started though. In the second part, we will not write any at all. Instead, we will talk about the robust Ajax API that comes with Drupal and which allows us to build some very dynamic functionalities that rely on JavaScript. To demonstrate how things work, we will revisit our Importer functionality started in Chapter 7, *Your Own Custom Entity and Plugin Types*, and improve it using Ajax.

Finally, we will also talk about the States system of the Form API, which allows us to make our form elements dynamic and dependent on others in a declarative way. Again, we won't even have to know any JavaScript to do what is actually quite complex client-side behavior.

JavaScript in Drupal

Drupal 8 relies on a number of JavaScript libraries and plugins to perform some of its frontend tasks. For example, the use of *Backbone.js* is another example of advancement from previous versions of Drupal when it comes to adopting established libraries rather than reinventing new ones. Of course, as we already saw, the ubiquitous *jQuery* library continues to be used in Drupal 8 as well. But of course, there's others.

Another thing I have already mentioned but which is helpful to bring up again is the fact that Drupal no longer loads things such as jQuery or its Ajax framework on all pages needlessly. For example, many pages serving anonymous users which do not require jQuery won't even load it. This can greatly improve performance. But it also means that when we define our libraries to include our own JavaScript files, we must always declare these as dependencies (if we need them). For example, jQuery is something you'll often depend on.

Drupal behaviors

One of the most important things you need to know when writing JavaScript files in Drupal is the concept of behaviors. But in order to understand that, let's get a bit of context.

When writing JavaScript code using jQuery, it's often standard to wrap our code inside a ready() method statement as follows:

```
$(document).ready(function () {
  // Essentially the entirety of your javscript code.
});
```

This ensures that your code runs only after the entire DOM has been loaded by the browser. Moreover, the use of jQuery for this helps a great deal with cross-browser compatibility and also allows us to place this code wherever we want on the page (header or footer).

In Drupal, however, we have a different solution which is better in the context of writing JavaScript, that works with Drupal as well (not just with the DOM). That comes in the form of Drupal behaviors. In a nutshell, behaviors are methods we declare which get called when the DOM loads fully, that is, when the document is ready. However, on top of that, they also get called by the Ajax framework when new data is loaded onto the page. Even when using BigPipe and placeholder, replacements are streamed.

Any Drupal site has a global `Drupal` object, which is used for many things we won't go into right now. However, the `Drupal.behaviours` object is where we declare behaviors, and typically any JavaScript code that we want to run should go inside a behavior. So, let's see an example, as it will be much easier to understand.

What we want is to show a little dynamic JavaScript clock next to the Hello World salutation, if the message is not coming from the configuration but is dependent on the time of day. While writing the code for our functionality, we'll talk about Drupal behaviors and how they are used.

Our library

In order to get our JavaScript file loaded, it needs to be in a library and attached to *something*. As you learned in Chapter 4, *Theming*, the libraries file has the name `hello_world.libraries.yml` and is located in the root folder of our module:

```
hello_world_clock:
  version: 1.x
  js:
    js/hello_world_clock.js: {}
  dependencies:
    - core/jquery
    - core/drupal
    - core/jquery.once
```

We only have a single JavaScript file that is needed for our purpose, located in the `js` directory of our module. But we do have some dependencies. First, we want jQuery loaded because we will use it. Second, we want to have the general Drupal JavaScript library, which handles a bunch of things, including behaviors. The last dependency we will talk about soon and it will make a bit more sense then.

Without these dependencies declared, in some cases (especially for anonymous users), Drupal would not have them loaded on the page and our JavaScript functionality will not work.

Now, let's attach this library to our salutation component found inside the `HelloWorldSalutation` service:

Right after these two lines:

```
$time = new \DateTime();
$render['#target'] = $this->t('world');
```

We can add the following:

```
$render['#attached'] = [
  'library' => [
    'hello_world/hello_world_clock'
  ]
];
```

This is nothing new for us but the point is we are only attaching the library if the component is showing the dynamic salutation message that depends on the time of day. If this message has been overridden, we don't even want to load these libraries, and that is pretty much it. We can dive in and create our `hello_world_clock.js` file.

The JavaScript

The first thing we need to do inside the JavaScript file is to wrap the entire code we write in the file into an immediately invoked function expression (IIFE). In doing this, we protect the scope of what we write from the global one and even use global variables with more commonly associated variable names inside our own scope. This is how this looks:

```
(function (Drupal, $) {

  "use strict";

  // Our code here.

}) (Drupal, jQuery);
```

The most important thing here is that inside this function we can now use the dollar sign ($) as a reference to the global jQuery object without interfering with other libraries that might use the same variable name. Also, we added the `use strict` declaration to ensure we write semantically correct code (and it's also part of the JavaScript coding standards for Drupal 8).

Let's now add the meat of our functionality and explain how it works:

```
Drupal.behaviors.helloWorldClock = {
  attach: function (context, settings) {
    function ticker() {
      var date = new Date();
      $(context).find('.clock').html(date.toLocaleTimeString());
    }

    var clock = '<div>The time is <span class="clock"></span></div>';

    $(context).find('.salutation').append(clock);

    setInterval(function() {
      ticker();
    }, 1000);
  }
};
```

First of all, we are defining a new behavior, which is an object on the `Drupal.behaviours` object and needs to have a unique name. You can look at a single behavior as one piece of functionality. We only need one function on this object called `attach`, which receives two parameters--`context` (the page or part of the page that is being loaded) and `settings` (the variable containing data passed from PHP).

This function gets invoked by Drupal whenever behaviors need to be attached--`Drupal.attachBehaviors()`. This happens when the page gets loaded for the first time (in which case `context` is the entire DOM) or after an Ajax request (in which case `context` contains only the newly loaded parts of the page). Therefore, using the `context` instead of the entire document for looking up elements is best practice because it's more performant (especially after an Ajax request) and prevents other side effects.

Inside the `attach` function, we have our logic for creating a clock. First, we define a simple function that looks for the element with the class `.clock`and puts the current time into it. You'll notice that we used `context` to look for the element. Next, we create this element ourselves and append it to our salutation message element. Lastly, we set an interval every second to keep calling our `ticker()` function, essentially updating the time every second, giving the illusion of a clock. This is all pretty standard.

 Be aware that the strings we are printing to the user via JavaScript are not run through the translation system and that is not good practice (even if the site is not multilingual). In a later chapter, we will see how we need to handle it instead.

Clearing the cache and navigating to our /hello page, we can already see the new clock appearing (if we don't have the salutation message overridden). So we're done, right? Well, not really.

If we open up the browser's developer tools, namely the console, and try to attach the behaviors again:

```
Drupal.attachBehaviors();
```

We notice that our clock element gets appended again (it has been duplicated). Well, that's not right because if we have an Ajax request we run the risk of having this happen. This is where jQuery.once comes in.

The jQuery.once library is a plugin for jQuery, which allows us to track and make sure we are performing something only once. It's actually very simple to use. All we have to do is replace this line:

```
$(context).find('.salutation').append(clock);
```

With this:

```
$(context).find('.salutation').once('helloWorldClock').append(clock);
```

So basically, before doing the actual thing, we call the .once() method with an ID to use for tracking. This will ensure that whatever comes next in the chain is only applied to the elements onto which it has not been already applied. And now you also see why we wanted our library to depend on core/jquery.once one.

And with this, our clock is ready.

Drupal settings

Another powerful thing we can do (and something we often need to do) is pass values from our PHP code to the JavaScript layer. In custom PHP applications, this can get messy, but Drupal has a robust API that transforms PHP arrays into JavaScript objects. These can be found inside the settings object passed to the behavior's attach() function.

Again, the easiest way to understand this is through an example. So let's say we want to print an extra message after the salutation if we are in the afternoon. Of course, we can use JavaScript to determine that as well, but so far it has been the responsibility of our PHP code, so let's keep it that way. So then we need a way to tell our JavaScript that it is afternoon, and we can do this by setting a flag if that is this case, as follows:

```
if ((int) $time->format('G') >= 12 && (int) $time->format('G') < 18) {
    $render['#salutation']['#markup'] = $this->t('Good afternoon');
$render['#attached']['drupalSettings']['hello_world']['hello_world_clock'][
'afternoon'] = TRUE;
    return $render;
}
```

New here is the second line from within the *if conditional*, namely, the one where we attach something to the render array. In this case, though, it's not a library but *drupalSettings* in a big multidimensional array. The best practice is to *namespace* our settings hierarchically like so--our module name -> the functionality the settings it belongs to -> the setting name. In JavaScript, this array will be transformed into an object.

> To get the *drupalSettings* to work, we need to make sure the core/drupalSettings library is loaded. In our case, this is because the core/drupalone lists it as a dependency.

Now that we pass this flag (which could be much more complex if needed), we can make use of it in JavaScript:

```
var clock = '<div>The time is <span class="clock"></span></div>';
if (settings.hello_world != undefined &&
settings.hello_world.hello_world_clock.afternoon != undefined) {
    clock += 'Are you having a nice day?';
}
```

That is pretty much it. We managed to easily pass values from PHP into JavaScript can and use them in client-side logic.

Ajax API

Now that you are on your way and ready to write whatever JavaScript you need for your application, and you are able to integrate this with the Drupal backend APIs, let's take a look at the Ajax framework. There's a lot we can do on the client side without having to write a single line of JavaScript code.

The Drupal Ajax API is a robust system that allows us to define client-side interactions via PHP. The most common time we use Ajax is when we interact with forms--triggering certain actions that change the DOM without having to reload the page. We will demonstrate how all this works by expanding a bit more on the importer functionality we built in `Chapter 7`, *Your Own Custom Entity and Plugin Types*. Before, though, let's take a quick look at the simpler use case of Ajax in Drupal 8.

Ajax links

The simplest way to interact with Drupal's Ajax API is to add the class `use-ajax` to any link. This will cause the link to make an Ajax request to the path of the link rather than moving the browser to it. A similar thing can be done with the submit button of a form using the class `use-ajax-submit`. This makes the form submit via Ajax to the path defined in the form's action.

The most important thing, however, is what we do on the other end of the process. Clicking a link which triggers an Ajax request won't do anything if we don't handle that request accordingly. What we have to do is return an `AjaxResponse` object with some jQuery *commands* that instruct the browser on the changes it needs to make to the DOM. So, let's see an example.

Remember in `Chapter 2`, *Creating Your First Module*, we created our first block that simply rendered the salutation message from the service? It did't use the theme hook we created in `Chapter 4`, *Theming*, but simply delegated to the `getSalutation()` method of the `HelloWorldSalutation` service. Let's say we want to add a link after the message we can click on, and which hides the block entirely. There are few easy steps we need to do to achieve this.

First, we need to alter the `build()` method of the block to get something like this:

```
/**
 * {@inheritdoc}
 */
public function build() {
$build = [];
```

```
$build[] = [
  '#theme' => 'container',
  '#children' => [
    '#markup' => $this->salutation->getSalutation(),
  ]
];

$url = Url::fromRoute('hello_world.hide_block');
$url->setOption('attributes', ['class' => 'use-ajax']);
$build[] = [
  '#type' => 'link',
  '#url' => $url,
  '#title' => $this->t('Remove'),
];

return $build;
}
```

The first thing we do is wrap our original simple #markup-based array into a Drupal core
container theme hook, just so it wraps it with some divs and we don't have to create our
own theme hook. After all, we are doing proof-of-concept work here. Next, below the
message, we print a link to a new route we have to define. And on that link we add the
use-ajax class, as we talked about. You'll notice that we can add attributes (refer back to
Chapter 4, *Theming*, for more info on those) straight onto the Url object, and they will be
added to the rendered link element.

Second, we need to define this new route. Nothing could be simpler:

```
hello_world.hide_block:
  path: '/hide-block'
  defaults:
    _controller:
'\Drupal\hello_world\Controller\HelloWorldController::hideBlock'
  requirements:
    _permission: 'access content'
```

We map it to a new method on the same Controller class we've been using and allow all
users access to it.

Third (and last), we need to define the Controller method:

```
/**
 * Route callback for hiding the Salutation block.
 * Only works for Ajax calls.
 *
 * @param \Symfony\Component\HttpFoundation\Request $request
 *
```

```
 * @return \Drupal\Core\Ajax\AjaxResponse
 */
public function hideBlock(Request $request) {
  if (!$request->isXmlHttpRequest()) {
    throw new NotFoundHttpException();
  }

  $response = new AjaxResponse();
  $command = new RemoveCommand('.block-hello-world');
  $response->addCommand($command);
  return $response;
}
```

The first thing you'll notice is the `$request` parameter to this method, and you may be wondering where it's coming from. Drupal passes the current request object to any Controller method which simply type hints a parameter with that name and interface. So, we don't have to inject it into our Controller. The reason we need it is so we can check if the request to this route is made via Ajax. Because if not, we don't want to handle it, that is, we throw a `NotFoundHttException`, which results in a regular Drupal 404.

Then comes the fun stuff relating to the Ajax API, namely, the building of an `AjaxResponse` full of commands back to the browser. In our example, there is only one command which instructs it to run the jQuery `remove()` method on the elements that match the selector that is passed to it. In our case, this is the class of the block wrapper. And with this our functionality is in place. We can clear our cache and the block should now print a link that removes the block via Ajax.

You may be thinking--why do we need a trip back to the server for a job that can be done on the client-side alone? And the answer is--we actually don't. However, it serves as a good example of how the Ajax responses work. And I encourage you to check the documentation page (`https://api.drupal.org/api/drupal/core!core.api.php/group/ajax/8.3.x`)for the Ajax API, where you can find a list of all the available commands. For example, we could have used the `ReplaceCommand` to replace the block with something else that comes back from the server, or the `HtmlCommand` to insert some data into an element on the page, or even an `AlertCommand`to trigger a JavaScript alert with some data coming from the server. The cool thing is that the response can process multiple commands so we are not restricted to only using one.

Ajax in forms

The most common use of Ajax in Drupal is through the Form API, where we can create dynamic interactions between the server and client with ease. To demonstrate how this works, we will go through an example. This will be a rework of the Importer configuration entity form we created in Chapter 7, *Your Own Custom Entity and Plugin Types*.

If you remember, we said that tying certain configuration values to the generic entity does not make sense, as importer plugins might be different. The first Importer we wrote loads a JSON file from a remote URL. So, it stands to reason that the configuration value for the URL is tied to the plugin and not the configuration entity (even if the latter actually stores it). Because if we want to create a CSV importer, for example, we don't need the URL. So, let's refactor our work to make this happen.

Here is an outline of the steps we need to do for this refactoring:

- Importer plugins need to provide their own configuration form elements
- The Importer configuration form needs to read these elements depending on which plugin is selected (this is where the Ajax API comes into play)
- We need to alter the storage and configuration schema of the values that are specific to plugins

Let's start by giving the plugin `ImporterInterface` and new method:

```
/**
 * Returns the form array for configuring this plugin.
 *
 * @param \Drupal\products\Entity\ImporterInterface $importer
 *
 * @return array
 */
public function
getConfigurationForm(\Drupal\products\Entity\ImporterInterface $importer);
```

This is responsible for getting the form elements needed for this plugin. As an argument, it receives the Importer configuration entity, which can be inspected for default values.

Next, on the `ImporterInterface` of the configuration entity, we need to remove the `getUrl()` method (since that is specific to the `JsonImporter` plugin) and replace it with a generic method for retrieving all the configuration values pertaining to the plugin selected for the entity:

```
/**
 * Returns the configuration specific to the chosen plugin.
 *
 * @return array
 */
public function getPluginConfiguration();
```

And of course, in the `Importer` entity class, we reflect this change as well:

```
/**
 * The configuration specific to the plugin.
 *
 * @var array
 */
protected $plugin_configuration;
```

And the actual getter method with respect to the interface:

```
/**
 * {@inheritdoc}
 */
public function getPluginConfiguration() {
    return $this->plugin_configuration;
}
```

So far so good, nothing complicated going on. We are replacing the plugin specific configuration values with a generic one in which values specific to the selected plugin will be stored.

Now, let's turn to the `ImporterForm` and make all the adjustments there. But before we do that, let's move the form element for the `url` field into the `JsonImporter`, where we have to implement the new `getConfigurationForm()` method:

```
/**
 * {@inheritdoc}
 */
public function
getConfigurationForm(\Drupal\products\Entity\ImporterInterface $importer) {
    $form = [];
    $config = $importer->getPluginConfiguration();
    $form['url'] = [
      '#type' => 'url',
```

```
      '#default_value' => isset($config['url']) ? $config['url'] : '',
      '#title' => $this->t('Url'),
      '#description' => $this->t('The URL to the import resource'),
      '#required' => TRUE,
    ];
    return $form;
  }
```

You'll notice some differences in getting the default value. Instead of calling the now removed getUrl() method on the configuration entity, we use the new getPluginConfiguration() method and check inside the resulting array. Also, since we use the $this->t() method to ensure the translation of the strings, we should use the StringTranslationTrait as well (inside the class as it is a Trait):

```
use StringTranslationTrait;
```

Let's not forget that we are actually using the URL in the import, so we need to make some adjustments to the getData() method as well:

```
/**
 * Loads the product data from the remote URL.
 *
 * @return \stdClass
 */
private function getData() {
  /** @var ImporterInterface $importer_config */
  $importer_config = $this->configuration['config'];
  $config = $importer_config->getPluginConfiguration();
  $url = isset($config['url']) ? $config['url'] : NULL;
  if (!$url) {
    return NULL;
  }
  $request = $this->httpClient->get($url);
  $string = $request->getBody();
  return json_decode($string);
}
```

With this, we can adjust our ImporterForm (where we no longer have the form element for the URL field).

There are two main things we need to do:

- Expose the plugin selection element to Ajax, that is, trigger an Ajax request when the user makes a selection
- Add the extra elements to the form depending on the chosen plugin

This is what the new `plugin` element looks like:

```
$form['plugin'] = [
  '#type' => 'select',
  '#title' => $this->t('Plugin'),
  '#default_value' => $importer->getPluginId(),
  '#options' => $options,
  '#description' => $this->t('The plugin to be used with this importer.'),
  '#required' => TRUE,
  '#empty_option' => $this->t('Please select a plugin'),
  '#ajax' => array(
    'callback' => [$this, 'pluginConfigAjaxCallback'],
    'wrapper' => 'plugin-configuration-wrapper'
  ),
];
```

There are two noticeable changes--we've added an `#empty_option` key (to be used as the option shown if the user has not made any choice) and the `#ajax` key (which we will discuss in a bit more detail).

What we did is pretty simple--we declared a callback method to be triggered when a user makes a change to this form element, and we declared the HTML ID of the element which should be replaced with the result of the Ajax callback. And in the latter case (which is a simple method on the same class), all we have to do is this:

```
/**
 * Ajax callback for the plugin configuration form elements.
 *
 * @param $form
 * @param \Drupal\Core\Form\FormStateInterface $form_state
 *
 * @return array
 */
public function pluginConfigAjaxCallback($form, FormStateInterface
$form_state) {
  return $form['plugin_configuration'];
}
```

We return a form element (which we still have to define). An important lesson here is that Ajax responses in forms can return content as well (in the form of render arrays or even strings), which will be used to replace the HTML found by the ID specified in the `wrapper` key of the Ajax declaration. Alternatively, an `AjaxResponse` full of commands can also be returned to do more complex things, as we saw in the previous section.

Before we look at this new `plugin_configuration` form element, let's look at some of the other options that can be used inside the `#ajax` array:

- `method`: This indicates the jQuery method to use when interacting with the `wrapper` element (if specified). The default is `replaceWith()`, but you can also use `append()`, `html()`, and others.
- `event`: This shows which event should be used to trigger the Ajax call. By default, the form element in question decides that. For example, when selecting an option in a select element or when typing something into a textfield.
- `progress`: This defines the indicator to be used while the Ajax request is taking place.
- `url`: A URL to trigger the Ajax request in case the `callback` was not specified. Typically, using the latter is more powerful as the entire `$form` and `$form_state` are passed as parameters and can be used in processing.

I recommend you check out the documentation page (`https://api.drupal.org/api/drupal/core!core.api.php/group/ajax/8.3.x`) for the Ajax API for more information about these options and the other ones that are available.

With that out of the way, we can go back to our form definition and add our missing parts, right after the `plugin` element:

```php
$form['plugin_configuration'] = [
  '#type' => 'hidden',
  '#prefix' => '<div id="plugin-configuration-wrapper">',
  '#suffix' => '</div>',
];

$plugin_id = NULL;
if ($importer->getPluginId()) {
  $plugin_id = $importer->getPluginId();
}
if ($form_state->getValue('plugin') && $plugin_id !==
$form_state->getValue('plugin')) {
  $plugin_id = $form_state->getValue('plugin');
}

if ($plugin_id) {
  /** @var \Drupal\products\Plugin\ImporterInterface $plugin */
  $plugin = $this->importerManager->createInstance($plugin_id, ['config' =>
$importer]);
  $form['plugin_configuration']['#type'] = 'details';
  $form['plugin_configuration']['#tree'] = TRUE;
  $form['plugin_configuration']['#open'] = TRUE;
```

```
  $form['plugin_configuration']['#title'] = $this->t('Plugin configuration
for <em>@plugin</em>', ['@plugin' =>
$plugin->getPluginDefinition()['label']]);
  $form['plugin_configuration']['plugin'] =
$plugin->getConfigurationForm($importer);
}
```

First, we define the `plugin_configuration` form element as a `hidden` type. This means it will not be visible to users when the page loads for the first time. However, we do use the `#prefix` and `#suffix` options (common practice with the Drupal Form API) to wrap this element with a DIV that has the ID we indicated as the `wrapper` of our Ajax declaration. So, the goal is to have this element replaced each time an Ajax request is made, that is, each time a plugin is selected.

Next, we try to get the ID of the chosen plugin. First, we load it from the configuration entity in case we are looking at an edit form. However, we also check in the form state to see if one has been selected (and is different than the one in the entity). And if you are wondering how we can have the plugin in the form state, the answer is that after an Ajax call is made (triggered by the user selecting a plugin), the form gets rebuilt. Now, we can see what's in the form state and retrieve the plugin ID that was chosen.

Even more than that, if we get our hands on a plugin ID, we can completely change the `plugin_configuration` element, which in turn then gets returned by the Ajax callback to be used to replace our wrapper. So to sum up:

- Page loads for the first time (on a new form). The element is hidden.
- User selects a plugin. Ajax request is triggered, which rebuilds the form.
- As the form is rebuilt, we check for the selected plugin and alter the `plugin_configuration` element to reflect the selected plugin.
- The Ajax response replaces the old element with the new potentially changed one.

The new `plugin_configuration` element becomes a `details` one (a collapsible container for multiple elements), open by default and which has one key called `plugin`, onto which we add all the elements coming from the plugin. Moreover, we use the `#tree` property to indicate that when the form is submitted, the values of the elements are sent and stored in a tree that reflects the form element (a multidimensional array, basically). Otherwise, the form state values that are submitted get flattened and we lose their connection to the `plugin_configuration` element (which is also the Importer configuration entity field name we want to store the data under).

We are almost there. We can already go create an Importer entity, and when to use the JSON Importer, the new fieldset containing the URL field should show up below. But we still have one problem. If we save the form, the URL value will be stored inside an array keyed by `plugin`, inside the `plugin_configuration` field. So, we need to clean things up a bit, and we can do so inside the `save()` method.

Right before saving the entity, we can do this:

```
$importer->set('plugin_configuration',
$importer->getPluginConfiguration()['plugin']);
```

So, we basically move the values one array up, removing the superfluous `plugin` level in the array (which was only needed to neatly organise the form tree).

With this, we are done. Well, not really, as we still need to handle the configuration schema aspect. Yes, remember those from `Chapter 6`, *Data Modeling and Storage*, and `Chapter 7`, *Your Own Custom Entity and Plugin Types*? We are now going to see how we can work with our own dynamic configuration schema, similar to how we did with the ones needed for the field plugins in `Chapter 9`, *Custom Fields*. But why do we need a dynamic configuration schema?

Before this refactoring, we knew the exact the fields on the Importer configuration entity and we could declare the schema for each easily (as we did). However, now plugins can come with their own individual fields, so we need to make sure they can provide their own schema definitions for the respective data. So how can we do this?

First, inside our `importer.schema.yml` file, we need to remove the `url` field schema definition as it no longer exists. We replace it, however, with one for the new field we created, namely the `plugin_configuration` array of values that came from the plugin:

```
plugin_configuration:
   type: products.importer.plugin.[%parent.plugin]
```

Here is where things become interesting. We don't know what fields there will be inside, so we instead reference another type (our own). Moreover, the name of the type is dynamic. We have a prefix (`products.importer.plugin.`) followed by a variable name given by the value of the plugin field of the parent *(the main configuration entity)*. So basically, if a given configuration entity uses the `json` plugin, the type of schema definition will be `products.importer.plugin.json`. So now, it's the responsibility of whoever creates new plugins to also provide their own schema definitions for their own fields (like we did in `Chapter 9`, *Custom Fields*, when we defined field plugins).

But before that can happen, we need to define this new type we created:

```
products.importer.plugin.*:
  type: mapping
  label: 'Plugin configuration'
```

So essentially, our new type extends from `mapping` and has a simple label. Of course it applies to all that start with that name (hence the wildcard we encountered before).

Now, we can add the schema definition for our single `json` Importer plugin:

```
products.importer.plugin.json:
  type: mapping
  label: Plugin configuration for the Json importer plugin
  mapping:
    url:
      type: uri
      label: Uri
```

As you can see, we now have our first instance of the `products.importer.plugin` type, which contains the `url` field which is inside the `plugin_configuration` field of the configuration entity--reflecting a simple array hierarchy.

But the point of this dynamic declaration is that other modules that define new plugins can now also define their own instances of the `products.importer.plugin.*` schema definitions to map their own fields. It is no longer the responsibility of the configuration entity (schema) to "guess" what field types are being used on each plugin.

With this, our refactoring is complete. Drupal is well aware of the type of data the configuration entity is saving, even if it is in part relating to external input (the selected plugin). So that means we can create (if we want) another importer plugin which uses a CSV file for the product data. But we'll see how to do that in a later chapter when we talk about file handling.

States (Form) system

The last thing we are going to look at in this chapter is the States system of the Form API (not to be confused with the State API we covered in `Chapter 6`, *Data Modeling and Storage*). This allows us to define our form elements to behave somewhat dynamically based on the user interaction with the form. It doesn't use Ajax but relies on JavaScript to handle the manipulations. This is another great example of client-side behavior where we don't have to write a single line of JavaScript. So, let's see what this is.

The #states are simple properties we can add onto form elements, which have the role of changing them depending on the *state* of other elements. The best way to understand this is through some examples. Imagine these two form elements:

```
$form['kids'] = [
  '#type' => 'checkbox',
  '#title' => $this->t('Do you have kids?'),
];

$form['kid_number'] = [
  '#type' => 'textfield',
  '#title' => $this->t('How many kids do you have?'),
];
```

In the first we ask the user if they have kids (using a simple checkbox) while in the latter we ask them how many kids they have. But why should the user actually see the second element if they don't have kids? This is where the #states property comes into play, and its role is to manipulate an element depending on the *state* of another. So instead, we can have this:

```
$form['kid_number'] = [
  '#type' => 'textfield',
  '#title' => $this->t('How many kids do you have?'),
  '#states' => [
    'visible' => [
      'input[name="kids"]' => ['checked' => TRUE],
    ],
  ],
];
```

Now, the element for specifying the number of kids is only going to be visible if the *state* of the kid element is checked.

The #states property is an array whose key is the actual *state* that needs to be applied to the current element if the conditions inside are met. And the conditions can vary, but they all depend on a CSS selector (in our case input[name="kids"] matching another element).

Our example can also be written with this reverse logic:

```
'#states' => array(
  'invisible' => array(
    'input[name="kids"]' => array('checked' => FALSE),
  ),
),
```

Apart from `visible` and `invisible`, the following *states* can be also applied to form elements--`enabled`, `disabled`, `required`, `optional`, `checked`, `unchecked`, `expanded` and `collapsed`. As for the conditions that can "trigger" these *states*, we can have the following (apart from `checked`)--`empty`, `filled`, `unchecked`, `expanded`, `collapsed` and `value`.

So, for example, we can even control the *state* of an element depending on the value the user selected on another. Combining these possibilities can greatly improve our forms when it comes to user experience, decluttering, and even building logical form trees.

Summary

In this chapter, we took on the client-side and talked about JavaScript and client-side capabilities in Drupal 8. We started with the approach we need to take when writing JavaScript in a Drupal context. You learned about behaviors, why they are important, and how to use them. We also saw how we can pass around data from the server (Drupal) to the client-side and make use of it in JavaScript.

Funnily enough, we then we switched to a no-JavaScript allowed policy for the rest of the chapter. We did this to prove how powerful the Drupal Ajax API is, in who we can perform complex server-to-client interactions even if we are not frontend developers that can write JavaScript code. And to demonstrate the API, we first looked at how simple links can be turned into Ajax requests. We followed that up with an important refactor to our earlier products importer functionality that relied on Ajax to make the Importer configuration entity form dynamic (dependent on the selected plugin). Let's not forget another nugget of information--dynamic configuration schema--which allows us to decouple the configuration entity data definitions from that of their selected plugins.

Finally, we finished by looking at the States system of the Form API, which allows us to declaratively code client-side manipulations onto our form elements, essentially making them dependent on the user's interaction with the form.

In the next chapter, we are going to talk about internationalization and translations to make sure our applications can be used anywhere around the globe.

13
Internationalization and Languages

Even though there have been great advancements across the board, Drupal 8 has a couple of almost revolutionary developments compared to its predecessor. Notable among these are the configuration API and the caching system, which are both light-years ahead of what was capable in Drupal 7. Another one is the multilingual initiative that sought to make Drupal fully multilingual out of the box--rather than having to use 20 contributed modules to achieve results that don't even come close. This also includes the internationalization (i18n: `https://www.w3.org/standards/webdesign/i18n`) aspect that allows sites to be translated in any of the installed languages.

In this chapter, we are going to talk about internationalization and multilingual features in Drupal 8 from the point of view of a module developer. Many of the built-in capabilities of this system are oriented toward site builders--enabling languages, translating content and configuration entities as well as the Drupal interface (for administrators and visitors alike). Our focus will be what we as module developers need to do programmatically to ensure that site builders and editors can use the aforementioned features. To that end, this chapter will be more of a reference guide with various tips, techniques, and even rules we need to follow when writing our code. Notwithstanding, we will also talk a bit about how we can work with languages programmatically.

First, however, we will start with an introduction to the multilingual ecosystem that comes out of the box and the modules responsible for various parts of it.

Introduction

The multilingual and internationalization system is based on four Drupal core modules. Let's quickly go through them and see what they do:

- Language
- Content Translation
- Configuration Translation
- Interface Translation

Language

The *Language* module is responsible for dealing with the available languages on the site. Site builders can choose to install one or more languages from a wide selection. They can even create their own custom language if necessary. The installed languages can then be added to things such as entities and menu links in order to control their visibility, depending on the current language. Apart from the installed ones, Drupal 8 comes with two extra special languages as well--*Not Specified* and *Not Applicable*.

The modules also handles the contextual language selection based on various criteria, as well as provides a language switcher to change the current language of the site.

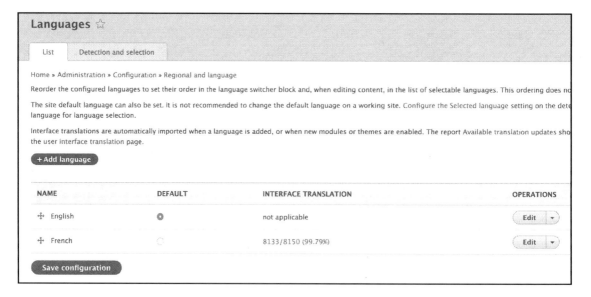

Content Translation

The *Content Translation* module is responsible for the functionality that allows users to translate content. Content entities are the principle vehicle for content, and with this module, the data inside can be translated (and granularly configured for it at a field level). In other words, users can control which fields and which entity type bundles should be translatable.

Configuration Translation

The *Configuration Translation* module is responsible for providing the interface via which users can translate configuration values. These can be from simple configuration objects or configuration entities. We've already seen how we can ensure that our configuration values can be translated in previous chapters, so we won't dive into that again here.

I recommend you reference the section on configuration schemas from `Chapter 6`, *Data Modeling and Storage*.

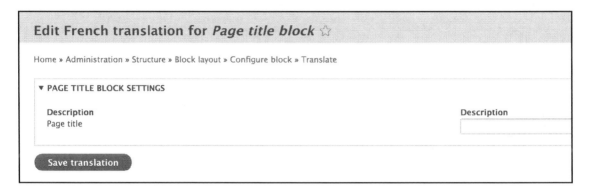

Interface Translation

The *Interface Translation* module is responsible for providing an interface that allows users to translate any string or text output on the website, in all the languages that are installed. Moreover, it provides a connection to the `localize.drupal.org` platform, from which it can download translations for many languages of the more common interface strings that come with Drupal.

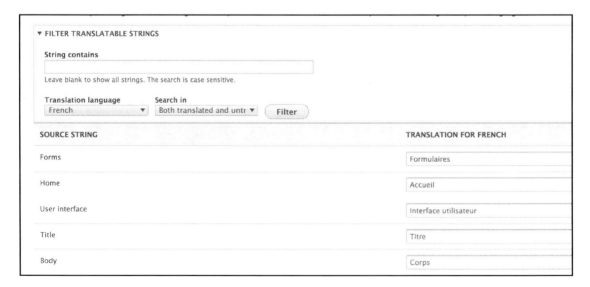

These four modules are not alone in the multilingual system but rely on a cross-application standard of ensuring that all the written code works well with it. In other words, the entire Drupal codebase is intertwined with the multilingual system at various levels, and is written in such a way that anything that should be translatable or localizable can be. This means that all the code we write needs to respect the same standard.

Internationalization

The idea behind internationalization is to ensure that everything that gets output on the site can be translated into the enabled languages through a common mechanism--in this case, using the Interface Translation module. This refers to content, visible configuration values, and the strings and texts that come out of modules and themes. But there are many different ways this can happen, so let's see how in each of these cases we would ensure that our information can be translated.

A principle *rule* when writing Drupal modules or themes is to always use English as the code language. This is to ensure consistency and keep open the possibility that other developers will work on the same codebase, which may not speak a particular language. This is also the case for text used to be displayed in the UI. It should not be the responsibility of the code to output the translated text, but rather to always keep it consistent, that is, in English.

Of course, this is dependent on it being done right, in order to allow it to be translated via interface translation. There are multiple ways this can be ensured, depending on the circumstances.

The most common scenario we need to be aware of is when we have to print out to the user, in a PHP, string of text. Drupal 7 developers should already be familiar with the t() function through which these strings are run. This function still exists and should be used whenever we are not inside a class context:

```
return t('The quick brown fox');
```

However, when we are inside a class, we should check if any of the parents are using the StringTranslationTrait. If not, we should use it in our class and then we'll be able to do this instead:

```
return $this->t('The quick brown fox');
```

Even better still, we should inject the `TranslationManager` service into our class because the preceding mentioned trait makes use of it.

None of the examples given before should be new to us, as we've been using these throughout the code we've been writing in this book. But what actually happens behind the scenes?

The `t()` and `StringTranslationTrait::t()` functions both create and return an instance of `TranslatableMarkup` (essentially delegating to its constructor), which upon rendering (being cast to a string), will return the formatted and translated string. The responsibility of the actual translation is delegated to the `TranslationManager` service. This process has two parts. Static analyzers pick up on these text strings and add them to the database in the list of strings that need to be localized. These can then be translated by users via the user interface. Second, at runtime, the strings get formatted and the translated version is shown, depending on the current language context. Because of the first part, we should never do something like this:

```
return $this->t($my_text);
```

The reason is that static analyzers can no longer pick up on the strings that need to be translated. Moreover, if the text is coming from user input, it can lead to XSS attacks if not properly sanitized before.

That being said, we can still have dynamic, that is, formatted, text output using this method, and we've seen this in action as well:

```
$count = 5;
return $this->t('The quick brown fox jumped @count times', ['@count' =>
$count]);
```

In this case, we have a dynamic variable (which can be part of user input), which will be used to replace the placeholder `@count` from the text. Drupal takes care of sanitizing the variable before outputting the string to the user. Alternatively, we can also use the `%` prefix to define a placeholder we want Drupal to wrap with `<em class="placeholder">`. The cool thing is that, when performing translations, users can shift the placeholder in the sentence to accommodate language specificity.

One of the intended consequences of the static analyzer picking out and storing the strings that need to be translated is that, by default, each individual string is only translated once. This is good in many cases but also poses some problems when the same English string has different meanings (which map to different translations in other languages). To counter this issue, we can specify a context to the string that needs to be translated so that we can identify which meaning we actually want to translate. This is where the third parameter of the `t()` function (and method) we saw in the previous paragraphs comes into play.

For example, let's consider the word Book, which is translated by default in its meaning as a noun. But we may have a submit button on a form that has the value Book, which clearly has a different meaning as a call to action. So in the latter case, we could do it like this:

```
t('Book', [], ['context' => 'The verb "to book"']);
```

Now in the interface translation, we will have both versions available.

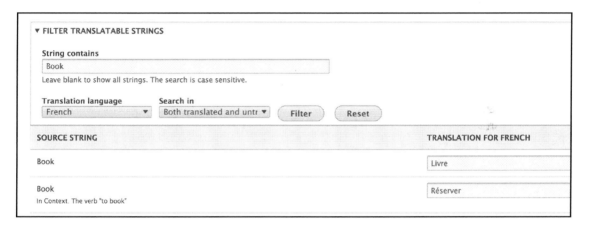

Another helpful tip is that we can also account for plurals in the string translations. The StringTranslationTrait::formatPlural() helps with this by creating a PluralTranslatableMarkup object similar to the TranslatableMarkup, but with some extra parameters to account for differences when it comes to plurals. This comes in very handy in our preceding example with the brown fox jumping a number of times, because if the fox jumps only once, the resulting string would not be grammatically correct anymore. So instead, we can do the following:

```
$count = 5;
return $this->formatPlural($count, 'The quick brown fox jumped 1 time',
'The quick brown fox jumped @count times')];
```

The first parameter is the actual count (the differentiator between singular and plural). The second and third parameters are the singular and plural versions respectively. You'll also notice that since we specified the count already, we don't have to specify it again in the arguments array. It's important to note that the placeholder name inside the string needs to be @count if we want the renderer to understand its purpose.

The string translation techniques we discussed so far also work in other places--not just in PHP code. For example, in JavaScript we would do something like this:

```
Drupal.t('The quick brown fox jumped @count times', {'@count': 5});
Drupal.formatPlural(5, 'The quick brown fox jumped 1 time', 'The quick
brown fox jumped @count times');
```

So, based on this knowledge, I encourage you to go back and fix our incorrect use of the string output in JavaScript in the previous chapter.

In Twig, we'd have something like this (for simple translations):

```
{{ 'Hello World.'|trans }}
{{ 'Hello World.'|t }}
```

Both of the above lines do the same thing. To handle plurals (and placeholders), we can use the {% trans %} block:

```
{% set count = 5 %}
{% trans %}
  The quick brown fox jumped 1 time.
{% plural count %}
  The quick brown fox jumped {{ count }} times.
{% endtrans %}
```

Finally, the string context is also possible like so:

```
{% trans with {'context': 'The verb "to book"'} %}
  Book
{% endtrans %}
```

In annotations, we have the @Translation() wrapper, as we've seen already a few times when creating plugins or defining entity types.

Finally, in YAML files, some of the strings are translatable by default (so we don't have to do anything):

- Module names and descriptions in .info.yml files
- The _title (together with the optional _title_context) key values under the defaults section of .routing.yml files
- The title (together with the optional title_context) key values in .links.action.yml, .links.task.yml and .links.contextual.yml files

Dates are also potentially problematic when it comes to localization, as different locales show dates differently. Luckily, Drupal provides the `DateFormatter` service, which handles this for us. For example:

```
\Drupal::service('date.formatter')->format(time(), 'medium');
```

The first parameter of this formatter is the UNIX timestamp of the date we want to format. The second parameter indicates the format to use (either one of the existing formats or `custom`). Drupal comes with a few predefined date formats, but site builders can define others as well as, which can be used here. However, if the format is custom, the third parameter is a a PHP date format string suitable for input to `date()`. The fourth parameter is a time zone identifier we want to format the date in, and the final parameter can be used to specify the language to localize to directly (regardless of the current language of the site).

Content entities and the Translation API

So far in this chapter, we've mostly talked about how to ensure that our modules output only text that can also be translated. The Drupal best practice is to always use these techniques regardless of whether the site is multilingual or not. You never know if you'll ever need to add a new language.

In this section, we are going to talk a bit about how we can interact with the language system programmatically and work with entity translations.

A potentially important thing you'll often want to do is check the current language of the site. Depending on the language negotiation in place, this can either be determined by the browser language, a domain, a URL prefix, or others. The `LanguageManager` is the service we use to figure this out. We can inject it using the `language_manager` key or use it via the static shorthand:

```
$manager = \Drupal::languageManager();
```

To get the current language, we do this:

```
$language = $manager->getCurrentLanguage();
```

Where `$language` is an instance of the `Language` class which holds some information about the given language (such as the language code and name). The language code is probably the most important as it is used everywhere to indicate what language a given *thing* is.

There are other useful methods with this service that you can use. For example, we can get a list of all the installed languages with `getLanguages()` or the site default language with `getDefaultLanguage()`. I encourage you to check out the `LanguageManager` for all the available API methods.

When it comes to content entities, there is an API we can use to interact with the data inside them in different languages. So, for example, we have figured out the current language with the preceding method, so we can now get some field values in that language. The way this works is that we ask for a *copy* of the node entity in the respective language:

```
$translation = $node->getTranslation($language->getId());
```

`$translation` is now almost the same as `$node`, but with the default language set to the one we requested. From there, we can access field values normally. However, not all nodes have to have a translation, so it's better to first check if one exists:

```
if ($node->hasTranslation($language->getId())) {
    $translation = $node->getTranslation($language->getId());
}
```

Since we can configure entity translatability at the field level (allowing only the fields that make sense to be translated), we can also check which of these fields can have translated values:

```
$fields = $node->getTranslatableFields();
```

Finally, we can also check which languages there are translations for:

```
$languages = $node->getTranslationLanguages();
```

Since it's up to the editors to add translations to an entity, we cannot guarantee in code that one exists.

Summary

In this short chapter, we talked about the Drupal 8 multilingual and internationalization system from a module developer perspective. We started with an introduction to the four main modules responsible for languages and translating content, and configuration entities as well as interface text.

Then, we focused on the rules and techniques we need to respect in order to ensure that our output text can be translated. We saw how we can do this in PHP code, Twig, and YAML files, and even in JavaScript. Finally, we looked a bit at the language manager and Translation API to see how we can work with content entities that have been translated.

The main takeaway from this chapter should be that languages are important in Drupal 8 even if our site is only in one language. So, in developing modules, especially if we want to contribute them back to the community, we need to ensure that our functionality can be translated as needed.

In the next chapter, we are going to talk about data processing using batches and queues, as well as the cron system that comes with Drupal.

14

Batches, Queues, and Cron

If in the previous chapter we kept things a bit more theoretical with me throwing "rules" at you, but in this chapter I am going to make up for it, and we are going to have some fun. This means we are going to write some code that demonstrates concepts related to data processing, especially larger amounts of it. And in doing so, we are going to cover a few topics.

First, we are going to look back at the `hook_update_N()` hook we saw in `Chapter 8`, *The Database API*, when we talked about the Database API. More specifically, we are going to see how the `&$sandbox` parameter can be used in order to handle updates that need to process some data, which may take a bit longer and should be split across multiple requests. Next up, we are going to look at standalone *batches* (which basically use the same system) to process data in batches across multiple requests. And what better example to illustrate this technique than with our `Chapter 7`, *Your Own Custom Entity and Plugin Types* Importer that needs to process an undefined number of products?

We will take a look at a related subsystem that allows us to queue *things* for later processing (either in batches, during cron, or in simple requests). Since we are talking about cron, we will also go a bit into detail and see how this system works in Drupal. Finally, we will finish this chapter by taking a look at the Lock API in Drupal 8, that allows us to ensure multiple requests don't run certain processes at the same time.

By the end of this chapter, you will be a lean, mean, data processing machine. So, let's get to it.

Batch powered update hooks

The first thing we are going to look at is update hooks, revisiting of our previous Sports module created in `Chapter 8`, *The Database API*. We will focus on the `&$sandbox` parameter we didn't use then. The goal is to run an update on each of our records in the `players` table and mark them as *retired*. The point is to illustrate how we can process each of these records one at the time in individual requests to prevent a PHP timeout, in case we have many records.

So to get us going, here is all the code, and we'll see right after what everything means:

```
/**
 * Update all the players to mark them as retired.
 */
function sports_update_8002(&$sandbox) {
  $database = \Drupal::database();

  if (empty($sandbox)) {
    $results = $database->query("SELECT id FROM
{players}")->fetchAllAssoc('id');
    $sandbox['progress'] = 0;
    $sandbox['ids'] = array_keys($results);
    $sandbox['max'] = count($results);
  }

  $id = $sandbox['ids'] ? array_shift($sandbox['ids']) : NULL;

  $player = $database->query("SELECT * FROM {players} WHERE id = :id",
[':id' => $id])->fetch();
  $data = $player->data ? unserialize($player->data) : [];
  $data['retired'] = TRUE;
  $database->update('players')
   ->fields(['data' => serialize($data)])
   ->condition('id', $id)
   ->execute();
  $sandbox['progress']++;
  $sandbox['#finished'] = $sandbox['progress'] / $sandbox['max'];
}
```

If you remember, the function name contains the new schema version for the module, which will be set once this is run. Refer back to `Chapter 8`, *The Database API*, for more information.

When this hook is fired, the $sandbox argument (passed by reference) is empty. Its goal is to act as temporary storage between the requests needed to process everything inside the function. We can use it to store arbitrary data, but we should be mindful of the size as it has to fit inside a *LONGBLOB* table column.

The first thing we are doing is getting our hands on the database service to make queries to our players table. But more importantly, we are checking if the $sandbox variable is empty, which indicates that this is the start of the process. If it is, we add some data to it specific to our process. In this case, we want to store the progress (this is quite common), the IDs of the players that need to be updated, and the total number of records (also quite common). To do this, we make a simple query.

Once the sandbox is set, we can get the first ID in the list while also removing it so that iteratively we have less records to process. Based on that ID, we load the relevant player, add our data to it, and update it back in the database. Once that is done, we increment the progress by one (as we processed one record). Finally, the #finished key in the sandbox is what Drupal looks at to determine whether the process is finished. It expects an integer between zero and one, the latter signifying that we are done. If anything below one is found, the function gets called again and the $sandbox array will contain the data as we left it (incremented progress and one less ID to process). In which case, the main body of the function runs again, processing the next record, and so on, until the progress divided by the maximum number of records is equal to one. If we have 100 records, when the progress reaches 100, the following is true:

$$100 / 100 == 1.$$

Then, Drupal knows to finish the process and not call the function again.

This process is also called batching in Drupal terms and is very useful because Drupal will make as many requests as needed to finish it. We can control the workload each request needs to make in one request. The preceding example might be a bit overkill in the sense that a request is perfectly capable of processing more than one player. We are actually losing time because like this, Drupal needs to bootstrap itself again and again for each request. So, it's up to us to find that sweet spot. In our previous example, what we could have done was break up the array of IDs into chunks of maybe five, and allowed a request to process five records instead of one. That would surely increase the speed, but I encourage you to go ahead and try that on your own now that you understand the principles behind using $sandbox for batching.

Batch operations

Now that we have a basic understanding of Drupal's capabilities to do multi-request processing, let's switch gears and look at the Batch API.

In order to demonstrate how this works, we are going to rebuild the way our product `JsonImporter` plugin processes the product data it retrieves. Currently, we simply load all the products into an array of objects and loop through each, saving them to the database. So if there are 100,000 products in the JSON response, we might get into trouble with this approach. To be fair, if the remote provider has so many products, it usually provides a paginated way of requesting them by passing an offset and a limit. This keeps the payloads smaller (which is good for both communicating servers) and makes it easier on the processing. On our side, we can treat it as we would treat a database. But for now, we'll go with the assumption that the number of returned products is large, but not too large as to pose problems with the communication or with the ability of PHP to store them in memory.

Moreover, while illustrating the Batch API, we will also perform an operation we "forgot" in `Chapter 7`, *Your Own Custom Entity and Plugin Types*. During the import, we also want to delete any products, which have been previously carried over but which are no longer in the JSON. It is a kind of synchronization between the two data sources, if you will. So, let's get to it.

Creating the batch

Inside the `JsonImporter::import()` method, once we get our hands on the `$products` array, let's replace the loop with the following:

```
$batch = [
  'title' => $this->t('Importing products'),
  'operations' => [
    [[$this, 'clearMissing'], [$products]],
    [[$this, 'importProducts'], [$products]],
  ],
  'finished' => [$this, 'importProductsFinished'],
];
batch_set($batch);
```

Creating a batch involves a number of steps, the first one being the creation of a batch definition, which is nothing more than an array with some data. The `title` option sets the title to be used on the progress page. Similarly, we also have the optional `init_message`, `progress_message` and `error_message`, which have some sensible defaults, so we won't set them here. For more information as to what exactly you can do with them, and what other options you have, make sure you check out the documentation of the `batch_set()` function.

The most important part of the batch definition is the `operations` array in which we list the operations that need to take place in the batch. These are defined as any kind of valid PHP callback and an array of arguments to pass to these callbacks. If the latter resides in a file that is has not been loaded, the `file` options can also be set to specify the file path to include. Each operation runs on its own PHP request; in the sequence, they are defined. Moreover, each operation can also run across multiple requests, similar to how we wrote our update hook earlier.

Our first operation will be responsible for removing from Drupal the products which no longer exist in the JSON response, while the latter will do the import. Both of these receive only one parameter--the array of products.

The `finished` key is another callback that gets fired at the end of the batch processing, after all the operations are done.

Finally, we call the global `batch_set()` method, which statically sets the batch definition and marks it as ready to be run. There is just one more step to trigger the batch, and that is a call to `batch_process()`. But the reason we have not used it is because if the import runs as part of a form submission, the Form API triggers it automatically. So it won't work if we trigger it here as well. The reason why the Form API does it for us is because most of the time we want batches to run only as a result of an action being taken. Usually, this is done via forms. However, the other major possibility is to trigger the batch via a Drush command (which we can actually do). In this case, we need to use the `drush_backend_batch_process()` function instead.

So, what we will do is first is check that we are in a command-line environment (aka Drush) and trigger it only in that case:

```
if (PHP_SAPI == 'cli') {
  drush_backend_batch_process();
}
```

Otherwise, we leave it up to the Form API. In doing this, we can trigger the import both from a Form submit handler and via Drush, and we can have plugins that don't necessarily use batches.

Batch operations

Now that we have our batch definition in place, we are missing those three callback methods we are referencing in it. So, let's see the first one:

```
/**
 * Batch operation to remove the products which are no longer in the list
of
 * products coming from the JSON file.
 *
 * @param $products
 * @param $context
 */
public function clearMissing($products, &$context) {
  if (!isset($context['results']['cleared'])) {
    $context['results']['cleared'] = [];
  }
  if (!$products) {
    return;
  }

  $ids = [];
  foreach ($products as $product) {
    $ids[] = $product->id;
  }

  $ids = $this->entityTypeManager->getStorage('product')->getQuery()
    ->condition('remote_id', $ids, 'NOT IN')
    ->execute();
  if (!$ids) {
    $context['results']['cleared'] = [];
    return;
  }

  $entities =
$this->entityTypeManager->getStorage('product')->loadMultiple($ids);

  /** @var ProductInterface $entity */
  foreach ($entities as $entity) {
    $context['results']['cleared'][] = $entity->getName();
  }
  $context['message'] = $this->t('Removing @count products', ['@count' =>
```

```
    count($entities)]);
      $this->entityTypeManager->getStorage('product')->delete($entities);
  }
```

This is the first operation in the batch process. As an argument, it receives all the variables we defined in the batch definition (in our case, the products array). But it also gets a `$context` array variable passed by a reference, which we can use similar to how we used `$sandbox` in the update hook (with some extra capabilities).

The task at hand is pretty simple. We prepare a list of IDs of all the products in the JSON, and based on those, we query our product entities for the those which are `NOT IN` that list. If any are found, we delete them. You'll notice already that in this operation we are not relying on the actual multi-request capabilities of Drupal's Batch API because we expect the workload to be minimal. After all, how many products could be missing at any given time and would need to be deleted? We'll assume not many for our use case.

But while we are doing all this, we are interacting somewhat with the batch processing. You'll notice that the `$context` array has a `results` key. This is used to store information related to the outcome of each operation in the batch. We are not supposed to use it for managing progress but instead to keep track of what was done so that at the end we can present the user with some useful information as to what has happened. So in our example, we create an array keyed by `cleared` (to namespace the data for this particular operation), in which we put in the names of each product that has been deleted.

Moreover, we also have a `message` key that we use to print a message as the action is happening. This gets printed out in "real time" to indicate to the user what is currently being processed. If the batch is run via the UI through a form, it very well might be that you won't see all the messages due to the speed of the processing. However, if triggered by Drush (as it will be in our case), each of these messages will be printed to the terminal screen.

With this, our first operation is done. It's time to look at the second, more complex one:

```
/**
 * Batch operation to import the products from the JSON file.
 *
 * @param $products
 * @param $context
 */
public function importProducts($products, &$context) {
  if (!isset($context['results']['imported'])) {
    $context['results']['imported'] = [];
  }

  if (!$products) {
```

```
      return;
  }

  $sandbox = &$context['sandbox'];
  if (!$sandbox) {
    $sandbox['progress'] = 0;
    $sandbox['max'] = count($products);
    $sandbox['products'] = $products;
  }

  $slice = array_splice($sandbox['products'], 0, 3);
  foreach ($slice as $product) {
    $context['message'] = $this->t('Importing product @name', ['@name' =>
$product->name]);
    $this->persistProduct($product);
    $context['results']['imported'][] = $product->name;
    $sandbox['progress']++;
  }

  $context['finished'] = $sandbox['progress'] / $sandbox['max'];
}
```

The arguments it receives are exactly the same as with our previous operation since we defined them in the same way.

Here, again is we ensure we have some products and start up our `results` array, this time to keep track of the imported records. But we also work with the `sandbox` key of the `$context` array this time in order to use the multirequest processing capabilities. The approach is similar to what we did in the update hook--we keep a progress count, store the maximum number of products, and then we calculate the `$context['finished']` key based on the division between the two. However, in this case, we opt to process three products at a time instead of one, as we did with our player records. Again, as with our previous operation, we are using the `message` key to inform the user as to what is going on and the `results` key to compile a list of products that have been imported.

Before moving on, let's talk a bit about the way we are importing the products. Had the JSON resource been able to return paginated results, we would have had to change our approach. First, we could not have deleted the missing products in the same way. Instead, we would have had to keep track of the IDs of the products that would have been imported only after deleting the other ones. So the order of two operations would have been reversed.

Second, the retrieval of the products would have been done from inside the `importProducts` operation using an offset and a limit stored in the sandbox. So, each Drupal batch request would have made a new request to the JSON resource. Of course, we would have had to keep track of all the processed products so that we would know which ones were able to be deleted.

Finally, let's take a look at the callback used when the batch processing finishes:

```
/**
 * Callback for when the batch processing completes.
 *
 * @param $success
 * @param $results
 * @param $operations
 */
public function importProductsFinished($success, $results, $operations) {
  if (!$success) {
    drupal_set_message($this->t('There was a problem with the batch'),
'error');
    return;
  }

  $cleared = count($results['cleared']);
  if ($cleared == 0) {
    drupal_set_message($this->t('No products had to be deleted.'));
  }
  else {
    drupal_set_message($this->formatPlural($cleared, '1 product had to be
deleted.', '@count products had to be deleted.'));
  }

  $imported = count($results['imported']);
  if ($imported == 0) {
    drupal_set_message($this->t('No products found to be imported.'));
  }
  else {
    drupal_set_message($this->formatPlural($imported, '1 product
imported.', '@count products imported.'));
  }
}
```

This callback receives three parameters--a boolean indicating whether the processing was successful or not, the results array we used inside our $context to keep track of what has been done, and the array of operations. What we are doing is actually pretty simple. We first print a generic message if the batch has failed. In this case, we also return early. Otherwise, we print relevant messages to the operations we have done, using the $results array. Note the use of the t() and formatPlural() methods you learned about in the previous chapter.

Or reworked JSON Importer now uses batching to make the process more stable in case the number of records it needs to process gets too big. Before we can try it out, we need to do one last step, and that is to use the DependencySerializationTrait inside the ImporterBase plugin class:

```
use DependencySerializationTrait;
```

The reason is that when the batch runs, Drupal stores some information about the object that runs it. In order to do so, it needs to serialize it. However, since it has dependencies such as the EntityTypeManager, Drupal needs a way to handle these in the serialization process. The preceding trait helps with that. Moreover, we can use it in the base class so that all plugin classes can use batching easily without having to worry about this step.

But now if we run the Drush command we wrote in Chapter 7, *Your Own Custom Entity and Plugin Types*, to trigger our importer, we get an output like this:

```
vagrant@vagrant:/var/www$ drush products-import-run --importer=json
Importing product TV
Importing product VCR
Importing product Stereo
Importing product Bike
Importing product Speakers
Importing product Gameboy
No products had to be deleted.
6 products imported.
The "json" importer has been run.
```

We notice the messages set when importing each record, as well as the messages we set at the end of the process, which provides kind of a summary of what went down.

When calling `batch_process()`, we can also pass in a URL to redirect to when the processing has finished. However, a better way is to return a `RedirectResponse` inside the `finished` callback. And it goes without saying that if we trigger the batch from Drush there will be no actual redirect. However, it will work just fine in a form context.

Cron

In the previous section, we created an awesome multirequest batch processing of our JSON product import. In the next section, we'll jump into the Queue API and see how we can plan the processing of multiple items at a later stage. However, before we dive into that, let's talk a bit about how the Drupal 8 cron works and what we can do with it. This is because our discussion about the Queue API is closely related to it.

First of all, Drupal doesn't actually have a fully fledged cron system. That is because it's an application and not a server capable of scheduling tasks that run at specified times of the day at intervals. However, what it has is a cron-like system, which can come very close, especially on busy websites. Often, it is affectionately referred to as the poor man's cron. Why? Since Drupal cannot by itself do anything without any sort of impetus, it relies on visitors coming to the website to trigger the cron tasks. So, even if we can configure the frequency of Drupal's cron, we are relying on visitors coming to the website and triggering it inadvertently. Drupal then keeps track of when the cron ran and ensures that the next time it runs is only after the configured amount of time has lapsed. So in essence, if the cron is set to run every hour but the next visitor only comes in three hours, it will only run then:

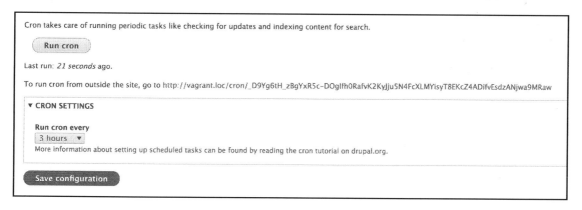

The Drupal cron is very useful for maintenance tasks and relatively small jobs that don't take too many resources away from the site visitors. It can be triggered manually from the UI, from an outside script, or even with Drush, by using the following command:

```
drush cron
```

There are many Drupal core and contributed modules that rely on this system to perform various tasks, and we as module developers can do the same by implementing `hook_cron()`. The latter gets fired every time the cron runs, so basically Drupal's cron is a collection of function calls to various modules. For this reason, we must avoid overloading the request with heavy processing, otherwise the request might crash. But as we will see in the next section, we can do something to control this if we have such jobs to run.

First though, let's look at an example implementation and see how it works. What we want to accomplish is that whenever cron runs, we delete all the records in the `teams` table (we created in Chapter 8, *The Database API*) that are no longer referenced by any player. Essentially, if the teams don't have any players, they need to go. So, we could do something simple like this:

```
/**
 * Implements hook_cron().
 */
function sports_cron() {
  $database = \Drupal::database();
  $result = $database->query("SELECT id FROM {teams} WHERE id NOT IN
(SELECT team_id FROM {players} WHERE team_id IS NOT
NULL)")->fetchAllAssoc('id');
  if (!$result) {
    return;
  }

  $ids = array_keys($result);
  $database->delete('teams')
    ->condition('id', $ids, 'IN')
    ->execute();
}
```

We are implementing `hook_cron()`, and inside, we basically figure out which teams have no players and delete them. You'll notice the query to do the former is actually a more complex one, as we are using a subquery, but it is still not rocket science. Feel free to check Chapter 8, *The Database API*, for a refresher on the Drupal 8 database API.

This function will then be fired every time our Drupal cron runs, and we could argue that doing this task is not such a big strain on our resources. However, in the next chapter, we will see how we can handle cases like those. Moreover, we'll see why that approach might even be better than this one, regardless of resource intensiveness.

Queues

It's finally time to talk a bit about the Queue API, how it works, and what it's main components are; the theory, basically. We will do this before diving into code examples that we all thoroughly enjoy.

Introduction to the Queue API

The main purpose of the Queue API is to provide a way for us to add items to a *queue* in order to have them processed at a later time. In charge of processing these items are the *queue worker* plugins, which can be enlisted either automatically by the Drupal cron, manually (programmatically) by us, or by Drush. We will look at an example of all three.

The central player in this API is the implementation of the `QueueInterface`, which is the actual queue into which we put items. There are two types of queues Drupal can handle-- reliable and unreliable. The first preserves the order in which the items are processed (first in, first out) and guarantees that each item gets processed at least once. In this chapter, we will focus only on this type of queue. But there is also the possibility of working with unreliable queues which give their best effort when maintaining the item order and do not guarantee that all items get processed.

By default, when we working with queues in Drupal 8, we use a reliable queue that is based on a database table to store the items. This is represented by the `DatabaseQueue` implementation. The Batch API in fact uses a type of queue that extends from the default one Drupal comes with. Okay, but what does a queue do?

A queue has three main roles:

- It create items (adds *stuff* to a list that needs processing at some point).
- It claims items (puts a hold on them while a worker does the processing).
- It deletes items (removes the items from the queue once they have finished processing). Alternatively, it can also release them if another worker needs to process them or something went wrong and it should be retrieved later on.

We will soon see a practical example of how this works. But first, let's look at how a queue comes about.

The `QueueInterface` implementation is created with the help of the `QueueFactory` service, keyed as `queue`. The factory delegates to another factory service specific to the type of queue being created. By default this is the `QueueDatabaseFactory` service (keyed `queue.database`), which expectedly returns an instance of the `DatabaseQueue` class. The table used by the latter is simply called `queue`.

Finally, the crux of the Queue API for us module developers is the system of `QueueWorker` plugins, which are responsible for processing a single item in the queue. These can be written in two ways. The simplest approach is to have them triggered by cron. In this case, the plugin ID needs to match the name of the queue it needs to process items for. This way, we don't have to worry about claiming, releasing, or deleting items. The cron system does it for us. However, a more flexible approach is the one in which we actually do that. We don't rely on cron, but process the items ourselves whenever we want. Moreover, both types of queue workers can be enlisted via Drush using a command that triggers the processing of a queue with a given name.

Cron based queue

In the previous section, we wrote the `sports_cron()` implementation, which at each run looks for teams that no longer have players and deletes them from the database. However, if we run the Drupal cron every hour, we keep running that query even if we are pretty certain that teams don't loose all their players so often. Moreover, we also go by the simple assumption (a functionality we have not written so far) that there is some code responsible for removing a player from a team. This would actually be the ideal place to check if that team has lost all its players. The idea, then, is to check if the team has been left empty and add it to a queue to be deleted later (whenever the cron runs).

We won't go into the code specific to player and team management, but instead focus on the part which adds the team that needs to be deleted to the queue.

The first thing we need to do is get our hands on the `QueueFactory` service:

```
/** @var QueueFactory $queue_factory */
$queue_factory = \Drupal::service('queue');
```

Then, we need to create an instance of the default `QueueInterface` (database) with the name of our future worker plugin ID:

```
/** @var QueueInterface $queue */
$queue = $queue_factory->get('team_cleaner');
```

This is obviously the static approach of loading services, and you should be injecting it instead. But if you cannot, there is also the following shorthand which can achieve the same thing in one line:

```
$queue = \Drupal::queue('team_cleaner');
```

`$queue` is an instance of `DatabaseQueue` with the name `team_cleaner`.

The next thing we need to do is add items to it (assuming that we've identified a team without players):

```
$item = new \stdClass();
$item->id = $team_id;
$queue->createItem($item);
```

It's standard practice to create a PHP object to wrap the data for the queue item. Inside, we can put anything we want that can serialize properly, and that's all. We can now turn to our `TeamCleaner` worker plugin, that naturally goes in the `Plugin/QueueWorker` namespace of our module:

```
namespace Drupal\sports\Plugin\QueueWorker;

use Drupal\Core\Database\Connection;
use Drupal\Core\Plugin\ContainerFactoryPluginInterface;
use Drupal\Core\Queue\QueueWorkerBase;
use Symfony\Component\DependencyInjection\ContainerInterface;

/**
 * A worker plugin that removes a team from the database. Normally used to clear
 * teams that have run out of players.
 *
 * @QueueWorker(
 *   id = "team_cleaner",
 *   title = @Translation("Team Cleaner"),
 *   cron = {"time" = 10}
 * )
 */
class TeamCleaner extends QueueWorkerBase implements
ContainerFactoryPluginInterface {
```

```
/**
 * @var \Drupal\Core\Database\Connection
 */
protected $database;

/**
 * Constructs a TeamCleaner worker.
 *
 * @param array $configuration
 * @param string $plugin_id
 * @param mixed $plugin_definition
 * @param \Drupal\Core\Database\Connection $database
 */
public function __construct(array $configuration, $plugin_id,
$plugin_definition, Connection $database) {
    parent::__construct($configuration, $plugin_id, $plugin_definition);
    $this->database = $database;
}

/**
 * {@inheritdoc}
 */
public static function create(ContainerInterface $container, array
$configuration, $plugin_id, $plugin_definition) {
    return new static(
        $configuration,
        $plugin_id,
        $plugin_definition,
        $container->get('database')
    );
}

/**
 * {@inheritdoc}
 */
public function processItem($data) {
    $id = isset($data->id) && $data->id ? $data->id : NULL;
    if (!$id) {
        throw new \Exception('Missing team ID');
        return;
    }

    $this->database->delete('teams')
        ->condition('id', $id)
        ->execute();
}
}
```

As we're already used to it, our plugin extends the base plugin class of its type to inherit any potential base functionality. In our case, this is limited to the implementation of the `QueueWorkerInterface`, which has one method whose name easily describe its responsibility--`processItem($data)`. Also not new to us is the implementation of `ContainerFactoryPluginInterface`, which allows us to inject the `database` service into our plugin that, in turn, we use to delete the queued team.

All the action in fact happens in the `processItem()` method, where we simply look into the `$data` object and delete the team with the specified ID. We also throw a simple exception if something goes wrong. We'll talk about exceptions in queue processing shortly.

Somewhat more interesting for the Queue API, however, is the plugin annotation. Apart from the standard expected plugin definition, we also encounter the following:

```
cron = {"time" = 10}
```

This simply indicates that this plugin should be used by the cron system. In other words, when the Drupal cron runs, it loads all the worker plugin definitions, and whichever has this information get processed. And the key here is the `time` information which we have set to 10 seconds. This essentially means that when the cron runs, we are saying--*go ahead and process as many queue items as you can within 10 seconds. Once that time limit is up, stop and continue with the rest of the cron tasks.* This is actually very powerful because we allocated an amount of time from the PHP request and dedicated it to our queue. This means that we don't have to guess how many items to allocate for a request (as we did with the batching). However, it also means that the rest of the time left needs to be enough for everything else. So, we need to adjust this carefully. As for the queue items that don't fit into those 10 seconds, they will simply be processed at the next cron run.

This approach is better than our previous one, in which we ourselves implemented `hook_cron()` because we don't want to always keep checking teams for players, but can instead create queue items and defer the deletion until a later time, as needed.

Very similarly, we could refactor our JSON product importer. When calling the `import()` method, the products would get queued, and then a separate worker plugin would handle the product data creation/update whenever cron runs. This of course depends on whether we are okay with splitting the import functionality into two classes, which is not a big deal. We are actually fine with the way things are at the moment, so to illustrate the programmatic processing of the queue, we will use another example.

Processing a queue programmatically

Now that we have our queue worker that deletes teams (for all it knows, the teams don't even have to be without any players), we can explore how we can process this queue ourselves if we don't want the cron option. If we wanted it to be processed using a Drush command, we would not have to write that ourselves. Drush comes with one, and it would work like this:

```
drush queue-run team_cleaner
```

However, we may want to create an admin interface, a form of some kind, which allows the user to trigger the queue processing. In that case, we could do something like this:

```
$queue = \Drupal::queue('team_cleaner');
/** @var QueueWorkerInterface $queue_worker */
$queue_worker =
\Drupal::service('plugin.manager.queue_worker')->createInstance('team_clean
er');

while($item = $queue->claimItem()) {
  try {
    $queue_worker->processItem($item->data);
    $queue->deleteItem($item);
  }
  catch (SuspendQueueException $e) {
    $queue->releaseItem($item);
    break;
  }
  catch (\Exception $e) {
    // Log the exception.
  }
}
```

In this example, we get our QueueInterface object just like we did before. But then, we also create an instance of our own QueueWorker plugin. Next, we use the claimItem() method inside a while loop, which returns an object that contains the data to be passed to the queue worker. Additionally, it blocks the item from being usable by another worker for a period of (lease) time (by default an hour).

Then, we try to use the worker to process the item, and if no exception is thrown, we delete the item. It's done! However, if we catch a `SuspendQueueException`, it means we expect the entire queue to be problematic. This exception type is thrown when there is the expectation that all other items are also likely to fail, in which case we release the item and break out of the loop. Releasing the item means that other workers are now free to process it using the `claimItem()` method. Or even better, our own worker can try it later on. Finally, we also catch any other exceptions, in which case we simply log the error but do not release the item to prevent an infinite loop. For the moment, that particular item cannot be processed, so we need to skip to the next one; it needs to stay blocked until our loop finishes. The latter can only happen when `$queue->claimItem()` doesn't return anything anymore.

And that is pretty much the logic behind processing a queue ourselves--we claim an item, throw it to a worker, and delete it. If something goes wrong, we work with exceptions to determine if the queue can be continued or if it should be skipped altogether.

Lock API

Whenever we process data on a regular basis, especially if it takes a while to complete, we might run into a situation in which parallel requests want to trigger that process again-- while the first is still running. Most of the time, this is not a good thing, as it can lead to conflicts and/or data corruption. A good example from Drupal core in which this can happen is the cron. If we start it, the process can end up taking a few good seconds. Remember, it needs to pull together the `hook_cron()` implementations and run them all. So while that is happening, if we trigger another cron run, it will give us a nice message asking us to chill because the cron is already running. It does this with the help of the Lock API.

The Lock API is a low-level Drupal solution for ensuring that processes don't trample each other. Since in this chapter we are talking about things such as batch operations, queues, and other kinds of potentially time-consuming processes, let's look at the Lock API to see how we can leverage it for our custom code. But first, let's get an understanding of how this locking works.

The concept is very simple. Before starting a process, we *acquire* a lock based on a given name. This means we check if, by any chance, this process has not already been started. If we get the green light (we *acquired* the lock), we go ahead and start the process. The API at this point locks down this process so that other requests cannot *acquire* it again until the initial one has *released* it. This normally happens when the process is finished, and other requests may then start it up again. Before that, though, we get a red light that tells us we cannot start it, to maintain the analogy of traffic lights. Speaking of which, the main Lock API implementation in Drupal, namely the one using the database, takes this analogy to heart as it names the table where the locks are being stored `semaphore`.

The API is actually pretty simple. We have a Lock service, which is an implementation of `LockBackendInterface`. By default, Drupal 8 comes with two--the `DatabaseLockBackend` and `PersistentDatabaseLockBackend`. Usually, the former is used. The difference between the two is that the latter can be used to keep a lock across multiple requests. The former in fact releases all the locks at the end of the request. We'll be using this one to demonstrate how the API works, as that is what Drupal core uses mostly, as well.

If you remember from `Chapter 7`, *Your Own Custom Entity and Plugin Types*, we created a Drush command that would run all of our Product importers. Of course, we so far have only created one plugin. But what we want to do is ensure that if this Drush command is executed multiple times at more or less the same time (before the actual import finishes), we don't run the imports simultaneously. It's probably not the most realistic example, as Drush commands have to be actually run by someone so there is good control over their timing. However, the same approach, as we will see, can be applied to processes triggered by unpredictable requests.

We defined the `_products_products_import_run_plugin()` helper function that runs the import for a specific plugin. We can wrap this trigger with a *lock block*. First, though, we need to load the service, and we can get to it using the `lock` key or the static shorthand:

```
$lock = \Drupal::lock();
```

This will yield the database powered locking backend.

So instead of just running the `import()` method on the plugin, we can first have this:

```
if (!$lock->acquire($plugin->getPluginId())) {
  drush_log(t('The plugin %plugin is already running.', ['%plugin' =>
$plugin->getPluginDefinition()['label']]));
  return;
}
```

We try to *acquire* the lock by passing an arbitrary name (in this case, our plugin ID). We are sticking to one plugin at the time here, so multiple plugins should in fact be able to run at the same time. If the `acquire()` method returns FALSE, it means we have a red light, a lock has already been *acquired*. In this case, we print a message to that effect and get out of there. However, if not, it means we have a green light and we can proceed with the rest of our code as it was. The `acquire()` method has locked it down, and other requests can no longer *acquire* it until we *release* it. Speaking of which, there is one thing we need to add at the end (after the import):

```
$lock->release($plugin->getPluginId());
```

We need to *release* the lock so other requests can run it again if they like. That is pretty much it. If we run our Drush command twice, more or less simultaneously, we will have something like this in the terminal:

As you can see, only one call to the Drush command actually went through. As expected.

But we can also do it a bit differently. Let's say that we want to wait with the second request until the first one is finished, and then still run it. After all, we don't want to miss out on any updates. We can do this using the `wait()` method of `LockBackendInterface`. The rework is minor:

```
if (!$lock->acquire($plugin->getPluginId())) {
  drush_log(t('The plugin %plugin is already running. Waiting for it to
finish.', ['%plugin' => $plugin->getPluginDefinition()['label']]));
  if ($lock->wait($plugin->getPluginId())) {
    drush_log(t('The wait is killing me. Giving up.'));
    return;
  }
}
```

So basically, if we don't *acquire* a lock, we print a message that we are waiting for the go ahead. Then, we use the `wait()` method, which puts the request to sleep for a maximum of 30 seconds. Within that timeframe, it will continuously check every 25 milliseconds (until it reaches 500 milliseconds, when it starts checking every 500 milliseconds) if the lock has become available. If it has, it breaks out of the loop and returns FALSE (meaning that we can go ahead, as the lock has become available). Otherwise, if the 30 seconds have passed, it returns TRUE, which means that we still need to wait. At this point we give up. Guess what, the second parameter of the `wait()` method is the number of maximum seconds to wait, so we can control that as well. I recommend you check out the code to better understand what it does.

Like this, we can run our two Drush commands in parallel and ensure that the second one requested only runs after the first finishes. If it takes longer than 30 seconds, we give up, because probably something went wrong. Then, we have the Lock API.

Summary

In this chapter, we looked at some of the ways we as module developers can set up simple and complex data processing tasks that can run at any time we want.

We started by looking into using the multirequest capabilities of the update hooks. This was a continuation from `Chapter 8`, *The Database API*, where we introduced them for the first time, and we have now seen how we can expand on their capabilities. Then, we turned to the more complex Batch API that uses similar, albeit more complex, techniques. This system allowed us to construct a series of operations that leveraged Drupal's multirequest capabilities. Our playground was the JSON products Importer, which now can handle large amounts of data without the concern of PHP memory timeouts. Next, we looked at how Drupal's cron system works and why it is there, and even saw an example of how as module developers we can hook into it and process our own tasks whenever it runs. But then, we took things to the next level with the introduction of the Queue API, which allowed us to add items to a queue so that they can get processed at a later stage. This processing, as we saw, can be triggered by cron or we can take matters into our own hands and handle them one by one. Not to mention the Drush option that can also make things easy. Finally, we looked at the Lock API, which allows us to get control over the triggering of certain processes that take longer to complete. All this is done in order to prevent them being run multiple times simultaneously, causing errors or data corruption.

In the next chapter we are going to talk about Views and how we can programmatically interact with these as module developers.

15
Views

Views has always been a staple module for any Drupal site. It was so popular and needed that it ended up being incorporated into Drupal 8 core. So now, each new Drupal site ships with Views out of the box, fully integrated with the rest of the system and powering a great number of core features.

Essentially, Views is a tool for creating and displaying lists of data. This data can be almost anything, but we mostly use Drupal entities as they are now so robust. It provides the architecture to build and manipulate complex queries through the UI as well as many different ways of outputting the resulting data. From a module developer's point of View (yes, pun intended), much of this power has been broken down into multiple layers of building blocks, abstracted as plugins. Moreover, in keeping with tradition, there are also a multitude of hooks that are fired at different stages, with which we can programmatically contribute to or influence Views.

In this chapter, we will look at the Views ecosystem from a module developer's perspective. As such, we won't be spending that much time with its site-building capabilities as one can easily argue an entire book could be dedicated just to that. Instead, we will focus on what we as module developers can do to empower site builders to have even more capabilities at their finger-tips, as well as manipulating Views to behave the way our functionality needs them to.

So, what will we actually do in this chapter? We will first start with integrating our Product entity type with Views. The entity system and Views can work very closely together, and all we need to do is point them to one another. Then, we will switch gears and expose our own custom player and team data (from Chapter 8 , *The Database API*) to Views so our site builders can build Views that list this information, complete with filters, sorts, arguments, and the *whole shebang*. From there, we will look at how we can also alter data that has been exposed to Views by other modules, like entity data such as Nodes.

Next, you will learn how to create your own `ViewsField`, `ViewsFilter`, and `ViewsArgument` plugins to account for those occasional requirements for which the existing ones are a bit lacking. Finally, we will talk a little bit about theming Views and the main components that play a role in this, just to get you going in the right direction, and applying the lessons from `Chapter 4`, *Theming*.

By the end of this chapter, you will get a pretty good understanding of how to leverage Views on top of your own data, as well as modifying or contributing to how other modules leverage it. You should also get a pretty good understanding of the Views plugin ecosystem, even if quite a bit of work will have to be done on your own, studying the available plugins of all types.

So, let's get to it.

Entities in Views

Even in Drupal 7, Views had a pretty good integration with the entity system. But seeing as there was no robust entity API to speak of, this integration was not so organic. It required more contributed modules and some custom code to make an entity type work with Views.

In Drupal 8, however, the two are very closely linked and it's a breeze exposing new content entities to Views. If you've followed along with `Chapter 7`, *Your Own Custom Entity and Plugin Types*, and have the Product entity type set up, you'll notice that if you try to create a View, you will have no option to make it based on products. That is because in the entity type definition, we did not specify it should be exposed to Views. That's all there is to it, actually. We just have to reference a new handler:

```
"views_data" = "Drupal\views\EntityViewsData"
```

That is it. Clearing the cache, we are now able to create Views with products that can show any of the fields, can filter and sort by them, and can even render them using View modes. All of these work consistently with the other entity types (at least fundamentally, as we will see in a moment).

You'll notice that we referenced the `EntityViewsData` data handler which ensures basic logic for entities of all types. If we want to, we can extend this class and add some of our own specificities to the data that is being exposed to Views (or alter the existing ones). This is done inside the `getViewsData()` method, and we will see an example later on. But if you already want to see an example, check out the `NodeViewsData` handler for the Node entity type, as it has quite a lot of extra stuff in there. Much of it probably won't make a lot of sense quite yet, so let's slowly get into how Views works by exposing our own custom data to it.

Exposing custom data to Views

To get a better understanding of how Views works, we are going to look at an example of totally custom data and how we can expose it to Views. Based on that, we will begin understanding the role of various plugins and can begin to create our own. Additionally, we'll be able to expand on our Product entity type data to enrich its Views interaction.

To exemplify all of this, we are going to revisit our sports module in which we declared the `players` and `teams` tables of data and which we will now be exposing to Views. The goal is to allow site builders to create dynamic listings of this data as they see fit. The lessons learned from this example can be applied to other data sources as well, even things such as remote APIs (with some extra work).

Views data

Whenever we want to expose data to Views, we need to define this data in a way Views can understand it. That is actually what `EntityViewsData::getViewsData()` does for content entities. However, since we are dealing with something custom, we can do so by implementing `hook_views_data()`. A lot can go into it, but we'll start things simple.

Let's implement this hook and simply describe our first table (that of the players) and only one field, namely, the player ID, to start with.

In Views lingo, the term `field` does not have to relate necessarily to entity fields or anything like that, but rather to an individual piece of data from a data source (real or not). A typical example to consider is a column in a table, but it can also be something like a property from a remote API resource. Moreover, the same term is used to describe the *responsibility* of that piece of data of being somehow output. Other such responsibilities it can have are `filter`, `sort`, `relationship`, and more. Each of these responsibilities are handled by a specific type of Views plugin (also known as a handler in older versions of Views).

So, the basic implementation can look like this:

```
/**
 * Implements hook_views_data().
 */
function sports_views_data() {
  $data = [];

  // Players table
  $data['players'] = [];
  $data['players']['table']['group'] = t('Sports');
  $data['players']['table']['base'] = array(
    'field' => 'id',
    'title' => t('Players'),
    'help' => t('Holds player data.'),
  );

  // Player fields
  $data['players']['id'] = array(
    'title' => t('ID'),
    'help' => t('The unique player ID.'),
    'field' => array(
      'id' => 'numeric',
    ),
  );

  return $data;
}
```

This hook needs to return a multi-dimensional associative array that describes various things, the most important being the table and its fields. The table doesn't have to be an actual database table, but can also mean something similar to an external resource. Of course, Views already knows how to query the database table, which makes things easy for us. Otherwise, we'd have to create also the logic for querying that external resource (by implementing a `ViewsQuery` plugin).

So, we start by defining the `players` table, which goes into the `Sports` group. This label can be found in the Views admin as the prefix to the fields we want to add. Next, we define our first *base* table called `players` (mapping to the actual database table with the same name). The *base* table is the one used for *basing* a View on when creating it. In other words, whatever you select in the following screentext:

The base table definition contains some information such as the `field`, which refers to the column that contains the unique identifier for the records. The `title` and `help`, both mandatory, are used in the UI. Moreover, it can also contain `query_id`, which references the plugin ID of a `ViewsQuery` plugin responsible for returning the data from the source in an intelligible way. Since in our case we are using the database (hence SQL), omitting this property will make it default to the `views_query` plugin (the `Sql` class if you want to check it out).

Views fields

But in order to actually use this table, we need to define one or more fields that can output some of its data. So, we start with a simple one, the player IDs. Anything that comes under the `$data['table_name']` array (that is not keyed by `table`, as we've seen) is responsible for defining Views fields. The keys are their machine names. `title` and `help` are there again and are used in the UI when we try to add the respective fields:

The most important part of this definition, however, is the `field` key which basically says for this piece of data, we want a Views field that uses the `ViewsField` plugin with the ID `numeric` (`NumericField`). So, we don't actually have to write our own plugin because Views already has a good one for us and it will treat our IDs according to the type of data they are. Of course, when defining Views fields (or any other types of data responsibilities, that is, plugins or handlers), we can have more options than just the ID of the plugin to use.

 You can check out all the existing Views plugins defined by the module itself (which are quite a lot and fit many many use cases) by looking at the `Drupal\views\Plugin\views` namespace. There are many plugin types that handle different responsibilities, but it's good to know where you can look because more often than not, one will already exist for your needs.

With this, we are done. Clearing the cache, we can now go into the Views UI and create our first View that shows player data. To it, we can add the ID field, which will then naturally just show a list of IDs. Not more, as we haven't defined anything else. So, let's go ahead and expose the player name in the same way:

```
$data['players']['name'] = array(
  'title' => t('Name'),
  'help' => t('The name of the player.'),
  'field' => array(
    'id' => 'standard',
  ),
);
```

This time, we are using the `standard` plugin, which is the simplest one we can use. It essentially just outputs the data as it is found in the data source (with the proper sanitization in place). In the case of our player names, that is enough. Now, we can add this new field to the View as well.

If you remember, the other column on our `players` table is one that can store arbitrary data in a serialized way. Obviously, this cannot be used for filtering or sorting, but we can still output some of that data as a field. There are two ways we can go about doing this, depending on our data and what we want accomplished. First, we can use the exiting `Serialized` plugin, which allows us to display the serialized data or even a given key from the resulting array (depending on the field configuration). But for more complex situations (especially when the data is arbitrary), we can write our own field plugin.

Let's start by creating a simple `data` field that can output a printed version of our serialized data since we cannot rely on the actual data being stored:

```
$data['players']['data'] = array(
  'title' => t('Data'),
  'help' => t('The player data.'),
  'field' => array(
    'id' => 'serialized',
  ),
);
```

In the field configuration, we then have these options to choose from:

With this, you should already get a picture of how to define fields for output in Views. Let's now see how we can bring our teams into the loop and show some data about the teams the players belong to.

Views relationships

The fact that the data about the teams our players belong to is stored in a different table means that at a database level a join will have to be created to pull them together. In Views lingo this is a `relationship` in the sense that one table relates to another and the way these are declared is directional from a field to another from the joined table. So, let's see how we can define the `team_id` field from the `players` table to join with the `teams` table on its `id` field:

```
$data['players']['team_id'] = array(
  'title' => t('Team ID'),
  'help' => t('The unique team ID of the player.'),
  'field' => array(
    'id' => 'numeric',
  ),
  'relationship' => array(
```

```
        'base' => 'teams',
        'base field' => 'id',
        'id' => 'standard',
        'label' => t('Player team'),
    ),
);
```

First of all, we define it to Views as a field. Then, because we also might want to display the team ID, we can define it as a `field` as well using the `numeric` plugin, the same way we defined the ID of the player records themselves. But here comes another *responsibility* of this field in the form of a `relationship`, and the latter requires four pieces of information:

- `base`: The name of the table we are joining
- `base field`: The name of the field on the table we are joining, which will be used to join
- `id`: The `ViewsRelationship` plugin ID to use for the relationship
- `label`: How this relationship will be labeled in the UI

Usually the `standard` relationship plugin will suffice, but we can always create one ourselves if we need to. It's doubtful you will ever need to, though.

This definition now allows us to add a relationship to the `teams` table in Views. However, even if the database engine joins the two tables, we haven't achieved anything as we also want to output some fields from the new table. So for that, we first have to define the table itself, as we did for the players:

```
// Teams table
$data['teams'] = [];
$data['teams']['table']['group'] = t('Sports');
```

Note that it is not mandatory to define it as a `base` table if we don't want to create Views that are basing themselves on this table. In our case, it can be secondary to player information. Then, just as we did before, we can define a couple of team fields:

```
// Teams fields
$data['teams']['name'] = array(
    'title' => t('Name'),
    'help' => t('The name of the team.'),
    'field' => array(
        'id' => 'standard',
    ),
);

$data['teams']['description'] = array(
    'title' => t('Description'),
```

```
  'help' => t('The description of the team.'),
  'field' => array(
    'id' => 'standard',
  ),
);
```

There is nothing new here, just the basic data output for our two columns. But now, with our relationship added to the View, we can include the name and description of the teams our players belong to. Neat.

Views sorts and filters

Let's go ahead and enrich the *responsibilities* of the team name field by making our list of players filterable and sortable by it; for example, to only show the players of a given team or sort the players alphabetically by the team name. It could not be easier. We just have to add these to the field definition (like we added the `relationship` to the players team_id field):

```
'sort' => array(
  'id' => 'standard',
),
'filter' => array(
  'id' => 'string',
),
```

So basically, we are using the `Standard` sort plugin for sorting (which basically defaults to whatever MySQL can do). As for the filter, we are using the `StringFilter` plugin, which is quite configurable from the Views UI. It even allows us various filtering possibilities like partial matching. With this, we can now sort and filter by the team name.

Views arguments

The last type of *responsibility* a View field can have is to be used as an argument (or a contextual filter for Drupal veterans). In other words, configuring the View to be filterable by a parameter that is dynamically passed to it. Let's face it, most of the time if we want to filter by a team, we won't rely on the actual string name as that can change. Instead, we tie everything to the record (by its ID). So that means we'll add the `argument` key to the team_id field of the `players` table (which also means that the query won't require a join so it will be more performant):

```
'argument' => array(
  'id' => 'numeric',
),
```

In this case, we use the `NumericArgument` plugin, which does pretty much all we need for our data type--it filters by what is expected to be a numerical data type. We are finished with that as well. We can now dynamically filter our players view by the ID of the teams they belong to.

Altering Views data

We saw how we can expose to Views our own data that is totally custom. However, we can also alter existing data definitions provided by Drupal core or other modules by implementing `hook_views_data_alter()`. The `$data` parameter passed by the reference will contain everything that has been defined and can be changed as needed.

Moreover, we can also use this implementation to create some new Views fields or filters on other tables that do not "belong" to us. This is actually more common than exposing totally custom tables or other kinds of resources. For example, we may want to create a new Views field that shows something related to the Node in the results. So, let's look at an example.

Do you remember in Chapter 6, *Data Modeling and Storage*, we saw how to create a *pseudo field*, which outputs a disclaimer message at the bottom of each Node? If our View is configured to render Node entities, that will work. However, if it's using fields, it cannot do that. So, let's see how we can expose this message also as a Views field.

First, we need to implement `hook_views_data_alter()` and define a new field on the Node entity type data table:

```
/**
 * Implements hook_views_data_alter().
 */
function module_name_views_data_alter(&$data) {
  $data['node_field_data']['disclaimer'] = [
    'title' => t('Disclaimer'),
    'help' => t('Shows a disclaimer message'),
    'field' => [
      'id' => 'custom',
    ],
  ];
}
```

In this case, we are adding our new Views field onto the Node data table (`node_field_data`). But then, we have a choice as to what plugin to use to render our message. We can of course create one ourselves (as we will do in the next section). This is actually very simple, especially since it doesn't even need to use any of the information from the resulting Nodes. However, if that's the case, we might as well use the existing `Custom` plugin, which has two main advantages. For one, we don't have to write any more code. Second, it allows the site builder to specify (and modify as needed) the disclaimer message through the UI. Because basically, this plugin exposes a configuration form which we can add the text we want displayed for each row:

Shows a disclaimer message

☐ Create a label

☐ Exclude from display
    Enable to load this field as hidden. Often used to group fields, or to use as token in ano

Text

The content provided is for general information purposes only.

The text to display for this field. You may include HTML or Twig. You may enter data from

Of course, there are some drawbacks to this approach as well. If we wanted to ensure consistency between the message here and the one we used in the *pseudo field*, we would probably want to write our own plugin and get the message from this unique place. The same applies if we wanted the message to be strictly in code, especially if we needed some sort of data from the Node in the View results. So, the choice depends on the actual use case, but it's good to look into the existing Views plugins and see what already exists before creating our own.

Custom Views field

Now that we have seen how data is exposed to Views, we can start understanding the `NodeViewsData` handler I mentioned earlier (even if not quite everything) a bit better. But this also provides a good segue back to our `Product` entity type's `views_data` handler, where we can now see what the responsibility of `getViewsData()` is. It needs to return the definition for all the tables and fields, as well as what they can do. Luckily for us, the base class already provides everything we need to turn our product data into Views fields, filters, sorts, arguments, and potentially relationships, all out of the box.

But let's say we want to add some more Views fields that make sense to us in the context of our product-related functionality. For example, each product has a `source` field that is populated by the Importer entity from it's own `source` field. This is just to keep track of where they come from. So we may want to create a Views field that simply renders the name of the Importer that has imported the product.

You'll be quick to ask,"But hey, that is not a column on the products table! What gives?" As we will see, we can define Views fields that render whatever data we want (that can relate to the record or not). Of course, this also means that the resulting data cannot be used inside a sort or filter because MySQL doesn't have access to it when building the query. So we are a bit less flexible.

In this section, you will learn two things. First, we'll see how to create our own `views_data` handler for our Product Entity type. By now, you should be quite familiar with this process. More importantly though, we'll use this handler to create a new Views field for our product that renders something no existing `ViewsField` plugin can offer--the name of the related Importer entity. That means our own custom plugin. How exciting!

There are two quick steps to create our own `views_data` handler. First, we need the class:

```
namespace Drupal\products\Entity;

use Drupal\views\EntityViewsData;

/**
 * Provides Views data for Product entities.
 */
class ProductViewsData extends EntityViewsData {

  /**
   * {@inheritdoc}
   */
  public function getViewsData() {
    $data = parent::getViewsData();
```

```
      // Add stuff.
      return $data;
   }
}
```

As you can see, we are extending the base `EntityViewsData` class we had been referencing in the Product entity type annotation before. Inside, we are overriding the `getViewsData()` method to add our own definitions (which will go where you can see the comment).

Second, we need to change the handler reference to this new class in the entity type annotation:

```
"views_data" = "Drupal\products\Entity\ProductViewsData",
```

That's it. We can now define our own custom fields, and we can start with the definition:

```
$data['product']['importer'] = [
  'title' => t('Importer'),
  'help' => t('Information about the Product importer.'),
  'field' => array(
    'id' => 'product_importer',
  ),
];
```

Simple stuff, like we did with the players. Except in this case, we are adding it to the `product` table and we are using a `ViewsField` plugin which doesn't exist. Yet. So, let's create it.

As you may have noticed if you checked some of the existing ones, Views plugins go in the `Plugin\views\[plugin_type]` namespace of the modules, where `[plugin_type]` in this case is `field`, as we are creating a `ViewsField` plugin. So, we can start with the plugin class scaffolding:

```
namespace Drupal\products\Plugin\views\field;

use Drupal\views\Plugin\views\field\FieldPluginBase;
use Drupal\views\ResultRow;

/**
 * Field plugin that renders data about the Importer that imported the
Product.
 *
 * @ViewsField("product_importer")
 */
class ProductImporter extends FieldPluginBase {
```

```
/**
 * {@inheritdoc}
 */
public function render(ResultRow $values) {
  // Render something more meaningful.
  return '';
}
}
```

Just like any other field plugin, we are extending the `FieldPluginBase` class, which provides all the common defaults and base functionalities the fields need. Of course, you notice the admittedly small annotation, which simply contains the plugin ID. Our main job is to work in the `render()` method and output something, preferably using the `$values` object, that contains all the data in the respective row.

 Inside the `ResultRow` object, we can find the values from the Views row which can contain multiple fields. In case it's a View that lists entities, we also have an `_entity` key, which references the entity object itself.

Clearing the cache, we will now be able to add the new *Product Importer* field to a View for products. But if we do, we will notice an error. Views is trying to add to the query the `product_importer` field we defined, and which doesn't actually exist. That isn't right! This happens because even though Views can be made to work with any data source, it still has a preference for the SQL database, so we can encounter these issues every once in a while. Not to worry though, as we can simply tell our plugin not to include the field in any query-- it will show totally custom data. We do so by overriding the `query()` method:

```
/**
 * {@inheritdoc}
 */
public function query() {
  // Leave empty to avoid a query on this field.
}
```

That's it. Now, our field is going to render an empty string--`''`. Let's change it to look for the related Importer entity and show its label. But in order to do that, we'll need the `EntityTypeManager` service to use for querying. Let's inject it:

```
/**
 * @var \Drupal\Core\Entity\EntityTypeManager
 */
protected $entityTypeManager;

/**
 * Constructs a ProductImporter object.
```

```
 *
 * @param array $configuration
 *   A configuration array containing information about the plugin
instance.
 * @param string $plugin_id
 *   The plugin_id for the plugin instance.
 * @param mixed $plugin_definition
 *   The plugin implementation definition.
 * @param \Drupal\Core\Entity\EntityTypeManager $entityTypeManager
 */
public function __construct(array $configuration, $plugin_id,
$plugin_definition, EntityTypeManager $entityTypeManager) {
  parent::__construct($configuration, $plugin_id, $plugin_definition);
  $this->entityTypeManager = $entityTypeManager;
}

/**
 * {@inheritdoc}
 */
public static function create(ContainerInterface $container, array
$configuration, $plugin_id, $plugin_definition) {
  return new static(
    $configuration,
    $plugin_id,
    $plugin_definition,
    $container->get('entity_type.manager')
  );
}
```

Since we are operating inside a plugin, we need to make sure we are implementing the
`ContainerFactoryPluginInterface` in order to make use of the `create()` method. But
luckily, a parent class does so already, namely
`Drupal\views\Plugin\views\PluginBase`, so we're good. We can now proceed with
the `render()` method:

```
public function render(ResultRow $values) {
  /** @var \Drupal\products\Entity\ProductInterface $product */
  $product = $values->_entity;
  $source = $product->getSource();
  $importers =
$this->entityTypeManager->getStorage('importer')->loadByProperties(['source
' => $source]);
  if (!$importers) {
    return NULL;
  }

  // We'll assume one importer per source.
```

```
    /** @var \Drupal\products\Entity\ImporterInterface $importer */
    $importer = reset($importers);
    return $this->sanitizeValue($importer->label());
}
```

Here, we simply get the Product entity of the current row and the query for the Importer configuration entities that have the source referenced on the product. We assume there is only one (even if we did not do a proper job ensuring this is the case) and simply return its label. We also pass it through the helper `sanitizeValue()` method, which takes care of ensuring the output is safe against XSS attacks and such. So now our products View can show, for each product, the name of the Importer that brought them into world.

If we take a step back and try to understand what is going on, a word of caution becomes evident. Views perform one big query that returns a list of product entities and some data. But then, when that data is output, we perform a query for the Importer entity corresponding to each product in the result set (and we load those entities). So if we have 100 products returned, that means 100 more queries. Try to keep this in mind when creating custom fields to ensure you are not getting a huge performance hit, which might often not even be worth it.

Field configuration

We got our field working, but let's say we want to make it a bit more dynamic. It's called *Product Importer,* and we are showing the title of the Importer entity. But let's make it configurable so that we can choose which title to show--that of the entity or that of the actual Importer plugin--in the UI.

There's a few simple steps for making the field plugin configurable. These work similarly to other Views plugin types. They are also quite similar in concept to what we did in Chapter 9 , *Custom Fields,* when we made the entity fields configurable.

First, we need to define some default options by overriding a method:

```
    /**
     * {@inheritdoc}
     */
    protected function defineOptions() {
        $options = parent::defineOptions();
        $options['importer'] = array('default' => 'entity');

        return $options;
    }
```

As you can see, we are adding to the options defined by the parent class (which are quite a few) our own `importer` one. And we set its default to the string `entity`. Our choice.

Second, we need to define the form element for our new option, and we can do this with another method override:

```
/**
 * {@inheritdoc}
 */
public function buildOptionsForm(&$form, FormStateInterface $form_state) {

  $form['importer'] = array(
    '#type' => 'select',
    '#title' => $this->t('Importer'),
    '#description' => $this->t('Which importer label to use?'),
    '#options' => [
      'entity' => $this->t('Entity'),
      'plugin' => $this->t('Plugin')
    ],
    '#default_value' => $this->options['importer'],
  );

  parent::buildOptionsForm($form, $form_state);
}
```

Nothing special here, we are simply defining a selected list form element on the main options form. We can see that the `$options` class property contains all the plugin options where we can check for the default value of our `importer` one. Finally, we of course add onto the form all the other elements from the parent definition.

Next, inside the `render()` method, once we get our hands on the Importer entity we can make a change to this effect:

```
// If we want to show the entity label.
if ($this->options['importer'] == 'entity') {
  return $this->sanitizeValue($importer->label());
}

// Otherwise we show the plugin label.
$definition =
$this->importerManager->getDefinition($importer->getPluginId());
return $this->sanitizeValue($definition['label']);
```

Pretty simple. We either show the entity label or that of the plugin. But of course--and we skipped this--the Importer plugin manager also needs to be injected into the class. I'll let you handle that on your own.

Finally, one last thing we need to do is define the configuration schema. Since our View (which is a configuration entity) is now being saved with an extra option, we need to define the schema for the latter. We can do this inside a new `products.schema.yml` file (in the `config/schema` folder of our module):

```
views.field.product_importer:
  type: views_field
  label: 'Product Importer'
  mapping:
    importer:
      type: string
      label: 'Which importer label to use: entity or plugin'
```

This should be already familiar to you, including the dynamic nature of defining configuration schemas. We pretty much did the same in `Chapter 9`, *Custom Fields*, for the options on our field type, widget, and formatter plugins. This time, though, the type is `views_field`, from which we basically inherit a bunch of definitions and to which we add our own (the `importer` string). That's it. If we configure our new Views field, we should see this new option:

Custom Views filter

In a previous section we exposed our `players` and `teams` tables to Views, as well as made the team name a possible string filter to limit the resulting players by team. But this was not the best way we could have accomplished this because site builders may not necessarily know all the teams that are in the database nor their exact names. So we can create our own `ViewsFilter` to turn it into a selection of teams the user can choose from. Kind of like a taxonomy term filter. So let's see how it's done.

First, we need to alter our data definition for the team name field to change the plugin ID that will be used for the filtering (inside `hook_views_data()`):

```
'filter' => array(
  'id' => 'team_filter',
),
```

Now we just have to create that plugin. And naturally, it goes in the `Plugin/views/filter` namespace of our module:

```
namespace Drupal\sports\Plugin\views\filter;

use Drupal\Core\Database\Connection;
use Drupal\views\Plugin\views\filter\InOperator;
use Drupal\views\ViewExecutable;
use Drupal\views\Plugin\views\display\DisplayPluginBase;
use Symfony\Component\DependencyInjection\ContainerInterface;

/**
 * Filter class which filters by the available teams.
 *
 * @ViewsFilter("team_filter")
 */
class TeamFilter extends InOperator {

  /**
   * @var \Drupal\Core\Database\Connection
   */
  protected $database;

  /**
   * Constructs a Bundle object.
   *
   * @param array $configuration
   *   A configuration array containing information about the plugin
instance.
   * @param string $plugin_id
```

```
 *    The plugin_id for the plugin instance.
 * @param mixed $plugin_definition
 *    The plugin implementation definition.
 */
public function __construct(array $configuration, $plugin_id,
$plugin_definition, Connection $database) {
   parent::__construct($configuration, $plugin_id, $plugin_definition);
   $this->database = $database;
}

/**
 * {@inheritdoc}
 */
public static function create(ContainerInterface $container, array
$configuration, $plugin_id, $plugin_definition) {
   return new static(
     $configuration,
     $plugin_id,
     $plugin_definition,
     $container->get('database')
   );
}

/**
 * {@inheritdoc}
 */
public function init(ViewExecutable $view, DisplayPluginBase $display,
array &$options = NULL) {
   parent::init($view, $display, $options);
   $this->valueTitle = t('Teams');
   $this->definition['options callback'] = [$this, 'getTeams'];
}

/**
 * Generates the list of teams that can be used in the filter.
 */
public function getTeams() {
   $result = $this->database->query("SELECT name FROM
{teams}")->fetchAllAssoc('name');
   if (!$result) {
     return [];
   }

   $teams = array_keys($result);
   return array_combine($teams, $teams);
}
}
```

First and foremost, we see the annotation is in place to make this a plugin. Similar to the Views fields. Then, we use dependency injection to get our hands on the database connection service. Nothing new so far. However, you will notice that we extend from the `InOperator` class, which provides the base functionality for a Views filter that allows an `IN` type of filter. For example . . . `WHERE name IN(name1, name2)`. So, we extend from there to inherit much of this logic that applies to Views.

Then, we override the `init()` method (which initializes the plugin) in order to set the available values that site builders can choose from (the team names) and a title for the resulting form element. But we do so by specifying an `options callback` that will be used to retrieve the options at the right moment. This callback is a method on our class called `getTeams()`, which returns an array of all the team names. This array needs to be keyed by the value to use in the query filter. That is pretty much it. We don't need to worry about the options form or anything like that. The base class does it all for us.

Now, site builders can add this filter and choose a team (or more) to filter by, in an inclusive way. For example, to show the players that belong to a respective team:

Instead of using the `options callback`, we could have also directly overridden the `getValueOptions()` method of the parent (which in fact calls the options callback itself). The only caution here is that to prevent performance leaks, the values should be stored in the local `valueOptions` class property. So, they can be read multiple times.

Even if it's not that obvious, one last thing we need to do is define the configuration schema for our filter. You may be wondering why we are not creating any custom options. The answer is that when the user adds the filter and chooses a team to filter by, Drupal doesn't know what data type that value is. So, we need to tell it that it's a string. Inside our `sports.schema.yml` file, we can have this:

```
views.filter.team_filter:
  type: views_filter
  label: 'The teams to filter by'
  mapping:
    value:
      type: sequence
      label: 'Teams'
      sequence:
        type: string
        label: 'Team'
```

Similar to the Views field, we have a dynamic schema definition for the filter, of the type `views_filter`. In the mapping, we override the `value`field (which has already been defined by the `views_filter` data type). In our case, this is a sequence (an array with unimportant keys) whose individual values are strings.

Another way we can achieve the same (or similar) is like this:

```
views.filter_value.team_filter:
  type: sequence
  label: 'Teams'
  sequence:
    type: string
    label: 'Team'
```

This is because in the definition of the `value` key found in the `views_filter` schema, the type is set to `views.filter_value.[%parent.plugin_id]`. This means that we can simply define the `views.filter_value.team_filter` data type ourselves for it to use. If you remember, this is very similar to what we did ourselves in Chapter 12 , *JavaScript and Ajax API*. So, we can just define that missing bit as our sequence, rather than overriding the entire thing to change one small bit.

The existing Views filter classes provide a great deal of capability for either using them directly for custom data or extending to complement our own specificities. So, I recommend you check out all the existent filter plugins. However, the main concept of a filter is the alteration of the query being run by Views, which can be done inside the `query()` method of the plugin class. There, we can add extra conditions to the query based on what we need. You can check out this method on the `FilterPluginBase` class, which simply adds a condition (using the `addWhere()` method in the query object) based on the configured value and operator.

Custom Views argument

When we first exposed the player and team data to Views, we used an argument plugin so that we could have a contextual filter on the team ID a player belongs to. To do this, we used the existing `numeric` plugin on the actual `team_id` field of the `players` table. But what if we wanted an argument that works on more levels? For example, we don't exactly know what kind of data we'll receive, but we want to be able to handle nicely both a numeric one (team ID) and a textual one (team name). All in one argument. To achieve this, we can create a simple `ViewsArgument` plugin to handle this for us.

First thing, like always, is to define this field. We don't want to mess with the `team_id` field onto which we added the earlier argument as that can still be used. Instead, we'll create a new field, this time on the `teams` table, which we will simple call `team`:

```
$data['teams']['team'] = array(
  'title' => t('Team'),
  'help' => t('The team (either an ID or a team name).'),
  'argument' => array(
    'id' => 'team',
  ),
);
```

This time, though, we don't create a *field* for it as we don't need this displaying anything. Rather, we stick only to the `argument` responsibility, which will be handled by our new `team` plugin. You may also note that the `team` column doesn't actually exist in the database table.

So, let's see the plugin:

```
namespace Drupal\sports\Plugin\views\argument;

use Drupal\views\Plugin\views\argument\ArgumentPluginBase;

/**
 * Argument for filtering by a team.
 *
 * @ViewsArgument("team")
 */
class Team extends ArgumentPluginBase {

  /**
   * {@inheritdoc}
   */
  public function query($group_by = FALSE) {
    $this->ensureMyTable();
    $field = is_numeric($this->argument) ? 'id' : 'name';
    $this->query->addWhere(0, "$this->tableAlias.$field", $this->argument);
  }
}
```

As usual, we are extending from the base plugin class of its type and adding the proper annotation. Inside, we only deal with the query() method, which we override. Arguments are very similar to filters in the sense that they aim to restrict the result set via the query. The main difference is the actual value used to filter, which in this case is dynamic and can be found on the $argument property of the (parent) class, and what we do is simply add a query condition to the right field on the teams table (since that is the base table), depending on the type of data we are dealing with. But before we do that, we call the ensureMyTable() method, which simply ensures that the table our plugin needs is included in the query by Views.

That's it. We can now add our newly created argument to the View, and regardless of what we passed as contextual filter (ID or name), it will filter accordingly. Of course, we can also have options like most other Views plugin types, but I'll let you explore those on your own. There are also a lot more we can override from the parent class in order to integrate with Views. But that's a bit more advanced and it's unlikely you'll need to deal with for a good while. I definitely recommend exploring the code behind it.

Views theming

Frontend developers had many pain points in Drupal 7 and many of them were also related to theming Views output. Luckily, Drupal 8 has made things much easier to handle. We will look at a bit of that here in order to nudge you in the right direction when applying what you learned in `Chapter 4`, *Theming*.

Views is very complex and is made up of many pluggable layers. A View has a *display* (such as a Page or Block), which can render its content using a given *style* (such as an Unformatted list or Table). Styles can decide whether to control the rendering of a given result item (row) themselves or delegate this to a *row* plugin (such as Fields or Entity). Most, in fact, do the latter. The two most common scenarios for using *row* plugins is either using the `EntityRow` one which renders the resulting entities using a specified view mode or the `Fields` plugin, which uses individual `ViewField` plugins to render each field that is added to the View.

If we wanted to theme a View, there are all these points we can look at. Want the View to output a slideshow? Maybe create a new *style* plugin. Want to do something crazy with each entity in the result set? Maybe create a new *row* plugin, or even just create a new *field* plugin (as we did) to render one piece of data in any way you want. These techniques are more oriented towards module developers taking control over Views. But we also have the theming aspects we can play with.

Again from the top, *style* plugins are nothing more than glorified wrappers over a theme hook. For example, the *Unformatted list* plugin uses the `views_view_unformatted` theme hook, which means a few things--it can be overridden by a theme (or even module) and it can be preprocessed by a theme or module. Take a look at the default `template_preprocess_views_view_unformatted()` preprocessor and `views-view-unformatted.html.twig` template file for more information. Don't forget about the theme hook suggestions, as Views defines quite a lot of them. All you need to do is enable theme (Twig) debugging, and you'll see for each View *layer* which template is being used.

The *style* theme, however, only gets us to the wrapper around all the results. To go a bit deeper we need to know what kind of *row* plugin it uses. If entities are being rendered, it's the same thing as controlling how entities are built. See `Chapter 6`, *Data Modeling and Storage*, for a refresher on that. If the *row* plugin uses *field* plugins, we have some options. First of all, this is also a wrapper over a theme hook, namely `views_view_fields`, which renders together all the *field* plugins added to the View.

So, we can override that using the already known theming methods. But we can also override the default theme hook for each `field` plugin itself, namely `views_view_field`, responsible for wrapping the output of the plugin. This takes us to the *field* plugins themselves and whatever they end up rendering which can differ from one plugin to another. So, make sure you check that.

Views hooks

Views also comes with a lot of hooks. We've already see an important one that allowed us to expose our own data to Views. But there are many more, and you should check out the `views.api.php` file for more information.

Quite a few exist for altering plugin information for all sorts of plugin types. But there are also some important ones that deal with Views execution at runtime. The most notable of these is `hook_views_query_alter()`, which allows us to make alterations to the final query that is going to be run. There is also `hook_views_post_render()` and `hook_views_pre_render()`, which allow us to make alterations to the View results. For example, to change the order of the items or something like that.

I recommend you check out their respective documents and make yourself aware what you can do with these hooks. At times they can be helpful, even if with Drupal 8 most of the action happens in plugins and you can easily now write your own to handle your specific requirements. This is why we won't be going into great detail about these.

Summary

In this chapter, we looked at Views from all sorts of module developer-oriented angles. We saw how we can expose our product entity type to Views. That was a breeze. But then, we also saw how our custom player and team data from Chapter 8, *The Database API*, can also be exposed to Views. Even if we did have to write some code for that, much of it was quite boilerplate as we were able to leverage the existing Views plugin ecosystem for almost everything we wanted. However, since these are all plugins, we also saw how we can create our own field, filter, and argument plugins to handle those exceptional cases in which what exists may not be enough.

Closely tied to this, we also talked a bit about altering the way other modules expose their data to Views. The most notable example here was the ability to easily add more fields (and plugins) to entity based Views in order to enrich them with custom functionalities.

Finally, we talked a bit about how we can approach the theming aspect of Views. We saw the different layers that make one up, starting from the display all the way down to the *field*. We closed the chapter with a shout-out to the existing hooks the Views module invokes at various times, and via which we can also make changes to its normal operation.

In the next chapter, we are going to see how we can work with files and images in Drupal 8.

16
Working with Files and Images

Drupal comes with many capabilities for handling and manipulating files and images and has been adding to its toolset more and more with recent versions. Of course, this is not to say that media management has not been always a pain point for Drupal developers. In Drupal 7, a complicated suite of contributed modules was needed to achieve a basic level of functionality, something that users of "competitors" like WordPress enjoy out of the box. In Drupal 8, there is more emphasis placed on media management, however much of the work is still in the contributed sphere. But due to the new way Drupal development will work, it's expected that much of this effort will find its way into the core system with future versions.

In this chapter, we will look at how we can work with files and images in Drupal, supported by the core features. We are not going to go into topics such as media management but rather focus on the module developer tools that can be used for working with files. We will see some examples along the way. So, what are we going to discuss?

First, we are going to get an understanding of the Drupal *filesystems*. Developers from previous versions of Drupal should already be familiar with these in theory, and we will see how these work in Drupal 8. Related to this, we're going to talk about *stream wrappers* and how Drupal handles native PHP file operations. We will even create our own custom stream wrapper a bit later in the chapter.

Then, we will talk a bit about the different ways to handle files in Drupal, namely *managed* (tracked) and *unmanaged* files. In exemplifying the work with *managed* files, we will add an image field to our Product entity type and have images imported from a fictional remote environment. We will also create a brand new CSV-based importer by which the product data is imported from a CSV file we process. In this process, we will mention the Entity CRUD hooks, a very important extension point in Drupal 8, and see how we can use those in our example context.

We will end the chapter by seeing how we can work with various APIs that deal specifically with images; especially for manipulating them via image toolkits and working with image styles. So let's get to it.

The filesystem

Drupal defines four main types of file storage for any given site--the *public*, the *private*, the *temporary* and the *translation* filesystems. When installing Drupal, the folders that map to these filesystems are created automatically. In case that fails--most likely due to permission issues--we have to create them ourselves and give them the right permissions. Drupal takes care of the rest (for example, adds relevant .htaccess files for security reasons). Make sure you check out the documentation on Drupal.org for how to successfully install Drupal 8 if you are unsure how this works.

Public files are available to the world at large for viewing or downloading. This is where things such as image content, logos, and anything that can be downloaded are stored. Your public file directory must exist somewhere under Drupal's root, and it must be readable and writeable by whatever *user* your web server is running under. Public files have no access restrictions. Anyone, at anytime, can navigate directly to a public file and view or download it. This also means that accessing these files does not require Drupal to bootstrap.

We can configure the path to the public filesystem in our settings.php file:

```
$settings['file_public_path'] = 'sites/default/files';
```

Private files are not available to the world for general download. Therefore the private files' directory must not be accessible via the web. However, it still has to be writeable by the web server user. Isolating private files this way allows developers to control who can and can't access them. For instance, we could write a module that only allows users who have a specific role to access PDFs in the private filesystem.

We can configure the path to the private filesystem in our `settings.php` file:

```
$settings['file_private_path'] = 'sites/default/private';
```

Temporary file storage is typically only used by Drupal for internal operations. When files are first saved by Drupal, they are initially written into the temporary filesystem so they can be checked for security issues. After they have been deemed safe, they are written to their final location.

We can configure the path to the temporary filesystem through the UI:

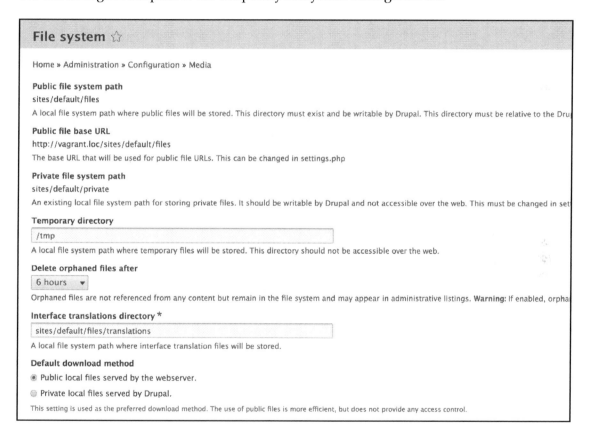

On the same configuration screen, we can also specify the default file download method for the site. By default, this is set to the public filesystem.

Finally, the translation file storage is used by Drupal for storing the `.po` files, which contain string translation values that can be imported into the system in bulk. As with the temporary file storage, we can configure the location of translation files through the UI.

Stream wrappers

If you've been writing PHP for a long time, you may have needed to work with local or remote files at some point. The following PHP code is a common way to read a file into a variable that you can do something with:

```
$contents = '';
$handle = fopen("/local/path/to/file/image.jpg", "rb");
while (!feof($handle)) {
 $contents .= fread($handle, 8192);
}
fclose($handle);
```

This is pretty straightforward. We get a handle to a local file using `fopen()` and read 8KB chunks of the file using `fread()` until `feof()` indicates that we've reached the end of the file. At that point, we use `fclose()` to close the handle. The contents of the file are now in the variable `$contents`.

In addition to local files, we can also access remote ones through `fopen()` in the same exact way but by specifying the actual remote path instead of the local one we saw before (starting with `http(s)://`).

Data that we can access this way is streamable, meaning we can open it, close it, or seek to an arbitrary place in it.

Stream wrappers are an abstraction layer on top of these streams that tell PHP how to handle specific types of data. When using a stream wrapper, we refer to the file just like a traditional URL--`scheme://target`. As a matter of fact, the preceding example uses one of PHP's built-in stream wrappers: the `file://` wrapper, for accessing files on local storage. It is actually the default scheme when none is specified, so that is why we got away with omitting it and just adding the file path. Had the file been on a remote location, we would have used something like `http://example.com/file/path/image.jpg`. That is another PHP built-in stream wrapper--`http://` (for the HTTP protocol).

If that's not enough, PHP also allows us to define our own wrappers for schemes that PHP does not handle out of the box; the Drupal File API was built to take advantage of this. This is where we link back to the different types of file storage we talked about earlier, as they all have their own stream wrappers defined by Drupal.

The public filesystem uses the rather known `public://` stream wrapper, the private one uses `private://`, the temporary one `temporary://`, and the translation one `translations://`. These map to the local file paths that we defined in the `settings.php` (or UI). Later in the chapter, we will see how we can define our own stream wrapper and what some of the things that go into it are. First, though, let's talk a bit about the different ways we can manage files in Drupal 8.

Managed versus unmanaged files

The Drupal File API allows us to handle files in two different ways. Files essentially boil down to two categories: they are either *managed* or *unmanaged*. The difference between the two lies in the way the files are used.

Managed files work hand in hand with the Entity system and are in fact tied to File entities. So whenever we create a *managed* file, an entity gets created for it as well, which we can use in all sorts of ways. And the table where these records are stored is called `file_managed`. Moreover, a key aspect of *managed* files is the fact that their usage is tracked. This means that if we attach them to another entity, reference them, or even manually indicate that we use them, this usage is tracked in a secondary table called `file_usage`. This way, we can see where each file is used and how many times, and Drupal even provides a way to delete "orphaned" files after a specific time in case they are no longer needed.

A notable example of using *managed* files is the simple `Image` field type that we can add to an entity type. Using these fields, we can upload a file and *attach* it to the respective entity. This attachment is nothing more than a special (tracked) entity reference between the two entities.

By understanding how *managed* files are used, it's not difficult to anticipate what *unmanaged* files are. The latter are the files we upload to make use of for various reasons but which--of course--do not need to be *attached* to any entity or have their usage tracked.

Using the File and Image fields

In order to demonstrate how to work with *managed* files, we will go back to our Product entity importer and bring in some images for each product. However, in order to store them, we need to create a field on the Product entity. This will be an *image* field.

Instead of creating this field through the UI and attaching it to a bundle, let's do it the programmatic way and make it a base field (available on all bundles). We won't need to do anything complex, for now we are only interested in a basic field that we can use to store the images we bring in from the remote API. It can look something like this:

```
$fields['image'] = BaseFieldDefinition::create('image')
  ->setLabel(t('Image'))
  ->setDescription(t('The product image.'))
  ->setDisplayOptions('form', array(
    'type' => 'image_image',
    'weight' => 5,
  ));
```

If you remember from `Chapter 6`, *Data Modeling and Storage* and `Chapter 7`, *Your Own Custom Entity and Plugin Types*, how this works is we are creating a base field definition which, in this case, is of the type `image`. This is the `FieldType` plugin ID of the `ImageItem` field. So that is where we need to look and see what kind of field and storage options we may have. For example, we can have a file extension limitation (which by default contains `png`, `gif`, `jpg`, and `jpeg`) and things like `alt` and `title` attributes, as well as image dimension configuration. Do check out `ImageItem` to get an idea of the possible storage and field settings. But alas, we are fine with the defaults in this case, so we don't even have any field settings.

Another interesting thing to notice is that `ImageItem` extends the `FileItem` field type, which is a standalone `FieldType` plugin that we can use. However, it is more generic and lends itself for use with any kind of file upload situation. Since we are dealing with images, we might as well take advantage of the specific field type.

For the moment, we do not configure our image field to have any kind of display. We'll look into that a bit later. However, we do specify the widget it should use on the entity form, namely the `FieldWidget` plugin with the ID of `image_image`. This maps to the default `ImageWidget` class. But again, we are fine with the setting defaults, so we don't specify anything extra.

With this our field definition is done; all we need to do is create the interface methods for easily accessing and setting the images:

```
/**
 * Gets the Product image.
 *
 * @return \Drupal\file\FileInterface
 */
public function getImage();

/**
 * Sets the Product image.
 *
 * @param int $image
 *
 * @return \Drupal\products\Entity\ProductInterface
 *   The called Product entity.
 */
public function setImage($image);
```

The getter method is supposed to return a `FileInterface` object (which is the actual File entity) while the setter is supposed to receive the ID (`fid`) of the image to save. As for the implementations, it should not be anything new to us:

```
/**
 * {@inheritdoc}
 */
public function getImage() {
  return $this->get('image')->entity;
}

/**
 * {@inheritdoc}
 */
public function setImage($image) {
  $this->set('image', $image);
  return $this;
}
```

With this, we are ready to proceed with the import of images from the remote API.

Working with managed files

In this section, we will look at two examples of working with managed files. First, we will see how we can import product images from our fictional remote JSON-based API. Second, we will see how to create a custom form element that allows us to upload a file, and use it in a brand new CSV based importer.

Attaching managed files to entities

Now that we have our product image field in place and we can store images, let's revisit our JSON response that contains the product data and assume it looks something like this now:

```
{
  "products" : [
    {
      "id" : 1,
      "name": "TV",
      "number": 341,
      "image": "tv.jpg"
    },
    {
      "id" : 2,
      "name": "VCR",
      "number": 123,
      "image": "vcr.jpg"
    }
  ]
}
```

What's new is the addition of the `image` key for each product, which simply references a filename for the image that goes with the respective product. The actual location of the images is at some other path we need to include in the code.

Going back to our `JsonImporter::persistProduct()` method, let's delegate the handling of the image import to a helper method called `handleProductImage()`. We need to call this method both if we are creating a new Product entity and if we are updating an existing one (right before saving):

```
$this->handleProductImage($data, $product);
```

And this is what the actual method looks like:

```
/**
 * Imports the image of the product and adds it to the Product entity.
 *
 * @param $data
 * @param ProductInterface $product
 */
private function handleProductImage($data, ProductInterface $product) {
    $name = $data->image;
    // This needs to be hardcoded for the moment.
    $image_path = '';
    $image = file_get_contents($image_path . '/' . $name);
    if (!$image) {
        // Perhaps log something.
        return;
    }

    /** @var \Drupal\file\FileInterface $file */
    $file = file_save_data($image, 'public://product_images/' . $name,
FILE_EXISTS_REPLACE);
    if (!$file) {
        // Something went wrong, perhaps log it.
        return;
    }

    $product->setImage($file->id());
}
```

First, we get the name of the image. Then we construct the path to where the product images are stored. In the preceding example it's left blank, but if the example were to work, we'd have to add a real path there. I leave that up to you for now. If you want to test it out, create a local folder with some images and reference that.

Using the native `file_get_contents()` function, we load the data of the image from the remote environment into a string. We then pass this string to the `file_save_data()` function which saves a new *managed* file to the public filesystem. This function takes three parameters--the data to be saved, the URI of the destination, and a flag indicating what to do if a file with the same name already exists. You'll notice that we used the Drupal `public://` stream wrapper to build the URI and we already know which folder this maps to.

As for the third parameter, we chose to replace the file in case one already exists. The alternative would have been to either use `FILE_EXISTS_RENAME` or `FILE_EXISTS_ERROR`. The first would have created a new file whose name would have gotten a number appended until the name became unique. The second would simply not do anything and return FALSE.

If all goes well, this function returns a `File` entity (that implements `FileInterface`) whose ID we can use in the Product image setter method. With that in place, we can synchronise also the individual product images. Moreover, in our database, a record is created in the `file_usage` table to indicate that this file is being used on the respective Product entity. If we delete the Product entity or remove the image from its field, the File entity looses this usage. If it's no longer used anywhere else, it will be deleted at the next cron run. Whether this happens actually depends on the filesystem configuration:

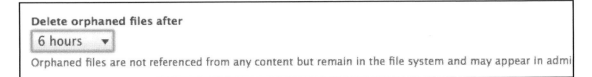

We can set a period for which files can stay orphaned for before they get deleted, or even prevent any files from being removed.

Helpful functions for dealing with managed files

Apart from the staple `file_save_data()` function, we have a few other ones that can come in handy if we are dealing with *managed* files. Here's a few of them.

If we want to copy a file from one place to another while making sure a new database record is created, we can use `file_copy()`. It takes three parameters:

- The `FileInterface` entity that needs to be copied
- The destination URI where it should go
- The flag indicating what to do in case a file with the same name exists

The parameters are the same as for `file_save_data()`.

Apart from the actual copying, this function also invokes `hook_file_copy()` which allows modules to respond to files being copied.

Very similarly to `file_copy()`, we also have `file_move()` that takes the same set of parameters but instead performs a file move. The database entry of the File entity gets updated to reflect the new file path. And `hook_file_move()` is invoked to allow modules to respond to this action.

Not strictly related to *managed* files but rather useful in all cases, we also have a `file_prepare_directory()` function which we can use to ensure the file destination is correct. It takes two arguments--the directory (a string representation of the path or stream URI) and a flag indicating what to do about the folder:

- `FILE_CREATE_DIRECTORY` : Will create the directory if it doesn't already exist
- `FILE_MODIFY_PERMISSION` : Will make the directory writable if it is found to be read-only

This function returns TRUE if the folder is good to go as a destination or FALSE if something went wrong or the folder doesn't exist.

Managed file uploads

Next, we are going to look at how we can work with *managed* files using a custom form element. And to demonstrate this, we are finally going to create another Product importer plugin. This time, instead of a remote JSON resource, we will allow users to upload a CSV file that contains product data and imports that into Product entities. This is what the example CSV data looks like:

```
id,name,number
1,Car,45345
2,Motorbike,54534
```

It basically has the same kind of data as the JSON resource we've been looking at so far, but without the image reference. So let's get going with our new plugin class.

Here is our starting point:

```
namespace Drupal\products\Plugin\Importer;

use Drupal\Core\Entity\EntityTypeManager;
use Drupal\Core\StreamWrapper\StreamWrapperManagerInterface;
use Drupal\Core\StringTranslation\StringTranslationTrait;
use Drupal\products\Entity\ImporterInterface;
use Drupal\products\Entity\ProductInterface;
use Drupal\products\Plugin\ImporterBase;
use GuzzleHttp\Client;
```

```php
use Symfony\Component\DependencyInjection\ContainerInterface;

/**
 * Product importer from a JSON format.
 *
 * @Importer(
 *   id = "csv",
 *   label = @Translation("CSV Importer")
 * )
 */
class CsvImporter extends ImporterBase {

  use StringTranslationTrait;

  /**
   * {@inheritdoc}
   */
  public function import() {
    $products = $this->getData();
    if (!$products) {
      return FALSE;
    }

    foreach ($products as $product) {
      $this->persistProduct($product);
    }

    return TRUE;
  }
}
```

The *used* files at the top also include the ones we will use as we flesh out the class, so one by one they will start making sense. In terms of our starting point, we extend from the ImporterBase class and implement the obligatory import() method. Like before, we delegate to getData() to retrieve the product information, but in this case we simply loop over the resulting records and use the persistProduct() method to save the Product entities. So no batch operations. Apart from no longer saving images, this latter method looks exactly like the one from the JsonImporter, so I won't be copying it over again. But, it makes for a good homework assignment to try to move it to the base class and abstract away the dynamic portions.

Managed file form element

The other obligatory method we need to implement is `getConfigurationForm()`, by which we define the form elements needed to configure this particular plugin. Here, we will create the `file` field allowing users to upload the CSV file:

```
/**
 * {@inheritdoc}
 */
public function
getConfigurationForm(\Drupal\products\Entity\ImporterInterface $importer) {
  $form = [];
  $config = $importer->getPluginConfiguration();
  $form['file'] = [
    '#type' => 'managed_file',
    '#default_value' => isset($config['file']) ? $config['file'] : '',
    '#title' => $this->t('File'),
    '#description' => $this->t('The CSV file containing the product
records.'),
    '#required' => TRUE,
  ];

  return $form;
}
```

The form element type is called `managed_file` (implemented by the `ManagedFile` form element class). The rest of the definition is straightforward. However, there are a couple of problems.

First, by default, using this form element, files are uploaded to the `temporary://` file system of Drupal. Since we don't want that, we need to specify an upload location:

```
'#upload_location' => 'public://'
```

The root of our public files folder will suffice for this example as we assume the file does not contain any sensitive information. If so, we could upload it to the `private://` one and control who gets access. We'll talk about how that works later in the chapter.

Second, by default, using this form element, the allowed file extensions for upload are limited to `jpg jpeg gif png txt doc xls pdf ppt pps odt ods odp`. So if we want to allow CSV files, we need to specify the extension in a list of allowed upload extensions. And we do this by overriding the default upload validators:

```
'#upload_validators' => [
  'file_validate_extensions' => ['csv'],
],
```

This is an array of validator callbacks we want Drupal to run when the file is uploaded. And allowing only CSV files is enough for our purposes. But another handy validator we could use is `file_validate_size()`. Moreover, we can implement `hook_file_validate()` ourselves and perform any custom validation to the files being uploaded. So, that's also something to keep in mind.

With this our plugin configuration form is in place; it looks something like this:

However, there is still something we need to do in order for the uploaded file to be *managed* properly. When using this form element, the file gets correctly uploaded and a record is added to the `file_managed` table. So we get our `File` entity. However, its status is not permanent because it doesn't have any usages. There are no records for it in the `file_usage` table. How could there be? So what we need to do is handle that ourselves and basically tell Drupal that the file uploaded in this form is *used* by the respective Importer configuration entity. And to do this, we need to know when the file is saved onto the entity, changed, and deleted.

With this we can also learn about something very important we skipped in Chapter 6 ,*Data Modeling and Storage* and Chapter 7, *Your Own Custom Entity and Plugin Types*--Entity CRUD hooks. But right before we jump into that, let's not forget about the configuration schema of this new configuration item--the file key of the plugin configuration:

```
products.importer.plugin.csv:
  type: mapping
  label: Plugin configuration for the CSV importer plugin
  mapping:
    file:
      type: sequence
      label: File IDs
      sequence:
        type: integer
        label: CSV File ID
```

We are doing the same as we did for the url key of the JSON importer but in this case we need to account for the fact that file is actually an array. So we define it as a sequence whose individual items are integers. Feel free to check Chapter 6, *Data Modeling and Storage*, for more information on configuration schemas whenever you need a reminder.

Entity CRUD hooks

Whenever entities are created, updated, or deleted, a set of hooks are fired that allow us to act on this information. We can use these hooks simply to perform some actions whenever this happens or even make changes to the entity being saved. So, let's see what we have.

A very useful one is hook_entity_presave(), which gets fired during the saving process of an entity (both content and configuration). This applies to both when the entity is first created, as well as when it is being updated. Moreover, it allows us to inspect the original entity and detect changes made to it. And finally, since the entity has not yet been persisted, it allows us to make changes to it ourselves. So very powerful stuff.

Since Drupal 8 is very flexible, we also have the hook_ENTITY_TYPE_presave() version which allows us to specifically target any entity type we want. We've already discussed the benefit of using more specific hooks to keep our code more organised as well as a little bit more performant. And this applies to all the entity CRUD hooks we are going to talk about next.

Then we have `hook_entity_insert()` and `hook_entity_update()`, which gets fired after an entity is created for the first time and after an entity is updated, respectively. We cannot make changes to the entity itself as it has already been saved, but they can come in handy at other times. The latter also gives us access to the original entity if we want to compare any changes. And similarly, we have `hook_entity_delete()`, which gets fired when an entity is deleted.

Finally, we also have `hook_entity_load()` which allows us to perform actions whenever an entity is loaded. For example, we can tack on additional information if we want. So keep in mind these hooks as they are going to be a very important tool in your module developer arsenal.

Managed file usage service

Now that we have an idea of the available entity CRUD hooks, we can implement three of them to handle our *managed* file problem. Because if you remember, *managed* files are actually represented by the `File` entity type, so the Entity CRUD hooks get fired for these as well.

To mark a file as being used by something, we can use the `DatabaseFileUsageBackend` service (`file.usage`), which is an implementation of the `FileUsageInterface`. This has a few handy methods that allow us to add a usage or delete it. That is actually what we are going to do next.

What we want to do first is add a file usage whenever a new Importer entity gets created (and a file uploaded with it):

```
/**
 * Implements hook_ENTITY_TYPE_insert() for the Importer config entity
type.
 */
function products_importer_insert(EntityInterface $entity) {
  if ($entity->getPluginId() != 'csv') {
    return;
  }

  // Mark the current File as being used.
  $fid = _products_importer_get_fid_from_entity($entity);
  $file = Drupal::entityTypeManager()->getStorage('file')->load($fid);
  \Drupal::service('file.usage')->add($file, 'products', 'config:importer',
$entity->id());
}
```

We are implementing the specific version of `hook_entity_insert()` for our own entity type, and the first thing we are checking is if we are looking at one using the CSV plugin. We're not interested in an Importers that don't have a CSV file upload. If so, we get the File entity ID from the importer using a private helper function:

```
/**
 * Given an Importer entity using the CSV plugin, return the File ID of the
CSV
 * file.
 *
 * @param EntityInterface $entity
 *
 * @return int
 */
function _products_importer_get_fid_from_entity(EntityInterface $entity) {
  $fids = $entity->getPluginConfiguration()['file'];
  $fid = reset($fids);
  return $fid;
}
```

You'll notice that the `file` key in our plugin configuration array is also an array of File IDs, even if we only uploaded one single file. That is just something we need to account for here (we did so in our configuration schema earlier on).

Then, we load the File entity based on this ID and use the `file.usage` service to add a usage to it. The first parameter of the `add()` method is the File entity itself, the second is the module name that marks this usage, the third is the type of *thing* the file is used by, while the fourth is the ID of this *thing*. The latter two depend on the use case; we choose to go with our own `config:importer` to make it clear that we are talking about a configuration entity of the type `importer`. Of course, we used the ID of the entity.

With this, a new record will get created in the `file_usage` table whenever we save such an Importer entity for the first time. Now let's handle the case in which we delete this entity-- we don't want this file usage lingering around, do we?

```
/**
 * Implements hook_ENTITY_TYPE_delete() for the Importer config entity
type.
 */
function products_importer_delete(EntityInterface $entity) {
  if ($entity->getPluginId() != 'csv') {
    return;
  }

  $fid = _products_importer_get_fid_from_entity($entity);
  $file = Drupal::entityTypeManager()->getStorage('file')->load($fid);
```

```
    \Drupal::service('file.usage')->delete($file, 'products',
  'config:importer', $entity->id());
  }
```

Most of what we are doing in this specific version of `hook_entity_delete()` is the same as before. However, we are using the `delete()` method of the `file.usage` service but passing the same arguments. These `$type` and `$id` parameters are actually optional so we can "un-use" multiple files at once. Moreover, we have an optional fifth parameter (the count) whereby we can specifically choose to remove more than one usage from this file. By default, this is one, and that makes sense for us.

Finally, we also want to account for the cases in which the user edits the importer entity and changes the CSV file. We want to make sure the old one is no longer marked as used for this Importer. And we can do this with `hook_entity_update()`:

```
/**
 * Implements hook_ENTITY_TYPE_update() for the Importer config entity
type.
 */
function products_importer_update(EntityInterface $entity) {
  if ($entity->getPluginId() != 'csv') {
    return;
  }

  /** @var \Drupal\products\Entity\ImporterInterface $original */
  $original = $entity->original;
  $original_fid = _products_importer_get_fid_from_entity($original);
  if ($original_fid !== _products_importer_get_fid_from_entity($entity)) {
    $original_file =
Drupal::entityTypeManager()->getStorage('file')->load($original_fid);
    \Drupal::service('file.usage')->delete($original_file, 'products',
  'config:importer', $entity->id());
  }
}
```

More correctly, we are using the specific variant of this hook which only gets fired for Importer entities. Just like we've been doing so far. And as I mentioned, we can access the original entity (before the changes have been made to it) like so:

```
$original = $entity->original;
```

And if the File ID that was on the original entity is not the same as the one we are currently saving with it (meaning the file was changed), we can delete the usage of that old File ID.

Remember, when we delete the usage of a file and its usage count reaches zero, the file is marked as temporary. This does not mean it gets moved to the `temporary://` file system but that it will be deleted at the next cron run (if this is configured to happen).

Processing the CSV file

Now that our plugin configuration works--and uploaded files are properly managed and marked as used--its time to implement the `getData()` method by which we process the CSV file of the importer entity. The result needs to be an array of product information as expected by the `import()` method we saw earlier. So we can have something like this:

```
/**
 * Loads the product data from the remote URL.
 *
 * @return array
 */
private function getData() {
  /** @var ImporterInterface $importer_config */
  $importer_config = $this->configuration['config'];
  $config = $importer_config->getPluginConfiguration();
  $fids = isset($config['file']) ? $config['file'] : [];
  if (!$fids) {
    return NULL;
  }

  $fid = reset($fids);
  /** @var \Drupal\file\FileInterface $file */
  $file = $this->entityTypeManager->getStorage('file')->load($fid);
  $wrapper = $this->streamWrapperManager->getViaUri($file->getFileUri());
  if (!$wrapper) {
    return NULL;
  }

  $url = $wrapper->getExternalUrl();
  $spl = new \SplFileObject($url, 'r');
  $data = [];
  while (!$spl->eof()) {
    $data[] = $spl->fgetcsv();
  }

  $products = [];
  $header = [];
  foreach ($data as $key => $row) {
    if ($key == 0) {
      $header = $row;
      continue;
```

```
      }

      if ($row[0] == "") {
        continue;
      }

      $product = new \stdClass();
      foreach ($header as $header_key => $label) {
        $product->{$label} = $row[$header_key];
      }
      $products[] = $product;
    }

    return $products;
  }
```

First, quite expectedly, we check for the existence of the File ID in the Importer entity and load the corresponding File entity based on that. To do this we use the entity manager we injected in the plugin base class. But then comes something new.

Once we have the File entity, we can ask it its URI, which will return something like this-- `public://products.csv`. This is what is stored in the database. But in order to turn that into something useful, we need to use the *stream wrapper* that defines this file system. And to get that, we use the `StreamWrapperManager` service (`stream_wrapper_manager`) which has a handy method of returning the *stream wrapper* instance responsible for a given URI--`getViaUri()`. And once we have our `StreamWrapperInterface`, we can use its `getExternalUrl()` method to get the web accessible URL for the resource. This can be a local file path or even something external. We will come back to *stream wrappers* a bit later in this chapter and it will make more sense. But for the moment, it's enough to understand that we are translating a URI in the format `scheme://target` into a useful path which we can use to create a new PHP native `SplFileObject` instance, that in turn we can use to process the CSV file easily.

When creating the `SplFileObject`, we used the external URL of the file; this worked just fine and we were able to also demonstrate how we can get our hands on the external URL if we ever need to. But as we will see in the next chapter, it will also work directly with the stream URI, and we will switch to this approach instead.

With three lines of code we are basically done getting all the rows from the CSV into the `$data` array. However, we also want to make this data look a bit more like what the JSON resource looked like--a map where the keys are the field names and the values are the respective product data. And we also want this map to contain PHP standard objects instead of arrays. So we loop through the data, establish the CSV header values, and use those as the keys in each row of a new `$products` array of objects. Our end result will look exactly like the product information coming from the decoded JSON response.

And with this we are done. Well, not quite. We still need to inject the `StreamWrapperManager` service into our plugin. And to do that, we need to make sure we are injecting also all the things that the parent class needs and passing them along:

```
/**
 * {@inheritdoc}
 */
public function __construct(array $configuration, $plugin_id,
$plugin_definition, EntityTypeManager $entityTypeManager, Client
$httpClient, StreamWrapperManagerInterface $streamWrapperManager) {
  parent::__construct($configuration, $plugin_id, $plugin_definition,
$entityTypeManager, $httpClient);
  $this->streamWrapperManager = $streamWrapperManager;
}

/**
 * {@inheritdoc}
 */
public static function create(ContainerInterface $container, array
$configuration, $plugin_id, $plugin_definition) {
  return new static(
    $configuration,
    $plugin_id,
    $plugin_definition,
    $container->get('entity_type.manager'),
    $container->get('http_client'),
    $container->get('stream_wrapper_manager')
  );
}
```

Nothing we don't yet know how to do. However, there is one thing I'd like to point out here. In `Chapter 7`, *Your Own Custom Entity and Plugin Types*, I mentioned how at the time I believed the Guzzle HTTP Client is a service that would be useful to all Importer plugins. Well, I was clearly wrong, as the CSV-based one we just created now doesn't need it. So there is no reason why it should be injected into it. What we need to do here is remove this dependency from the base plugin class and only use it in the JSON importer. However, I leave this up to you as homework.

Our CSV Importer plugin is now complete. If we did everything correctly, we can now create a new Importer entity that uses it, upload a correct CSV file, and import some Product entities via our Drush command. How neat.

Our own stream wrapper

At the beginning of this chapter, we briefly talked about stream wrappers and what they are used for. We saw that Drupal comes with four mainstream wrappers that map to the various types of file storage it needs. Now its time to see how we can create our own. And the main reason why we would want to implement one is to expose resources at a specific location to PHPs native file system functions.

In this example, we will create a very simple stream wrapper that can basically only read the data from the resource. Just to keep things simple. And the data resource will be the product images hosted remotely (the ones we are importing via the JSON Importer). So there will be some rework there, as well, to use the new stream wrapper instead of the absolute URLs. Moreover, we will also learn how to use the site-wide settings service by which we can have environment specific configurations set in the settings.php file and then read by our code.

The native way of registering a stream wrapper in PHP is by using the stream_wrapper_register() function. However, in Drupal 8 we have an abstraction layer on top of that in the form of services. So a stream wrapper is a simple tagged service, albeit with many potential methods. So let's see its definition which we add to the products.services.yml file:

```
products.images_stream_wrapper:
  class: Drupal\products\StreamWrapper\ProductsStreamWrapper
  tags:
    - { name: stream_wrapper, scheme: products }
```

Nothing too complicated. The service is tagged with stream_wrapper and we use the scheme key to indicate--you guessed it--the scheme of the wrapper. So the URIs will be in this format:

```
products://target
```

One important thing to note about stream wrapper services is that we cannot pass dependencies to them. The reason is that they are not instantiated the normal way (by the container) but arbitrarily by PHP whenever some of its methods need to be called. So if we need to use some services, we'll have to use the static way of loading them.

The stream wrapper service class needs to implement `StreamWrapperInterface` which comes with a lot of methods. There are many possible file system interactions that PHP can do and these methods need to account for all. However, we will only be focusing on a few specific ones that have to do with reading data. After all, our resources are remote and we don't even have a clue how to make changes to them over there. So for the rest of the methods, we will be returning FALSE to indicate that the operation cannot be performed.

Let's see this big class then:

```php
namespace Drupal\products\StreamWrapper;

use Drupal\Component\Utility\UrlHelper;
use Drupal\Core\StreamWrapper\StreamWrapperInterface;
use Drupal\Core\StringTranslation\StringTranslationTrait;

/**
 * Stream wrapper for the remote product image paths used by the JSON
 * Importer.
 */
class ProductsStreamWrapper implements StreamWrapperInterface {

  use StringTranslationTrait;

  /**
   * The Stream URI
   *
   * @var string
   */
  protected $uri;

  /**
   * @var \Drupal\Core\Site\Settings
   */
  protected $settings;

  /**
   * Resource handle
   *
   * @var resource
   */
  protected $handle;
```

```
/**
 * ProductsStreamWrapper constructor.
 */
public function __construct() {
  // Dependency injection does not work with stream wrappers.
  $this->settings = \Drupal::service('settings');
}

/**
 * {@inheritdoc}
 */
public function getName() {
  return $this->t('Product images stream wrapper');
}

/**
 * {@inheritdoc}
 */
public function getDescription() {
  return $this->t('Stream wrapper for the remote location where product
images can be found by the JSON Importer.');
}

/**
 * {@inheritdoc}
 */
public static function getType() {
  return StreamWrapperInterface::HIDDEN;
}

/**
 * {@inheritdoc}
 */
public function setUri($uri) {
  $this->uri = $uri;
}

/**
 * {@inheritdoc}
 */
public function getUri() {
  return $this->uri;
}

/**
 * Helper method that returns the local writable target of the resource
within the stream.
 *
```

```php
   * @param null $uri
   *
   * @return string
   */
  public function getTarget($uri = NULL) {
    if (!isset($uri)) {
      $uri = $this->uri;
    }

    list($scheme, $target) = explode('://', $uri, 2);
    return trim($target, '\/');
  }

  /**
   * {@inheritdoc}
   */
  public function getExternalUrl() {
    $path = str_replace('\\', '/', $this->getTarget());
    return $this->settings->get('product_images_path') . '/' .
UrlHelper::encodePath($path);
  }

  /**
   * {@inheritdoc}
   */
  public function realpath() {
    return $this->getTarget();
  }

  /**
   * {@inheritdoc}
   */
  public function stream_open($path, $mode, $options, &$opened_path) {
    $allowed_modes = array('r', 'rb');
    if (!in_array($mode, $allowed_modes)) {
      return FALSE;
    }
    $this->uri = $path;
    $url = $this->getExternalUrl();
    $this->handle = ($options && STREAM_REPORT_ERRORS) ? fopen($url, $mode)
: @fopen($url, $mode);
    return (bool) $this->handle;
  }

  /**
   * {@inheritdoc}
   */
  public function dir_closedir() {
```

```
    return FALSE;
  }

  /**
   * {@inheritdoc}
   */
  public function dir_opendir($path, $options) {
    return FALSE;
  }

  /**
   * {@inheritdoc}
   */
  public function dir_readdir() {
    return FALSE;
  }

  /**
   * {@inheritdoc}
   */
  public function dir_rewinddir() {
    return FALSE;
  }

  /**
   * {@inheritdoc}
   */
  public function mkdir($path, $mode, $options) {
    return FALSE;
  }

  /**
   * {@inheritdoc}
   */
  public function rename($path_from, $path_to) {
    return FALSE;
  }

  /**
   * {@inheritdoc}
   */
  public function rmdir($path, $options) {
    return FALSE;
  }

  /**
   * {@inheritdoc}
   */
```

```php
public function stream_cast($cast_as) {
    return FALSE;
}

/**
 * {@inheritdoc}
 */
public function stream_close() {
    return fclose($this->handle);
}

/**
 * {@inheritdoc}
 */
public function stream_eof() {
    return feof($this->handle);
}

/**
 * {@inheritdoc}
 */
public function stream_flush() {
    return FALSE;
}

/**
 * {@inheritdoc}
 */
public function stream_lock($operation) {
    return FALSE;
}

/**
 * {@inheritdoc}
 */
public function stream_metadata($path, $option, $value) {
    return FALSE;
}

/**
 * {@inheritdoc}
 */
public function stream_read($count) {
    return fread($this->handle, $count);
}

/**
 * {@inheritdoc}
```

```
 */
public function stream_seek($offset, $whence = SEEK_SET) {
  return FALSE;
}

/**
 * {@inheritdoc}
 */
public function stream_set_option($option, $arg1, $arg2) {
  return FALSE;
}

/**
 * {@inheritdoc}
 */
public function stream_stat() {
  return FALSE;
}

/**
 * {@inheritdoc}
 */
public function stream_tell() {
  return FALSE;
}

/**
 * {@inheritdoc}
 */
public function stream_truncate($new_size) {
  return FALSE;
}

/**
 * {@inheritdoc}
 */
public function stream_write($data) {
  return FALSE;
}

/**
 * {@inheritdoc}
 */
public function unlink($path) {
  return FALSE;
}

/**
```

```
   * {@inheritdoc}
   */
  public function url_stat($path, $flags) {
    return FALSE;
  }

  /**
   * {@inheritdoc}
   */
  public function dirname($uri = NULL) {
    return FALSE;
  }
}
```

The first thing to look at is the constructor in which we statically load the Settings service and store it as a class property. And speaking of which, we also define a $uri property to hold the actual URI this wrapper *wraps* and a $handle property to hold a generic PHP resource handle.

The getName() and getDescription() are pretty straightforward methods used for identifying the stream wrapper, while the getType() method returns the type of stream. We'll go with the hidden type because we don't want it visible in the UI. It's strictly for programmatic use so we can read our product images. Do check out the available types and their meanings by looking at the StreamWrapperInterface constants.

Then we have a getter and setter for the $uri property by which the Drupal StreamWrapperManager can create an instance of our wrapper based on a given URI. The getTarget() method is actually not in the interface but is a helper to extract a clean target from the URI (the target being the second part of the URI that comes after scheme://). And we use this method in the getExternalUrl(), which is quite an important method responsible for returning an absolute URL to the resource in question. But here we also use our Settings service to get the product_images_path key. If you remember in the beginning of the chapter, we saw that the path to the public file system is defined in the settings.php file like so:

```
$settings['file_public_path'] = 'sites/default/files';
```

That $settings variable is the data array that is wrapped by the Settings service. So we want to do the same for defining our own remote path to the product images:

```
$settings['product_images_path'] =
'http://path/to/the/remote/product/images';
```

This way we are not committing to Git the actual remote URL and we can also change it later if we want. And this is the URL we are reading inside the getExternalUrl() method.

The other pillar of our read-only stream wrapper is the ability to open a file handle to the resource and allow us to read the data from it. And the stream_open() method does this as it gets called when we run either file_get_contents() or fopen() on our URI. Using the $mode parameter, we ensure that the operation is read-only and return FALSE otherwise--we do not support *write* or other flags.

 Any mode can have b appended to it to indicate that the file should be opened in binary mode. So where r indicates read-only, rb indicates read-only in binary mode.

The third argument is a bitmask of options defined by PHP. The one we're dealing with here is STREAM_REPORT_ERRORS, which indicates whether or not PHP errors should be suppressed (for instance if a file is not found). The second is STREAM_USE_PATH, which indicates whether PHP's include path should be checked if a file is not found. This is not relevant to us, so we ignore it. If a file is found on the include path, then the fourth argument ($opened_url) should be set with the file's real path.

What we do then is translate the URI into the absolute URL of the external resource so that we can open a file handle on it. And in doing so we make use of the STREAM_REPORT_ERRORS option to either prepend the @ to the fopen() function or not (doing so suppresses errors). Finally, we store the reference to the resource handle and return a boolean based on it to indicate whether the operation succeeded or not.

Finally, we also implement the stream_read(), stream_eof() and stream_close() methods so that we can actually also stream the resources if we want to. As for the rest of the methods, as already mentioned we return FALSE.

All we have to do now is clear the cache and make use of our stream. As long as we have a valid URL declared in the settings.php file, our stream should work fine. And here are the kinds of things we could do with a URI like this:

```
$uri = 'products//tv.jpg';
```

To get the entire file content into a string, we can do this:

```
$contents = file_get_contents($uri);
```

Or we can use the example from the beginning of the chapter and stream the file bit by bit:

```
$handle = fopen($uri, 'r');
$contents = '';
while (!feof($handle)) {
  $contents .= fread($handle, 8192);
}
fclose($handle);
```

All these file operations such as opening, reading, checking the end of a file, and closing is possible due to our `stream_*()` method implementations from the wrapper.

And finally, maybe now it's also a bit clearer what we did when writing the CSV Importer and using the `StreamWrapperManager` to identify the stream wrapper responsible for a given URI, and based on that, the external URL of the URI. There is also a shorter version of doing this, useful especially in a context in which we cannot inject the stream wrapper manager service:

```
$url = file_create_url($uri);
```

Internally, this will do it for us and give us the URL as returned by the `getExternalUrl()` of the responsible `StreamWrapperInterface` implementation.

To end the section on stream wrapper, let's do some clean-up work by refactoring a bit our `JsonImporter::handleProductImage()` method. Our logic there involved hardcoding the URL to the remote API which is really not a good idea. Instead, now that we have our stream wrapper, we can go ahead and use it. We can replace this:

```
// This needs to be hardcoded for the moment.
$image_path = '';
$image = file_get_contents($image_path . '/' . $name);
```

With this:

```
$image = file_get_contents('products://' . $name);
```

It's that simple. And now we can control the remote URL from outside the Git repository and if it changes, we don't even have to alter our code. Granted, solely for this purpose implementing a stream wrapper seems a bit excessive. After all, you can simply inject the `Settings` service and use the URL in the Importer plugin itself allowing for the same kind of flexibility. But we used the opportunity to learn about stream wrappers and how to create our own and even managed to find a small use case in the process.

Working with unmanaged files

Working with *unmanaged* files is actually pretty similar to doing so with *managed* files, except that they are not tracked in the database using the File entity type. There is a set of helper functions similar to what we've seen for *managed* files that do the same things--but they have the word *unmanaged* in them. Let's see some examples.

To save a new file, we do almost like we did before:

```
$image = file_get_contents('products://tv.jpg');
$path = file_unmanaged_save_data($image, 'public://tv.jpg',
FILE_EXISTS_REPLACE);
```

We load the file data from wherever and use the `file_unmanaged_save_data()` the same way as we did `file_save_data()`. The difference is that the file is going to be saved but no database record is created. So the only way to use it is to rely on the path it is saved at and either try to access it from the browser or use it for whatever purpose we need. The `file_unmanaged_save_data()` returns the URI of where the file is now saved or FALSE if there was a problem with the operation. So if all went well with the preceding example, `$path` would now be--`public://tv.jpg`.

And just like with the *managed* files, we also have a few other helpful functions such as `file_unmanaged_move()`, `file_unmanaged_copy()` and `file_unmanaged_delete()`.

Private file system

The private file system is used whenever we want to control access to the files being downloaded. Using the default public storage, users can get to the files simply by pointing to them in the browser, thereby bypassing Drupal completely. However, `.htaccess` rules prevent users from directly accessing any files in the private storage making it necessary to create a route that delivers the requested file. It goes without saying that the latter is a hell of a lot less performant as Drupal needs to be loaded for each file. So it's important to only use it really when files should be restricted based on certain criteria.

Drupal already comes with a route and Controller ready to download private files but we can create one as well if we really need to. For example, the image module does so in order to control the creation and download of image styles--`ImageStyleDownloadController`.

The route definition for the default Drupal path looks like this:

```
system.files:
  path: '/system/files/{scheme}'
  defaults:
    _controller: 'Drupal\system\FileDownloadController::download'
    scheme: private
  requirements:
    _access: 'TRUE'
```

This is a bit of an odd route definition. We have a `{scheme}` parameter but which will be the actual file path requested for download. The URI scheme itself defaults to `private` as illustrated by the signature of `FileDownloadController::download()`. Moreover, access is allowed at all times as Drupal delegates this check to other modules --as we will see in a minute.

If we look in the `FileDownloadController::download()` Controller, we can see that it isn't actually much that it is doing itself. However, we also note that in the first line it looks for the query parameter called `file` in order to get the URI of the requested file:

```
$target = $request->query->get('file');
```

But based on the route definition, we don't even have this parameter. This is where *Path Processors* come into play, more specific implementations of `InboundPathProcessorInterface`. These are tagged services that get invoked by the routing system when building up the routes by the requested path. And essentially, they allow the alteration of a given path as it comes in. For Drupal 7 veterans these can be likened to implementations of `hook_url_inbound_alter()`.

The core *System* module implements its own path processor for the purpose of handling the download of private files:

```
path_processor.files:
  class: Drupal\system\PathProcessor\PathProcessorFiles
  tags:
    - { name: path_processor_inbound, priority: 200 }
```

It's a simple tagged service definition whose class needs to implement the correct interface that has one method. In the case of `PathProcessorFiles`, it looks like this:

```
/**
 * {@inheritdoc}
 */
public function processInbound($path, Request $request) {
  if (strpos($path, '/system/files/') === 0 &&
!$request->query->has('file')) {
```

```
      $file_path = preg_replace('|^\/system\/files\/|', '', $path);
      $request->query->set('file', $file_path);
      return '/system/files';
   }
   return $path;
}
```

The goal of this method is to return a path which can be the same as the one requested or changed for whatever reason. And what Drupal does here is checks if the path is the one defined earlier (starts with /system/files/) and extracts the requested file path that comes as the first argument after that. It takes that and adds it to the current request parameter keyed by file. Finally, it returns a cleaner path called simply /system/files. So this is why the FileDownloadController::download() method looks there for the file path.

Turning back to the Controller, we see that it essentially checks for the file and if it is not found, throws a 404 (NotFoundHttpException). Otherwise, it invokes hook_file_download() that allows all modules to control the access to the file. And these can do so in two ways--either by returning −1 which denies access or by returning an array of headers to control the download for that specific file. By default, files in the private file system cannot be downloaded unless a specific module allows this to happen.

 A quick note on invoking hooks. You remember from Chapter 2, *Creating Your First Module*, how we used the ModuleHandler service to invoke *alter* hooks. Well, we can use the same service to invoke regular hooks as well by using the invokeAll() method. This will return the merged result of all module implementations of that hook. In previous versions of Drupal, this was the main extension point available for modules. However, with the introduction of plugins and the Event Dispatcher, Drupal has removed this technique from the limelight.

So what does this mean? If we have a file in the private file system, we need to implement hook_file_download() and control access to it. Let's see an example of how this might work by assuming we have a folder called /pdfs whose files we want to make accessible to users which have the administer site configuration permission:

```
/**
 * Implements hook_file_download().
 */
function module_name_file_download($uri) {
  $file_system = \Drupal::service('file_system');
  $dir = $file_system->dirname($uri);
  if ($dir !== 'private://pdfs') {
    return NULL;
```

```
    }

    if (!\Drupal::currentUser()->hasPermission('administer site
configuration')) {
        return -1;
    }

    return [
        'Content-type' => 'application/pdf',
    ];
}
```

This hook receives as an argument the URI of the file being requested. And based on that, we try to get the folder name it belongs to. To do this, we use the `file_system` service which contains some helper methods for interacting with the file system. I encourage you to check it out, and the `FileSystemInterface`, for more information on what you can do with it.

If the file is not in the private file system inside the `/pdfs` folder, we simply return NULL to signify that we don't control the access to this file. Other modules may do so (and if none do, access is denied). If it is our file, we check for the permission we want and return −1 if the user doesn't have it. This will deny access. Finally, if access is allowed, we return an array of headers we want to use in the file delivery. In our case, we simply use the PDF-specific headers that facilitate the display of the PDF file in the browser. If we wanted to trigger a file download, we could do something like this instead:

```
$name = $file_system->basename($uri);
return [
    'Content-Disposition' => "attachment;filename='$name'"
];
```

We use the file system service to determine the file name being requested and adjust our headers accordingly to treat it like an attachment that has to be downloaded.

And that is all there is to it. If we wanted more control (or a different path to download the files) we can implement our own route and follow the same approach. Without, of course, the need to invoke a hook but simply handling the download inside the controller method. For example, this is what `FileDownloadController::download()` does to handle the actual response:

```
return new BinaryFileResponse($uri, 200, $headers, $scheme !== 'private');
```

This type of response is used when we want to deliver files to the browser and it comes straight from Symfony.

Images

In this section, we are going a bit deeper into the world of images in Drupal 8 while keeping the focus on module developers.

Image toolkits

The Drupal 8 Image toolkits provide an abstraction layer over the most common operations used for manipulating images. By default, Drupal uses the GD image management library that is included with PHP. However, it also offers the ability to switch to a different library if needed by using the `ImageToolkit` plugins.

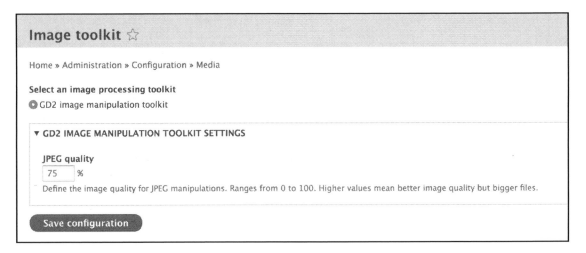

For instance, a contributed module could implement the `ImageMagick` library for developers who needed support for additional image types such as TIFF, which GD does not support. However, only one library can be used at a time as it needs to be configured site-wide.

Programmatically manipulating images using a toolkit involves instantiating an `ImageInterface` object that wraps an image file. This interface (implemented by the `Image` class) contains all the needed methods for applying the common manipulations to images, as well as saving the resulting image to the file system. And to get our hands on such an object, we use the `ImageFactory` service:

```
$factory = \Drupal::service('image.factory');
```

The role of this factory is to create instances of `Image` using a given toolkit. And it works like this:

```
$image = $factory->get($uri);
```

The second parameter to this method is the `ImageToolkit` plugin ID we want the `Image` object to work with. By default, it uses the default toolkit configured for the entire application.

And now we can use the manipulation methods on the `ImageInterface` to change the file:

```
$image->scale(50, 50);
$image->save('public://thumbnail.jpg');
```

In the preceding example, we scale the image to 50x50 and save it to a new path. Omitting the destination in the `save()` method would mean overwriting the original file with the changed version. If you need to perform such manipulations manually, I encourage you to explore the `ImageInterface` for all the available options.

Image styles

Even though as we've seen we can handle image manipulations programmatically ourselves, typically, this is done as part of *Image Styles* which can be created and configured via the UI. These work similarly as they did in Drupal 7 and involve the application of several possible *Image Effects* in order to create image variations used in different places. Drupal 8 comes with the same three default image styles as did Drupal 7:

The image styles themselves are configuration entities which store configuration specific to the *ImageEffect* plugins they work with. Once they are created in the UI, we can make use of them in various ways. The most typical way is to use the image style in the *display* configuration of an entity field or even in Views when rendering an image field.

If you remember in the beginning of the chapter we created the image field on the Product entity but we did not configure a display. So for the moment, the imported images do not show up on the main product page. But we can add some display configuration to our base field definition so that images are shown with a specific image style:

```
->setDisplayOptions('view', array(
  'type' => 'image',
  'weight' => 10,
  'settings' => [
    'image_style' => 'large'
  ]
))
```

In this example, we are using the default `image` field formatter plugin which can be configured to use an image style. So under the `settings` key, we reference the `large` image style configuration entity that actually comes with Drupal core. Omitting this would simply just render the original image. Make sure you check back `Chapter 7`, *Your Own Custom Entity and Plugin Types* and `Chapter 9`, *Custom Fields* if you are a bit fuzzy on the base field definitions.

Rendering images

In `Chapter 4`, *Theming*, we talked about theme hooks and how we use them in render arrays to build output. And we also saw a few examples of theme hooks that come with Drupal core and which can be used for common things (such as links or tables). But images are also something we'll often end up rendering and there are two ways we can do so (both using theme hooks defined by Drupal core).

First, we can use the `image` theme hook to simply render an original image. And it's pretty simple to use it:

```
return [
  '#theme' => 'image',
  '#uri' => 'public://image.jpg',
];
```

And this will render the image as is. We can also pass some more options like the *alt*, *title*, *width* or *height* which will be applied to the image tag as attributes, as well as an array of any other kinds of attributes we may want. Check out `template_preprocess_image()` for more information on how this works.

Alternatively, the *Image* module defines the `image_style` theme hook which we can use to render the image using a given image style:

```
return [
  '#theme' => 'image_style',
  '#uri' => 'public://image.jpg',
  '#style_name' => 'large',
];
```

This theme hook works pretty much the same way except that it has an extra parameter for the ID of the `ImageStyle` entity we want to use. And the rest of the parameters we find on the `image` theme hook can also be found here. In fact, `image_style` delegates to the `image` theme hook under the hood.

Finally, we may also find ourselves in a situation in which we need to get our hands on the URL of an image using a given image style. We need to work with the `ImageStyle` configuration entity for this:

```
$style =
\Drupal::entityTypeManager()->getStorage('image_style')->load('thumbnail');
$url = $style->buildUrl('public://image.jpg');
```

Once we load the image style we want, we simply call its `buildUrl()` method to which we pass the URI of the file for which we want the URL. The first time this URL is accessed, the image variation gets created and stored to disk. Future requests will load it directly from there for improved performance.

Summary

We are closing this chapter after covering a lot of different topics that have to do with working with files in Drupal 8.

We started with a couple of introductory sections in which we introduced some general concepts such as the various file systems (storages) that Drupal 8 uses, as well the how stream wrappers come into play for working with them. We also introduced the different ways to work with files--*managed* vs *unmanaged*.

Next, we dove into working with *managed files* and created an image field on our Product entity type so that we could import images into it. The other example of working with *managed* files had us create a new Product importer based on a CSV file of data and we also saw how to upload, read and process such a file, as well as manually track its usage. As a parenthesis, we introduced a very powerful feature of Drupal 8 that allows us to hook into the entity CRUD operations and perform actions whenever these are fired. This is a majorly important technique module developers typically use in Drupal.

We then switched gears and implemented our own stream wrapper to serve our imaginary remote API that stored the product images. Moreover, we talked about working with *unmanaged* files and some of the functions we can use for this--things similar to *managed* files except the function names are different and there are no File entities or usage tracking to them.

We continued with the private file system and a talk about what this serves and how we can work with it to control access to our own files. As opposed to allowing users to bypass Drupal and download files from the public file system.

Finally, we finished the chapter with a look at the APIs surrounding images and how we can use toolkits to process images, both manually and as part of image styles. And even more useful, we saw how we can render images in all sorts of ways in Drupal 8 and get our hands on image style URLs.

In the next and final chapter, we will look at automated testing and how we can ensure that our code works and that we don't introduce regressions along the way.

17
Automated Testing

Automated testing is a process by which we rely on special software to continuously run pre-defined tests that verify the integrity of our application. To this end, automated tests are a collection of steps that cover the functionality of an application and compare triggered outcomes to the expected ones.

Manual testing and review is a great way to ensure that a piece of written functionality works as expected. The main problem encountered by most adopters of this strategy and those who use it exclusively is a regression. Once a piece of functionality is tested, the only way they can guarantee regressions (or bugs) were not introduced by another piece of functionality is by retesting it. Also, as the application grows, it becomes impossible to handle. This is where automated tests come in.

Automated testing uses special software that has an API which allows us to automate the steps involved with testing the functionality. This means that we can rely on machines to run these tests as many times as we want, and the only thing stopping us from having a fully-working application is the lack of proper test coverage with well-defined tests.

There is much different software available for performing such tests and they are usually geared towards specific types of automated testing. For example, Behat is a powerful PHP-based open source behavior testing framework that allows the scripting of tests that mirror quite closely what a manual tester would do--interact with the application through the browser and test its behavior. There are other testing frameworks that go much lower down in the level of their testing target. For example, the PHP industry standard tool, PHPUnit, is widely used for performing unit tests. This type of testing focuses on the actual code at the lowest possible level; it tests that class methods work properly by verifying their output after providing them with different inputs. A strong argument in favor of this kind of testing is that it encourages better code architecture which can be (partly) measured by the ease with which unit testing can be written for it.

We also have functional or integration tests which fall somewhere in between the two examples given before. These go higher than the code level and enlist application subsystems in order to test more comprehensive sets of functionality, without necessarily considering browser behavior and user interaction.

It is not difficult to agree that a well-tested application features a combination of the different testing methodologies. For example, testing the individual architectural units of an application does not guarantee that the entire subsystem works, just as testing only the subsystem does not guarantee that its individual components will work properly under all circumstances. Also, the same is true for certain subsystems that depend on user interaction--these require test coverage as well.

In this chapter, we will see how automated testing works in Drupal 8. More specifically, we will go through and explain all testing methodologies available for us as module developers and exemplify them with two tests each. By the end of this chapter, you'll be ready to write your own tests and be familiar enough with the code to further explore the available testing capabilities.

Testing methodologies in Drupal 8

Like many other development aspects, automated testing has been greatly improved in Drupal 8. In the previous version, the testing framework was a custom one built specifically for testing Drupal applications--*Simpletest*. Its main testing capability focused on functional testing with a strong emphasis on user interaction with a pseudo-browser. However, it was quite strong and allowed a wide-range of functionality to be tested.

Drupal 8 development started with *Simpletest* as well, lots of older tests still using this framework. However, with the adoption of PHPUnit, Drupal is moving away from it and is in the process of deprecating it. To replace it, there is a host of different types of tests--all run by PHPUnit--that can cover more testing methodologies. So let's see what these are.

Drupal 8 comes with the following types of testing:

- Simpletest: Existing for legacy reasons but no longer used to create new tests. This will most likely be removed in Drupal 9.
- Unit: Low-level class testing with minimal dependencies (usually mocked).
- Kernel: Functional testing with the kernel bootstrapped, access to the database and only a few loaded modules.

- Functional: Functional testing with a bootstrapped Drupal instance, a few installed modules and using a Mink-based browser emulator (Goutte driver).
- Functional JavaScript: Functional testing like the previous, using the Phantom.js driver (`http://phantomjs.org/`) for Mink that allows for testing JavaScript powered functionality

Apart from Simpletest, all of these test suites are built on top of PHPUnit and are consequently run by it. Based on the namespace the test classes reside in, as well as the directory placement, Drupal can discover these tests and know what type they are.

In this chapter, we will see examples of all of them (except Simpletest) as we go about testing some of the functionality we've been writing in this book.

PHPUnit

Apart from the old and more or less deprecated *Simpletest*, Drupal 8 uses PHPUnit as the testing framework for all types of tests. In this section, we will see how we can work with it to run tests.

On your development environment (or wherever you want to run the tests), make sure you have the composer dependencies installed with the --dev flag. This will include PHPUnit. Keep in mind not to ever do this on your production environment as you can compromise the security of your application.

Although Drupal has a UI interface for running tests, PHPUnit is not well integrated with this. So, it's recommended that we should run them using the command line instead. However, it's actually very easy to do so. To run the entire test suite (of a certain type), we have to navigate to the Drupal core folder:

```
cd core
```

Run the following command:

```
../vendor/bin/phpunit --testsuite=unit
```

This command goes back a folder through the vendor directory and uses the installed `phpunit` executable. As an option, in the preceding example, we have specified that we only want to run unit tests. Omitting that we would run all types of tests, however, for most others, there will be some configuration needed as we will see in the respective sections.

If we wanted to run a specific test, we can pass it as an argument to the `phpunit` command (the path to the file):

```
../vendor/bin/phpunit tests/Drupal/Tests/Core/Routing/UrlGeneratorTest.php
```

In this example, we run a Drupal core test that tests the `UrlGenerator` class.

Alternatively, we can run multiple tests that belong to the same *group* (we will see how tests are added to a group soon):

```
../vendor/bin/phpunit --group Routing
```

This runs all the tests from the `Routing` group which actually contains the `UrlGeneratorTest` we saw earlier. We can run tests from multiple groups if we separate them by a comma.

Also, to check what are the available groups, we can run the following command:

```
../vendor/bin/phpunit --list-groups
```

This will list all the groups that have been registered with PHPUnit.

Finally, we can also run a specific method found inside a test by using the `--filter` argument:

```
../vendor/bin/phpunit --filter=testAliasGenerationUsingInterfaceConstants
```

This is one of the test methods from the same `UrlGeneratorTest`, we saw before and is the only one that would run.

Registering tests

There are certain commonalities between the various test suite types regarding what we need to do in order for Drupal (and PHPUnit) to be able to discover and run them.

First, we have the directory placement where the test classes should go in. The pattern is this--`tests/src/[suite_type]` where `[suite_type]` is a name of the test suite type this test should be. Also, it can be one of the following:

```
Unit
Kernel
Functional
FunctionalJavascript
```

So, for example, unit tests would go inside the `tests/src/Unit` folder of our module.

Second, the test classes need to respect a namespace structure as well:

```
namespace Drupal\Tests\[module_name]\[suite_type]
```

This is also pretty straightforward to understand.

Third, there is a certain metadata that we need to have in the test class PHPDoc. Every class must have a summary line describing what the test class is for. Only classes that use the `@coversDefaultClass` attribute can omit the summary line. Moreover, all test classes must have the `@group` PHPDoc annotation indicating the group they are part of. This is how PHPUnit can run tests that belong to certain groups only.

So now that we know how to register and run tests, let's look at unit tests and see how we can write our own.

Unit tests

As briefly mentioned in the beginning, unit tests are used for testing single *units* that make up the code architecture. In practice, this means testing individual classes, especially the methods they contain and what they should be doing. Since the testing happens at such low level, they are by far the fastest tests that can be run.

The logic behind unit tests is quite simple--after providing input, the test asserts that the method output is correct. Typically, the more *input -> output* scenarios it covers, the more stable the tested code is. For example, tests should also cover unexpected scenarios as well as exercise all the code contained in the tested methods (such as forks created by *if/else* statements).

The programming pattern of dependency injection--objects should receive as dependency other objects they might need--becomes critical when it comes to unit testing. The reason is that if class methods work with the global scope or instantiate other objects, we can no longer test them cleanly. Instead, if they require dependencies, we can *mock* them and pass these within the context of the executed tests. We will see some examples shortly. But before we do that, let's create a simple class which can be easily tested using a unit test.

A typical example is a simple calculator class. It will take two numbers as arguments to its constructor and have four methods for performing basic arithmetic on those numbers. We'll put this into our Hello World module:

```
namespace Drupal\hello_world;

/**
 * Class used to demonstrate a simple Unit test.
 */
class Calculator {

  private $a;
  private $b;

  public function __construct($a, $b) {
    $this->a = $a;
    $this->b = $b;
  }

  public function add() {
    return $this->a + $this->b;
  }

  public function subtract() {
    return $this->a - $this->b;
  }

  public function multiply() {
    return $this->a * $this->b;
  }

  public function divide() {
    return $this->a / $this->b;
  }
}
```

Nothing so complicated here. You could argue that a calculator class should not get any dependencies but instead pass the numbers to the actual arithmetic methods. However, this will work just as fine for our example and is a bit less repetitive.

Now, let's create the first unit test to make sure that this class behaves as we expect it. In the previous section, we saw which directory these need to go in. So, in our case, it will be /tests/src/Unit. Also, the test class looks like this:

```
namespace Drupal\Tests\hello_world\Unit;

use Drupal\hello_world\Calculator;
use Drupal\Tests\UnitTestCase;

/**
 * Tests the Calculator class methods.
 *
 * @group hello_world
 */
class CalculatorTest extends UnitTestCase {

  /**
   * Tests the Calculator::add() method.
   */
  public function testAdd() {
    $calculator = new Calculator(10, 5);
    $this->assertEquals(15, $calculator->add());
  }

  /**
   * Tests the Calculator::subtract() method.
   */
  public function testSubtract() {
    $calculator = new Calculator(10, 5);
    $this->assertEquals(5, $calculator->subtract());
  }

  /**
   * Tests the Calculator::multiply() method.
   */
  public function testMultiply() {
    $calculator = new Calculator(10, 5);
    $this->assertEquals(50, $calculator->multiply());
  }

  /**
   * Tests the Calculator::divide() method.
   */
```

```
  public function testDivide() {
    $calculator = new Calculator(10, 5);
    $this->assertEquals(2, $calculator->divide());
  }

}
```

First of all, you notice the namespace corresponds to the pattern what we saw in the previous chapter. Second of all, the PHPDoc contains the required information--a summary and the `@group` tag. Third of all, the class name ends with the word `Test`. Finally, the class extends `UnitTestCase`, which is the base class we need to extend for all unit tests.

 All types of test class names in Drupal 8 need to end with the word *Test* and extend the relevant base class that provides specific code for that type of test.

Then, we have the actual methods that test various aspects of the `Calculator` class and which always have to start with the word `test`. This is what tells PHPUnit that they need to be run. These methods are the actual standalone tests themselves, meaning that the `CalculatorTest` class has four tests. Moreover, each of these tests runs independently of the other.

Since the `Calculator` arithmetic is very simple, it's not difficult to understand what we are doing to test it. For each method, we are instantiating a new instance with some numbers, and then we *assert* that the result from the arithmetic operation equals to what we expect. The base class provides a multitude of different assertion methods that we can use in our tests. Since there are so many of them, we are not going to cover them all here. We will see more as we write more tests but I strongly recommend, you check the base classes of the various types of test suites for methods that start with the word `assert`. A great way is also to use an IDE that autocompletes as you type the method name. It can be very handy.

With this, we can already run the test and see if it passes. Normally, it should because that we can do math in our heads and we know it's correct:

```
../vendor/bin/phpunit
../modules/custom/hello_world/tests/src/Unit/CalculatorTest.php
```

The result should be green:

```
OK (4 tests, 4 assertions)
```

However, earlier I mentioned that a good test also accounts for unexpected situations and negative responses. However, we have not done so very well in our example. If we look at `testAdd()`, we can see that the assertion is correct with those two numbers. But what if we later go to the `Calculator::add()` method and change it to this by accident:

```
return 15;
```

The test will still pass but will it actually be a true positive? Not really because if we pass different numbers, the calculation won't match anymore. So, we should test these methods with more than just one set of numbers to actually prove that the math behind the `Calculator` class is valid.

So instead, we can do something like this:

```
$calculator = new Calculator(10, 5);
$this->assertEquals(15, $calculator->add());
$calculator = new Calculator(10, 6);
$this->assertEquals(16, $calculator->add());
```

Like this, we are sure that the addition operation works correctly. One trade-off in this is that we have a bit of repetitive code, especially if we have to do this for all the other operations as well.

Generally, when writing tests, repetition is a bit more accepted than when writing the actual code. Many times there is nothing you can do about it, a code will seem very repetitive. However, in our case, we can actually do something by using the `setUp()` method that is called by PHPUnit before each test method runs. Its purpose is to perform various preparation tasks that are common for all the tests in the class. However, don't take this to mean that it runs only once and then is used by all. In fact, it runs before each individual test method.

So, what we can do is something like this:

```
/**
 * @var Calculator
 */
protected $calculatorOne;

/**
 * @var Calculator
 */
protected $calculatorTwo;

/**
 * {@inheritdoc}
 */
```

```
public function setUp() {
  parent::setUp();
  $this->calculatorOne = new Calculator(10, 5);
  $this->calculatorTwo = new Calculator(10, 2);
}
```

We create two class properties and inside the `setUp()` method, we assign them to our calculator objects. A very important thing to keep in mind is to always call the parent call of this method because it does very important things for the environment setup. Especially, as we move to Kernel and Functional tests.

Now, the `testAdd()` method can look like this:

```
public function testAdd() {
  $this->assertEquals(15, $this->calculatorOne->add());
  $this->assertEquals(12, $this->calculatorTwo->add());
}
```

Much cleaner and less repetitive. Based on this, you can extrapolate and apply the same changes to the other methods yourself.

Mocked dependencies

Seldom, some tested classes are so simple as our calculator class and most of the times they will have dependencies which in turn also have dependencies. So, unit testing becomes a bit more complicated. In fact, the ease with which unit tests are written has become a litmus test for the quality of the code being tested--the less complicated the unit test, the better the code.

As our second example of writing unit tests, let's go into the "real world" and test one of the classes we wrote in this book, namely the `UserTypesAccess` class. If you remember from `Chapter 10`, *Access control*, we created this service to be used on routes as an access checker. Although we can write functional tests that verify that it works well as a part of the access system, we can also write a unit test to check the actual code in the `access()` method. So let's get started.

The first thing we need to do is to create the class (respecting the directory placement as well as the class namespace):

```
namespace Drupal\Tests\user_types\Unit;

use Drupal\Core\Session\UserSession;
use Drupal\Tests\UnitTestCase;
use Drupal\user_types\Access\UserTypesAccess;
use Symfony\Component\Routing\Route;

/**
 * Tests the UserTypesAccess class methods.
 *
 * @group user_types
 */
class UserTypesAccessTest extends UnitTestCase {}
```

So far things look like our previous example--we have the PHPDoc information and we are extending the UnitTestCase class. So let's write a test for the access() method of the UserTypesAccess class. However, if you remember, this method takes two arguments (a user account and a route object) and also uses the entity type manager which is injected in the class. So that is where the bulk of our complication lies. What we need to test is the return value of the method depending on these arguments. Basically, whether it will allow or deny access if the user account has certain values found on the route.

In unit testing, dependencies are usually mocked. This means PHPUnit will create empty look-alike objects that behave as we describe them too and we can use these as the dependencies. The way to create a simple mock object is this:

```
$user = $this->getMock('Drupal\user\Entity\User');
```

The $user object will now be a mock of the Drupal 8 User entity class. It, of course, won't do anything but it can be used as a dependency. But to actually make it useful, we need to prescribe some behavior to it based on what the tested code does with it. For example, if it calls its id() method, we need to prescribe this behavior. We can do this with expectations:

```
$user->expects($this->any())
  ->method('id')
  ->will($this->returnValue(1));
```

This tells the mock object that for every call to the `id()` method on it, it should return the value 1. The `expects()` method takes in a matcher, which can be even more restrictive. For example, instead of `$this->any()`, we can use `$this->once()` which means that the mock object can have its `id()` method called only once. Check out the base class for the other available options, as well as what you can pass to the `will()` method--although `$this->returnValue()` is going to be the most common one. Finally, if the `id()` method takes an argument, we can also have the `->with()` method to which we pass the value of the expected argument in the matcher.

A more complex way of creating a mock is by using the mock builder:

```
$user = $this->getMockBuilder('Drupal\user\Entity\User')
  ->getMock();
```

This will get the same mock object but allow for some more options in its construction. I recommend checking out the PHPUnit documentation for more information as this is as deep as we are going to go in this book on mocking objects.

Now that we understand a bit about mocking, we can proceed with writing our test. To do this, we need to think about the end goal and work our way back to all the method calls we need to mock. Just as a reminder, this is the code that we need to test:

```
public function access(AccountInterface $account, Route $route) {
  $user_types = $route->getOption('_user_types');
  if (!$user_types) {
    return AccessResult::forbidden();
  }
  if ($account->isAnonymous()) {
    return AccessResult::forbidden();
  }
  $user =
$this->entityTypeManager->getStorage('user')->load($account->id());
  $type = $user->get('field_user_type')->value;
  return in_array($type, $user_types) ? AccessResult::allowed() :
AccessResult::forbidden();
}
```

So, at the first glance, we need to mock `EntityTypeManager`. The method arguments we will instantiate manually with some dummy data inside. However, mocking `EntityTypeManager` is going to be quite complicated. A call to its `getStorage()` method needs to return a `UserStorage` object. This needs to also be mocked because a call on its `load()` method needs to return a `User` entity object. Finally, we also need to mock that because a call to its `get()` method is also expected to return a value object.

As I mentioned, we will proceed by going back from our end goal. So we can start with instantiating the types of `AccountInterface` objects we want to pass, as well as the route objects:

```
/**
 * Tests the UserTypesAccess::access() method.
 */
public function testAccess() {
  // User accounts
  $anonymous = new UserSession(['uid' => 0]);
  $registered = new UserSession(['uid' => 2]);

  // Route definitions.
  $manager_route = new Route('/test_manager', [], [], ['_user_types' =>
['manager']]);
  $board_route = new Route('/test_board', [], [], ['_user_types' =>
['board']]);
  $none_route = new Route('/test_board');
}
```

Basically, we want to test what happens for both types of users--anonymous and registered. When instantiating the `UserSession` objects (which implement `AccountInterface`) we pass in some data to be stored with it. In our case, we need the user `uid` because it will be requested by the tested code when checking if the user is anonymous or not.

Then, we create three routes--one where managers should have access, one where board members should have access, and one where no one should have access (as indicated by the _user_types option on the route). Do check back in Chapter 10, *Access Control,* if you don't remember what this functionality is about.

Once this is done, it follows to instantiate our `UserTypesAccess` class, in view of calling its `access()` method with various combinations of our account and route objects:

```
$access = new UserTypesAccess($entity_type_manager);
```

However, we don't yet have an entity type manager, so we need to mock it. Here is all the code we need to mock the entity type manager to work for our tested code (this goes before the code we wrote so far in this test):

```
// User entity mock.
$type = new \stdClass();
$type->value = 'manager';
$user = $this->getMockBuilder('Drupal\user\Entity\User')
  ->disableOriginalConstructor()
  ->getMock();
$user->expects($this->any())
```

```
    ->method('get')
    ->will($this->returnValue($type));

// User storage mock
$user_storage = $this->getMockBuilder('Drupal\user\UserStorage')
  ->disableOriginalConstructor()
  ->getMock();
$user_storage->expects($this->any())
  ->method('load')
  ->will($this->returnValue($user));

// Entity type manager mock.
$entity_type_manager =
$this->getMockBuilder('Drupal\Core\Entity\EntityTypeManager')
  ->disableOriginalConstructor()
  ->getMock();
$entity_type_manager->expects($this->any())
  ->method('getStorage')
  ->will($this->returnValue($user_storage));
```

First of all, you will notice that the entity type manager is only mocked at the very end. We first need to start the call chain which ends with a User entity object field value. So, the first block mocks the User entity object which expects any number of calls to its `get()` method to which it will always return a `stdClass()` object with the property `value` that equals to the `manager` string. This way we are mocking the entity field system accessor.

 While using the mock builder for creating our mocks, we can use the `disableOriginalConstructor()` method to prevent PHPUnit from calling the constructor of the original class. This is important to prevent the need for all sorts of other dependencies which don't actually impact the tested code.

Now that we have the User entity mock, we can use it as the return value of the `UserStorage` object mock's `load()` method. This, in turn, is the return value of the entity type manager mock's `getStorage()` method. So, all of the code we wrote means that we have mocked the following chain:

```
$this->entityTypeManager->getStorage('user')->load($account->id());
```

It doesn't really matter what we pass to the `load()` method, as we will always have that one user entity which has the `manager` user type.

Now that everything is mocked, we can use the `$access` object we created earlier and make assertions based on calls to its `access()` method:

```
// Access denied due to lack of route option.
$this->assertInstanceOf('Drupal\Core\Access\AccessResultForbidden',
$access->access($registered, $none_route));

// Access denied due to user being anonymous on any of the routes
$this->assertInstanceOf('Drupal\Core\Access\AccessResultForbidden',
$access->access($anonymous, $manager_route));
$this->assertInstanceOf('Drupal\Core\Access\AccessResultForbidden',
$access->access($anonymous, $board_route));

// Access denied due to user not having proper field value
$this->assertInstanceOf('Drupal\Core\Access\AccessResultForbidden',
$access->access($registered, $board_route));

// Access allowed due to user having the proper field value.
$this->assertInstanceOf('Drupal\Core\Access\AccessResultAllowed',
$access->access($registered, $manager_route));
```

The return value is always an object that implements an interface-- either `AccessResultAllowed` or `AccessResultForbidden`, so that is what we need to assert. We are checking four different use cases:

- Access denied, if there is no route option
- Access denied, for anonymous user on any of the routes
- Access denied, for registered user with wrong user type
- Access allowed, for registered user with proper user type

So with this we can run the test and should hopefully get a green result:

```
../vendor/bin/phpunit
../modules/custom/user_types/tests/src/Unit/UserTypesAccessTest.php
```

This is the basics of writing unit tests. There are a lot more types of assertions and you'll end up mocking quite a lot of dependencies in Drupal 8. But don't be put off by the slow pace encountered at first as things will become faster as you get more experience.

Kernel tests

Kernel tests are the immediate higher level of testing methodology we can have in Drupal 8 and are actually integration tests which focus on testing various components. They are faster than regular Functional tests as they don't do a full Drupal install, but use an in-memory pseudo installation that is much faster to bootstrap. For this reason they also don't handle any browser interactions and don't install any modules automatically.

Apart from the code itself, Kernel tests also work with the database and allow us to load the modules that we need for running the test. However, unlike the Functional tests we will see next, Kernel tests also require us to manually trigger the installation of any database schemas we need. But we will see how we can do this in the two examples we cover in this section.

Before we can work with Kernel tests though, we need to make sure we have a connection to the database and PHPUnit is aware of this. Inside the `core` folder of our Drupal installation we find a `phpunit.xml.dist` file which we need to duplicate and rename to `phpunit.xml`. This is the PHPUnit configuration file. Normally this file should already be ignored by Git so no need to worry about committing it to the repository.

In this file, we find an environment variable called `SIMPLETEST_DB` where we can specify the connection to the database, using the format exemplified in the preceding commented code:

```
mysql://username:password@localhost/databasename#table_prefix
```

Once that is in, PHPUnit will be able to connect to the database in order to install Drupal for Kernel tests as well as Functional and FunctionalJavascript tests.

 As a rule of thumb, you should always opt for Kernel tests over Functional tests whenever browser interactions are not involved and Kernel tests are enough to do the job. This is because a suite full of tests can end up taking a long time to run so you should make it as performant as possible.

TeamCleaner test

Now that we have that covered, it's time to write our first Kernel test. And a nice simple example can be to test the `TeamCleaner QueueWorker` plugin we created in Chapter 14, *Batches ,Queues and Cron*. If you are wondering why this cannot be tested using the ultra-fast unit testing methodology, the answer is that its one method doesn't return anything. Instead, it alters database values which we need to access in order to check it happened correctly.

The test class goes naturally in the `tests/src/Kernel` folder of our module and can start off like this:

```
namespace Drupal\Tests\sports\Kernel;

use Drupal\KernelTests\KernelTestBase;
use Drupal\sports\Plugin\QueueWorker\TeamCleaner;

/**
 * Test the TeamCleaner QueueWorker plugin.
 *
 * @group sports
 */
class TeamCleanerTest extends KernelTestBase {}
```

The namespace conforms to the ones we've seen so far, and we have the correct PHPDoc annotations to register the test. Moreover, this time, we are extending from `KernelTestBase`. Do pay attention to the actual version of this class because the one that comes from the old Simpletest framework is also called like `KernelTestBase`. So make sure you extend the correct one as seen in the preceding *use* statement.

The first thing we need to do is specify which modules we want loaded when running this test. For our case this is the `sports` module so we can add a class property that contains this name:

```
/**
 * Modules to enable.
 *
 * @var array
 */
protected static $modules = ['sports'];
```

Specifying a list of modules here does not actually install them but simply loads and adds them to the service container. So yes, we have access to the module and code as well as the container. But that also means that schemas defined by these modules are not actually created so we need to do that manually. And we can do it in the setUp() method or in the actual test method itself. We'll opt for the latter because in this case we only have test method in the class. And the whole thing can look like this:

```
/**
 * Tests the TeamCleaner::processItem() method.
 */
public function testProcessItem() {
  $this->installSchema('sports', 'teams');
  $database = $this->container->get('database');
  $fields = ['name' => 'Team name'];
  $id = $database->insert('teams')
    ->fields($fields)
    ->execute();

  $records = $database->query("SELECT id FROM {teams} WHERE id = :id",
[':id' => $id])->fetchAll();
  $this->assertNotEmpty($records);

  $worker = new TeamCleaner([], NULL, NULL, $database);
  $data = new \stdClass();
  $data->id = $id;
  $worker->processItem($data);
  $records = $database->query("SELECT id FROM {teams} WHERE id = :id",
[':id' => $id])->fetchAll();
  $this->assertEmpty($records);
}
```

Since the `TeamCleaner` plugin removes teams, it's enough to only install that table. We can do that using the parent `installSchema()` method to which we pass the module name and table we want installed. We don't actually deal with players so we should avoid doing unnecessary work like the creation of the `players` table.

Then, very similar to how we do it in real code, we get the `database` service from the container and add a record to the `teams` table. This will be the test record which we delete so we remember its `$id`. But before we test this, we want to make absolutely sure that our record got saved. So we query for it and assert that the result is not empty. The `assertNotEmpty()` method is another helpful assertion that we can use when dealing with arrays.

Now that we are certain the record is in the database, we can "process" it using our plugin. So we instantiate a `TeamCleaner` object, passing all its required dependencies --most importantly the database service. Then we create a simple object that mimics what the `processItem()` method expects and call the later while passing the former to it. At this point, if our plugin did its job correctly, the team record should be deleted from the database. So we can query for it and this time assert the opposite of what we did before-- that the query comes back empty.

And with this our test is finished. As always, we should actually run it and make sure it passes:

```
../vendor/bin/phpunit
../modules/custom/sports/tests/src/Kernel/TeamCleanerTest.php
```

And that is a very simple example of using Kernel tests for testing a component, particularly one that integrates with the database. We could have used a Functional test as well but would have been an overkill--would run slower and we made no use of the benefits that it offers over Kernel testing, namely browser integration.

CsvImporter test

After this simple example, let's write another test that illustrates a more complex scenario. And we will write one that tests the `CsvImporter` plugin we created in the previous chapter.

There is quite a lot of functionality that goes into this plugin and working with it--we have the actual importing, the plugin and configuration entity creation, the user interface for doing so and so on. And it's a very good example of functionality that can benefit from a multi-methodology test coverage. And in this respect, we start with testing its underlying purpose, that of the product import, for which we don't need browser interactions. This means that we can use a Kernel test.

Similar to how we wrote the previous test, we can start with the class like so (this time in the `products` module):

```
namespace Drupal\Tests\products\Kernel;

use Drupal\KernelTests\KernelTestBase;

/**
 * Tests the CSV Product Importer
 *
 * @group products
```

```
 */
class CsvImporterTest extends KernelTestBase {}
```

Nothing new so far.

Next, we need to specify the modules we need loaded. And here we have a bigger list:

```
/**
 * Modules to enable.
 *
 * @var array
 */
protected static $modules = ['system', 'csv_importer_test', 'products',
'image', 'file', 'user'];
```

Only the `products` module may seem obvious to you at this point, but all the rest are also needed. The `system`, `image`, `file` and `user` are all somehow needed for dealing with the file upload and storage process that is needed for the `CsvImporter` plugin.

It's not always so easy to figure out which modules are needed and it will involve a bit of a trial and error, at least in the beginning. A typical scenario is to run the test and notice failures due to missing functionality. Tracking this functionality to a module and specifying this module in the list is how you usually end up with a complete module list — especially when the test is complex and needs a wide range of subsystems with dependencies.

But you may be wondering what's with the `csv_importer_test` module there. Often times you may need to create modules used only for the tests--most of the time because they contain some configuration you want to use in your testing. In our case, we did so to demonstrate where these modules would go and to add a `products.csv` test file that we can use in our tests.

Tests modules go inside the `tests/modules` folder of the module that contains the tests that use them. So in our case we have the `csv_importer_test` with its `info.yml` file:

```
name: CSV Importer Test
description: Used for testing the CSV Importer
core: 8.x
type: module
```

And the mentioned CSV file we will use is right next to it:

```
id,name,number
1,Car,45345
2,Motorbike,54534
```

Now that we covered that, we can write the test method:

```
/**
 * Tests the import of the CSV based plugin.
 */
public function testImport() {
  $this->installEntitySchema('product');
  $this->installEntitySchema('file');
  $this->installSchema('file', 'file_usage');
  $manager = $this->container->get('entity_type.manager');
  $products = $manager->getStorage('product')->loadMultiple();
  $this->assertEmpty($products);

  $csv_path = drupal_get_path('module', 'csv_importer_test') .
'/products.csv';
  $csv_contents = file_get_contents($csv_path);
  $file = file_save_data($csv_contents, 'public://simpletest-products.csv',
FILE_EXISTS_REPLACE);
  $config = $manager->getStorage('importer')->create([
    'id' => 'csv',
    'label' => 'CSV',
    'plugin' => 'csv',
    'plugin_configuration' => [
      'file' => [$file->id()]
    ],
    'source' => 'Testing',
    'bundle' => 'goods',
    'update_existing' => true
  ]);
  $config->save();

  $plugin =
$this->container->get('products.importer_manager')->createInstanceFromConfi
g('csv');
  $plugin->import();
  $products = $manager->getStorage('product')->loadMultiple();
  $this->assertCount(2, $products);

  $products = $manager->getStorage('product')->loadByProperties(['number'
=> 45345]);
  $this->assertNotEmpty($products);
  $this->assertCount(1, $products);
```

```
}
```

The initial set-up here is a bit more complicated, partly because of Kernel tests not installing module schemas. Using the parent `installEntitySchema()` method we can install all the necessary tables for the Product and File content entities. However, since we are working with managed files, we also need to install the `file_usage` table manually. It is not technically an entity table. Again, there is no shame in arriving at these steps using trial and error.

Now that we have the basics set up, we do a sanity check and ensure that we don't have any product entities in the database. There is no reason why we should have any, but it doesn't hurt to ensure it. This guarantees a valid test since our goal will be to later assert the existence of products.

Then we create a managed File entity by using the `products.csv` file from the `csv_importer_test` module. The `drupal_get_path()` function is a very common way of retrieving the relative path to a module or a theme, regardless of where it is actually located. And we save the contents of this file into the `public://` file system of the testing environment. Keep in mind, though, that after the test runs successfully, this file gets removed as Drupal cleans up after itself.

Next, we need to create an Importer configuration entity that uses the CSV based plugin to run the import. And instead of doing it through the UI, we do it programmatically. Using the storage manager we create the entity as we learned in Chapter 6, *Data Modeling and Storage*. Once we have that, we use the Importer plugin manager to create an instance based on this configuration entity (to which we gave the ID `csv`). And finally, we run the import of the products.

Now for the assertions, we do a double check. Since our test CSV contains two rows, we load all the Product entities again and assert that we have a total of two. No more, no less. And here we see another useful assertion method for working with arrays: `assertCount()`. But then we get a bit more specific and try to load a Product which has a field value (the `number`) equal to an expected number from the test CSV file. And assert that it is in fact found as well.

We could even do some more assertions. For example, we can check that all the Product field values have been set appropriately. I'll let you explore ways in which you can do this-- either by querying based on these values or asserting equality between field values and their expected ones. But it's important to not go overboard as it will impact speed and in some cases add insufficient value to the test coverage to compensate for it. The trick is to find the right balance.

Finally, with our test in place, we can actually run it:

```
../vendor/bin/phpunit
../modules/custom/products/tests/src/Kernel/CsvImporterTest.php
```

But this time, we get an error that looks something like this:

```
RuntimeException:
SplFileObject::__construct(http://localhost/vfs://root/sites/simpletest/255
55814/files/simpletest-products.csv): failed to open stream: HTTP request
failed! HTTP/1.0 404 Not Found
```

This is caused by the fact that in `CsvImporter` we try to instantiate a new `\SplFileObject` using the full URL of the file we get from the respective stream wrapper:

```
$url = $wrapper->getExternalUrl();
$spl = new \SplFileObject($url, 'r');
```

And although this worked when we wrote our functionality, and still does in the browser, in the test environment it doesn't. And that is because in the testing environment the file system is a virtual one (vfs) and uses a different base URL. However, the `SplFileObject` class can also be instantiated using the URI of the file. So all we have to do is change our code to this:

```
$spl = new \SplFileObject($file->getFileUri(), 'r');
```

And the test should now pass. And of course, the code will work the same way in the browser as well.

Functional tests

In the previous section, we looked at Kernel tests and said that they are basically integration tests which focus on components rather than interactions with the browser. In this section, we'll go one level up and talk about the fully-fledged Functional tests, otherwise called browser tests (from the name of the base class we need to extend).

Functional tests in Drupal 8 use a simulated browser (using the popular Mink emulator) that allows users to click links, navigate to pages, work with forms and make assertions regarding HTML elements on the page. What they don't allow us is to test JavaScript based interactions (see next section for those).

In Drupal 7, Functional tests were the most common type of tests used, most classes extending from Simpletest's `WebTestBase` class. But in Drupal 8 we have the `BrowserTestBase` class which is integrated with PHPUnit like the ones we've seen before. And the base class contains loads of methods both for asserting things and shortcuts to performing Drupal (and web) related tasks--creating users, entities, navigating to pages, filling in and submitting forms, logging in, and so on. And just like before, each test (class method), runs in isolation so things like content and users cannot be shared across multiple tests but would have to be recreated (perhaps using the `setUp()` method as we've already seen).

Browser tests perform a full Drupal installation with a minimal number of modules (using the *Testing* installation profile). This means that we can specify to install other modules as well, and the schema for these also gets installed. Moreover, it's also important to understand that the resulting installation has got nothing in common with our current development site. Any configuration we need, we have to create. There are no users, no content and no files. So it is a brand new, parallel installation, that runs for the duration of one single test and gets cleaned up as it finishes.

Configuration for functional tests

Before writing our functional tests we need to turn back to our `phpunit.xml` file and change some environment variables. Apart from the `SIMPLETEST_DB` variable we adjusted earlier, we also have the `SIMPLETEST_BASE_URL` and `BROWSERTEST_OUTPUT_DIRECTORY`. The first is used to know where can the application be accessed in the browser. The latter is the directory where output data can be saved by PHPUnit and needs to be an absolute local path (for example a folder in the local `files` folder):

```
/var/www/sites/default/files/browser-output
```

Moreover, make sure the user running the test has permissions to write into the `sites/simpletest` folder as that is where the virtual file system is created for each test. The easiest way to do it is to change the folder ownership to the web server user that runs the process. In case of Apache, this is usually `www-data`.

Hello World page test

The first Functional test we will write is for the *Hello World* page we created and the functionality behind it. We will test if the page shows the correct *Hello World* message, also depending on the value found in the configuration. So let's create the class for it, naturally in the `hello_world` module, inside the `tests/src/Functional` folder:

```
namespace Drupal\Tests\hello_world\Functional;

use Drupal\Tests\BrowserTestBase;

/**
 * Basic testing of the main Hello World page.
 *
 * @group hello_world
 */
class HelloWorldPageTest extends BrowserTestBase {}
```

You can really see the consistency with the other types of tests. But in this case, as mentioned, we extend from `BrowserTestBase`.

Also, like before, we can configure a number of modules we want installed:

```
/**
 * Modules to enable.
 *
 * @var array
 */
protected static $modules = ['hello_world', 'user'];
```

The User module we will need for the second test we run which will go in the same class as this one. But let's proceed with the first, easier test:

```
/**
 * Tests the main Hello World page.
 */
public function testPage() {
  $expected = $this->assertDefaultSalutation();
  $config = $this->config('hello_world.custom_salutation');
  $config->set('salutation', 'Testing salutation');
  $config->save();

  $this->drupalGet('/hello');
  $this->assertSession()->pageTextNotContains($expected);
  $expected = 'Testing salutation';
  $this->assertSession()->pageTextContains($expected);
}
```

If you remember, our /hello page shows a greeting depending on the time of day, unless an administrator has overridden that message through a configuration form. So we start this test by asserting that with a fresh install that has no override, we see the time based greeting. And for that we create a separate assertion message since it's a bit wordy and we will reuse it:

```
/**
 * Helper function to assert that the default salutation is present on the
page.
 *
 * Returns the message so we can reuse it in multiple places.
 */
private function assertDefaultSalutation() {
  $this->drupalGet('/hello');
  $this->assertSession()->pageTextContains('Our first route');
  $time = new \DateTime();
  $expected = '';
  if ((int) $time->format('G') >= 06 && (int) $time->format('G') < 12) {
    $expected = 'Good morning';
  }

  if ((int) $time->format('G') >= 12 && (int) $time->format('G') < 18) {
    $expected = 'Good afternoon';
  }

  if ((int) $time->format('G') >= 18) {
    $expected = 'Good evening';
  }
  $expected .= ' world';
  $this->assertSession()->pageTextContains($expected);
  return $expected;
}
```

The very first thing we do here is use the drupalGet() method to navigate to a path on the site. Do check out the method signature for all the options you can pass to it. And the first assertion we make is that the page contains the text *Our first route* (which is the page title). The parent assertSession() method returns an instance of WebAssert which contains all sorts of methods for asserting the presence of elements on the current page in the Mink session. One such method is the generic pageTextContains() with which we simply check that the given text can be found anywhere on the page.

Although in quite a lot of cases asserting the presence of a text string is enough, you may want to ensure that it is actually the right one (to avoid false positives). For example, in our case, we could check that it is really the page title which is rendered inside an <h1> tag. We can do it like so:

```
$this->assertSession()->elementTextContains('css', 'h1', 'Our first route');
```

The elementTextContains() method can be used to find an element on the page based on a locator (CSS selector or xpath) and assert that it contains the specified text. In our example we use the CSS selector locator and we try to find the <h1> element.

If all that is okay, we proceed to asserting that the actual salutation message is present on the page. Unfortunately we have to duplicate quite some code because it is dependent on the time of day. A good homework for you would be to extract this logic to a service that determines the message and use this service both here and in the actual code. And since we need this message later, we also return it.

Going back to our actual test method, we can proceed knowing that the message is showing correctly on the page. And the next thing we want to test is that if there is a hello_world.custom_salutation configuration object with a salutation value, that is what is shown. So we programmatically create it. Next, we again navigate to the same path (we essentially reload the page) and check that the old message is not shown anymore and that the new one is instead.

So if we actually run this test:

```
../vendor/bin/phpunit
../modules/custom/hello_world/tests/src/Functional/HelloWorldPageTest.php
```

...darn. We get an error:

```
Behat\Mink\Exception\ResponseTextException: The text "Good evening world"
appears in the text of this page, but it should not.
```

It's as if we didn't even override the salutation message. But we did.

The problem is caching. Keep in mind, we are navigating these pages as anonymous users and caching is enabled on the site like in normal scenarios. When we were writing Chapter 11, *Caching* and talked about caching, we had a note about this particular problem--the max-age property only bubbles up to the page level for the dynamic page cache (logged-in users) and not for anonymous users.

This is a great example of automated testing shedding light on mistakes we introduce while developing and that we don't notice. We most likely wrote our functionality while having caching disabled and/or always visiting the page as a logged-in user. So it's an easy mistake to make. Luckily, automated testing comes to the rescue.

The solution to this problem can be found using an all-out cache kill switch. This means that we need to alter a bit our logic to tell Drupal to never cache the pages where our salutation component is shown. This is the price we have to pay for the highly dynamic nature of our functionality and it's always a good exercise to evaluate if it is worth it.

The kill switch is actually easy to use. It's a service that we need to inject into our `HelloWorldSalutation` service:

```
/**
 * @var \Drupal\Core\PageCache\ResponsePolicy\KillSwitch
 */
protected $killSwitch;

/**
 * HelloWorldSalutation constructor.
 *
 * @param \Drupal\Core\Config\ConfigFactoryInterface $config_factory
 * @param \Symfony\Component\EventDispatcher\EventDispatcherInterface
 $eventDispatcher
 * @param \Drupal\Core\PageCache\ResponsePolicy\KillSwitch $killSwitch
 */
public function __construct(ConfigFactoryInterface $config_factory,
EventDispatcherInterface $eventDispatcher, KillSwitch $killSwitch) {
  $this->configFactory = $config_factory;
  $this->eventDispatcher = $eventDispatcher;
  $this->killSwitch = $killSwitch;
}
```

Making sure we also have the appropriate *use* statement at the top:

```
use Drupal\Core\PageCache\ResponsePolicy\KillSwitch;
```

And at the beginning of both the `getSalutation()` and `getSalutationComponent()` methods we simply have to add this line:

```
$this->killSwitch->trigger();
```

This will tell Drupal's internal page cache to never cache this page. But before we go running the test again, we mustn't forget to add the `page_cache_kill_switch` service as a dependency to the `HelloWorldSalutation` service inside `hello_world.services.yml`. And now if we run this test, we should get a green result.

Hello World form test

The second Functional test we will write should test the salutation override form itself. In the previous one, we interacted with the configuration API directly to make changes to the configuration value. Now we will see if the form to do so actually works. But since we can reuse quite a lot from the previous test, and they are very closely related, we can add it to the same class:

```
/**
 * Tests that the configuration form for overriding the message works.
 */
public function testForm() {
  $expected = $this->assertDefaultSalutation();
  $this->drupalGet('/admin/config/salutation-configuration');
  $this->assertSession()->statusCodeEquals(403);
  $account = $this->drupalCreateUser(['administer site configuration']);
  $this->drupalLogin($account);
  $this->drupalGet('/admin/config/salutation-configuration');
  $this->assertSession()->statusCodeEquals(200);
  $this->assertSession()->pageTextContains('Salutation configuration');
  $this->assertSession()->elementExists('css', '#edit-salutation');

  $edit = [
    'salutation' => 'My custom salutation',
  ];

  $this->drupalPostForm(NULL, $edit, 'op');
  $this->assertSession()->pageTextContains('The configuration options have
been saved');
  $this->drupalGet('/hello');
  $this->assertSession()->pageTextNotContains($expected);
  $this->assertSession()->pageTextContains('My custom salutation');
}
```

We start this test, in the same way, asserting that the hour dependent message is shown. This also proves that each test runs in its own independent environment and changes to the configuration in one test has no impact on the other. They all start with a blank slate.

Then we navigate to the configuration form page and assert that we do not have access. For this we use the `statusCodeEquals()` assertion method to check the response code. This is good because we need to be logged in with a user that has a certain permission.

 The access restrictions on the configuration form allow any user which have a certain permission. For this reason, our test should focus on that permission rather than something else that may indirectly include this permission. For example, it should not assume that a user with the administrator role has that permission.

So we create a new user account using the handy `drupalCreateUser()` method whose first parameter is an array of permissions the user should have. We can then use the resulting User entity with the `drupalLogin()` method to log in. Under the hood, this navigates to the user login page, submits the form and then asserts that everything went well. Now we can go back to the configuration form page and should have access--something that we also assert. In addition, we assert that we have the page title and that we have the salutation text field HTML element on the page. We do so using the `elementExists()` method, using the CSS selector locator as we had done in the previous test. Again, check out `WebAssert` for all sorts of assertion methods that help you identify things on the page.

Now it's time to submit the form and override the salutation message. And we do this with `drupalPostForm()` whose most important parameter is an array of values to fill in the form elements, keyed by the `name` parameter of the individual form HTML element. In our case, we only have one. Do check out the documentation of this method for more information on all the things you can do with it. Once the form is submitted, the page will reload and we can assert the presence of the confirmation message. And finally, we can go back to the `/hello` path and assert that the old message is no longer showing but the new overridden one does so instead.

Running the test class again should now include this new test as well and everything should be green. And noticeably much slower as two full Drupal installations are done. In the next section, we'll bring JavaScript into the picture so that we can also test the more dynamic browser integrations. But already you can notice that due to performance hits, Kernel tests are much faster to run if you don't need to interact with a browser.

Functional JavaScript tests

The last type of tests we can write in Drupal 8 is the JavaScript-powered Functional tests. FunctionalJavascript tests are useful when we want to test more dynamic client-side functionality such as JavaScript behaviors or Ajax interactions.

They are an extension of the regular Functional tests but which use the Phantom.js driver instead of Goutte for Mink in emulating the browser. This also means that in order to run these tests we need to install Phantom.js.

Installing Phantom.js is very simple. We have to go to the website (`http://phantomjs.org/download.html`) and download the package somewhere onto our system. Since we are using a Linux system so we can pull the archive into our home folder (the following link may change for you depending on the version):

```
wget
https://bitbucket.org/ariya/phantomjs/downloads/phantomjs-2.1.1-linux-x86_6
4.tar.bz2
```

Then we can *untar* the archive:

```
tar xjf phantomjs-2.1.1-linux-x86_64.tar.bz2
```

This will unpack the archive into the current folder. And that is it.

To run Phantom.js, we need to run the executable with the following command (from within the Drupal `core` folder):

```
~/path/to/the/phantomjs/executable --ssl-protocol=any --ignore-ssl-
errors=true ../vendor/jcalderonzumba/gastonjs/src/Client/main.js 8510 1024
768
```

This will start Phantom.js in the current terminal window where we can see the output as tests are running. So to run tests, we need to open another terminal window. Alternatively, we can start it and have it run in the background by appending the following to the preceding command:

```
2>&1 >> /dev/null &
```

Now we can also run the tests in the current window as Phantom.js runs in the background.

Now that we have Phantom.js running, we can write some tests.

Time test

If you remember from `Chapter 12`, *JavaScript and Ajax API*, we added to our Hello World salutation component a little time widget that displays the current hour in real time, if the salutation is not overridden. This component is powered by JavaScript, and more importantly, appended to the page using JavaScript.

Moreover, in the previous section, we wrote a Functional test for the Hello World page in which we asserted the presence of the salutation message. However, the actual time widget would never show up there because the Mink driver used in these types of tests do not support JavaScript. So if we want to test that, we need to write a FunctionalJavascript test.

As expected, these types of tests follow the same patterns for the directory placement and namespaces. So our first test class can start like this:

```
namespace Drupal\Tests\hello_world\FunctionalJavascript;

use Drupal\FunctionalJavascriptTests\JavascriptTestBase;

/**
 * Testing the simple Javascript timer on the Hello World page.
 *
 * @group hello_world
 */
class TimeTest extends JavascriptTestBase {}
```

By now most of the above code should be clear. However, the base class we extend this time is the `JavascriptTestBase` class which itself is a child of `BrowserTestBase`. Interestingly, it doesn't actually add much to the mix apart from configuring the test to use Phantom.js and adding a few JavaScript specific helper methods. This is to demonstrate that most of the difference between Functional and FunctionalJavascript tests is given by the actual Mink driver.

One extremely handy addition, though, is the ability to take screenshots. Many times when testing frontend interactions, things don't go as we thought and we don't understand why. The parent `createScreenshot()` method allows us to save a full page screenshot at any given moment that we can investigate for debugging purposes. All we have to do is pass in the name of the file we want to be saved. So do check that out.

Moving on with our test, let's add the modules we want to be enabled:

```
/**
 * Modules to enable.
 *
 * @var array
 */
protected static $modules = ['hello_world'];
```

As expected, the `Hello World` module is enough. And the very simple test method can look like this:

```
/**
 * Tests the time component.
 */
public function testTime() {
  $this->drupalGet('/hello');
  $this->assertSession()->pageTextContains('The time is');

  $config = $this->config('hello_world.custom_salutation');
  $config->set('salutation', 'Testing salutation');
  $config->save();

  $this->drupalGet('/hello');
  $this->assertSession()->pageTextNotContains('The time is');
}
```

We are using the exact same assertion techniques as before, but because JavaScript is enabled, the time widget text should show up now. And like before, we also test that if the salutation method is overridden, the time widget does not show up.

CsvImporter test

When learning about Kernel tests, we wrote a test for the `CsvImporter` that focused on the importing functionality given an existing Importer configuration entity (which we created programmatically). However, another important angle of this functionality is the process of creating this configuration entity as we are relying on Ajax to dynamically inject form elements related to the selected Importer plugin. So let's write a test for that as well.

Just as before, the test class can start with something like this:

```
namespace Drupal\Tests\products\FunctionalJavascript;

use Drupal\file\Entity\File;
use Drupal\FunctionalJavascriptTests\JavascriptTestBase;
use Drupal\products\Entity\Importer;
use Drupal\products\Entity\ProductType;

/**
 * Testing the creation/edit of Importer configuration entities using the
 * CSV importer
 *
 * @group products
 */
```

```
class ImporterFormTest extends JavascriptTestBase {}
```

The *use* statements will be used in the code we write so they will make sense in a minute.

And like always, let's enable some modules:

```
/**
 * Modules to enable.
 *
 * @var array
 */
protected static $modules = ['image', 'file'];
```

You may be wondering why, for example, the `products` module is not in that list. At the time of writing, it did not work, as a dependency related error was being thrown when enabling it (missing plugin defined by the `image` module). So instead, we can also enable modules directly in our test or `setUp()` methods. And that is exactly what we will do.

Even though we only write one test method, for now, there is quite a bit of preparation for it which we might want to reuse elsewhere and which also looks cleaner to be separated from the actual test method. So we can add it to the `setUp()` method instead:

```
/**
 * {@inheritdoc}
 */
public function setUp() {
  parent::setUp();
  $this->container->get('module_installer')->install(['products',
'csv_importer_test']);
  $csv_path = drupal_get_path('module', 'csv_importer_test') .
'/products.csv';
  $csv_contents = file_get_contents($csv_path);
  $this->file = file_save_data($csv_contents, 'public://simpletest-
products.csv', FILE_EXISTS_REPLACE);
  $this->admin = $this->drupalCreateUser(['administer site
configuration']);
  $this->bundle = ProductType::create(['id' => 'goods', 'label' =>
'Goods']);
  $this->bundle->save();
}
```

As expected, the first thing we do is install the `products` and `csv_importer_test` modules. We use the `ModuleInstaller` service for that. Then, we do the same thing as we did in the previous test--load the test CSV file from the `csv_importer_test` module and "upload" it to Drupal creating a new managed File entity.

Then, we create an administrator user account which has the permission needed for creating Importer configuration entities, as well as a bundle for the Product entity so that we can actually create products. We didn't need to worry about the bundle in the previous test because we created the Importer configuration programmatically. But now, through the UI, a bundle needs to exist in order to select it.

The resulting File entity, admin user account and ProductType configuration entity we store on class properties so we should also define those:

```
/**
 * @var \Drupal\file\FileInterface
 */
protected $file;

/**
 * @var \Drupal\Core\Session\AccountInterface
 */
protected $admin;

/**
 * @var \Drupal\products\Entity\ProductType
 */
protected $bundle;
```

And with this we are ready to write our empty test method and start filling it up step by step:

```
/**
 * Tests the importer form.
 */
public function testForm() {}
```

We can start with the basics:

```
$this->drupalGet('/admin/structure/importer/add');
$assert = $this->assertSession();
$assert->statusCodeEquals(403);
```

We navigate to the form for creating Importer configuration entities and assert that the user does not have access. This is because by default we are browsing as anonymous users. Next, we need to login and try this again:

```
$this->drupalLogin($this->admin);
$this->drupalGet('/admin/structure/importer/add');
$assert->pageTextContains('Add importer');
$assert->elementExists('css', '#edit-label');
$assert->elementExists('css', '#edit-plugin');
```

```
$assert->elementExists('css', '#edit-update-existing');
$assert->elementExists('css', '#edit-source');
$assert->elementExists('css', '#edit-bundle');
$assert->elementNotExists('css',
'input[name="files[plugin_configuration_plugin_file]"]');
```

We use the same `drupalLogin()` method and navigate back to the form. This time we assert that we have the title as well as various HTML elements--the form elements used for creating the entity. Moreover, we also assert that we do not have the element for uploading the CSV file because that should only show up if we select we want to use the CSV Importer plugin.

It follows we do just that:

```
$page = $this->getSession()->getPage();
$page->selectFieldOption('plugin', 'csv');
$this->assertSession()->assertWaitOnAjaxRequest();
$assert->elementExists('css',
'input[name="files[plugin_configuration_plugin_file]"]');
```

Using the `getSession()` method we get the current Mink session, from which we can get the object representing the actual page we are looking at. This is a `DocumentElement` object which can be traversed, inspected and manipulated in all sorts of ways and I recommend you check out the `TraversableElement` class for all the available methods.

One such method is `selectFieldOption()` by which we can specify the locator of an HTML select element (ID, name or label) and a value, and it will trigger the selection. As you know, this is supposed to make an Ajax request bringing in our new form elements. And using the `assertWaitOnAjaxRequest()` on the `JSWebAssert` object we can wait until that is complete. Finally, we can now assert that the file upload field is present on the page.

Next, we proceed with filling in the form:

```
$page->fillField('label', 'Test CSV Importer');
$page->fillField('id', 'test_csv_importer');
$page->checkField('update_existing');
$page->fillField('source', 'testing');
$page->fillField('bundle', $this->bundle->id());
$wrapper =
$this->container->get('stream_wrapper_manager')->getViaUri($this->file->get
FileUri());
$page->attachFileToField('files[plugin_configuration_plugin_file]',
$wrapper->realpath());
$this->assertSession()->assertWaitOnAjaxRequest();
$page->pressButton('Save');
```

```
$assert->pageTextContains('Created the Test CSV Importer Importer.');
```

The generic `fillField()` is useful for things like text fields while the `checkField()` is expectedly useful for checkboxes. The locator for both is again either the ID, the name or the label of the element. The more complicated field is the file upload field which again uses Ajax. With the help of the stream wrapper of the file that we uploaded and more specifically its `realpath()` method, we attach the file to the field using the `attachFileToField()` ;method. This triggers an Ajax request which again we wait for to complete. Lastly, we use the `pressButton()` method to click on the submit button and then assert that we have a confirmation message printed out (the form has been saved and the page refreshed).

Now the check that the operation actually went through properly:

```
$config = Importer::load('test_csv_importer');
$this->assertInstanceOf('Drupal\products\Entity\ImporterInterface',
$config);

$fids = $config->getPluginConfiguration()['file'];
$fid = reset($fids);
$file = File::load($fid);
$this->assertInstanceOf('Drupal\file\FileInterface', $file);
```

We load the configuration entity using the ID we gave it and then assert that the resulting object is an instance of the correct interface. This checks we actually did save the entity. Next, we load the File entity based on the ID found in the Importer configuration entity and assert that it itself also implements the correct interface. This proves that the file actually got saved and the configuration is correct.

Instead of checking the rest of the field values programmatically, in the same way, we opt for navigating to the edit form of the Importer entity and asserting that the values are pre-filled correctly:

```
$this->drupalGet('admin/structure/importer/test_csv_importer/edit');
$assert->pageTextContains('Edit Test CSV Importer');
$assert->fieldValueEquals('label', 'Test CSV Importer');
$assert->fieldValueEquals('plugin', 'csv');
$assert->checkboxChecked('update_existing');
$assert->fieldValueEquals('source', 'testing');
$page->hasLink('products.csv');
$bundle_field = $this->bundle->label() . ' (' . $this->bundle->id() . ')';
$assert->fieldValueEquals('bundle', $bundle_field);
```

The `fieldValueEquals()` and `checkboxChecked()` methods are handy for checking field values. Moreover, we also use the `hasLink()` method to check if there is a link with that name on the page. This is actually to prove the uploaded file is shown correctly:

And finally, since the bundle field is a reference field and not a simple text field, we need to construct the value the testing framework actually sees there and which is in this pattern-- `Label (ID)`.

And with this our test is complete and we can run it in its entirety:

```
../vendor/bin/phpunit
../modules/custom/products/tests/src/Kernel/CsvImporterTest.php
```

Summary

In this chapter, we talked a bit about automated testing in Drupal 8. We started with an introduction about why it's useful and actually important to write automated tests, and then briefly covered also a few of the more popular types of software development testing methodologies.

Drupal 8 comes with advantages in this field over its predecessor by integrating with the PHPUnit framework for all the different types of testing it does. And there is a capability for quite a lot of methodologies as we've seen exemplified. We have unit tests--the lowest level form of testing that focuses on single architectural units and which are by far the fastest running tests of them all. Then we have Kernel tests which are integration tests focusing on lower level components and their interactions. Next, we have Functional tests, which are higher level tests that focus on interactions with the browser. And finally, we have the FunctionalJavascript tests which extend on the latter and bring in `Phantom.js` to allow for the testing of functionalities that depend on JavaScript.

We've also seen that all these different types of tests are integrated with PHPUnit so we can run them all using this tool. This means that all the different types of tests follow the same "rules" for registering them with Drupal, namely the directory placement, the namespacing, and the PHPDoc information. Moreover, there is an ongoing process of moving a lot of legacy tests written in the Drupal-specific Simpletest framework to the new system. So it is expected that Simpletest will be shortly deprecated.

The world of automated testing is huge and there can be no single chapter in a book that can cover all the different ways something can be tested. For this reason, especially for beginners, the journey towards good test coverage is full of trial and error when reading Drupal and PHPUnit code and documentation, and even has the occasional frustration. But out of this, we get stable code that works always and that is protected from regressions.

Drupal 8 Security

Writing secure code is an important aspect of any web application. Preventing ever-so-creative hacking techniques can be really daunting, and this is partly the reason why we as developers sometimes choose a well-established framework with solid and up-to-date security measures baked right in.

Drupal is a CMS that takes security very seriously. The community has a dedicated security team that is always on the lookout for vulnerabilities and advises core contributors and module developers on ways to fix potential vectors of attack. It is also responsible for the fast mitigation of any such issue and disseminating the correct information to the affected parties.

When it comes to out-of-the-box installation, Drupal 8 has come a long way in addressing many security concerns present in previous versions, to the point where much of what Drupal 7 developers had to worry about can now be taken for granted. For this reason, in this annex, we will talk about some of the most prominent security features that Drupal 8 comes with out-of-the-box and that are directly related to our work as module developers. Moreover, we will take a look at some tips for ensuring that the modules we write respect the security standards Drupal prides itself on.

Cross-Site Scripting (XSS)

Drupal 7 was not inherently vulnerable to XSS attacks, but made it easy for novice developers to open such vulnerabilities. The PHP-based templating system, in particular, made it easy for developers to forget to properly sanitize user input and any other kind of data before outputting it. Moreover, it allowed novice developers to perform all kinds of business logic directly in the template. Apart from not keeping a separation of concerns (business logic vs presentation), this also meant that third-party themes were much more difficult to validate and could easily include security holes.

Most of these concerns have been addressed in Drupal 8, in principle with the adoption of Twig as the templating system. There are two main consequences of this adoption. The first one addresses the need for separating presentation from business logic. In other words, themers and developers can no longer directly access Drupal's APIs nor can they run SQL queries from templates. To expose any such functionality, Twig extensions and filters can be used, but they require the logic to be encapsulated inside a module.

The second consequence is in the form of Twig auto-escaping. This means that any string not specifically marked as safe will be escaped by Twig using the native PHP `htmlspecialchars()` function. This provides a level of safety that previously had to be actively sought manually by themers and developers using functions such as `check_plain()`.

Sanitization methods in Drupal 8

Twig auto-escapes any string that is outputted using the normal notation, as follows:

```
{{ variable_name }}
```

However, there are cases in which the variable has already been marked safe, and Twig does not escape it anymore. This is usually in the case of `MarkupInterface` objects--such as `FilteredMarkup` or `FormattableMarkup`--we saw in Chapter 12, *JavaScript and the Ajax API*, when we discussed translations (extended by `TranslatableMarkup`). In these cases, Twig assumes that the strings they wrap have already been sanitized and that they can be outputted as they are. Of course, it is then up to us, as module developers, to ensure that we don't use any such objects with strings that contain an unsanitized user input.

Let's look at a popular example of such an object we use all the time, and then we will talk about the different ways we can sanitize our user input.

If you remember, in Chapter 12, *JavaScript and the Ajax API*, we talked about the `t()` function (and the `StringTranslationTrait` method) that returns a `TranslatableMarkup` object used for translating strings. Printing such an object inside Twig will prevent auto-escaping because Twig already considers it safe. Moreover, if you remember, this applies to the main string only, as any placeholders we use do get escaped:

```
$object = t('This does not get escaped but this does: @safe', ['@safe' =>
'This can be unsafe as it will be escaped'])
```

Even if there were no security implications, we should not be passing user input or variables to `TranslatableMarkup`, as that hinders the actual purpose of these objects--to translate the string. However, for other `MarkupInterface` objects, there are a few ways we can treat user input or strings of a dubious origin in order to prepare them for Twig:

- `Drupal\Component\Utility\Html::escape()`: This is the strictest sanitization function used to print plain text. It uses PHP's `htmlspecialchars()` to convert special characters to HTML entities.
- `Drupal\Component\Utility\Xss::filter()`: This filters HTML to prevent XSS attacks. It also allows a few basic HTML elements.
- `Drupal\Component\Utility\Xss::filterAdmin()`: This is a very permissive XSS filter that allows through most HTML elements apart from things like `<script>` or `<style>`. It should be used only for known and safe sources of input.
- `Drupal\Component\Utility\UrlHelper::filterBadProtocol()`: This strips dangerous protocols from URLs. It should be used before printing the HTML attribute value when the URLs are obtained from user input or unsafe sources.

So, depending on the case, using one of the preceding sanitization methods will prevent XSS attacks when dealing with markup that Twig doesn't escape.

Double escaping

Since Twig already does much of the work for us, it's also important not to go overboard with escaping. Veteran Drupal 7 developers may have a tendency to escape things like there is no tomorrow, but this can have unintended consequences. For example, imagine the following scenario:

```
return [
  '#theme' => 'my_custom_theme',
  '#title' => 'The cow\'s got milk.',
];
```

Since Twig is auto-escaping, the following string will be printed:

```
The cow's got milk.
```

So, there is no visible change as the string was safe. However, imagine that we were overzealous with our sanitization and did this:

```
return [
  '#theme' => 'my_custom_theme',
  '#title' => Html::escape('The cow\'s got milk.'),
];
```

Then, we would get the following title:

```
The cow's got milk.
```

That is because the first time it is escaped, Drupal turns the apostrophe into an HTML entity ('). However, the browser renders it correctly so we don't actually see it. The second escaping turns the individual characters from that HTML entity into *their* respective HTML entities. In this case, the & character gets turned into &. So, the entire string is no longer properly readable by the browser.

I now draw your attention for a moment to Chapter 4, *Theming,*. In that chapter, we saw that the #markup and #plain_text properties already serve to sanitize the user input passed through them. The first uses the Xss::filterAdmin() method, whereas the latter uses the Html::escape() method. So, keep in mind that if you use those as part of your render arrays, you may not need further sanitization.

SQL Injection

SQL Injection still remains a very popular vector attack on unsuspecting vulnerable applications that incorrectly make use of database drivers. Luckily, using the Drupal 8 database abstraction layer, we go a long way toward ensuring protection against such vulnerabilities. All we have to do is use it correctly.

When it comes to Entity queries, there isn't much we can do wrong. However, when using the Database API directly as we did in Chapter 8, *The Database API*, we have to pay attention.

Most of the time, vulnerabilities have to do with improper placeholder management. For example, we should never do things like this:

```
$database->query('SELECT column FROM {table} t WHERE t.name = ' .
$variable);
```

This is regardless of what `$variable` is--direct user input or otherwise. Because by using that direct concatenation, malicious users may inject their own instructions and complete the statement in a different way than intended. Instead, we should use code like we did in `Chapter 8`, *The Database API*:

```
$database->query("SELECT column FROM {table} t WHERE t.name = :name",
[':name' => $variable]);
```

In other words, use placeholders which will then be sanitized by the API to ensure that no characters are allowed to form malicious statements.

Drupal 8 comes with an additional security improvement when it comes to SQL injection vulnerabilities--single statement executions. Up until recently, the PHP PDO driver (which Drupal extended since Drupal 7) did not have a flag in place to inform MySQL to execute only a single statement at a time. Theoretically, vulnerabilities caused by appending multiple statements were possible (with one painful example of an attack that marked the Drupal community forever--SA-CORE-2014-005). However, this has been changed, and Drupal now sends this flag via PDO to the database engine to prevent multiple statements from being executed at once. So, we get this extra bit of protection.

Cross-Site Request Forgery (CSRF)

CSRF attacks are another popular way applications can be overtaken, by forcing a user with elevated privileges to execute unwanted actions on their own site. Usually, this happens when certain URLs on the application trigger a process simply by being accessed through the browser (and being authenticated)--for example, deleting a resource.

The most important thing to consider in this respect is to never have such actions happening simply by accessing a URL. To help with this, we have the powerful Form API, which already had token-based CSRF protection embedded from previous versions of Drupal. So basically you can create forms whose submit handlers perform the potentially damaging actions (as we learned in `Chapter 2`, *Creating Your First Module*) or even add a second layer using a confirmation form (as we saw in `Chapter 6`, *Data Modeling and Storage*, and `Chapter 7`, *Your Own Custom Entity and Plugin Types*, when talking about entities). The latter is actually recommended for when the action is irreversible or has greater implications.

Although the Form API should account for most use cases, we may also encounter the need to declare a callback URL that directly handles the process. And, to protect ourselves from CSRF attacks, we can use the CSRF token system as we saw in Chapter 10, *Access Control*, when we talked about the various types of access control. I recommend that you check out that chapter for more information on this topic.

Summary

Drupal 8 has come a long way with locking down its APIs to attack vulnerabilities. Of course, this does not mean it's perfect nor that a bad developer cannot create security holes. For this reason, it's extremely important to pay attention to the security implications of all the code you write, follow the standards (including the OWASP checklist), and be aware of what contributed modules you use (to at least be covered by the Drupal security team). Moreover, it's also very important to keep up to date with security announcements from the Drupal security team, as new vulnerabilities may be discovered and updates required to remedy them. These are more time-sensitive in some cases than others, but it's always good to stay up to date as quickly as possible (by following the communication from the Drupal security team). Luckily, though, historically speaking, Drupal has not had many security crises--at least not compared to other open source frameworks out there. So, from a security standpoint, it has a good reputation. However, do not take this to mean that you as a module developer are unburdened by the heavy responsibility for keeping your application safe.

In this chapter, we discussed three transitional vulnerabilities web applications usually face, how Drupal 8 stands against these, and what we as module developers can--and should--do to protect ourselves from them--XSS, SQL Injection, and CSRF. Of course, there are many more things that we can do from an application and server maintenance point of view. However, these fall outside the scope of what this book focuses on. I strongly encourage you, though, to read all the available documentation on security in Drupal 8 and keep yourself informed.

Index

modules 11, 12
plugins 12, 13
response, delivering to request 14, 15
services 14
themes 11, 12
Drupal behaviors
about 374
code, wrapping in file 376, 377
library 375, 376
Drupal Console
about 24
URL 24
Drupal Form API
reference 45
Drupal shell (Drush)
about 24
reference link 23
Drupal VM
URL 21
Drupal.org
reference 111, 262
Drupal
developing, tools used 21
for developers 8
reference 109
Drush command 253, 254, 255, 257

E

emails
altering 82, 83
sending 79, 81, 82
entity access
about 334, 335, 336
entity access hooks 338, 339
field access 340
in routes 341, 342
node access grants 342, 343, 344, 347, 349
services, injecting into Entity handlers 337
Entity API
content entities, rendering 196
content entity validation, summary 204
content entries, rendering 197
content entry validation 199, 203
entities, creating 195
entities, loading 186, 188

entities, manipulating 194
entities, querying 186
entities, reading 189, 191, 193
interacting with 185
pseudo-fields 198
queries, building 186
entity type plugin
about 165
bundles 166
database tables 167
fields 171
identifiers 166
links 168
summary 178
entity
about 163
configuration export 169
content, versus configuration entity type 163
handlers 170
in Views 428
keys 167
revisions 168
translation 168
Event Dispatcher
and redirects 60
EventDispatcher component
reference link 13
events
dispatching 65, 67

F

field formatter 301, 305
field settings 306, 307
field type 283, 284, 285, 286, 288, 289, 292
field widget 293, 294, 296, 299, 300
fields
configuration entity fields 172, 173
content entity fields 173
File fields
using 460, 461
filesystem 456, 457
form
about 42, 44, 47
altering 47
custom submit handlers 49

Made in the USA
Lexington, KY
11 June 2018